Their Home and Native Land

Their Home and Native Land

Robert MacBain

Robert MacBain Books
• 2017 •

Copyright © 2017, Robert MacBain
All rights reserved. This book contains material protected under International and Federal Copyright Laws and Treaties. Any unauthorized reprint or use of this material is prohibited. No part of this book may be reproduced or transmitted in any form or by any means, electronic or mechanical, including photocopying, recording, or by any information storage and retrieval system without the express written permission from the author.

David Moratto, interior and cover design
Teresa Miller Photography, author photo

Cover image:
A Blackfoot Travois
Edward S. Curtis
Courtesy of Library and Archives Canada
(C-026182)

Robert MacBain Books
www.RobertMacBainBooks.ca

Printed in United States of America.

Copyright Registration #1125222
October 19, 2015

Ebook ISBN 978-0-9918017-4-9
Paperback ISBN 978-0-9918017-3-2

*This book is dedicated to the memory of
Brian Benjamin Tuesday (Tibishkopiness),
a tortured Ojibway soul who was born on
May 22, 1944, at the Big Grassy River reserve
on the southeastern shore of the Lake of the Woods.
Brian died alone at Nestor Falls
on January 30, 2011.
He was 66.*

Contents

Foreword 1

1 First Aboriginal lawyer in Western Canada, oppressive Indian Act, 1969 White Paper, Pierre Trudeau backs down 7

2 Canada takes control of vast Hudson's Bay Company territories, state of the western tribes, loss of the buffalo herds, North-West Mounted Police establish law and order . . 39

3 Linking Thunder Bay to Winnipeg, "negotiating" with the Ojibways of Treaty #3, divide and conquer, no arable land, broken promises 65

4 Ojibways forced west, allegiance to the King of France, British takeover, Tecumseh, War of 1812 85

5 "Intractable" Blackfoot, refugee Sioux, Sitting Bull, Crowfoot and Red Crow 113

6   No "nation-to-nation" negotiations, British Indians
    on British soil, Chiefs made officers of the Queen,
    Christian Aboriginals, no title to land,
    hunting restricted, superintendencies. 125

7   Transition to farming, early successes,
    pushed off fertile land. 149

8   Entrepreneurial Cree woman, transition
    to urban life, preserving culture and tradition,
    forerunner to Assembly of First Nations. 163

9   Kahnawake Mohawks, Expo 67,
    culture clash, parting of the ways 175

10 Suicides, poisoned rivers, bureaucratic control,
    removing the children, a life once good,
    "they owe us", fish shipped in. 193

11 Discrimination, ongoing problems, first Aboriginal
    protest march, reasonable demands, a diverse people. 221

12 High-fashion furs, mutual aid, bureaucratic control,
    inferior education, no economic base, pregnant at 13,
    social breakdown, bands in debt, tourist economy in decline . . 245

13 Minister in buckskin, a gifted woman, questionable
    government spending, the cost of political life,
    plying chiefs with liquor. 269

14 Keeping her language, suicidal youth,
    sawmill and fish factory, friendly relations,
    building a better life, bureaucratic red tape,
    reclaiming their lands, band cooperation,
    remembering the past, divisions at Whitefish Bay. 287

15 *Cruiser and jingle dance, PM Trudeau threatens "bloodshed", back to the bush, effect of Indian residential schools, a tortured life* 305

16 *Dilapidated school, Charter of Rights and Freedoms, 28-day walk, Minaki Lodge, social discord, drug abuse, loss of language, police outreach* 323

17 *Counselling inmates, return to the drum, "a sacred building", work or starve, taking a stand, very little progress, restoring language/culture.* 339

18 *Oka factor, making do with less, $70 million settlement, entrepreneurial initiatives, restoring ceremony and tradition* . . 353

19 *Graduation ceremonies, leg lost, drinking again, $130 million solar project, hobbled ministers, reflections* . . . 361

Bibliography 369
Acknowledgements 371
About the Author 373

Foreword

Much of the current national discussion about the place of Aboriginal people in modern Canadian society is conducted in oversimplified black-and-white terms. Complex issues are reduced to the lowest possible common denominator. And, even at that, there is no agreed statement of facts.

By revising the 2015 edition of *Their Home and Native Land*, I have attempted to provide a narrative that will enable the reader to better understand some of the complicated issues that are being debated and to provide context and perspective.

While I present a considerable amount of research and documentation, the book is not intended to be read as an academic thesis. I wrote it as I would if I was still writing for the Toronto Star or the Globe and Mail. Every effort has been made not to let any bias on my part interfere with the telling of the story.

The book touches on the life of William (Bill) I.C. Wuttunee, the first Aboriginal lawyer in western Canada who went on to become one of the top litigators in Saskatchewan. He helped establish the National Indian Council in 1961. However, a culture clash between the chiefs on the Prairies, who had treaties with the Canadian government, and those in Quebec who didn't, led to the demise of the National Indian

Council which morphed into the National Indian Brotherhood in 1968 and, in 1982, today's Assembly of First Nations.

Bill Wuttunee, a lifelong proponent of integration over segregation, was banned from several reserves in northwestern Saskatchewan because of his public support of Prime Minister Pierre Elliott Trudeau's controversial 1969 White Paper which addressed the fact that Aboriginal people could not own their own homes or get a loan from the bank. They also had to get permission from an Indian agent before selling any of their chickens or cows and a faceless bureaucrat in Ottawa had final say on how their possessions would be disposed of after death.

Government-funded Aboriginal organizations across Canada were bitterly opposed to Trudeau's White Paper on the place of the Aboriginal people in modern Canadian society and the government backed down and abandoned the life-altering new approach.

Their Home and Native Land provides some historical context by taking the reader behind the scenes in the treaty-making process of 1871–77 with the scattered bands of Ojibways, Crees, Blackfoot and other tribes living on the former Hudson's Bay Company lands between Thunder Bay and the eastern slopes of the Rocky Mountains. Quotes from official documents describe what chiefs and representatives of the Canadian government—not of the British Queen—said and did during those negotiations.

The book documents that there were no "nation-to-nation" negotiations. The representatives of the Canadian government operated on the premise that they were dealing with "British Indians on British soil". All of the Aboriginals they dealt with were subjects of Queen Victoria and required to obey her laws. There was no talk of sharing the land as equals.

The natives were in dire straits and the government was offering, as a short-term measure only, to help them make the difficult transition from their nomadic lifestyle of hunting, fishing and gathering to supporting themselves by farming and/or raising cattle. The goal was that they would become a self-supporting population able to take care of themselves in the same manner as the white settlers without further assistance from the Canadian government.

The book details how bands who were making a successful transition to supporting themselves by cultivating the soil were forced off fertile land that had been reserved for them and their children under the treaties by greedy land speculators aided and abetted by corrupt government officials.

Their Home and Native Land describes the devastating effect on the lives of Ojibways in northwestern Ontario when their lakes and rivers were poisoned with mercury from a British-owned pulp and paper mill and the social breakdown that followed.

Some of those interviewed for the book describe the iron-clad control bureaucrats at the Department of Indian Affairs exercised over their lives and how well-meaning ministers of Indian affairs were hobbled by the bureaucrats in Ottawa.

The chief of one of the bands in the Kenora-Fort Frances area talks about how he and some of his colleagues would have gone to war, and died if necessary, if the Canadian Army had opened fire during the 78-day Mohawk standoff at Oka, Quebec, in 1990.

A former vice-president of the Native Council of Canada recalls Prime Minister Pierre Elliott Trudeau telling native leaders in 1983 there would be bloodshed if they tried to establish their own independent government.

The book describes an Ojibway band half way between Kenora and Fort Frances where most of the people are on welfare and without hope of getting a job while another band—just about an hour south—operated a computerized sawmill and a fish hatchery, manufactured windows and provided employment for everyone on the reserve plus natives from nearby reserves.

The reader will learn about bands torn apart by factionalism, girls getting pregnant at 13, people coming together as family at pow wows, and efforts to restore the language, culture and traditions of the Ojibway people.

The book profiles four Ojibway communities in northwestern Ontario. Several individuals describe what life was like on those reserves from the 1950s through to June, 2013, and how the Ojibways organized the first native protest march in Canadian history in 1965 and the events and circumstances leading up to it.

The reader will meet some truly remarkable and fascinating Ojibways, Mohawks and Crees and find that their positive approach to life—despite the conditions they live under—is truly inspirational. They have a story worth telling, worth reading.

While the book describes the life-destroying impact residential schools had on one tortured Ojibway soul and touches briefly on the experiences of others, I am saving the extensive research I have conducted on the Indian residential schools for the book I will release early in 2018.

Meanwhile, articles I have written about the Indian residential schools and information I have shared in radio interviews can be found on my website—www.RobertMacBainBooks.ca

It is my sincere hope that the information provided in this book will be of assistance to those who desire more knowledge and understanding about the place of the first peoples of this land in modern Canadian society.

—*Robert MacBain*
Toronto, Canada
September 26, 2017

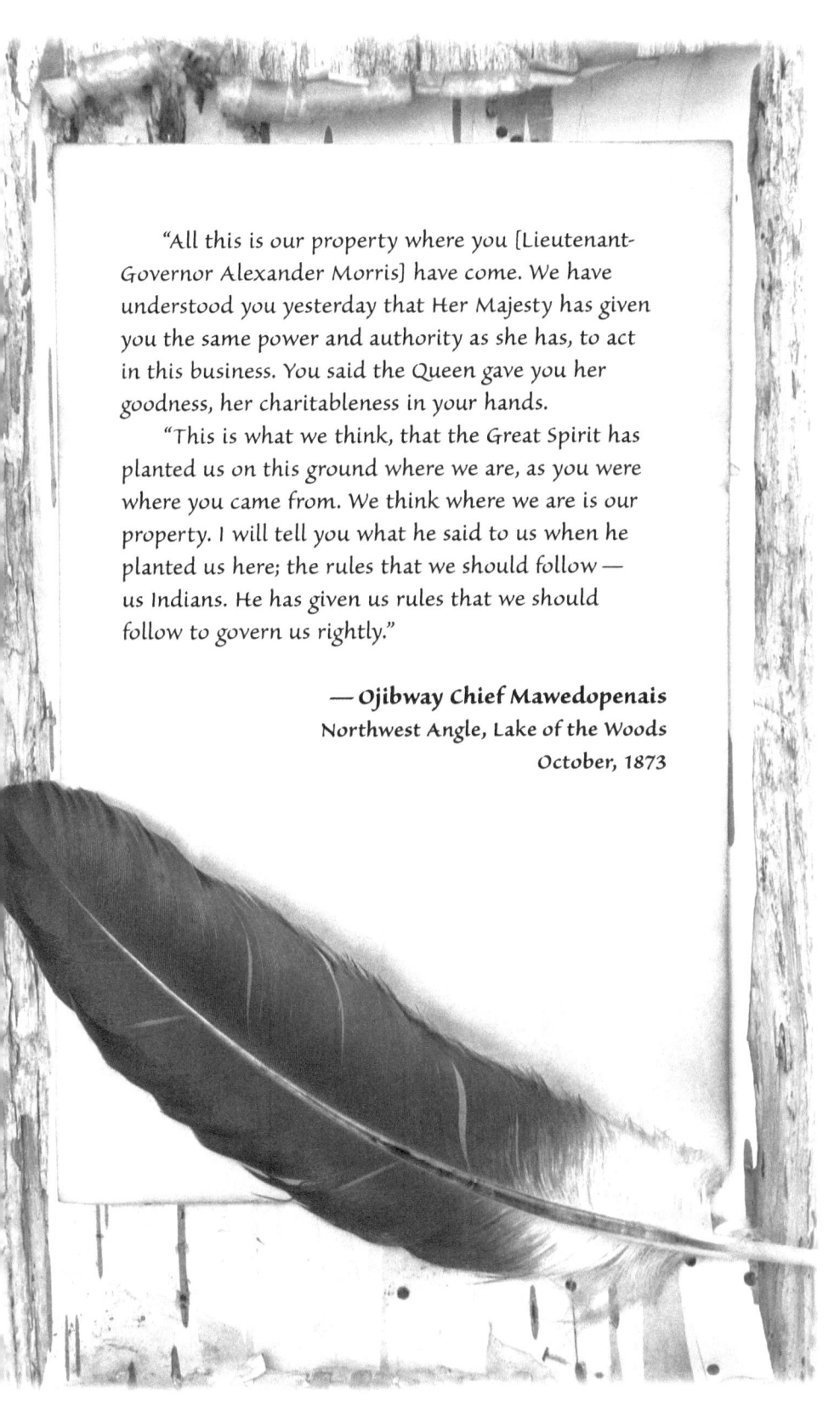

"All this is our property where you [Lieutenant-Governor Alexander Morris] have come. We have understood you yesterday that Her Majesty has given you the same power and authority as she has, to act in this business. You said the Queen gave you her goodness, her charitableness in your hands.

"This is what we think, that the Great Spirit has planted us on this ground where we are, as you were where you came from. We think where we are is our property. I will tell you what he said to us when he planted us here; the rules that we should follow — us Indians. He has given us rules that we should follow to govern us rightly."

— **Ojibway Chief Mawedopenais**
Northwest Angle, Lake of the Woods
October, 1873

Chapter 1

*I*magine not being allowed to own your own home, not being able to get a loan from the bank, requiring permission from a government agent to sell any of your chickens or cows, and having a faceless bureaucrat in Ottawa decide how your personal property should be disposed of after you're dead.

That's the situation 36-year-old Calgary lawyer William (Bill) I. C. Wuttunee — the first Aboriginal lawyer in western Canada — described when I interviewed him for an article published in the *Toronto Daily Star* on September 17, 1964.

Before going into private practice in Calgary in 1963, he had been one of the Saskatchewan government's top litigators and specialized in tort and insurance law. At the time that I interviewed him, he had just been re-elected as the president of the three-year-old National Indian Council which morphed into the National Indian Brotherhood in 1968 and today's Assembly of First Nations in 1982.

What bothered Bill Wuttunee the most at the time of our interview was the almost total lack of control Aboriginal people were allowed to exercise over their own lives. Indian agents and their political masters, from the very first day, considered them to be totally incapable of managing their own affairs. "My brother [at the Red Pheasant reserve] in Saskatchewan can't even sell a cow without the Indian agent's permission."

The procedure originated in the 1870s to protect Aboriginal people from unscrupulous white traders. However, Bill Wuttunee believed the time had come for the government to stop treating the estimated 220,000 people living on the reserves scattered across Canada like juvenile delinquents and let them manage their own affairs.

A smouldering bitterness overshadowed his face as he described the conditions Aboriginals in Canada were forced to endure when I interviewed him for that article. He believed strongly that their advancement was being held back because of the iron-clad control the Department of Indian Affairs exercised over their lives.

If something in dispute was covered by the Indian Act, it was held to be outside the bounds of discussion. That's why he believed that, if the lot of the first peoples of this land was to be improved, they would have to be given much more responsibility for their own lives than the framework of the Act allowed. "That Indian Act should be revamped and brought up to date so that my people are more free," he said.

He was convinced the odds were stacked against the average Aboriginal child being able to carve out a comfortable niche in Canadian society. "If he's born to very poor parents in a northern tent, he'll be darned lucky if he becomes an adult."

In that article in the *Toronto Daily Star*, Bill said the Aboriginal people were not opposed to receiving meaningful help or assistance from the white community when they moved to the urban centres. However, they were strongly opposed to unwanted help from well-intentioned whites.

"We aim to do things for ourselves," he said. "We build on what we have done, not on what others have done for us. Those people who try and set up friendship centres FOR the Indians and not WITH the Indians should stick to their housekeeping. These paternalistic do-gooders cause us the greatest headache in many cities."

The key words in his vocabulary at that time were self-help, self-sufficiency, self-respect and self-management.

Although his parents raised him as an Anglican, Bill Wuttunee developed a life-long interest in native culture and tradition. When he was about eight years old, he went to a sun dance and joined the singers.

"I was standing in front of this little sun dance lodge," he once told me, "and then I went in to do the drumming, just went in by myself and sat with the men, just a little guy. I took a stick and started singing and drumming. I learned the song. When you're young you learn very quickly. My Dad and Mother always supported the native traditions and although they were good Christian people—I was raised as a Christian and as a traditional person as well—I did that throughout my entire life."

In 1962, he went to a Piute ceremony and was quite impressed.. "It was an all-night ceremony. People were singing and praying continually all night long. I was exposed to that and it took me about three years to get in to do it."

That's one of the reasons he resented the almost total intolerance white churches and governments exhibited toward the sun dance, potlatch and other native customs and traditions.. "The religions, the Catholic Church, the Anglican Church, etc. didn't want natives participating in the sun dance so they influenced the government. The government then passed legislation prohibiting it and so the habit was to have it in kind of a secretive place."

He was deeply resentful of the manner in which the early missionaries set about the task of stripping the Aboriginal people of their ancient beliefs. The Aboriginals had been relegated to the role of pagan because of their ignorance of the Judeo-Christian tradition. That concept of the heathen savage exists to this day.

"The Indian believed in a God long before the arrival of the white man," Bill once said. "As a matter of fact, the Indians had one great spirit throughout all of the country. They never had more than one god. We believed in what is known as Gitchi Manitou, the Great Spirit. God was in the sun, in the moon, in mother earth, in the rain that made the grass grow. Manitou was a loving and merciful god to us. I learned about our Heaven, known as the 'happy hunting ground', where everyone goes whether you are good or bad. There is no such thing as Hell and this concept was alien to the Indian mind."

During the negotiations for Treaty #3 at the Northwest Angle of the Lake of the Woods in 1873, Chief Mawedopenais, the lead spokesperson for the Ojibways, said to Lieutenant-Governor Alexander Morris—who negotiated four of the seven treaties entered into between

1871 and 1877: "This is what we think, that the Great Spirit has planted us on this ground where we are, as you were where you came from. We think where we are is our property. I will tell you what he said to us when he planted us here. The rules that we should follow—us Indians. He has given us rules that we should follow to govern us rightly."

When they were negotiating the Qu'Appelle Treaty in October, 1874, Chief Chee-e-kuk (the Worthy One) said: "Just now the Great Spirit is watching over us. It is good. He who has strength and power is overlooking our doings. I want very much to be good in what we are going to talk about, and our Chiefs will take you by the hand just now."

But the Aboriginals never did manage to convince their pale-faced overlords that their religion and way of life was of a high standard prior to the "founding" of the so-called new-found land.

Something else Bill Wuttunee wanted to see changed was the Orphan Annie image most Canadians had of the native people.. This stemmed from the accepted belief that they were helpless wards of the federal government—another of the hundreds of misrepresentations that irritated the young Cree lawyer.

"It's an old-fashioned idea to say that Indians are wards of the federal government," he said. "When that is said, it is a disservice to the Indians. An Indian is as much a citizen of the province as anyone else and the government in Ottawa is not in the position of a special guardian for the Indians. It only means that where legislation is concerned with Indians' affairs, that comes from Ottawa."

Old-fashioned or not, the Aboriginal people seemed stuck with that false dependency image and Bill Wuttunee and the National Indian Council were trying to turn that image around.

Notwithstanding all of the problems the white settlers caused for his people and the hundreds of years of abuse, Bill Wuttunee was deeply proud of his Cree heritage. "We're more of a nation than the Canadians because we have a history, thousands of years," he once told me. "The Canadians have only just arrived here, just a short while ago. Within my father's time they came out west. My father said to me as he pointed out the land, 'this is our land, Bill.' He only said it once, but that was enough."

Despite being one of the top lawyers in Saskatchewan, Bill Wuttunee was often discriminated against because of his Cree heritage. During one of our many interviews, he recalled getting on a cargo-passenger plane at Prince Albert in 1958 and having to sit on the floor at the back with the other native people.

"This pilot put all the Indians in the back on the floor and all the white people in the seats. I had a friend of mine, Jimmy Griffin, a white lawyer, and I said, 'see what the hell that guy's doing?'. It was very obvious what he was doing. He didn't say 'all Indians at the back'; he didn't say that, but obviously everybody was directed to sit at the back because when I walked in there was no seats hardly in there and he just pointed me to the back of that plane. At that time I was working with [Saskatchewan Premier] T.C. Douglas with the provincial committee on minority groups so I had real access to him and I reported this man what he had done and he was fired immediately."

Bill described Scottish-born T.C. (Tommy) Douglas as "the only humane socially-conscious person who was a leader at that time and he made a lot of changes in Saskatchewan. They brought in [pub-lic] health care and did all kinds of new things, no-fault insurance, etc."

In her biography of Tommy Douglas, Doris French Shackleton wrote: "The practical, obvious 'solution' to Douglas...was to do away with the reserves and the degradation that went with 'wardship' and integrate the Indians with all speed into Canadian society."

"I helped Premier T.C. Douglas introduce the vote, the franchise, and liquor rights for Indians," Bill told me. "He made it into law in 1959. The federal government followed suit not long after and the other provinces as well. The politicians are interested in the votes of the people and of course there's a lot of Indian people living in those constituencies and that's the way I think it should be.

"T.C. Douglas wanted me to work with him and I was doing organizational work with the natives in Saskatchewan. So what I did there was, I had their support, in other words I had the government's support, right? When you have the government's support you're going to do things. So we organized a meeting at Fort Qu'Appelle, but before that I had to visit all the Indian chiefs and I went on my own and visited, no matter where they were. If they were in the bush, I'd go in the bush. If they were in the field, I'd go in the field to find the chief and talk with him and tell him what was afoot.

"I said to them, I said 'we're organizing a meeting in order to have the vote, the franchise', because we didn't have any vote either provincially or federally and also to have liquor rights, the right to consume liquor. So some of them were opposed, others weren't. Some others thought it was a very good idea."

Why did he think that making it legal for Indians to consume liquor was a good idea? "Well because they were left out. It's like inviting guests into your house and you leave one in the corner. You serve your dinner and…"

And you can't serve liquor to a native person. "Yeah, you don't, you couldn't participate."

And you also have all the bootlegging because of that. "That's right and a lot of people died from that. Now whether it was a good idea or not, is another question because liquor is such a problem with, not only Indian people, but with all people. Like in Alberta, here in Calgary, they drink like fish, especially on weekends and so the problem will always remain so long as the government supports liquor because they kind of push it.

"At that time, the Indians didn't have a vote and they had no liquor rights, etc. Now, in 1958, I started the Federation of Saskatchewan Indians, but when I say 'I', I mean 'I' because I don't get credit for what I have done and I want to make it abundantly clear what I did."

He travelled for six weeks through all of Saskatchewan, visited just about every chief and spoke to them about the vote and the liquor rights and then he organized a conference that fall and formed the Federation of Saskatchewan Indians.

"They asked me to be the president of the organization, wanted to nominate me and I said 'no'. I said John Tootoosis [from the Poundmaker reserve west of Battleford] should be the guy. So they nominated John and they had another round and they elected him, and he was president for a long time which was good because John was a good leader and he had done a lot of work and my father, James Wuttunee, used to work with John and my father was active with the

League of Indian Nations back around 1919, '20, in the '20s. So I was just carrying on that work and I remember John used to come to our house and meet with my dad. So I was involved with politics when I was just a little boy. Always interested me, native politics."

At that first meeting of the Federation of Saskatchewan Indians, Bill asked for those who had running water on their reserve to raise their hand. Only one hand went up. "We have running water," one participant said with a smile on his face. "We have the Saskatchewan River."

Shortly after the meeting, Bill phoned Saskatchewan Government Telephones and asked them to install a phone at the Red Pheasant reserve. They refused on the basis that the natives wouldn't pay the phone bill. After further negotiation, they agreed to install a pay phone in his brother's house, who was the chief at that time.

"So they put a pay phone in his place and then after a while they changed it to a regular phone. And then I asked the provincial government to install electricity. I said my brother lives just a stone's throw from the electricity line, they go right by the reserve, why don't you cut up a few posts and take it in there? I said go and put in lights in his place, even if you put just one bulb in there. So they brought electric light also to my brother's place. He was one of the first Indians to get a telephone and electricity on the reserve. It would have been 1959, somewhere in there.

"That was the beginning of how the services were extended by the province and no other province was doing it. They were all hands off completely. But that was the beginning, the beginning of extending social services to the native people."

Bill considered the effort he put into getting the natives the right to vote in Saskatchewan to be one of his most important accomplishments. "As a result of that [getting the vote] there was more interest in Indians because they had a franchise. They could now vote. Now the question was, of course, at that time, whether Indians should accept the vote because it may be that the provincial governments would want jurisdiction and, of course, that's exactly what's happening now."

Bill Wuttunee moved to Calgary in January, 1963, and practised law out of an office in the building owned by the *Calgary Herald* where I was working as a reporter.

"Because I'm native, the big firms didn't say 'well Bill Wuttunee come and work with us'. They didn't say that. I was never invited and so I had to just do it on my own. I didn't mind doing that because that's the way life is. I have no regrets concerning that. I'm glad I have the guts to go out and do it because when I did that, I had never practised law before.

"I had worked with the Saskatchewan Government in Regina and I had a lot of experience in litigation because that's all I had done for a period of about 10 years. So when I came here, I didn't hesitate to go into private practice although I'd never been in private practice, never, but I thought, well, I have experience as a lawyer, as in court, I would go to court any time. It would have been better had I started out with somebody else.

"The whole idea at that time was to not be dependent on anybody. That has always been my approach. You can't be dependent on people to get anywhere. You gotta do it yourself and forget about the rest."

The big law firms had no interest in him and neither had the big corporations. Most of his clients were dirt poor. "Indians they have no money. They have no money and even when they came to see me I thought they had no money and when they said to me they wanted me to work for them I just never thought that they really did have money and that they could really pay. But to go and act full time for a band, for example, I, in retrospect I could've done that. I could've been on a retainer. But I didn't want to be sidetracked because I was a lawyer for anybody who came through those doors. Not only Indians came. Most of my clients were white, but they're also poor whites."

The Indian residential school Bill Wuttunee was sent to was about 160 kilometres northwest of his home on the Red Pheasant reserve. "It was a long way from Red Pheasant, at least a hundred miles or more and in those days, of course, we had no cars," Bill recalled. "The only way you operated was by a horse and buggy, or teams, wagons. And it would have taken a long time to go and visit that place. We didn't have any phones so we couldn't phone and of course we weren't really allowed to phone. All we could do was write letters and they [school officials] would go over the letters to make sure we didn't say anything against the school. I don't have any bitterness in my life, my ideas, about that."

The thing that bothered him the most was the separation from his parents and his family. "I was just a boy of twelve years old and they took my freedom away because as soon as you went into that school they locked the door and we only went out when they unlocked the door. We weren't allowed to go out and run around on our own. We were always under lock and key. That was the bad thing.

"I was really in prison. I was serving time in prison when I hadn't done anything wrong. I had been a free boy on the reserve who would go horseback riding on the prairies, gallop or ride by the lake or over the hills. We had all kinds of freedom. The freedom to walk around and enjoy life. And, especially the young native children, we had more freedom really than ordinary white children because there are kinds of rules and regulations for them. For us, we had our independence early in life. That's what I missed most when I was there."

There were about 200 students from reserves across northern Saskatchewan at the school, about half male and half female. The school was on the Onion Lake Reserve on the border between Saskatchewan and Alberta and was operated by the Anglican Church. "About a mile and a half away there was a Roman Catholic school and we were never allowed to intermingle."

Onion Lake wasn't the only reserve where there were two church-run schools within a short distance of each other. In 1908, for example, there were seven Catholic Indian industrial schools across Canada. There were also seven Anglican Indian industrial schools. Twenty-five per cent of the boarding schools in Alberta and Saskatchewan were twinned—one Catholic, one Anglican—and were located within a matter of kilometres from each other.

As with most Indian residential schools, discipline was meted out unsparingly at the school that young Bill Wuttunee was forced to attend. "I remember a young boy being whipped for twenty minutes on his arms. I don't know what he had done, if he had done that much wrong, and I was there and I happened to have a watch, and I remember what time it was. It was eight o'clock when I went there and I had to leave and he was still being whipped at twenty minutes after eight by this woman, just the two of them in the room, and he was hollering and hollering and hollering and I thought what should I do but there was nothing I could do. I was just twelve years old and I thought well I'll just go back upstairs. Well, that's when I went back upstairs."

Bill Wuttunee was eighty when he recalled that painful incident when I interviewed him in Toronto in April, 2009. The memory was as fresh as yesterday. "The question was, what could I have done? What could a person do in those circumstances except maybe to grab the arm of the woman and say 'What are you doing with this? What's the situation?' She was the supervisor. She was a big woman. She wasn't slim or small. She was big. I mean, I was only twelve years old and she was BIG."

One of his teachers at the residential school was a former life insurance salesman. "He used *Time* magazine for spelling and consequently we became good spellers. But we spent most of our time computing annuities and life insurance premiums and reading *Time*. This was our education from an ex-life insurance salesman who could not have qualified as a teacher anywhere else," Bill recalled. "I did a lot of reading as a boy and I would also go to the library there and get a book and read. I was the only one [out of about 200] that used the library."

While inadequate educational facilities had handicapped thousands of Aboriginal students, poor health conditions had meant death for hundreds more. The most painful example of that was the tuberculosis outbreak at the end of the 19th century. Entire families were wiped out and Bill Wuttunee believed much of that loss could have been avoided if the Canadian government had honored what he considered to be its responsibilities under the treaties. "They just didn't provide hospitals for them," he said.

Bill Wuttunee believed strongly that the best route for his people was to integrate into Canadian society and become full-fledged Canadian citizens rather than subsisting on the apartheid-like reserves that crisscross the country.

Back in 1959, for example, he was very impressed by a presentation Chief Andrew E. Thompson of the Manitoba Indian Brotherhood made to a joint committee of the Senate and the House of Commons. Here's part of what Chief Thompson said:

> "I do not object to integration. I would like to see my children mixed in with white children, more than has been the case in the past. Of course, in respect to the reserve from which I come, there has been a mixed-up pattern. I was raised with white people for a long, long time. I could take you right back to the great grandfather of Chief Peguis. He was the man who helped to set up the Scots colonization [Red River Colony in Manitoba] and his children and his neighbour's children mixed in with the white people's children. These people are civilized. I do not want my people to turn back the clock. I want them to advance in their studies and to become something and to have good professions wherein they can compete with the white people."

In June, 1969,—a little less than five years after my article in the *Toronto Daily Star*—the Liberal government of Prime Minister Pierre Elliott Trudeau attempted to address some of the concerns Bill Wuttunee and others had raised about the place of Aboriginal people in modern Canadian society.

Sounding a lot like Bill Wuttunee, Indian Affairs Minister Jean Chretien—who would become Prime Minister of Canada in 1993—rose in the House of Commons on June 25, 1969, and said:

> "To be a Canadian Indian today is to be someone different in another way. It is to be someone apart—apart in law, apart in the provision of government services and, too often, apart in social contacts. To be an Indian is to lack power—the power to act as owner of your lands, the power to spend your own money and, too often, the power to change your own condition.
>
> "Not always, but too often, to be an Indian is to be without—without a job, a good house, or running water; without knowledge, training or technical skill and, above all, without those feelings of dignity and self-confidence that a man must have if he is to walk with his head held high ...
>
> "Obviously, the course of history must be changed. To be an Indian must be to be free—free to develop Indian cultures in an environment of legal, social and economic equality with other Canadians."

Speaking in Vancouver on August 8, 1969, Prime Minister Pierre Elliott Trudeau said:

> "We have set the Indians apart as a race. We've set them apart in our laws. We've set them apart in the ways the governments will deal with them. They're not citizens of the province as the rest of us are. They are wards of the federal government. They get their services from the federal government rather than from the provincial or municipal governments. They have been set apart in law. They have been set apart in the relations with government and they've been set apart socially too.
>
> "We can go on treating the Indians as having a special status. We can go on adding bricks of discrimination around the ghetto in which they live and at the same time perhaps helping them preserve certain cultural traits and certain ancestral rights. Or we can say you're at a crossroads—the time is now to decide whether the Indians will be a race apart in Canada or whether [they] will be Canadians of full status."

While addressing the Empire Club in Toronto on October 16, 1969, Indian Affairs Minister Chretien said:

> "I think that to have a Department of Indian Affairs is wrong, because we run a government within a government for a small group of citizens [approximately 250,000 out of a total population of 21 million] stretched from one end of the country to the other.
>
> "In many fields, such as education and welfare, the provinces are better equipped to provide the services to Indian people. The fact is that between the byzantine maze of administrative necessity and the Indian Act, there is a solid confusion that cannot be overcome ... We know that these proposals [1969 White Paper] are not magical solutions to the problems of the Indian people.
>
> "We know as well that if an effort is not made to change the present system under which Indian people live — separate legislation, separate land system, and separate administrations — that little progress will be made in breaking the pattern of separation and discrimination which has plagued Indian people for so long.
>
> "Whether we like to admit it or not, Indian people have been living in a kind of apartheid — living apart, separate from other Canadians. The government's proposals are designed to end the isolation of Indian people from the rest of Canadian society."

A background paper accompanying the statement the Minister of Indian Affairs delivered in June, 1969, said:

> "The Government believes that its policies must lead to the full, free and non-discriminatory participation of the Indian people in Canadian society. Such a goal requires a break with the past. It requires that the Indian people's role of dependence be replaced by a role of equal status, opportunity and responsibility, a role they can share with all other Canadians.

"This proposal is a recognition of the necessity made plain in a year's intensive discussions with Indian people throughout Canada. The Government believes that to continue its past course of action would not serve the interests of either the Indian people or their fellow Canadians.

"The policies proposed recognize the simple reality that the separate legal status of Indians and the policies which have flowed from it have kept the Indian people apart from and behind other Canadians. The Indian people have not been full citizens of the communities and provinces in which they live and have not enjoyed the equality and benefits that such participation offers.

"The treatment resulting from their different status has been often worse, sometimes equal and occasionally better than that accorded to their fellow citizens. What matters is that it has been different ...

"The legal and administrative discrimination in the treatment of Indian people has not given them an equal chance of success. It has exposed them to discrimination in the broadest and worse sense of the term — a discrimination that has profoundly affected their confidence that success can be theirs. Discrimination breeds discrimination by example, and the separateness of Indian people has affected the attitude of other Canadians towards them."

What became known as the 1969 White Paper recommended that the federal government take the following steps:

1. Propose to Parliament that the Indian Act be repealed and take such legislative steps as may be necessary to enable Aboriginals to control their lands and to acquire title to them.
2. Propose to the governments of the provinces that they take over the same responsibility for Aboriginals that they have for other citizens in their provinces. The takeover would be accompanied by the transfer

to the provinces of federal funds normally provided for programs for Aboriginals, augmented as may be necessary.
3. Make substantial funds available to Aboriginals for economic development as an interim measure.
4. Wind up that part of the Department of Indian Affairs and Northern Development dealing with Aboriginals. The residual responsibilities of the Federal Government for Aboriginal people would be transferred to other appropriate federal departments.

In addition, the Government proposed the appointment of a federal Commissioner to consult with the Aboriginals and to study and recommend acceptable procedures for the adjudication of land claims.

In consultation with representatives of the Aboriginal people, the Commissioner would "inquire into and report upon how claims arising in respect of the performance of the terms of treaties and agreements formally entered into by representatives of the Indians and the Crown, and the administration of moneys and lands pursuant to schemes established by legislation for the benefit of Indians may be adjudicated. The Commissioner will also classify the claims that in his judgment ought to be referred to the courts or any special quasi-judicial body that may be recommended."

The White Paper emphasized that nothing was going to change overnight. "Many years will be needed. Some efforts may fail, but learning comes from failure and from what is learned success may follow. All the partners have to learn; all will have to change."

The government said the underlying premise of its new policy was "the fundamental right of Indian people to full and equal participation in the cultural, social, economic and political life of Canada. To argue against this right is to argue for discrimination, isolation and separation. No Canadian should be excluded from participation in community life, and none should expect to withdraw and still enjoy the benefits that flow to those who participate."

The government stressed throughout that the success of the revolutionary new approach to the place of the Aboriginals in modern

Canadian society would require extensive consultation with the Aboriginal people.

>"The new policy looks to a better future for all Indian people wherever they may be. The measures for implementation are straightforward. They require discussion, consultation and negotiation with the Indian people — individuals, bands and associations and with provincial governments.
>
>"Success will depend upon the co-operation and assistance of the Indians and the provinces. The Government seeks this cooperation and will respond when it is offered.
>
>"To this end the Government proposes to invite the executives of the National Indian Brotherhood [established in 1968 by former members of the National Indian Council] and the various provincial associations to discuss the role they might play in the implementation of the new policy, and the financial resources they may require. The Government recognizes their need for independent advice, especially on legal matters.
>
>"The Government also recognizes that the discussions will place a heavy burden on Indian leaders during the adjustment period. Special arrangements will have to be made so that they may take the time needed to meet and discuss all aspects of the new policy and its implementation.
>
>"Needs and conditions vary greatly from province to province, since the adjustments would be different in each case, the bulk of the negotiations would likely be with the provincial bodies, regional groups and the bands themselves. There are those matters which are of concern to all, and the National Indian Brotherhood would be asked to act in liaison with the various provincial associations and with the federal departments which would have ongoing responsibilities.
>
>"The Government proposes to ask the associations to act as the principal agencies through which consultation

and negotiations would be conducted, but each band would be consulted about gaining ownership of its land holdings. Bands would be asked to designate the association through which their broad interests would be represented.

"Steps would be taken in consultation with representatives of the Indian people to transfer control of land to them. Because of the need to consult over five hundred bands the process would take some time."

Reaction to the 1969 White Paper from Aboriginal organizations across Canada was overwhelmingly negative. In a book that he published in 1970, Indian Association of Alberta president Harold Cardinal—the most vociferous and widely-publicized opponent who described the government's White Paper as "a thinly disguised programme of extermination through assimilation."—said: "In spite of all government attempts to convince Indians to accept the white paper, their efforts will fail, because Indians understand that the path outlined by the Department of Indian Affairs through its mouthpiece, the Honourable Mr. Chrétien, leads directly to cultural genocide. We will not walk this path."

The Indian Chiefs of Alberta released a paper in June, 1970, calling on the federal government to recognize Aboriginals as "Citizens Plus". In the preamble to their paper—released exactly one year after the government's White Paper—the chiefs said: "In Alberta, we have told the federal Minister of Indian Affairs [Jean Chretien] that we do not wish to discuss his White Paper with him until we reach a position where we can bring forth viable alternatives because we know that his paper is wrong and that it will harm our people. We refused to meet with him on his White Paper because we have been stung and hurt with his concept of consultation."

The paper went on to say: "We felt that with this concept of consultation held by the Minister and his department, that if we met with them to discuss the contents of his White Paper without being fully prepared, that even if we just talked about the weather, he would turn around and tell Parliament and the Canadian public that we accepted his White Paper."

It also said: "We say that the recognition of Indian status is essential for justice...The legal definition of Indian must remain." Their paper also contained a threat of violence if their demands were not met. "But, if for much longer the rights are not noticed, needs not met, or aspirations not filled, then no one — especially having regard to developments all over the globe — can be assured that the rank and file will continue to accept such pacific conduct from its leaders."

Prime Minister Trudeau took exception to the tone and thrust of the paper presented by the Indian Chiefs of Alberta. "You can say that the government doesn't understand, that it's stupid or ignorant," he told them after they made their presentation, "but do not say that we are dishonest and that we are trying to mislead you, because we're not."

Bill Wuttunee was banned from his home reserve southeast of North Battleford, Saskatchewan, and several other reserves because of his strong public support of the revolutionary shift in policy the Liberal government announced in June, 1969. He also lost some clients.

"The usual evils of nepotism and favoritism have cropped up in the organizations and in the councils of the bands," he said in his 1971 book, *Ruffled Feathers*. "The epitome of the Indian leadership across Canada is typified by my own treatment in 1970 at the hands of the Indian Chiefs and organizations in North Battleford, Saskatchewan. They banned me from the area when I spoke in favour of the government's White Paper on Indian Policy, without having given me the opportunity of presenting my arguments on the subject."

Being banned from his home reserve is a bit ironic in light of the fact that he was fired from his job with the federal government twice back in the days when he was leading the National Indian Council for speaking out on behalf of Aboriginal rights.

During the fiscal year 1970–71, the Indian Association of Alberta received a total $696,101 in funding from the federal government. Association president Harold Cardinal received a salary of $18,000 a year.

That's $3,000 a year more than I was making in 1969 as news director of Canada's second-largest radio station.

The executive director of the association was also being paid $18,000 and the executive secretary was receiving $28,800. Five non-Aboriginals had been hired at salaries ranging from $20,000 to $30,000 a year.

"It seems odd indeed," Bill Wuttunee wrote in *Ruffled Feathers*, "that the hierarchy of the Indian Association of Alberta should pay themselves such exorbitant salaries, bearing in mind the poverty in which so many Indian people live. It is interesting to note that none of these funds come from the tax exempt Indians themselves, but are all government grants."

He also noted that Harold Cardinal took his entire board of directors and executive team with him to Ottawa. "They spent $10,000 by way of travelling expenses, which would have been enough money to feed an entire northern community for a month."

In an interview I conducted with him in 1996, he said the authors of the Red Paper and other presentations that were made at the time concentrated all of their attention on Aboriginals living on the reserves and keeping them separate and apart from the rest of Canadian society.

"I thought that the only way that our people could survive would be to get an education and to take their place like any other Canadian and work," he said. "So that's why I said stop complaining and become part of this society. I didn't say that in order to insult them or to be cocky. I said it because I thought that that was the only way."

He had a right to be cocky. At the time that he was establishing a reputation as one of the Saskatchewan government's top litigators, he was the only Aboriginal lawyer in western Canada and had proven himself to be as good as, or better than, most of the white lawyers.

Holding fast to his long-stated conviction that Aboriginal people must accept more responsibility for their own lives, Bill went on to say in *Ruffled Feathers* that: "The mulcting [extracting money] of the white man and the white man's government is an extremely negative policy. Current Indian leaders are not prepared to do their share. They are not prepared to tell the Indian people to get an education and to pull their share of the load in Canada."

He said implementation of what became widely-known as the Red Paper would reverse the trend towards integration and result in further segregation of the Aboriginal people. "There is no mention of integration, and the whole theme of the Red Paper is against the involvement of Indians in the Canadian way of life. They wish primarily to develop their own culture and their institutions with the aid of provincial and federal funds. The Red Paper has concentrated on the recognition of the treaties, thereby reversing the previous trend towards a modern approach in relations between Indians and non-Indians."

In criticizing a paper put forward by the Union of British Columbia Indian Chiefs, he said they "are looking toward the reservations instead of outward to the rest of Canada. They do not appear cognizant of the fact that they are welcome to live in the cities and in other parts of the country and that they are not restricted to the reserves only."

The authors of such papers, he said, "disregard the trend towards urbanization, and the fact that at least one-third of those registered as Indians are not living on their reserves."

In *Ruffled Feathers,* Bill Wuttunee described programs the federal government had put in place to assist Aboriginals living on the reserves and those who wanted to make the transition from life on the reserve to living in the towns and cities.

"A great deal of help is available from the [Indian Affairs] Branch for any Indian who wants to make a success of it either on or off the reserve," he wrote. "If an Indian wants to farm and raise cattle, the Department will lend him 50 head of cattle for a period of 3 years. All he has to do during that time is to feed and shelter them, and at the end of 3 years he can retain all the calves and return the 50 head to the branch who will then re-assign the herd to some other Indian.

"If an Indian wants to leave the reserve [in 1970] and buy a house in the city, the Branch will provide him with a $10,000 mortgage loan. If he stays in the house for a certain period of time he doesn't have to pay off the mortgage at all. He can also obtain a $1,000 grant for the purchase of furniture.

"For those children attending high school in the city, the Branch will provide all educational expenses, clothing and spending allowances together with guidance counselling. If the Indian wishes to make a business investment, on or off the reserve, there is a fund of $2.65 million available from which he can borrow at the low interest rate of 4%, while the non-Indian has to pay as high as 9 or 10%.

"A cost-sharing welfare agreement has been entered into with the Province of Ontario. Child welfare agreements have been developed with Manitoba and Nova Scotia, and Indians receive social welfare on the same level as that provided to other residents of the provinces.

"It is upon education, however, that the Department has been concentrating. In 1970–71 it spent $100 million on education ... There appears to be a considerable lack of motivation for these children to obtain an education and they are not encouraged in any way by these Indian leaders who speak out against the dominant society. If there was a positive response to the dominant society on the part of the Indian leaders and by the parents themselves, children would continue their education through high school and university.

"In 1969 the Indian Affairs Branch spent $3,000,000 for transportation of Indian children to and from school, with over half the transportation contracts going to persons with Indian status. In 1968 alone the Branch assisted over 3,000 adults with a basic literacy program and another 9,600 with other adult programs. It assisted 3,800 others in vocational training and assisted over 11,000 Indians for employment relocation. The Branch also conducted adult education programs in at least 250 Indian communities.

"These facts and figures clearly indicate that the Department of Indian Affairs is vitally involved in the lives of the Indian people and that it is making great strides in educating them and encouraging them to fit into the Canadian society."

In stressing the need for Aboriginal children to receive a proper education, he wrote: "These children are going to have to compete with non-Indians in the race for employment, and they must also learn to live with the white man. What better 'setting and learning environment' than in the actual process of learning together as children?"

As a strong proponent of integration over segregation, Bill Wuttunee wrote: "There is certainly something good to be said about the value of people living together peacefully, mutually, for the benefit of one another. It is time to blast the arguments against integration and to speak in favour of it.

"Integration doesn't have to mean forced integration. Rather it can be a gradual process which will develop Indian men and women into independent, contributing members of Canadian society. It doesn't mean the wholesale displacement of Indian people, but individual attention to individual Indians and their problems. It means giving assistance to those Indians who are now helping themselves, rather than only helping the rebellious few.

"When we have re-examined our approach with a sincere desire to assist and to develop, it is possible that the 'Indian situation' can be solved within the next generation. Let the next century be one of development and self-fulfillment for Indian people. Let us establish a society within which an Indian and a white man can look each other in the eye, with mutual trust. Their concern must always be for those people and for their right to choose freely for themselves."

Given the progress that was being made in improving the lives of Aboriginals living on and off the reserves, Bill Wuttunee was bitterly critical of the negative position on the 1969 White Paper taken by the various Aboriginal organizations and, in particular, the Red Paper put forward by the Indian Chiefs of Alberta.

"What is the Indian cause as espoused by the Red Power advocates?" he asked. "It is the segregation of Indians from white people, the establishment of an administration financed by the Canadian taxpayer and run by Indian organizations. It is the promotion of a buckskin and feather culture and the attempt by Indian leaders to muzzle any criticism by their fellow Indians.

"It is the perpetual criticism of the Indian Affairs Branch, and the process of white witch-hunting. They believe it is the white society which is guilty and which should pay retribution for their pain and suffering. They blame everything on the white man and the Indian Agents. They don't like the words 'assimilation' and 'integration', and plainly they don't seem to like anything except the white man's money."

While it might not have been a deliberate policy of the federal government, he argued, giving unrestricted grants to the Aboriginal organizations "is resulting in the establishment of a new form of segregation."

He also criticized the Aboriginal organizations who were threatening the federal government "by waving verbal tomahawks over their heads in an apparent struggle for better treatment for the first peoples of this land. They are in fact exploiting their own people.

"The theory is that, if independence is to be given to the Indians, then it must be done even if they make mistakes and even if these mistakes are made at the expense of the Canadian taxpayers. This blank-cheque attitude goes only to support little red dictators. Surely there should be more effective controls placed on the spending of this money by the Indian organizations."

With regard to those who advocated reinterpreting the treaties the new Dominion of Canada entered into with the tribes living on the former Hudson's Bay Company lands between Thunder Bay and the eastern slopes of the Rocky Mountains and implementing them according to "the intent" rather than the literal text, Bill Wuttunee said: "It is not possible to turn back the hands of history or to rewrite those hundred-year-old documents."

He also had some strong words about the manner in which most Aboriginal organizations insist on having the people of Canada pay for the benefits they have received from developing the land on which their ancestors once roamed.

"Indians have always hopefully insisted that as original inhabitants of this land they should be reimbursed for the land that was taken away from them by the white man," he wrote. "In reaching this conclusion they have failed to appreciate that the white man conquered Canada without firing a shot. We did not have the fighting between Indians and whites as happened in the United States but, rather, the white man kept coming and the Indians of Canada were aware that if they didn't settle down peacefully it would mean war and they — the Indians — would have been the losers. This finally did happen in 1885 during the Riel Rebellion [which pitted about 500 Métis, Crees and Assiniboine against approximately 5,000 government soldiers and militia].

"At the time of the arrival of the white man, the Indian did not occupy all of the country. Therefore it cannot be said that the land was taken away from him. Those areas which were unoccupied were never taken away from anyone. Indians never owned Canada. They do not own it now, and they never will. Once this concept is clearly understood, there will be less torment in the hearts of Indians in assessing their relationship with the dominant society."

Aboriginal people, he pointed out, had accepted the benefits of the administration of the Indian Affairs Branch, the money of the federal government, and the protection of the North-West Mounted Police.

"So long as the treaties [described in the next chapter] are held in solemn reverence and so long as Indians continue to lick their wounds in the memories of the past," Bill said, "Canada will have the problem of a people unable to stand on their feet in a new society. The signing of the treaties hastened the crumbling of an old culture which had seen its day. It is always difficult to face the fact of having lost something as important as a way of life. If the treaties had not been signed by the Indian people, the white man would have continued his western migration anyway and would have pushed the Indian farther and farther away.

"The history of the negotiations which were conducted at the time of the treaties indicated that the Indians were not really about to refuse the offers of the Queen's Commissioners. They could see the writing on the wall — the buffalo was disappearing and their way of life was coming to an end. They were prepared to give up their nomadic way of life and settle themselves on the land, which is why they were anxious to have instructors in building houses and agriculture. They knew that their days were numbered and that their children would have to live in the new civilization ...

"Since the date of the treaties, the Indians have interpreted them to mean something quite different from what was envisaged by the Commissioners of the Crown.

"It was to the great advantage of the Indian people to be introduced and assisted in the ways of the new civilization. We cannot close our minds to the realities of the situation which confronted them at the time of the signing of the treaties. The treaties are full of humility and supplication of the Indian people in asking for the assistance of the government."

While the old ways have gone the way of the buffalo, Bill Wuttunee was full of hope that the Aboriginal people could adapt to the new realities and carve out a good life for themselves. But first, they would have to ditch the treaty mentality.

"If the treaties can be buried once and for all and if they can be relegated as tombstones to an ancient culture, Indians can build a new future. It is shocking to see Indian people standing in line for their pittance of $5.00 a year [annual treaty payments]. Such a performance is demeaning by present-day standards and must be discontinued. The government should at least mail out the treaty payments in the same way as the family allowance, without any great fanfare …

"One cannot overstress the significance of ending these treaties and of ending the treaty mentality which has spread throughout the country. It has embedded itself so firmly in the Indian mind that it clouds all his thinking and he cannot seem to see his way clearly, for his feelings work more strongly than his mind on this subject. The Indian people cannot keep living in the past. They can never rewrite what actually transpired at the signing of the treaties because the cold facts of history have indelibly written themselves in the hearts and minds of the people. We cannot reinterpret them. We cannot give more significance to either the one side or the other. We cannot improve the bargaining position of either side and neither can we take away. We can realistically look at the past, the present and the future, and learn from the hard lessons of history those truths which will assist us in facing the problems of the day.

"The people who negotiated the treaties have died and we should leave them in peace. They did the very best they could in the circumstances and they left to us a commission to fight new battles for a new era. It is our responsibility to settle this land peacefully and to look to the new boundaries. Let us then gather the old treaties, the Queen Victoria medals, the flags and the chiefs' uniforms and put them in the museums of our land, so that they can forever remind our children that this land was built and created out of the hopes and frustrations of ancestors who earnestly desired the peaceful development of Canada.

Let us consider them hereafter without frustration, and regard the treaty period as a necessary development in the process of fusing together the red and the white."

Bill Wuttunee fully supported the Trudeau government's proposal that individual Aboriginals be allowed to own their own land and criticized the organized opposition. "Once again, the Indians wish to deprive the residents of the reserves of the inherent birthright of every citizen, that is, the right of owning land. There is no reason why reserve lands should not be subdivided and registered in the names of the individual holders. Most of the leasing that has taken place has been to non-Indians who have developed the reserve for them. It appears that the Indians prefer to have someone else do the groundwork in developing their own reserves ...

"There are many band members who are qualified and who would like to hold land in fee simple rather than by the feudal system which is presently in use. It is the basic right of every individual to own land and probably it is contrary to the Bill of Rights for the Indian Act to forbid ownership to various Indians across the country, when they should have the chance to own the land which is rightfully theirs."

He was strongly opposed to the practice of having separate health and other services for Aboriginal people. "The provision of segregated services for Indian people, designed initially to facilitate their integration into the community, tends to work to their disadvantage. Hospitals and schools are prime examples. There is no reason why there should be a white hospital and an Indian hospital in the same community. However, by reason of the policies of the government there are separate health services for Indian people, which only promotes segregation and discrimination."

In supporting the Trudeau government's proposal that the Indian Act should be phased out over time, he said: "The provisions of the Indian Act do not give native people equality. They are saddled with disadvantages which hound them continually in their daily lives. It cannot be said that an Indian has equality before the law if he cannot enjoy his property and if he has to depend on a Minister in Ottawa to exercise and make decisions on his behalf.

"The Indian Act promotes a spirit of inferiority and dependence and, coupled with the treaty mentality, is one of the main reasons for the current difficult situation. Canada will continue to have this problem unless definite steps are taken to change the provisions of the Indian Act or to repeal the Act completely."

One of his main criticisms of the Aboriginal organizations opposed to the new policy was the manner in which they concentrated most of their attention on the isolated reserves scattered across Canada. "They [reserves] have caused nothing but hardship to their inhabitants, and the reserves have become cemeteries of once-brave tribes. Indians have a great love of their land which they regard as Mother Earth, but this love for the last remnants of their land has been their undoing. It had engendered a great devotion, to the point of heroic sacrifice, for a few acres of reserve land …

"Since there is absolutely nothing to do on some reserves, the people spend their time travelling back and forth to the nearest town. Because so many of them spend so much time in town, it is therefore evident that these Indians wish to be integrated and to be with the mainstream of society, rather than stuck back on the reserve …

"In fact, when they leave the reserve they are taking the first step to complete freedom. The reserve was a trap set in the 19th Century which continues to snap at the heels of the natives. If they can leave the reserve and remove from their hearts once and for all the last vestiges of any misplaced feelings of loyalty, they will then be happy in their new surroundings.

"Young people should be encouraged to leave the reserve as early as possible, and they should be helped to fit into the Canadian way of life. They don't have to give up their culture. If they wish to maintain their culture off the reserve they can probably more easily do so by living in better surroundings.

"Just because a culture dies does not mean that something good has died. People do not exist for culture's sake. Culture must be malleable to the wants and tastes of its living participants. Real Indian culture is just about dead on the reserves. To maintain Indian culture does not mean wearing feathers and hopping around on one foot. It means belief in the Great Spirit who inhabits the sun, the stars, the wind and all of nature. It means that one is honourable, brave, generous and kind. It means that one has a sense of responsibility to his immediate family and to the other members of the community with whom he is in contact ...

"If Indians are to become a part of the non-Indian society they cannot be museum pieces in buckskin and feathers. They must be dynamic participants in the society around them. Today, if buckskin and feathers are to be worn, they must be worn honourably and gracefully at functions which are truly native."

While agreeing wholeheartedly with those who believe that the Aboriginal people had suffered enormously as a result of colonization, Bill Wuttunee believed that the time had come to concentrate on the future rather than on the past.

"The past was very difficult for the Indian and he was many times forgotten by the government. But this is no longer the situation, and he is getting the prime attention of every government. Every effort is being made to change his status and to improve the conditions on the reserves and in the cities to which he is now moving. The problem does not lie with the white people anymore. The problem is squarely placed upon the shoulders of the Indian to reassess himself with regard to his position on integration ...

"The new breed of native cannot look at the past as a form of defeat, but only as a necessary period of transition. These people must look at today's events and the past from a viewpoint which will keep them going ever-forward into the mainstream of society. Indians had great leaders in the past, and there is no reason why they cannot continue to have great leaders in the future. If they continue only to cry about broken promises and broken treaties, they can never attain much for their people.

"Merely because some Indians have chosen to leave their reserves and their people does not mean that they have no use for the Indian culture or for their language or for their families. They have become tired of the poverty in which they have to live, and tired of the administration of the Indian Affairs Branch over their daily lives. They want freedom, a chance to live like an ordinary person, to grow old in peace and die without shackles.

"The desire for an improvement in the standard of living must carry with it the equal desire to make a contribution to society by way of taxation. Indians cannot expect to participate in the dominant society without the resulting obligations of hard work and taxation. Indians can no longer blame the white man for their own failures. At one time they had valid arguments against Canadians for having left them to rot on the reserves, but those times have disappeared.

"The Indian people will never regain this country from the white man. They can, however, effectively participate with the white man in its full development. Indians can work with the white men in partnership to develop a country which will provide for each of our children a legacy of great value. It is not necessary to separate from the white man, either physically or spiritually. The long period of segregation of the two races has now ended.

"Let us then unite in spirit, so that each of us can look forward to a peaceful old age in which we can see our children effectively participating in the creation of a new society. Many Indians have already taken the road ahead, to live in the land of the white man. They have paved the way for their brothers and sisters, on which they must learn to walk without fear.

"The hard knocks of history are pushing the Indian into a new way of life and he must learn to accept this new challenge with faith and with hope. History has taught a hard lesson, but history will vindicate itself one day when the Indian finally finds his place in Canadian society."

One of the principal architects of the 1969 White Paper was Toronto Member of Parliament Martin O'Connell, a truly gracious gentleman with a life-long interest in improving the lives of Canada's Aboriginal people.

Martin first got involved when he was a school teacher on Vancouver Island helping local bands deal more effectively with the bureaucracy and encouraging them to speak up about the conditions they were forced to live under.

He later became president of the Indian-Eskimo Association of Canada where he helped fund Indian Friendship Centres and organize workshops to discuss native housing and community and economic development. Aboriginals comprised 25% of the membership of the IEA and always had representation on the board of directors.

Martin, who had a successful career in finance before entering politics, got involved in drafting the 1969 White Paper because of a call he got from Minister without Portfolio Bob Andras, who had built up a successful car dealership in Thunder Bay, Ontario, before becoming an MP in 1965. While it was Jean Chretien, as Minister of Indian Affairs, who introduced the White Paper in the House of Commons, much of the thinking behind the paper was the work of Martin O'Connell and Bob Andras.

"We were trying to come up with a policy that would enable the native people to look after their own affairs," Martin recalled. "One of our first ideas was that we had to amend the Indian Act. The root objective was to put decisions back into the hands of the indigenous communities and trust them to come back with what they needed, their needs for a safe passage into a more integrated style of life."

Martin could recall saying on more than one occasion, and believing very strongly, that "the Indians cannot become Canadians unless they become Indians again. They have to be themselves and hopefully that's the way it's going to go. They have to become Indians again."

He was very firm in his belief that, whether they liked it or not, the Aboriginals were citizens of Canada and it was not in the cards for them to become a sovereign power unto themselves. "They are Canadian citizens," he told me. "They may deny it but they have to respect the fact of that citizenship. They can maintain all kinds of cultural and international and North American contacts and activities, but I don't think that it's in the cards that they can make their own laws. If they want to, they'll have to pay their own way.

"I think they could have a great deal of self-government but you will also have to avoid the prolongation of being kept, the funds which they don't earn. I think it would be a mistake in public policy to accept the continual subsidy for just being, living on a reserve. It would be a mistake to go to a state within a state. I can see reservations, Indian communities, being the equivalent of a municipality, no problem. But they have to also do that within the laws of that province and its statutes. You don't set up a separate state."

In the interview that I conducted with him in Toronto in 1997, Martin, who was appointed to Cabinet in 1971, said the government of Prime Minister Pierre Elliott Trudeau was quite taken aback by the negative, hostile, reaction of the Aboriginal organizations.

He said there "was a feeling of despair" in Cabinet when they saw how opposed most Aboriginal organizations were to the recommendations contained in the 1969 White Paper. "How to handle this situation was a genuine big problem in Cabinet," Martin said. "They had really struggled with it. They wanted to make the concept of the just society apply in the relationship between the government and the Indian people. There was a genuine attempt to 'well, let's give it to them now.'"

But that's not how the more militant Aboriginal organizations reacted. They rejected the White Paper out of hand. In fact, many, like the Indian Chiefs of Alberta, refused to discuss the issue with the government. "I remember saying in Cabinet that 'we offered them those lands that they would take over. We offered to give up the Indian Act which they don't like and they rejected it. What do we do next?'"

He also remembers saying, after much discussion around the Cabinet table: "'Leave the White Paper. Leave the Red Paper. Leave it all there, as if you just left it on the ground and probably, in a decade or two, you'll hear all that stuff coming back from them [Aboriginal people] and those parts only that they'd like to see'."

And that's exactly what the Trudeau government did. They bowed to the pressure from the Aboriginal organizations and shelved the 1969 White Paper. As a result, Aboriginal people still couldn't own their home, get a loan from the bank, or sell any of their chickens or cows without first getting permission from an Indian agent. And a bureaucrat in Ottawa still had final say on how their personal property should be disposed of after their death.

Chapter 2

Let's take a look at the treaties the Aboriginal organizations from western Canada put so much emphasis on despite Cree lawyer Bill Wuttunee's opinion that they really didn't amount to very much in the overall scheme of things.

Here's some background information. When the contiguous British colonies now known as the provinces of Ontario, Quebec, Nova Scotia and New Brunswick became the Dominion of Canada in July, 1867, vast areas of what is now Canada were under the control of the Hudson's Bay Company (HBC) which had its headquarters in London, England.

The 3.8 million square kilometer area the HBC controlled with its forts and soldiers included much of what is now northern Ontario and Quebec, all of Manitoba, most of Saskatchewan and southern Alberta and a portion of the Northwest Territories.

HBC had been granted exclusive trading rights to those vast territories by King Charles II in May, 1670. The company quickly established trading posts and forts throughout the area and developed a positive relationship with the scattered bands of Aboriginals who had lived on the land for centuries.

To advance and protect its trading relationship with the Aboriginals, the company built forts on James Bay and at the mouth of the

Nelson River. The French marched overland from Quebec in 1686 and took control of the posts on James Bay. That was the first of several battles between the French and the English in that area. Finally, under the Treaty of Utrecht, France conceded control of what was known as Rupert's Land to the British in 1713.

Most of the trapping was done during the fall and winter and the Aboriginals would travel to the company's trading posts and forts in summer to exchange their pelts for metal tools, guns, textiles, blankets, foodstuffs and other goods. The beaver and other furs came from as far west as Lake Athabasca and the Rocky Mountains.

The Hudson's Bay Company wrote a letter to the British government in 1811 in which it said:

> "The servants of the Hudson's Bay Company, employed in the fur-trade, have hitherto been fed with provisions exported from England. Of late years this expense has been so enormous, that it became desirable to try the practicability of raising provisions within the territory itself ... It did not appear that agriculture would be carried on with sufficient care and attention by servants in the immediate employ of the company; but by establishing independent settlers, and giving them freehold tenures of land, the company expected that they would obtain a certain supply of provisions at a moderate price. The company also entertained expectations of considerable eventual benefit from the improvement of their landed property by means of agricultural settlements ...
>
> "With these views, the company were induced in the year 1811 to dispose of a large tract of lands to the Earl of Selkirk in whose hands they trusted the experiment would be prosecuted with due attention, as the grant was made subject to adequate conditions of settlement."

Thomas Douglas, the 5th Earl of Selkirk, was born on June 20, 1771, in Kirkcubrightshire, Scotland, and studied law at the University of Edinburgh. Selkirk became increasingly concerned with the plight of tenant farmers who had been forced off lands their families had lived on for generations by landlords who could make more money with sheep than they could renting out their estates to the crofters. The practice became known as the Highland Clearances because, at times, entire valleys were being cleared of farm families to provide grazing land for the sheep.

On inheriting his father's estate in 1799, Selkirk set about the task of resettling displaced Scottish farmers in Canada. In 1803, he financed the passage of 800 Highlanders to land he had purchased in Prince Edward Island. In the following year, he moved 15 families from Kircudbrightshire to land on the north shore of Lake St. Clair.

The June 12, 1811, indenture of sale from the Hudson's Bay Company to Selkirk for the lands upon which the Red River Colony would be established stated:

> "Whereas the said Governor and Company are seized to them and their successors in fee simple [absolute ownership], as absolute Lords and proprietors of all the lands and territories situate upon the coasts and confines of the seas, streights, bays, lakes, rivers, creeks and sounds, within the entrance of the streights commonly called Hudson's Streights, in the north-west part of America, and which lands and territories are reputed as one of the plantations or colonies belonging or annexed to the United Kingdom of Great Britain and Ireland, and are called Rupert's Land..."

The first of several hundred Scottish settlers who arrived at what is now Winnipeg in 1812 had spent a bitterly cold winter on the southwestern shore of Hudson Bay before continuing their long journey from Scotland to the confluence of the Red and Assiniboine Rivers.

They met immediate resistance from the Montreal-based North West Company which was in fierce competition with the Hudson's Bay Company for the lucrative trade in furs in the northwest. They also met resistance from the Métis who were allies of the North West Company and rejected Selkirk's claim to ownership of the land he had purchased from the Hudson's Bay Company for the purpose of establishing a settlement.

Later, when the main group of settlers arrived, they were bitterly disappointed to find that the homes and gardens they had been promised had not been built. In an effort to alleviate their situation, Ojibway Chief Peguis took them with him on his band's annual trek to Fort Daer (Pembina, North Dakota) to hunt buffalo. Pequis also provided ponies for the children who were weak from the long journey from Scotland. When they got to the buffalo country, Pequis taught the settlers how to hunt.

Tension between Selkirk's settlers and the Métis came to a head in January, 1814, when the Governor of the Red River Colony issued the Pemmican Proclamation whereby all pemmican (dried buffalo, moose, elk or deer meat pounded into a coarse powder and mixed with melted fat and berries) was to be reserved for the exclusive use of the settlers. The Métis, who had been supplying pemmican to the traders of the North West Company, destroyed Fort Douglas and burned all the homes around it as an act of protest.

Two years later, a group of Métis seized a supply of pemmican from the Hudson's Bay Company warehouse and headed for a meeting of traders of the North West Company in order to sell it to them. They were intercepted by Robert Semple, the Governor of the Red River Colony and a group of Hudson's Bay Company men and some settlers at Seven Oaks, just south of the recently rebuilt Fort Douglas.

The Métis outnumbered Governor Semple and his group by a ratio of three to one. A heated argument over the pemmican led to a gunfight. Governor Semple and 21 of his outnumbered men were killed. There was only one Métis casualty.

On the next day, Chief Peguis and his warriors retrieved the body of Governor Semple and nine others and buried them in a mass grave in a grove of trees southwest of Fort Douglas. The rest of the dead were left at the scene of the battle.

Meanwhile, the North West Company took control of Fort Douglas, took several officers of the Hudson's Bay Company prisoner and transported them to its inland headquarters at Fort William (Thunder Bay.)

Settlers who survived the attack at Seven Oaks were provided assistance from Chief Peguis. In fact, he rescued the future grandmother of Métis leader Louis Riel and kept her and her children at his camp for several weeks.

Selkirk—after whom the town of Selkirk just north of Winnipeg was named—wrote a testimonial later in which he said Peguis "has been a steady friend of the settlement ever since its first establishment, and has never deserted its cause in its greatest reverses."

At the time of the altercation at Seven Oaks, Selkirk, was en route to the Red River Colony from Montreal with about 100 soldiers of the British Regiment de Meuron. He was told what had happened when he arrived at Sault Ste. Marie and immediately set out for the North West Company's inland headquarters at Fort William, arriving at Fort William shortly after 10:00 a.m. on the morning of August 12th. An eyewitness account provided by author/journalist Samuel Wilcocke said:

> "His Lordship came into the River Kaministiquiâ with four canoes, attended by a number of soldiers, and by his guard, with whom he encamped about 800 or 900 yards above the Fort, on the opposite shore. Within two or three hours, eleven boats full of men, in the uniform of De Meuron's Regiment, came into the River, and were followed by one boat and two canoes loaded with arms and stores, &c. The troops immediately joined Lord Selkirk at his encampment, Cannon were landed, and drawn up, pointed at the Fort, and balls were ready piled beside them, as prepared for a siege and bombardment."

After Selkirk and his soldiers captured the fort, he released those who had been captured at the Red River Colony and ordered the soldiers who would be remaining at the fort not to allow any canoes bearing the North West Company's goods to leave for the interior and to prevent any canoes from transporting furs to Montreal. This ban remained in effect for a year and resulted in enormous losses for the rival North West Company.

Selkirk took eight North West Company partners prisoner, including the head of the company, and dispatched them by canoe for

Montreal along with an armed escort. One of the overloaded canoes capsized on Lake Superior. Selkirk dispatched forces to capture the North West Company's forts at Lac la Pluie, Fond du Lac and Michipicoton.

The British government appointed Hon. W.B. Coltman to conduct an investigation into the incidents at Seven Oaks and Fort William. On July 17, 1817, Selkirk wrote a letter to Coltman in which he said:

> "You are aware that one of the allegations which have been made in vindication of the North West Company, is that the outrages committed here have risen from the jealousy of the native Indians against agricultural settlements, and their resentment against my settlers, for having possession of their lands without their consent or any purchase from them.
>
> "I believe you have already heard enough to be satisfied how little foundation there is for any such idea. But it would be still more satisfactory if the sentiments of the Indians on that point were explicitly and formally declared in your presence, and still more so if they would consent to a specific cession of a portion of their lands to be set aside for the express purpose of agricultural settlements.
>
> "With a view to obviate misrepresentation and to show in a more decided manner their sense of the benefits likely to arise from agricultural establishments, I would propose to them, not a sale but a gift. If a large quantity of goods were offered for the purchase, it might be said, that the temptation of immediate advantage had induced them to sacrifice their permanent interests.
>
> "I would therefore propose to them, merely a small annual present, in the nature of a quit rent, or acknowledgment of their right, and having specified what I intend to give in this way I would leave it to themselves to specify the boundaries of the lands, which they might agree to give up on that consideration, and to appropriate to country. But at all events the transaction would seem

to facilitate the settlement of the country under Crown grants, in the event of my title being found defective."

On the very next day, Selkirk signed an agreement with five chiefs —including Pequis—in which they surrendered all of their rights to a vast quantity of fertile land to "the Sovereign Lord, King George the Third."

In *The Treaties of Canada with the Indians of Manitoba and the North-West Territories* which was published in 1880, former Lieutenant-Governor Alexander Morris said the ceded territory "extended to Grand Forks [North Dakota] in what is now United States territory." Lieut.-Gov. Morris said the chiefs "were made to comprehend the depth of the land they were surrendering by being told that it was the greatest distance at which a horse on the level prairie could be seen or daylight seen under his belly between his legs."

That must have been one giant of a horse between whose legs the chiefs looked to see how much land they were surrendering to Lord Selkirk in exchange for "the payment of 100 pounds of good merchantable tobacco" to be paid to each tribe annually.

Meanwhile, the intense rivalry between the Hudson's Bay Company and the North West Company continued unabated until July, 1821, when, under pressure from the British government, the two companies merged under the Hudson's Bay Company name.

HBC surrendered control over Rupert's Land to the recently-established Dominion of Canada on November 19, 1869, in exchange for 300,000 British pounds, certain lands around its trading posts and forts and, eventually, 2.4 million hectares of farmland. Because of uncertainty caused by an uprising among the Métis who had proclaimed a provisional government in what is now Manitoba, the transfer did not come into effect until July 15, 1870.

At that point, the Parliament of Canada passed laws establishing the Province of Manitoba with a Lieutenant-Governor and Legislature. It also established the North-West Territories and made the Lieutenant-Governor of Manitoba the *ex officio* Lieutenant-Governor of the North-West Territories.

Between 1871 and 1877, the government of Canada negotiated seven treaties with the Ojibways, Crees, Blackfoot and other Aboriginals living on the former HBC lands between Thunder Bay and the eastern slopes of the Rocky Mountains. In *The Treaties of Canada with the Indians* former Lieut.-Gov. Alexander Morris wrote:

> "One of the gravest of the questions presented for solution by the Dominion of Canada, when the enormous region of country formerly known as the North-West Territories and Rupert's Land, was entrusted by the Empire of Great Britain and Ireland to her rule, was the securing of the alliance of the Indian tribes, and maintaining friendly relations with them.
>
> "The predecessors of Canada—the Company of Adventurers of England Trading into Hudson's Bay, popularly known as the Hudson's Bay Company—had, for long years, been eminently successful in securing the good-will of the Indians—but on their sway coming to an end, the Indian mind was disturbed.
>
> "The events, that transpired in the Red River region in the years 1869–1870, during the period when the provisional government was attempted to be established [by Métis leader Louis Riel], had perplexed the Indians.
>
> "They, moreover, had witnessed a sudden irruption into the country of whites from without. In the West, American traders poured into the land, and, freighted with fire-water, purchased their peltries [furs] and their horses, and impoverished the tribes.
>
> "In the east, white men took possession of the soil and made for themselves homes, and as time went on steamboats were placed on the inland waters—surveyors passed through the territories—and the 'speaking wires', as the Indian calls the telegraph, were erected.
>
> "What wonder that the Indian mind was disturbed, and what wonder was it that a Plain chief, as he looked upon the strange [telegraph] wires stretching through his land, exclaimed to his people, 'We have done wrong to

allow that wire to be placed there, before the Government obtained our leave to do so. There is a white chief at Red River [Winnipeg], and that wire speaks to him, and if we do anything wrong he will stretch out a long arm and take hold of us before we can get away.'"

On November 3, 1871, Indian Commissioner Wymess McKenzie Simpson wrote: "Already, settlers from the Provinces of Canada [Ontario and Quebec] and elsewhere are pushing their way beyond the limits of the Province of Manitoba; and there is nothing but the arbitrary limits of that Province, and certain water and wood advantages found in the territory beyond it, to distinguish one part of the country from the other."

Commissioner Simpson went on to say: "In the neighbourhood of Fort Edmonton, on the Saskatchewan, there is a rapidly increasing population of miners and other white people and it is the opinion of Mr. W. J. Christie, the [Hudson's Bay Company] officer in charge of the Saskatchewan district, that a treaty with the Indians of that country or at least an assurance during this coming year that a treaty will shortly be made is essential to the peace, if not the actual retention, of the country."

Commissioner Simpson described the preparations he had made for making a treaty with the bands in Manitoba. "I called upon Mr. [Lieutenant-Governor Adams G.] Archibald, and learned from him that the Indians were anxiously awaiting my arrival, and were much excited on the subject of their lands being occupied without attention being first given to their claims for compensation.

"Amongst the settlers, also, an uneasy feeling existed, arising partly from the often-repeated demands of the Indians for a treaty with themselves, and partly from the fact that certain settlers in the neighborhood of Portage la Prairie and other parts of the Province, had been warned by the Indians not to cut wood or otherwise take possession of their lands upon which they were squatting.

"The Indians, it appeared, consented to their remaining on their holdings until sufficient time had been allowed for my arrival, and the conclusion of a treaty; but they were unwilling to allow the settlers the free use of the country for themselves or their cattle."

In a letter to government authorities dated April 13, 1871, W. J. Christie, Chief Factor, Saskatchewan District, Hudson's Bay Company, said: "I take this opportunity of most earnestly soliciting, on behalf of the [Hudson's Bay] Company's servants, and settlers in this district, that protection be afforded to life and property here as soon as possible, and that Commissioners be sent to speak to the Indians on behalf of the Canadian Government."

Mr. Christie described a recent meeting with some Cree chiefs who had come to visit him at the HBC fort. "They referred to the epidemic [smallpox] that had raged throughout the past summer and the subsequent starvation, the poverty of their country, the visible diminution of the buffalo, their sole support."

He said the chiefs had ended the meeting by requesting certain "presents" at once and asking that he present their case to 'Her Majesty's representative at Fort Garry'.

"Had I not complied with the demands of the Indians—giving them some little presents—and otherwise satisfied them, I have no doubt that they would have proceeded to acts of violence, and once that had commenced, there would have been the beginning of an Indian war, which it is difficult to say when it would have ended.

"The buffalo will soon be exterminated, and when starvation comes, these Plain Indian tribes will fall back on the Hudson's Bay Forts and settlements for relief and assistance. If not complied with, or no steps taken to make some provisions for them, they will most assuredly help themselves; and there being no force or any law up there to protect the settlers, they must either quietly submit to be pillaged, or lose their lives in the defence of their families and property, against such fearful odds that will leave no hope for their side.

"Gold may be discovered in paying quantities, any day, on the eastern slopes of the Rocky Mountains. We have, in Montana, and in the mining settlements close to our boundary line, a large mixed frontier population, who are now only waiting and watching to hear of gold discoveries to rush into the Saskatchewan, and, without any force of Government or established law up here, or force to protect whites or Indians, it is very plain what will be the result.

"I think that the establishment of law and order in the Saskatchewan district, as early as possible, is of most vital importance to the future of the country and the interest of Canada and also the making of some treaty or settlement with the Indians who inhabit the Saskatchewan district."

In a report that he wrote describing the negotiations with the Crees at Stone Fort (Lower Fort Garry) and Manitoba Post (at the north end of Lake Winnipeg) in 1871, Lieutenant-Governor Adams G. Archibald said: "We told them that whether they wished it or not, immigrants would come in and fill up this country. That every year from this one twice as many in number as their whole people there assembled would pour into the Province [Manitoba], and in a little while would spread all over it, and that now was the time for them to come to an arrangement that would secure homes and annuities for themselves and their children."

Speaking to the Crees near Fort Qu'Appelle, Saskatchewan, on September 11, 1874, Lieut.-Gov. Morris said: "The Queen knows that you are poor. The Queen knows that it is hard to find food for yourselves and children. She knows that the winters are cold and your children are often hungry. She has always cared for her red children as much as for her white. Out of her generous heart and liberal hand she wants to do something for you, so that when the buffalo get scarcer, and they are scarce enough now, you may be able to do something for yourselves."

In a letter to Lieut.-Gov. Morris dated October 23, 1875, Reverend George McDougall, a Wesleyan Methodist missionary who had spent about 14 years living among the Crees, said: "Though they [the Crees and Plains Assiniboines] deplored the necessity of resorting to extreme measures, yet they were unanimous in their determination to oppose the running of [telegraph] lines, or the making of roads through their country, until a settlement between the Government and them has been effected.

"I was further informed that the danger of a collision with the whites was likely to arise from the officious conduct of minor Chiefs who were anxious to make themselves conspicuous, the principal men of the large camps being much more moderate in their demands."

In his annual report for 1876, Hon. David Mills, Minister of the

Interior, said: "Official reports received last year from His Honor Governor [Alexander] Morris and Colonel French, the officer then in command of the [North-West] Mounted Police Force, and from other parties, showed that a feeling of discontent and uneasiness prevailed very generally amongst the Assiniboines and Crees lying in the unceded territory between the Saskatchewan River and the Rocky Mountains.

"This state of feeling, which had prevailed amongst these Indians for some years past, had been increased by the presence, last summer, in their territory of the parties engaged in the construction of the telegraph line, and in the survey of the Pacific Railway line, and also of a party belonging to the Geological Survey.

"To allay this state of feeling, and to prevent the threatened hostility of the Indian tribes to the parties then employed by the Government, His Honor Governor Morris requested and obtained authority to dispatch a messenger to convey to these Indians the assurances that Commissioners would be sent this summer, to negotiate a treaty with them, as had already been done with their brethren further east."

Speaking to the Crees at Fort Carlton on August 19, 1876, Lieut.-Gov. Morris said: "The country is wide and you are scattered, other people will come in. Now unless the places where you would like to live are secured soon there might be difficulty. The white man might come and settle on the very place where you would like to be."

One reason for the ever-increasing number of settlers was the Dominion Lands Act of 1872 which offered free homesteads of 65 hectares to farm families on the condition that they clear four hectares and build a house within three years.

In a report that he wrote after all of the treaties had been signed, Lieut.-Gov. Morris said: "The Indians were apprehensive of their future. They saw the food supply, the buffalo, passing away, and they were anxious and distressed. They knew the large terms granted to their Indians by the United States, but they had confidence in their great Mother, the Queen, and her benevolence. They desired to be fed. Smallpox had destroyed them by hundreds a few years before, and they dreaded pestilence and famine."

In a letter that was sent to Lieutenant-Governor Adams G. Archibald in the summer of 1876, Sweet Grass, the principal chief of the Plains

Crees, said: "Our country is getting ruined of fur-bearing animals, hitherto our sole support, and now we are poor and want help—we want you to pity us. We want cattle, tools, agricultural implements, and assistance in everything when we come to settle—our country is no longer able to support us.

"Make provisions for us against years of starvation. We have had great starvation, this past winter, and the small-pox took away many of our people, the old, young, and children.

"We want you to stop the Americans from coming to trade on our lands, and giving firewater [whiskey], ammunition and arms to our enemies the Blackfeet.

"We made a peace this winter with the Blackfeet. Our young men are foolish, it may not last long."

Three other chiefs added their comments to the letter.

> Ki-He-Win (The Eagle): "Great Father. Let us be friendly. We never shed any white man's blood and have always been friendly with the whites and want workmen, carpenters and farmers to assist us when we settle. I want all my brother Sweet Grass asks. That is all."
>
> The Little Hunter. "You my brother the Great Chief in Red River, treat me as a brother, that is, as a Great Chief."
>
> Kas-ki-on or Short Tail. "My brother that is coming close. I look upon you as if I saw you. I want you to pity me and I want help to cultivate the ground for myself and descendants. Come and see us."

Ten months before the start of the negotiations with the Cree Chiefs at Forts Carlton and Pitt in August, 1876, Reverend George McDougall visited most of the bands and delivered a message from Lieut.-Gov. Morris along with some presents. With the exception of Big Bear, an Ojibway chief from Jack Fish Lake who commanded a band of approximately 500, most of the chiefs welcomed the opportunity to negotiate a treaty.

Despite the protestations of Big Bear, the treaty was supported by a significant majority and signed accordingly. Chief See-kahs-kootch

(The Cut Arm) said: "I am glad of the goodness of the Great Queen. I recognize now that this that I once dreaded most is coming to my aid and doing for me what I could not do for myself."

Chief Tus-tuk-ee-skuas, then said: "I am truly glad that the Queen has made a new country for me. I am glad that all my friends and children will not be in want of food hereafter. I am glad that we have everything which we had before still extended to us."

Wah-wee-kah-nihk-kah-oo-tah-mah-hote (the man you strike in the back) said: "Pity the voice of the Indian. If you grant what we request the sound will echo through the land. Open the way. I speak for the children that they may be glad. The land is wide. There is plenty of room. Have compassion on the manner in which I was brought up. Let our children be clothed.

"Let us now stand in the light of day to see our way on this earth. Long ago it was good when we first were made. I wish the same were back again. But now the law has come, and in that I wish to walk. What God has said, and our mother here [the earth], and these our brethren, let it be so."

Chief Sweet Grass said: "I thank you [Lieut.-Gov. Morris] for this day, and also I thank you for what I have seen and heard. I also thank the Queen for sending you to act for our good. I am glad to have a brother and friend in you, which undoubtedly will raise us above our present condition. I am glad for your offers and speak from my heart.

"I speak this in the presence of the Divine Being. It is all for our good. I see nothing to be afraid of. I therefore accept of it gladly and take your hand to my heart. May this continue as long as this earth stands and the river flows. The Great King [William IV who died in 1837] our Father, is now looking upon us this day. He regards all the people equal with one another. He has mercy on the whole earth. He has opened a new world to us.

"I have pity on all those who have to live by the buffalo. If I am spared until this time next year [he was accidentally shot and killed by his brother-in-law six months later] I want this my brother to commence to act for me, thinking therefore that the buffalo might be protected. It is for that reason that I give you my hand. If spared, I shall commence at once to clear a small piece of land for myself and others of my kinsmen will do the same. We will commence hand in hand to protect the buffalo.

"When I hold your hand I feel as if the Great Father [King William IV] were looking on us both as brothers. I am thankful. May this earth here never see the white man's blood spilt on it. I thank God that we stand together, that you all see us. I am thankful that I can raise up my hand, and the white man and red man can stand together as long as the sun shines.

"When I hold your hands and touch your heart, as I do now [at that point he placed his hand on Lieut.-Gov. Morris's chest], let us be as one. Use your utmost to help me and help my children, so that they may prosper."

According to Lieut.-Gov. Morris, what Sweet Grass had to say "was assented to by the people with a peculiar guttural sound which takes with them the place of the British cheer [Hip Hip Hooray]."

In reply, the Lieutenant-Governor said: "I rise with a glad heart. We have come together and understood each other. I am glad that you have seen the right way. I am glad that you have accepted so unanimously the offer made. I will tell the Queen's Councillors what good hearts their Indian children have. I will tell them that they think of the good of their children's children."

At the negotiations at Fort Carlton, Kah-mee-yis-too-ways (The Beardy) said: "I feel grateful for this day, and I hope we will be blessed. I am glad that I see something that will be of use. I wish that we all as a people may be benefitted by this. I want that all these things should be preserved in a manner that they might be useful to us all. It is in the power of men to help each other.

"We should not act foolishly with the things that are given us to live by. I think some things [offered] are too little, they will not be sufficient for our wants. I do not want very much more than what has been promised, only a little thing. I will be glad if you will help me by writing my request down.

"On account of the buffalo I am getting anxious. I wish that each one should have an equal share, if that could be managed. Perhaps this is not the only time that we shall see each other. Now I suppose another can say what he wishes."

Say-sway-kus then said: "What my brother has said, I say the same, but I want to tell him and our Mother the Queen, that although we understand the help they offer us, I am getting alarmed when I look at the buffalo. It appears to me as if there was only one. I trust to the Queen and to the Governor. It is only through their aid we can manage and preserve them."

Concern about the alarming rate at which the buffalo were disappearing was well grounded. In the winter of 1846, for example, an American Indian agent on the Missouri River reported that the Assiniboines of the northern plains had been reduced to starvation. They subsisted for a time on deer, elk, and wolves, but these were either too few or too insubstantial to sustain them. After consuming their reserves of dried meat, berries and roots, they started to eat their dogs and horses.

It was reported that the population of all of the Plains tribes on the American side of the border fell from 142,000 in 1780 to 53,000 in 1890, in large part because of disease and starvation. Lodges in which whole families lay dead lined the trails.

And, consider this from the 1883 report of Canada's Indian Affairs Branch: "The majority of deaths during the year have been from consumption. This is owing, in a great extent, to their want of clothing ... All this is caused by the disappearance of the buffalo and other game from which they formerly obtained their covering and lodges. The latter are now made of very thin [store-bought] cotton, and are utterly inadequate to protect them from the severe winter climate."

The buffalo-based economy had been completely destroyed and, no longer having anything to trade, destitute bands of disease-ravaged Aboriginals had no option but to camp beside the trading posts and hope some white man would take pity on them.

This might be a good point to tell you something about the manner in which the bands on the prairies slaughtered the buffalo by the hundreds at kill sites. The principal method of mass killing was by stampeding the buffalo at full gallop from their grazing grounds toward high cliffs, called buffalo jumps. The bulls, cows and young calves, would cascade over the edge of the cliff and tumble about 10 metres down onto the rocks below. The Aboriginal males would then make their way into the mass of broken bones and mangled bodies and slaughter the animals with spears. And then the women and children would move in to skin them and separate the meat.

Another method was described by British surveyor Henry Youle Hind who witnessed a band of Crees hunting buffalo in 1857: "In hunting the buffalo, they are wild with excitement, but no scene or incident seems to have such a maddening effect upon them as when the buffalo are successfully driven into a pound [corral]. Until the herd is brought in by the skilled hunters, the utmost silence is preserved around the fence of the pound. Men, women and children with pent up feelings, hold their robes so as to close every orifice through which the terrified animals might endeavour to escape. The herd, once in the pound, a scene of diabolical butchery and excitement begins. Men, women and children climb on the fences and shoot arrows or thrust spears at the bewildered buffalo with shouts, screams and yells horrible to hear."

However, it was the arrival of the white hunters on the great plains of North America in the mid-19th century that led to the rapid and brutal extermination of the buffalo herds. Consider this excerpt from "Major" Israel McCreight's *Buffalo Bone Days* which was published in 1939. "From 1868 to 1881 more than two million five hundred thousand dollars was paid out for buffalo bones in the Kansas section alone … this tonnage accounted for thirty one million animals. If we take Major Inman's count for the thirteen years from '68 to '81, we must also assume that gathering of bones began in 1868 and was completed by 1881, in the territory served by the Kansas Pacific-Santa Fe railroads in that district. But that by no means indicates that all the bones had been collected in the Kansas-Nebraska country during that period. Main and branch lines were being pushed out in many directions and the settlement by incoming pioneers continued for many years,—and likewise the gathering of bones followed until the entire farming area of the two states, was under cultivation."

McCreight—a white man from Pennsylvania who traded with the

Lakota Sioux in the Dakota Territory—went on to say: "In the middle 70's it was not uncommon for the lone still-hunter to shoot down 150 or 200 [buffalo] without moving from his hiding place. One man claimed to have killed 1,500 buffalo in seven days, and that he killed 250 in a single day; another is quoted who said he shot down 120 animals in forty minutes, and it is claimed that nearly four million animals were killed and their hides shipped out over the Sante Fe railroad, while the carcasses were left to rot on the plains—all in two years.

"When one contemplates that this kind of slaughter was going on at like rate from the Canadian border to lower Texas it is no wonder that it took but a few years to exterminate the nation's entire herds of the bison ... Compilations rendered by the Santa Fe [Railway] show that during the three years 1871–1874 that railroad shipped from points on its lines in Kansas 459,453 buffalo hides, and 10,793,350 pounds of buffalo bones, and from other lines in tile [sic] same sections and for the same years, there were shipped out 918,906 hides and 21,586,700 pounds of buffalo bones."

A letter included in McCreight's book states: "Hard upon the crack of the rifle came the buffalo skinners, with their worn I. Wilson knives, long iron pickets and skinning teams. They slit the hide down the belly and about the neck, picketed the buffalo's nose to the ground and hitched the skinning team to a tab on the rough neck hide. At the crack of the whip the horses lunged forward, and the skin was off.

"Millions of tons of meat were left on the plains to rot—food for maggots and wolves. Only the stark ribs remained. In the '50's and '60's the plains from the Pan-Handle and northern Arkansas to the Canadian line were frosted white as alkali flats in spots with bleaching bones. The rime was thickest in western Kansas, spreading north to the Platte and west into eastern Wyoming and Colorado.

"No one seeing the endless mass of bones dreamed that any use would ever be made of them. But with the completion of the Union Pacific railroad, and later the Santa Fe line, new industry sprang up. Hundreds of merchants established a regular trade and did a lively business buying and shipping buffalo bones to eastern markets. In ten years the trade in bones amounted to fully two and a half million dollars, averaging $8 per ton.

"Upon the heels of the vanishing buffalo came the homesteader, often with only an old wagon, a skinny team, several children and a few dogs. Many got a start by collecting buffalo bones. In the lean years of the '70s when the hot winds blew over Kansas and Nebraska, the settlers fitted out their wagons, pushed into the unclaimed prairies and braved the rattle snakes lurking about the old 'critters' to gather the bones and trade them for flour and calico at the nearest store."

And consider this excerpt from an article written by Arthur C. Bill who was engaged in the buffalo bones trade in Kansas back in the early 1870s. "Government freighters hauling on way south were glad to haul for us on their return trip north. We piled the bones along the trail with our numbers on same. They hauled the bones to Dodge City and piled them along the A. T. & S. Fe tracks from where they were loaded into cattle cars and shipped to St. Louis to be used in refining sugar; their hoofs used to make glue; the horns to make buttons, combs, knife handles, etc. We received from $7 to $9 per ton f.o.b. for the plain bones, and $12 to $15 for the hoofs and horns ...

"We made good gathering buffalo bones—would often come to a place where the hunters had succeeded in getting a stand on the herd and would kill them all. The hunters watched for the leader before doing any shooting. The leader, always a cow buffalo, with a number of buffalo in her family, would be dropped in her tracks the first shot; then the whole herd would stand still for a while, regardless of how many were killed. Then another cow would take the lead; she was shot down at once. After that the whole herd would stand still and all be shot down.

"The noble beasts of the plains were slaughtered unmercifully, for no gain. The hunter realized but little for his share. Following the hunters were the skinners—skinning the buffalo and staking the hide to the ground, flesh side up; then came the rustlers, gathering up the pelts and hauling them to the railroads where they brought but little—seventy-five cents apiece or less.

"The buffalo furnished a living for the Indians of the plains. The Indians only killed the buffalo for use of food and raiment. His tents, his beds, his moccasins, his lariats, his thread and many other useful articles, not forgetting his food. The only good that came from destroying the buffalo was to rid the country of the Indians—if we may call that good."

A bone of contention with the chiefs on the prairies was the fact that the new government of Canada had paid 300,000 British pounds to the Hudson's Bay Company when they assumed control of the vast territories over which the company had previously exercised complete control.

"We heard our lands were sold and we did not like it," Chief Sweet Grass said during the treaty negotiations at Fort Carlton, Saskatchewan. "We don't want to sell our lands. It is our property and no one has a right to sell them."

This attitude toward the Hudson's Bay Company was a definite stumbling block at the start of the negotiations near Fort Qu'Appelle, Saskatchewan, in September, 1874. When the chiefs appeared reluctant to speak, Lieut.-Gov. Alexander Morris said: "Why are your Chiefs dumb? They can speak. One of them is called 'Loud Voice'. He must have been heard in the councils of the nation. Then I ask myself, why do they not answer? It cannot be that you are afraid. You are not women."

Pointing to an officer of the Hudson's Bay Company, Chief Pis-qua (the plain) said: "You told me you had sold your land for so much money, 300,000 pounds. We want that money."

In response, Lieut.-Gov. Morris said: "I wish our Indian brother had spoken before what was on his mind. He has been going here and there and we never knew what he meant. I told you that many years ago the Queen's father gave the Company the right to trade in the country from the frozen ocean [Hudson Bay] to the United States boundary line, and from the Atlantic Ocean to the Pacific.

"The Company grew strong and wanted no one to trade in the country but themselves. The Queen's people said, 'no, the land is not yours, the Queen's father gave you rights to trade, it is time those rights should stop.' You may go and trade like any other merchant, but as it was worth money to you to say to this trader you shall not buy furs at any post, the Queen would not act unjustly to the Company. She would not take rights away from them any more than from you;

and to settle the question, she took all the lands into her own hands and gave the Company a sum of money in place of the rights which she had taken from them.

"She is ready to deal with you justly. We are here today to make to you her good offers. We have nothing to hide, nothing to conceal. The Queen acts in daylight. I think it is time you are going to talk with us about the offers we have made."

Nevertheless, the chiefs held firm to the belief that "their land" had been sold and the money should have been given to them.

The Canadian government's decision to establish the North-West Mounted Police in 1874 and have them headquartered at Fort Macleod in southern Alberta made an enormous difference in the lives of the Aboriginals and of the settlers.

In addition to stamping out the ruinous trade in firewater and providing protection for the settlers and the Aboriginals, the North-West Mounted Police served as a deterrent to any plans on the part of the Americans to annex the sparsely-populated area which had only recently come under Canadian control.

Here's how a missionary priest by the name of Father Constantine Scollen put it on September 8, 1876: "But this [1874] was the year of their [Blackfoot] salvation. That very summer the [North-West] Mounted Police were struggling against the difficulties of a long journey across the barren plains in order to bring them help.

"This noble corps reached their destination that same fall, and with magic effect put an entire stop to the abominable traffic of whiskey with the Indians. Since that time the Blackfeet Indians are becoming more and more prosperous. They are now well clothed and well furnished with horses and guns. During the last two years I have calculated they have bought two thousand horses to replace those they had given away for whiskey.

"They are forced to acknowledge that the arrival of the Red Coats has been to them a great boon. But, although they are externally so friendly to the Police and other strangers who now inhabit their country, yet underneath this friendship remains hidden some of that dread which they have always had of the white man's intention to cheat them."

While addressing the Crees near Fort Qu'Appelle in September, 1874, Lieut.-Gov. Morris provided further evidence of the benefit to the Blackfoot, Cree and other tribes of having the North-West Mounted Police in the territory. "I am now quite willing to tell you all about Fort Pelly [a Hudson's Bay Company post in east-central Saskatchewan]. The Queen heard that Americans had come into the country and were treating her Indian children badly. I myself sent her word that twenty-five of her Indian children, men, women and children, had been shot down by the American traders. Then she resolved to protect her red children.

"For that reason she had determined to have a body of men on horses as policemen to keep all the bad people, white or red, in order. She will not allow her red children to be made drunk and shot down again as some of them were a few months ago. Now you ought to be glad that you have a Queen who takes such an interest in you.

"In this country, now, no man need be afraid. If a white man does wrong to an Indian, the Queen will punish them. The other day at Fort Ellice, a white man, it is said, stole some furs from an Indian. The Queen's policemen took him at once, sent him down to Red River, and he is lying in jail now. And if the Indians prove that he did wrong, he will be punished. And it will be the same if an Indian does wrong to the white man.

"The red and white man must live together and be good friends and the Indians must live together like brothers with each other and the white man."

That was quite a contrast to the lawless situation that existed when the Canadian government sent Major William Butler of the British Army into the newly-acquired North-West Territories in 1871 to examine and report upon the state of affairs in that region. In a report to Lieutenant-Governor Adams G. Archibald, he said that "law and order are wholly unknown in the region of the Saskatchewan, in so much as the country is without any executive organization and destitute of any means of enforcing the law."

During the negotiations at Fort Pitt, Saskatchewan, on September 13, 1876, Lieut.-Gov. Morris said: "Look at the condition of the Blackfeet. Before the red-coats went, the Americans were taking their furs and [buffalo] robes and giving them whiskey. We stopped it. They have been able to buy back two thousand horses. Before that, robes would have gone to the Americans for whiskey."

In his 1877 annual report, Interior Minister David Mills said: "I may here remark, that another great benefit has resulted from the judicious steps taken by the Canadian government, and that is the cessation of warfare between the various tribes, which was before of constant occurrence."

In their book, *First Peoples in Canada,* Professors Alan D. McMillan and Eldon Yellowhorn, who was born and raised on the Peigan Reserve in Alberta, wrote: "By the beginning of the 19th century, as the Cree and Assiniboine pushed west and encroached on Blackfoot lands, they became embroiled in bitter hostilities. Warfare became continual on the western plains until the reserve period. The last major battle between the Blackfoot and Cree was fought near Fort Hoop-Up near Lethbridge Alberta in 1870. ...

"Eventually armed with European weapons obtained in trade on Hudson Bay and allied with the Assiniboine, the Cree pushed across the southern plains to the Rockies. Other groups were displaced in front of them until smallpox and the acquisition of firearms by their enemies finally halted their advance.

"The plains Cree along with their Assiniboine allies established themselves as intermediaries between the post on Hudson Bay and the western tribes. They could make huge profits by taking furs to the post and bringing back European goods to trade to more distant groups. Later when the [Hudson's Bay] company set up posts across the plains, the Cree and Ojibwa became major suppliers of pemmican and bison [buffalo] hides. Their close association with the fur trade led to the rise of the Métis from unions between male fur traders and Cree or Ojibwa women ...

"With their Plains Cree allies, the Assiniboine waged continued war against the tribes of the Blackfoot Confederacy to the west. To the south the bitter enmity with their Dakota relatives simmered for centuries. War parties of Assiniboine, plains Cree and plains Ojibwa combined to do battle with these foes.

"At the end of the horse days, the Assiniboine were distributed across southern Saskatchewan and northern Montana. Their reserves in Saskatchewan today are generally shared with the Cree. Closely related to the Assiniboine, are the Stoney, who split from the main group and established a separate identity, possibly in the 18th century. They pushed west to the Rockies where they battled the Blackfoot for possession of the foothills and eastern mountain slopes. There they hunted bison on the plains and elk and other large game in the mountains and they traded at [Hudson's Bay Company] posts such as Rocky Mountain House."

The plains Cree and their Assiniboine and Ojibway allies forced the Gros Ventre south into Montana. A state of warfare existed between the Ojibways and the Sioux when Treaty #3 was being negotiated in 1873. "At the [Northwest] Angle [of the Lake of the Woods]," Lieut.-Gov. Alexander Morris wrote, "but for the presence of the troops, the Chippewas would have fled, it having been circulated among them, that the Sioux were coming to attack them."

In talking about the establishment of the North-West Mounted Police, Lieut.-Gov. Morris said: "An intelligent Ojibbeway Indian trader told me, that the change was wonderful. 'Before,' he said, 'the Queen's government came, we were never safe, and now,' he said, 'I can sleep in my tent anywhere, and have no fear. I can go to the Blackfeet, and Cree camps, and they treat me as a friend.'"

Here's how Lieutenant-Governor David Laird described his long journey in the summer of 1877 from Government House at Battleford, Saskatchewan, to Fort Macleod in order to negotiate a treaty with the Blackfoot and other tribes. "The Crees [on the journey through Treaty 6 territory] appeared friendly, but were not so demonstrative as the Blackfeet who always rode up at once with a smile on their countenances and shook hands with us. They knew the uniform of the Mounted Police at a distance and at once recognized and approached them as friends."

During the negotiations for the Blackfeet Treaty at the Blackfoot Crossing in September, 1877, Button Chief said: "The Great Spirit sent the white man across the great waters to carry out His ends. The Great Spirit, and not the Great [white] Mother, gave us this land. The Great Mother sent Stamixotokon [Colonel James Farquharson Macleod] and the Police put an end to the traffic in firewater. I can now sleep safely. Before the arrival of the Police, when I laid my head down at night, every sound frightened me. My sleep was broken. Now I can sleep sound and I am not afraid. The Great Mother sent you to this country, and we hope she will be good to us for many years."

Chief Crowfoot said: "The advice given me and my people has proved to be very good. If the Police had not come to the country, where would be all now? Bad men and whiskey were killing us so fast that very few, indeed, of us would have been left today. The Police have protected us as the feathers of the bird protect it from the frosts of winter. I wish them all good, and trust that all our hearts will increase in goodness from this time forward. I am satisfied. I will sign the treaty."

In his report about the negotiations leading up to the signing of the Blackfeet Treaty, Lieutenant-Governor David Laird said: "The leading Chiefs of the Blackfeet and kindred tribes, declared publicly at the treaty that, had it not been for the Mounted Police they would all have been dead ere this time."

He went on to say: "I cannot speak too highly of the kind manner in which the officers and men of the Mounted Police at Fort McLeod [sic] treat their Indian visitors. I never heard a harsh word employed in asking them to retire. The beneficial effects of this treatment, of the exclusion of intoxicants from the country, and of impartially administering justice to whites and Indians alike were apparent in all my interviews with the Indians. They always spoke of the officers of the Police in the highest terms and of the Commander of the Fort, Lieut-Col. McLeod [sic] especially as their great benefactor."

Colonel Macleod, after whom a major thoroughfare in Calgary is named, was born in Scotland in 1836 and was educated at Upper Canada College in Toronto, Queen's College, Kingston, and at Osgoode Hall, in Toronto. He practised law in Bowmanville and joined the Volunteer Militia Field Battery in Kingston. He was mentioned in dispatches while serving under Colonel Garnet Joseph Wolseley in the

Red River Expedition of 1870 and was promoted to Lieutenant-Colonel in the 45th Battalion of Infantry.

In 1874, he led his troops across the prairies and established Fort Macleod at a crossroads near Lethbridge, Alberta, that hosted wagon trains, Aboriginal encampments, and grazing grounds for buffalo. The buffalo head on the insignia of the Royal Canadian Mounted Police was first suggested by Colonel Macleod.

Chapter 3

For quite some time before the Hudson's Bay Company transferred its vast territories to the new Dominion of Canada, traders had been using a route of lakes, creeks, rivers and portages in order to get from what is now Thunder Bay to Winnipeg. Doing so required permission from the scattered bands of Ojibways living in the area who were very protective of their territory. On more than one occasion, they warned white men not to depart from the established route.

In July, 1857, for example, a survey party was intercepted by an Ojibway chief leading a war party returning home from a foray into Sioux territory on the American side of the border. The chief was suspicious of their motives and insisted that the party stick to the common route that had been established by the fur traders. "The white man comes, looks at our flowers, our trees and our rivers," he said. "Others soon follow him. The lands of the Indians pass from their hands and they have a home nowhere. You must go by the way the white man has hitherto gone."

In a letter dated February 8, 1870, Indian agent Robert Pither said the Ojibways wanted an answer to a demand they had sent to him regarding payment they were to receive for allowing the Canadians to pass through their territory. He quoted the Ojibways as saying "we expect an answer to our demand sent to Mr. Pither during the winter so that we may know how to act and when to assemble for payment. For this we are willing to allow the Queen's subjects the right to pass through our lands, to build and run steamers, build canals and railroads and to take up sufficient land for buildings for Government use — but we will not allow farmers to settle on our lands. We want to see how the Red River [Winnipeg] Indians will be settled with and whether the soldiers will take away their lands — we will not take your presents, they are a bait and if we take them you will say we are bound to you."

In a letter to the Canadian government at that time, Simon J. Dawson, the man in charge of building what would become known as the Dawson Road, passed on a message he had received at a meeting with Ojibway chiefs. He quoted them as saying: "We want much that the white man has to give and the white man, on his part wants roads and land. When we meet next Summer you must be prepared to tell us where your roads are to pass and what lands you require ... We believe what you tell us when you say that, in your land [Ontario], the Indians have always been treated with clemency and justice, and we are not apprehensive for the future, but do not bring settlers and Surveyors amongst us, to measure and occupy our lands until a clear understanding has been arrived at, as to what our relations are to be in the time to come."

In another letter, Mr. Dawson wrote that the Ojibways were "tenacious of what they conceive to be their rights, but they have for some years past observed the white men in unaccustomed numbers pursuing their avocations quietly and unobtrusively, and if they are now disposed to enter into a treaty with the Government, as I believe them to be, I can safely say that it is in no small measure due to the fact that from observing the proceedings of the people on the Works (Dawson Route) they have begun to look with favour on the altered position in which they are being placed by the opening up of their country, and this, I may add, can very rarely be said of the first advance of civilization among the native tribes."

Obtaining free and unfettered access to the huge territory that would be covered by Treaty #3 was important for the proposed transcontinental Canadian Pacific Railway and for the protection of Canadian sovereignty over the United States/Canada border.

Mr. Dawson was fully aware of the many battles the Ojibways had engaged in to prevent encroachment on their lands by Sioux on the American side of the border. In emphasizing the urgent necessity of entering into a treaty with the Ojibways, he said: "They are sufficiently organized, numerous and warlike, to be dangerous if disposed to hostility; and standing as they do in the gateway to the territories of the North West, it is of the highest importance to cultivate amicable relations with them."

When the commissioners appointed by the Government of Canada first met with the chiefs representing the scattered bands of Ojibways living in the area in July, 1871, the chiefs said they would only agree to a right-of-way through their sparsely-populated territory. The commissioners told the chiefs that the British Queen wanted them to surrender all of their territorial rights in exchange for reserves of land and annual payments and asked them to consider the matter over the winter months.

In the summer of 1872, the leaders of the Ojibways said they were still not ready to enter into a treaty and the subject was put over to the following year.

In a letter to the Secretary of State for the Provinces dated July 17, 1872, Indian Commissioner Wemyss M. Simpson said: "They seem fully alive to their own interests and had no small amount of intelligence in maintaining their views. We have made them liberal presents of provisions, tobacco etc. and have parted with them on amicable terms, with the understanding that we are not to negotiate with separate bands, but that, if further propositions are to be made, we are to call a general council of the chiefs, but we do not believe that under existing circumstances any good could arise from further councils."

In his 1996 *Illustrated History of Canada's Native People*, Arthur J. Ray, professor emeritus in history at the University of British Columbia, says the Ojibways "looked for ways to profit from the new business possibilities in their district. By the early 1870s, as many as sixteen hundred people used the road annually to travel from Lake Superior to the Red River. The Ojibwa wanted to be paid for the right of passage through their territory, they expected compensation for the wood used in building construction along the Dawson Road and to fuel the steamboats, and they claimed that they owned the settlers' houses because the intruders had not paid for the timber they had used to build them. In addition, they wanted to lease access and resource rights, rather than sell their lands to the Crown."

In *The Treaties of Canada with the Indians*, former Lieut.-Gov. Alexander Morris outlined the reason why the Government of Canada wanted the scattered tribes of Ojibways living in what is now known as Treaty #3 to surrender all of their rights to approximately 88,500 square kilometres of forest, lakes and rivers: "This step had become necessary," he wrote, "in order to make the route known as the 'Dawson Route', extending from Prince Arthur's Landing [Thunder Bay] on Lake Superior to the North-West Angle of the Lake of the Woods, which was then being opened up, 'secure for the passage of emigrants and of the people of the Dominion generally', and also to enable the Government to throw open for settlement any portion of the land which might be susceptible of improvement and profitable occupation."

The final negotiations were held at the Northwest Angle of the Lake of the Woods — about 80 kilometres southwest of present-day Kenora. The chiefs had wanted to meet about 200 kilometres farther east at their traditional meeting place at Fort Frances. However, Lieut.-Gov. Morris insisted on having the meeting at the Northwest Angle which was closer to his home base at Upper Fort Garry (Winnipeg).

In a report that he wrote after the negotiations resulted in the Ojibway chiefs signing what came to be known as Treaty #3, Lieut.-Gov. Morris said the Ojibways along the lakes and rivers "were dissatisfied at the use of the waters which they considered theirs, having been taken without compensation." He said the extent of their dissatisfaction was such that "I believe if the treaty had not been made, the Government would have been compelled to place a [military] force on the line [Dawson Road] next year."

Here's how Lieut.-Gov. Morris described his first encounter with the Ojibway people at the Northwest Angle of the Lake of the Woods on September 25, 1873. "On arriving, the Indians, who were already there, came up to the [Hudson's Bay Company] house I occupied, in procession, headed by braves bearing a banner and a Union Jack, and accompanied by others beating drums. They asked leave to perform a dance in my honor, after which they presented me the pipe of peace. They were then supplied with provisions and returned to their camp."

Despite the almost regal welcome the Ojibway chiefs afforded Lieut.-Gov. Morris, they were quite skeptical of the white man's motives and were in no hurry to sign a treaty. Lieut.-Gov. Morris interpreted this well-founded reluctance on their part as a sign of division and lack of leadership among the Ojibways.

"The principal cause of the delay," he said later, "was divisions and jealousies among themselves. The [Ojibway] nation had not met for many years and some of them had never before been assembled together. They were very jealous of each other, and dreaded any of the Chiefs having individual communication with me, to prevent which they had guards on the approaches to my house and Mr. [Simon J.] Dawson's tent."

A report in the October 18, 1873, issue of the *Manitoban* newspaper describing the negotiations at the Northwest Angle said: "Divisions and local jealousies have taken possession of the Indian mind. The difficulties are the inability of the Indians to select a high or principal Chief from amongst themselves, and as to the matter and extent of the demands to be made …

"It is many years since these people had a general council, and in the interval many head men have died, while others have grown to man's estate, and feel ambitious to take part in the proceedings. But the fiat has gone forth, that unless a conclusion is arrived at to-morrow negotiations will be broken off for this year."

While the Ojibways did not appear to be of one mind as to what the terms of the treaty should be, they were most certainly in agreement that the white men were not to be trusted and that there was a great deal at stake in these negotiations.

Here's what one of the main chiefs said to Lieut.-Gov. Morris at the start of the negotiations. "My terms I am going to lay down before you. The decision of our Chiefs; ever since we came to a decision, you push it back. The sound of the rustling of the gold is under my feet where I stand. We have a rich country. It is the Great Spirit who gave us this. Where we stand upon is the Indians' property, and belongs to them. If you grant us our requests you will not go back without making a treaty."

Chief Mawindopenais, the lead spokesperson for the Ojibways, said: "All this is our property where you have come. We have understood you yesterday that Her Majesty has given you the same power and authority as she has, to act in this business. You said the Queen gave you her goodness, her charitableness in your hands.

"This is what we think, that the Great Spirit has planted us on this ground where we are, as you were where you came from. We think where we are is our property. I will tell you what he said to us when he planted us here; the rules that we should follow—us Indians. He has given us rules that we should follow to govern us rightly.

"We have understood that you have opened your charitable heart to us like a person taking off his garments and throwing them to all of us here."

Another chief said: "We understood yesterday that the Queen had given you the power to act upon, that you could do what you pleased, and that the riches of the Queen she had filled your head and body with, and you had only to throw them around about; but it seems it is not so, but that you have only half the power that she has, and that she has only half filled your head.

"It is your charitableness that you spoke of yesterday—Her majesty's charitableness that was given to you. It is our Chiefs, our young men, our children and great grandchildren, and those that are to be born, that I represent here, and it is for them I ask for terms.

"The white man has robbed us of our riches, and we don't wish to give them up again without getting something in their place."

The chief of the Fort Frances band said: "One thing I find, that deranges a little my kettle. In this [Rainy] river, where food used to be plentiful for our subsistence, I perceive it is getting scarce. We wish that the river should be left as it was formed from the beginning—that nothing be broken."

On the first day of the negotiations, Commissioner Simon J. Dawson reminded the chiefs of a large military expedition that had passed through their territory just three years earlier on its way west to crush the Red River Rebellion instigated by Métis leader Louis Riel who had set up a provisional government in Manitoba.

"It is now some years since the white men first came to this country," he said. "They came in the first place at the head of a great military expedition and when that expedition was passing through the country all the chiefs showed themselves to be true and loyal subjects—they showed themselves able and willing to support their great Mother the Queen."

The expedition of approximately 400 British regulars and 800 Ontario and Québec militiamen—complete with cannons and other instruments of war—was commanded by Colonel Garnet Joseph Wolseley, Deputy Quartermaster-General of the British forces in Canada.

Col. Wolseley had served with distinction as an officer in the British Army in the second Anglo-Burmese War, the Crimean War and putting down the mutiny of Muslim and Hindu soldiers in India in 1857 who had discovered that the cartridges they had to bite open for their new Enfield muskets were greased with animal fat. In 1860, he served under General James Hope Grant—along with 11,000 British troops, 6,700 French troops and 173 naval ships—in an attack against the Qing Dynasty in China.

Col. Wolseley was sent to Canada in 1861, the first year of the American Civil War, to prepare for the reception of British troops in the event that war broke out with the United States as a result of two Confederate envoys having been removed from a British mail steamer by a Union frigate operating in international waters.

After that matter was settled amicably, he remained in Canada and, in 1867, he was appointed deputy quartermaster-general of the British forces in Canada. When Treaty #3 was being negotiated at the Northwest Angle of the Lake of the Woods, Col. Wolseley was in Africa waging war against the Ashanti Empire in Gold Coast, which later became Ghana. His military exploits there made him a household name in England. He was promoted to Major-General, received the thanks of both houses of Parliament and was made an honorary D.C.L. of Oxford and LL.D. of Cambridge. When unrest broke out in the Colony of Natal, in south-eastern Africa, he was sent there as Governor and Commander of the British forces.

It took Col. Wolseley three months to lead the Red River Expedition from Toronto to Fort Garry. The trek through the heavily-wooded Treaty #3 area involved crossing a chain of small lakes and connecting rivers, creeks and portages. As the trip was made in the heat of summer, his troops were plagued with mosquitoes and black flies. Col. Wolseley had made quite an impression on the Ojibways when he led his 1,200-strong expedition through their territory.

Lieut.-Gov. Morris had been escorted to the Northwest Angle of the Lake of the Woods by a detachment of troops from Upper Fort Garry under the command of Captain A. Macdonald. That might help explain, in part, the following from a report in the *Manitoban* newspaper written at the time that Treaty #3 was being negotiated. "One very wonderful thing that forced itself on the attention of everyone was the perfect order that prevailed throughout the [Ojibway] camp, and which more particularly marked the proceedings in council. Whether the demands put forward were granted by the Governor [Alexander Morris] or not, there was no petulance, no ill-feeling, evinced; but everything was done with a calm dignity that was pleasing to behold, and which might be copied with advantage by more pretentious [white] deliberative assemblies."

In a report to his superiors, Lieut.-Gov. Morris commended the troops for "their soldierly bearing and excellent conduct while at the Angle. Their presence was of great value, and had the effect of deterring traders from bringing articles of illicit trade for sale to the Indians; and moreover exercised a moral influence which contributed materially to the success of the negotiations."

That ties in with something Lieutenant-Governor Adams G. Archibald wrote on July 22, 1871, when he was negotiating a treaty with the bands in Manitoba. "I have, amongst other things, asked Major Irvine to detail a few of his troops to be present at the opening of the treaty [negotiations]. Military display has always a great effect on savages, and the presence, even of a few troops, will have a good tendency."

Reporting on the negotiations that took place at Fort Carlton, Saskatchewan, in August, 1876, Lieut.-Gov. Morris said: "Late in the evening the escort of [North-West] Mounted Police was reinforced by a detachment, accompanied by their band, under command of Col. Jarvis, making a force of nearly one hundred men and officers."

In his report about the Blackfeet Treaty in 1876, Lieutenant-Governor David Laird said: "While the signing was being proceeded with a salute was fired from the field guns in honor of the successful conclusion of the negotiations."

One might well ask why the field guns were felt to be necessary in the first place.

In reporting on the negotiations that took place with the Crees near Fort Qu'Appelle, Saskatchewan, in August, 1874, Lieut.-Gov. Morris said: "The Commissioners had an escort of [more than 100] militia, under the command of Lieut-Col. [William] Osborne Smith, C.M.G. This force marched to and from Qu'Appelle, acquitted themselves with signal propriety, and proved of essential service. Their return march was made in excellent time. The distance, three hundred and fifty miles having been accomplished in sixteen and a half days."

Lieut.-Col. Smith had served in the British Army during the Crimean War. He was then transferred to Canada and commanded the Victoria Rifles on the American frontier at Detroit in 1864. When the Fenian Brotherhood started raiding British Army forts, customs offices and other targets, on the Canadian border in 1866 in order to pressure the British to withdraw from Ireland, he was in command of the frontier south of Montreal.

In writing about the negotiations at the Northwest Angle, Lieut.-Gov. Alexander Morris said: "The Chief of the Lac Seul band [northwest of Sioux Lookout] came forward to speak. The others tried to prevent him, but he was secured a hearing. He stated that he represented four hundred people in the north; that they wished a treaty; that they wished a school-master to be sent to teach their children the knowledge of the white man; that they had begun to cultivate the soil and were growing potatoes and Indian corn, but wished other grain for seed and some implements and cattle. This Chief spoke under evident apprehension as to the course he was taking in resisting the other Indians, and displayed much good sense and moral courage."

The chief of the Lac Seul band also said: "If I should try to stop you — it is not in my power to do so. Even the Hudson's Bay Company, that is a small power, I cannot gain my point with it. If you take what I ask, the time may come when I will ask you to lend me one of your daughters and one of your sons to live with us; and in return I will lend you one of my daughters and one of my sons for you to teach what is good, and after they have learned, to teach us. If you grant us what we ask, although I do not know you, I will shake hands with you. This is all I have to say."

The Ojibways were aware that their counterparts in the United States were receiving larger payments than were being offered by the Canadian government.

Lieut.-Gov. Morris responded to that by saying: "I ask you once more to think what you are doing and of those you have left at home and also those that may be born yet. And I ask you not to turn your backs on what is offered to you, and you ought to see by what the Queen is offering you that she loves her red subjects as much as her white.

"I think you are forgetting one thing, that what I offer you is to be while the water flows and the sun rises. You know that in the United States they only pay the Indians for 20 years, and you come here today and ask forever more more than they get for 20 years. Is that just?

"I think you ought to accept my offer and make a treaty with me as I ask you to do. I only ask you to think for yourselves and for your families and for your children and children's children and I know that if you do that you will shake hands with me today."

The chiefs wanted more. Much more. "On the 3rd October," Lieut.-Gov. Morris later reported, "the Chiefs again assembled and made a counter proposition, of which I enclose a copy, being the demand they had urged since 1869. I also enclose an estimate I had made of the money value of the demand, amounting to $125,000 per annum.

"On behalf of the Commissioners I at once peremptorily refused the demand. The spokesman returned to the Chiefs, who were arranged on benches, the people sitting on the ground behind them, and on their return they informed me that the Chiefs, warriors and braves were of one mind, that they would make a treaty only if we acceded to their demand. I told them if so the conference was over, that I would return and report that they had refused to make a reasonable treaty, and hereafter I would treat with those bands who were willing to treat, but that I would advise them to return to the council and reconsider their determination before the next morning, when, if not, I should certainly leave."

He went on to say: "The Chiefs were summoned to the conference [next morning] by the sound of a bugle and again met us, when they told me that the determination to adhere to their demands had been so strong a bond that they did not think it could be broken, but they had now determined to see if I would give them anything more."

Faced with such a pronounced degree of resistance, Lieut.-Gov. Morris decided that his best option was to divide and conquer. "I then told them that I had known all along they were not united as they had said; that they ought not to allow a few Chiefs to prevent a treaty, and that I wished to treat with them as a nation and not with separate bands, as they would otherwise compel me to do; and therefore urged them to return to their council, promising to remain another day to give them time for consideration."

Here's how the reporter for the *Manitoban* described the situation. "The Council broke up at this point, and it was extremely doubtful whether an agreement could be come to or not. The Rainy River Indians [on the American border] were careless about the treaty, because they could get plenty of money for cutting wood for the boats, but the northern and eastern bands were anxious for one. The Governor decided that he would make a treaty with those bands that were willing to accept his terms, leaving out the few disaffected ones."

The Lieutenant-Governor's divide-and-conquer strategy worked. "When the council broke up last night, 3rd October," the *Manitoban* reported, "it looked very improbable that an understanding could be arrived at, but the firmness of the Governor, and the prospect that he would make treaty with such of the bands as were willing to accept his terms, to the exclusion of the others, led them to reconsider their demands."

Under the terms of Treaty #3, the scattered bands of Ojibways did "hereby cede, release, surrender and yield up to the Government of the Dominion of Canada for Her Majesty the Queen and Her successors forever, all their rights, titles and privileges whatsoever" to 88,500 square kilometres of territory.

Before the treaty was signed, Hon. James McKay—a mixed-blood giant of a man who was a Member of the Manitoba Legislative Assembly and spoke several native languages and dialects—read the text to the Ojibways in their own language and explained the main points.

Chief Mawendopenais, who along with Chief Powhassan, had played the lead role in the negotiations, said: "Now you see me stand before you all. What has been done here today has been done openly before the Great Spirit, and before the nation, and I hope I may never hear any one say that this treaty has been done secretly. And so, in closing this Council, I take off my glove, and in giving you my hand, I deliver over my birthright and lands. And, in taking your hand, I hold fast all the promises you have made, and I hope they will last as long as the sun goes round and the water flows, as you have said."

While it can be argued that the Government of Canada got the better end of the bargain it reached with the various tribes between 1871 and 1877, it is important to note that all of the terms of the treaties were carefully explained in their own language and there is no evidence of any attempt to mislead or deceive.

In his book on the treaty-making process, Lieut.-Gov. Morris said certain verbal promises which had been made during the negotiations for Treaties #1 and #2 in Manitoba had not been included in the final text of the agreement—despite the fact they were outlined in a memorandum which had been attached to the document. "This, naturally, led to misunderstanding with the Indians," he wrote, "and to widespread dissatisfaction among them."

On being advised of the discrepancies, the Canadian government instructed the Indian Commissioner to fulfill all of the promises that had been made and then sent Lieut.-Gov. Morris to meet again with the chiefs and get them to sign a revised treaty—including all of the terms that had been promised to them.

"When the agreement was completed," Lieut.-Gov. Morris wrote, "I asked Mr. Cummings, the Interpreter, to read it to them, which he did. Three Indians, who understood English, and who had at an early period been selected by the Indians to check the interpretation of what was said, standing by ...

"The experience derived from this misunderstanding proved however, of benefit with regard to all of the treaties, subsequent to Treaties One and Two, as the greatest care was thereafter taken to have all promises fully set out in the treaties, and to have the treaties thoroughly and fully explained to the Indians, and understood by them to contain the whole agreement between them and the Crown."

The text of each of the numbered treaties records that the terms were explained to the chiefs in their own language. Treaty #3 says "read and explained by the Honorable James McKay." Treaty #4 says "read and explained by Charles Pratt." Treaty #5 says "having been first read and explained by the Honorable James McKay." Treaty #6 was "read and explained by Peter Erasmus, Peter Ballendine and Rev. John McKay." Same thing with Treaty #7 — "explained by James Bird, Interpreter."

The commissioners appointed by the Canadian government took steps to ensure that the chiefs representing the various bands during the negotiations were duly authorized to speak on their behalf. While negotiating the Stone Fort and Manitoba Post Treaties in July, 1871, Lieutenant-Governor Adams G. Archibald wrote a letter to the Secretary of State for the Provinces in which he said: "At the time of the [1817] treaty with the Earl of Selkirk, certain Indians signed as Chiefs and representatives of their people. Some of the Indians now deny that these men ever were Chiefs or had authority to sign the treaties.

"With a view therefore to avoid a recurrence of any such question, we asked the Indians, as a first step, to agree among themselves in selecting their Chiefs, and then to present them to us and have their names and authority recorded."

That process was followed at the beginning of negotiations for all of the treaties entered into between 1871 and 1877.

The text of Treaty #3 also said: "And with a view to show the satisfaction of Her Majesty with the behaviour and good conduct of her Indians, she hereby, through her Commissioners, makes them a present of twelve dollars for each man woman and child belonging to the bands here represented, in extinguishment of all claims heretofore preferred.

"And further, Her Majesty agrees to maintain schools for instruction in such reserves hereby made as to Her Government of Her Dominion of Canada may seem advisable whenever the Indians of the reserve shall desire it.

"It is further agreed between Her Majesty and the said Indians that the sum of fifteen hundred dollars per annum shall be yearly and every year expended by Her Majesty in the purchase of ammunition and twine for nets for the use of the said Indians."

An article in the *Manitoban* described the careful way in which the Ojibways handled the money that was given to them immediately after the signing of Treaty #3 — $12 for each man woman and child.

"As soon as the money was distributed the shops of the H.B. Co., and other resident traders were visited, as well as the tents of the numerous private traders, who had been attracted thither by the prospect of doing a good business. And while these shops all did a great trade — the H.B. [Hudson's Bay] Co. alone taking in $4,000 in thirty hours — it was a noticeable fact that many [Ojibways] took home with them nearly all of their money.

"When urged to buy goods there, a frequent reply was: 'If we spend all our money here and go home and want debt, we will be told to get our debt where we spent our money.' 'Debt' is used by them instead of the word 'credit'. Many others deposited money with white men and Half-breeds upon whose honor they could depend, to be called for and spent at Fort Garry when 'the ground froze'."

Every family of five was to receive 259 hectares of land. Every family actually cultivating the soil was to receive two hoes and one spade. For every 10 families, there was to be one plow and one harrow. For every 20 families, there was to be one scythe, one axe and one cross-cut saw.

Each band was to receive one hand-saw, one pit-saw, necessary files, one grindstone, one auger, one chest of ordinary carpenter's tools "and also for each band enough of wheat, barley, potatoes and oats to plant the land actually broken up for cultivation by such band; also for each band one yoke of oxen, one bull and four cows; all the aforesaid articles to be given **once for all** [emphasis added] for the encouragement of the practice of agriculture among the Indians."

It is worth taking note of a commitment Indian Commissioner J. A. N. Provencher made at the Northwest Angle in the Lieutenant-

Governor's absence. Here's what he said. "There will be another undertaking between the officers of the Government and the Indians among themselves for the selection of land. They will have enough of good farming land, they may be sure of that."

It was widely known at the time that most of the land covered by Treaty #3 was totally unsuitable for farming. Writing about the treaty covering most of Manitoba, for example, Lieutenant-Governor Adams G. Archibald said: "Nor indeed would it be right, if we look to what we receive, to measure the benefits we derive from coming into possession of the magnificent territory we are appropriating here, by what would be fair to allow for the rocks and swamps and muskegs of the lake country [Treaty #3] east of the Province."

Joseph Toma, an Ojibway who was present at the negotiations at Fort Carlton in 1876, said: "It is true the Governor says he takes responsibility on himself in granting the extra requests of the Indians, but let him consider on the quality of the land he has already treated for. There is no farming land whatever at the Northwest Angle."

In writing about Treaty #3 in his book, Lieut.-Gov. Morris said: "He [Colonel Dennis, Surveyor-General and now Deputy Minister of the Interior] advised [in 1874] that the local agents should have some practical knowledge of agriculture as he believed that the Indians would succeed in raising quantities of stock though the character of the country prevented their general success as farmers."

Here's how the reporter for the *Manitoban* described the adjournment of the proceedings: "On Sunday afternoon, the Governor presented an ox to the nation, and after it had been eaten [the ox was cut up and boiling in 50 pots half-an-hour after it was led into the encampment] a grand dance was indulged in. Monday morning the river Indians took passage on the steamer for Fort Francis [sic], and others left in their canoes for their winter quarters.

"The Governor and party left on Monday morning, the troops, under command of Captain McDonald, who had conducted themselves with the greatest propriety, and had contributed, by the moral effect of their presence, much to the success of the negotiation, having marched to Fort Garry on Saturday morning."

In a report to his superiors, Lieut.-Gov. Morris said: "This treaty was one of great importance, as it not only tranquilized the large Indian population affected by it, but eventually shaped the terms of all the treaties, four, five, six and seven, which have since been made with the Indians of the North-West Territories—who speedily became apprised of the concessions which had been granted to the Ojibbeway nation."

He also said that, as a result of the signing of the treaty, "a territory was enabled to be opened up of great importance to Canada embracing as it does the Pacific Railway route to the Northwest Territories—a wide extent of fertile lands and, as is believed, great mineral resources."

The western line of the Canadian Pacific Railway running between Kenora and Winnipeg was completed on June 11, 1882. The eastern line, connecting Kenora and Thunder Bay, was completed one year later. On July 1, 1886, the first transcontinental train passed though Kenora on its historic ocean-to-ocean journey.

This might be a good point to take a quick look at how things went for the Ojibways after they signed Treaty #3 in October, 1873, at the Northwest Angle of the Lake of the Woods. The actual text of the treaty says: "And further, Her Majesty agrees to maintain schools for instruction in such reserves hereby made as to Her Government of Her Dominion of Canada may seem advisable whenever the Indians of the reserve shall desire it."

Soon after the treaty was signed, government officials told Chief Mawindopenais' band they would have to build a school themselves before the government would supply a teacher. That's not what they were promised. When Chief Mawindopenais died 17 years after the treaty was signed, the government still hadn't provided the teacher and school Lieut.-Gov. Alexander Morris had promised during the treaty negotiations.

In 1892, the Grand Council of Treaty #3 complained about high water levels on the Lake of the Woods. "Ever since the dam has been put up in the river, the water keeps high, destroying the wild rice crop, which is the principal cause of our starving in winter time." In 1909, the Rainy Lake and Rainy River chiefs and councillors wrote a letter to the government saying: "We have now no hunting grounds, our privileges were never taken from us by Treaty. We may not kill moose now without someone interfering. We want to know the reason why. The White Man's laws do not stop the white man from destroying. We like to live & let live & use our meat for food. The time has come when we must have an understanding. Are your words & the words of the Great White Queen our Mother to be as smoke?"

They also said: "We also wish to fish for ourselves all the year and no reserve seasons, it's our daily food. We don't want to be stopped and we don't want game inspectors cutting our lines and taking our nets. In the Treaty [#3] paper we were allowed this privilege. It is our right. We only want to live. "

Chief Namaypock of the Rainy River band said: "Trees and bushes ... growing along this original beach but are now broken and fallen down and lying in the water. The water extends inland from one-half mile in some places to as much as two or three miles in other places. Logs and brush have been driven inland from the old beach as far as a mile in some places ... The land that is overflowed around the shore as above mentioned is good rich land and at one time had fine crops on it which made good hay. My understanding is that the dam built by the Canadians at the outlet of the lake has been the cause of water rising."

According to a position paper Ojibway lawyer Sara J. Mainville prepared for the Grand Council of Treaty #3 in September, 2012: "Buried ancestors' remains washed ashore in some communities which would have devastated Anishinaabe [Ojibway] people. Most property damage for the hard-working Anishinaabe families in the early twentieth century was not compensated. The Anishinaabe Nation in Treaty 3 and the Treaty 3 communities in both Ontario and Manitoba (some 20,000 square miles of Anishinaabe Aki is now west in the Province of Manitoba) have grievances against the Province of Ontario and the Federal Government of Canada. The flooding claims may also impugn, if only indirectly, the Province of Manitoba."

In 1929, H. J. Berry, Supervisor of Indian Timber Lands, wrote a letter to the Deputy Minister of Indian Affairs in which he said: "I desire to draw your attention to the deplorable state of affairs that is existing at present among the Indians of the Lake of the Woods area (Treaty No. 3) due entirely to the actions of the Province of Ontario in curtailing their hunting and fishing rights.

"I have seen many Indians practically starving on the shore, whilst they watched white men fishing commercially in the bays, adjacent to their reserves, the Indians themselves being refused fishing licenses by Ontario, although quite willing to pay the license fee and purchase their nets and equipment. Many instances of absolute persecution of Indians on the part of officious game wardens have been reported, the most glaring being the recent instance of Game Warden Hemphill descending on the Islington [Whitedog] band and confiscating all the deer meat that the Indians had taken for food, and also the deer skins which they required for moccasins.

"The Lake of the Woods Indians are physically suffering from the wrongful treatment mete out to them by the Province, but are patiently awaiting the time when their wrongs will be re-dressed and their rights vindicated... If this clause [the taking-up clause] means what it says, and the language is unequivocal, then the hunting and fishing privileges of the Indians are under the control of the Dominion Government solely, and any regulation that the Province of Ontario may see fit to make, is ultra vires, unless assented to in the first place by the Dominion ...

"I submit that we should insist upon the right of the Indians to take game and fish for food, only, at any time. The prior right of the Indians to commercial fishing in their own waters or waters adjacent to their reserves. The creation of trapping ground areas for the exclusive use of the Indians. The Indians of Treaty No. 3 area (Lake of the Woods) are possibly facing today the worst conditions of living that they have ever experienced.

"Prevented from hunting for food, restricted from commercial fishing, failing to secure a blueberry crop, they will assuredly need all the help and assistance that it's possible to give them to tide over the winters; but if besides financial help, they also receive the assurance from the Department that their grievances will be remedied so far as it is humanly possible to do so, then they will turn to the future with renewed hope and a conviction that treaties are inviolable documents, not susceptible to alteration or abrogation by parties who were not contributory signatories."

In 1938, the Indian Agent at Fort Frances wrote that the chiefs and headmen had appointed a small delegation to go to Ottawa "to interview the Department in respect of their Treaty, the greatest discussion was in regard to Fishing and Hunting because the Game Wardens are seizing their nets and boats or taking them up in court and being fined for fishing. The Indians cannot make a living unless they are permitted to sell a few fish, as fishing and trapping is the only way they have of making a living …

"If the Indians are not allowed to catch a few fish to sell, it will be as I was told by a few of my Indians, they said that if they could not sell a few fish to provide for their families, that they would have to go to jail, because they could not see their families starve, and I think they are telling the truth in that respect."

Ms. Mainville wrote in her 2012 paper: "Ontario's policy towards treaty harvesting rights was legally, morally and politically wrong. The Anishinaabe knew this, and there were several direct complaints and petitions amongst the many delegations to Ottawa."

Chapter 4

The ancestors of the Ojibway chiefs who signed Treaty #3 on October 3, 1873, were forced out of their ancient villages on the Atlantic seaboard of what is now the United States of America by Iroquois warriors who had acquired firearms from Dutch and English traders as early as 1639.

In his *History of the Ojibway People* which was published by the Minnesota Historical Society in 1885 William Whipple Warren wrote: "From the earliest period that their [Ojibway] historical traditions treat of, they tell of having carried on an exterminating war with the Iroquois, or Six Nations of New York, whom they term Naud-o-waig, or Adders. The name indicates the deadly nature of these, their old and powerful antagonists, whose concentrated strength and numbers, and first acquaintance with the use of the white man's murderous fire arms, caused them to leave their ancient village sites and trek westward for new homes."

A large body of Ojibways eventually settled between Sault Ste. Marie and the Mississippi River in present-day Minnesota which was the best hunting grounds of the Dakotas and the Foxes. "All this was the country of the Dakotas and Foxes," Warren—who was born the son of a white fur trader and an Ojibway-French mother on May 27, 1825 —wrote, "and bravely did they battle to beat back the encroaching

Ojibways from their best hunting grounds, but in vain; for the invaders, besides having increased in numbers, had become possessed of fearful weapons, against which they feared to battle with their primitive bow and arrow ...

"On an uninterrupted line from Selkirk's settlement [Winnipeg] to the mouth of the Wisconsin River, over a thousand miles in length, the Ojibways and Dakotas carried on against one another their implacable warfare, and whitened this vast frontier with each other's bones."

Among the stories and legends Warren recorded in numerous interviews with Ojibway elders in their own language were acts of extreme cruelty on both sides. He tells of a camp of Ojibways who were attacked early one morning by a large war party of Foxes who killed all of the men, women and children, with the exception of an old man and a young boy who got bogged down in a swamp while trying to escape.

They were captured and taken to the Foxes' village where the old man was wrapped in folds of combustible birch bark, set on fire and forced to run a gauntlet "amid their hellish whoops and screams covered with a perfect blaze of fire, and receiving withal a shower of blows, the old man soon expired." The young boy was next. He was made to run backwards and forwards on a pile of burning branches until the fire consumed him.

Warren tells of a canoe laden with young Dakota women floating leisurely down the Minnesota River "chatting and laughing in anticipation of the magnificent scalp dance which they were going to join, after having adorned their persons with profuse ornaments and painted their cheeks with vermilion." Much to their surprise, they were captured by a band of Ojibway warriors who scalped them alive and attached their scalp-locks to their belts to the delight of the Ojibway women who danced around their corpses.

And then there was the time when the Dakotas offered a young Dakota girl to Wa-son-aun-e-qua (Yellow Hair) to take the place of his young son whom they had killed. They dressed her in finery and ornaments hoping to appease the renowned Ojibway warrior. "The innocent little girl came forward," Warren writes, "but no sooner was she within reach of the avenger, than he grasped her by the hair of the head and loudly exclaiming — 'I sent for thee that I might do with you as your people did to my child. I wish to behold thee as I once beheld him' — he deliberately scalped her alive, and sent her shrieking back to her agonized parents."

Warren also tells the story of an Ojibway warrior who greatly impressed a war party of Dakotas by keeping them at bay and yelling a war whoop, despite blood oozing from several gaping wounds, until he was so weak that one of them was able to knock him to the ground and behead him with his scalp knife. "It is said that during the whole fight, the Ojibway warrior had laughed at his enemies, and his face, after the head had been separated from his body, was still wreathed in a smile. Such a high notion did the Dakotas entertain of his bravery, that they cut out his heart, which, being cut into small pieces, was swallowed by their warriors raw, in the belief that it would make them equally 'strong hearted.'"

On another occasion, an Ojibway camp was attacked by a Dakota war party and a handful of the outnumbered Ojibway warriors who survived the initial attack and took shelter near their wigwams were surrounded by the Dakotas. "After a brave, but hopeless, defence, their guns were silenced forever, and their scalps graced the belts of their victorious enemies. After annihilating the men, the Dakotas rushed into the perforated wigwams, and massacred the women and children who had escaped their bullets."

After the Ojibways had established a firm footing in the rich hunting grounds of the Upper Mississippi, Chief Bi-aus-wah entered into peace negotiations with the Foxes and the Dakotas. He got them to sign a treaty putting an end to the torture of prisoners and, from that point forward, the taking of captives became less frequent. Meanwhile, right up until 1662, the Lake Superior Ojibways were still at war with the Iroquois. That war ended once and for all when the Ojibways slaughtered an Iroquois war party near Sault Ste. Marie. That was the last time the Iroquois tried to penetrate what had then become Ojibway territory.

According to Warren, an envoy of the King of France met with Ke-che-ne-zuh-yauh of La Pointe, Wisconsin, in 1671 and named him chief of the Lake Superior Ojibways. As he placed a gold medal shaped like a heart on the chief's breast, he said: "Every morning you will look toward the rising of the sun and you shall see the fire of your French father reflecting towards you, to warm you and your people. If you are in trouble, you, the Crane, must arise in the skies and cry with your 'far sounding' voice, and I will hear you. The fire of your French father shall last forever, and warm his children."

From that time on, the French conducted the lucrative fur trade without interference and the Ojibways referred to the French king as "Father" and supported the French in their wars against the British. The Ojibways often travelled by canoe to Montreal and Quebec to trade their furs for goods.

According to Warren, Chief Ma-mong-e-se-da (Big Feet) made frequent visits to Montreal and Quebec and was known for his love of the French people. When he was first recognized as a chief, he was given a medal and a French flag. At that point in time, the Ojibways controlled all of the valuable hunting region stretching nearly 500 kilometres west from Lake Superior to just east of the Mississippi River.

The Ojibways were loyal to the King of France and willing to die in his name. During the North American part of the Seven Years' War of 1756–63 — which had Britain, Prussia and Portugal on one side and France, Russia, Austria and Spain on the other — Ojibway warriors from Sault Ste. Marie, Mackinaw and the shores of Lake Huron, fought along-side the French.

They were with the French army at Detroit, Fort Du Quesne, Niagara, Montreal and Quebec. In fact, they were involved in just about every battle in those bloody wars between the French and the British.

In *History of the Ojibway People*, William Warren says Chief Ma-mong-e-se-da delivered a message from General Louis-Joseph, Marquis de Montcalm, the commander of all French forces in North America, asking the Lake Superior Ojibways to come to his aid in the defence of Quebec. A war party of Ojibways travelled more than 3,000 kilometres to fight alongside Montcalm at the historic Battle of the Plains of Abraham. They fought on Montcalm's extreme left, near the woods along the cliffs.

According to British interpreter Jean-Baptiste Cadotte, the reason the Ojibways referred to the British as Shaug-un-aush—"to appear from the clouds" — was because of the sudden and unexpected manner in which more than 3,000 of the enemy climbed a cliff and appeared in force on the Plains of Abraham early on the morning of September 13, 1759, ready to do battle.

That battle was over in less than an hour — mainly because, after being held under siege by British General James Wolfe for three months, a frustrated Montcalm decided to come out from behind the protection of the great walls and fight in the open rather than wait for reinforcements that were on their way from nearby Beauport.

The overwhelmingly negative attitude of many of the French toward New France was summed up by Jeanne Antoinette Poisson, the mistress of King Louis XV, who, after receiving news of the defeat and death of Montcalm at Quebec, was quoted as saying: "Now that Montcalm is dead, the King will have some peace. It makes little difference. Canada is useful only to provide me with furs. Now the King can sleep. We can be happy without Canada."

While the French were victorious in several battles after Montcalm's defeat, the British kept control of Quebec City and the 15-minute battle on the Plains of Abraham marked the beginning of the end of New France. On September 6, 1760, Pierre de Rigaud de Vaudreuil de Cavagnia, the Governor-General of New France, formally surrendered to British General Jeffrey Amherst.

The Huron, Mohawk, Abenaki and other native allies of France had already entered into a peace agreement with the British under which they pledged that they would no longer fight alongside the French.

Under the terms of the 1763 Treaty of Paris, Britain restored Havana and Manila to Spain and France traded New France to the British in exchange for the rich sugar island of Guadeloupe. France also ceded the eastern half of Louisiana to Britain and Spain ceded Florida to Britain.

The Treaty guaranteed freedom of religion to all Catholics living in New France. It also stipulated that any residents of New France who wished to sell their possessions to British subjects and leave were free to do so.

France succeeded in retaining fishing rights off Newfoundland and keeping the tiny islands of Saint-Pierre and Miquelon at the edge of the Grand Banks where fishermen could repair their boats and dry their fish. That was all that was left — 242 square kilometres — of New France (1534–1763).

Renowned French philosopher Voltaire did not appear to regret the loss of New France. He was quoted as having said that, if one-tenth of the money that had been swallowed up by New France had been employed to reclaim uncultivated land in France, the gain would have been considerable.

Voltaire's comments were reflective of a pronounced negative attitude toward New France that had existed for quite some time. On January 5, 1666, for example, Jean-Baptiste Colbert, Minister of Finances of France, wrote to Jean Talon, Intendant of Justice, Public Order and Finances in Canada, Acadia and Newfoundland, saying: "His Majesty cannot concur in all the reasons you put forward for the formation of Canada into a great and powerful state finding that there are diverse obstacles that could only be surmounted by the passage of many years. Even granting that there were no other concerns and that the resources of the Kingdom…could be applied to Canada, it would not be prudent to depopulate his Kingdom…to populate Canada."

That message seemed to carry some weight at the Royal Palace. One year later, King Louis XIV stated quite emphatically: "To people Canada, it would be necessary to depopulate France." In an April 16, 1676, letter to Count Louis de Frontenac, the Governor General of New France, the king said: "Concerning these new discoveries, you must on no account encourage them unless there be a great need and some obvious advantage to be derived from them. You must hold to the maxim that it is far more worthwhile to occupy a smaller area and have it well populated than to spread out and have several feeble colonies which could easily be destroyed by all manner of accidents."

The king is quoted as having said sometime around 1702: "The Colony of Canada is good only inasmuch as it can be useful to the Kingdom."

On October 7, 1763, King George III signed a Royal Proclamation regarding the vast territories in North America that France had "ceded and confirmed" to Britain under the Treaty of Paris. The English King's Royal Proclamation stated that "the several Nations or Tribes of Indians with whom We are connected, and who live under our Protection, should not be molested or disturbed in the Possession of such Parts of Our Dominions and Territories as, not having been ceded to or purchased by Us, are reserved to them, or any of them, as their Hunting Grounds."

The Royal Proclamation did not apply to the vast territories controlled by the Hudson's Bay company which included what is now northern Ontario and Quebec, all of Manitoba, most of Saskatchewan and southern Alberta and a portion of the Northwest Territories.

The lands immediately west of the Thirteen Colonies on the Atlantic seaboard were to be reserved "under our Sovereignty, Protection, and Dominion" as hunting grounds for the natives "for the present, and until our further pleasure be known."

Because "great Frauds and Abuses have been committed in purchasing Lands of the Indians, to the great Prejudice of our Interests, and to the great Dissatisfaction of the said Indians," settlers were prohibited from purchasing any of the lands lying west of the Allegheny Mountains. Only the Crown could purchase or sell lands which had been reserved as hunting grounds for the western tribes. All trade with the native people was to be regulated by the Governor or Commander in Chief of a colony and all traders had to be licenced.

Evidence of the fact that King George III believed that he exercised sole authority over all of the lands that had been ceded to him by France is found in the following whereby he authorized: "All Officers whatever, as well Military as those Employed in the Management and Direction of Indian Affairs, within the Territories reserved as aforesaid for the use of the said Indians, to seize and apprehend all Persons whatever, who standing charged with Treason, Misprisions of Treason, Murders, or other Felonies or Misdemeanors, shall fly from Justice and take Refuge in the said Territory, and to send them under a proper guard to the Colony where the Crime was committed, of which they stand accused, in order to take their Trial for the same."

In other words, the King's men were authorized to pass in and out of the Indian Territory as they saw fit. No permission from the native people was required.

One of the key proponents of the Royal Proclamation of 1763 was Sir William Johnson, the British Superintendent of Indian Affairs for the Thirteen Colonies, who had commanded the Iroquois and other native allies during the war against the French.

Johnson was a wealthy landholder and slave owner. At the time of the Royal Proclamation, he was in possession of 32,375 hectares he had acquired from the Mohawks near present-day Schenectady, New York.

He saw the Royal Proclamation as a means of exercising greater Imperial control over settlers from the Thirteen Colonies who were anxious to move into the Ohio Valley now that France had surrendered the territory.

When Johnson negotiated the Treaty of Fort Stanwix with the Iroquois Confederacy at present-day Rome, New York, in November, 1768, he arbitrarily pushed the boundary established by the Royal Proclamation 644 kilometres farther to the west so he and other land speculators could acquire more land.

Despite criticism of Johnson for having acted without proper authorization, the new boundary line held—primarily because of the connections Johnson and other land speculators had with the British government.

At the time of his death on July 11, 1774, Johnson owned approximately 69,201 hectares and was one of the largest landholders in British America — which included Bermuda, Belize, the British West Indies and Guyana.

In that same year, the British Parliament passed the *Quebec Act* which extended the territory of the Province of Quebec south into much of what is now Illinois, Indiana, Michigan, Ohio, Wisconsin and parts of Minnesota.

This expanded territory included much of the lands between the Ohio and Mississippi rivers which the Royal Proclamation had reserved for the natives as hunting grounds. There is no mention in the *Quebec Act* of the natives living on those lands.

The legislation clearly stated that the territory in question was "ceded to his Majesty by the definitive Treaty of Peace concluded at Paris on the tenth day of February, one thousand seven hundred and sixty-three" and was comprised of lands "belonging to the Crown of Great Britain."

The Ojibways of the Lake Superior region were not at all happy when the defeated French ceded New France to the British and the English king asserted control over their traditional territories. Unlike the French who had treated them as friends and allies and did not attempt to dominate or control them, the British treated them as a conquered people and encouraged further intrusion into their lands.

Samuel de Champlain — a wealthy explorer/geographer/navigator/soldier who had a great deal of experience at sea — is a good example of the French approach. Prior to his first voyage to New France in March, 1603, Champlain had spent two years in the West Indies and Mexico. During that time, he wrote letters to King Henry IV with vivid pictures he had drawn of Aboriginals being burned alive by the Spanish Inquisi-tion, beaten by priests for not attending Mass and being exploited as forced laborers.

Champlain took an altogether different approach to the natives he encountered in New France. According to history professor David Hackett Fischer of Brandeis University, he went unarmed with one French friend and two native interpreters into the middle of a huge encampment of Montagnais, Algonquins, and Etchemins near where the Saguenay River joins the St. Lawrence.

Approaching the natives with respect and goodwill, he joined them in a tobacco feast and entered into an informal alliance that lasted for many years. He adopted the same approach in 1604 when he made peace with the Penobscot of Maine in what is now downtown Bangor. One year later, he entered into a peace agreement with the Mi'kmaq of Acadia and, in 1608, he made peace with the Hurons.

Unlike the Spaniards he had encountered in Mexico, Champlain made no attempt whatsoever to conquer or subjugate the natives. Nor did he or his fellow French explorers abuse them as the English did the natives in Virginia or drive them out of their ancient villages as was the case in New England.

He certainly didn't terrorize them as did Willem Kieft, the Director-General of New Netherland (New York State), who was held responsible for the brutal deaths of more than 1,000 natives, many of whom were burned alive.

When a hungry old Hackensack woman took some peaches off the land she had once picked berries on in 1643, Kieft sent 129 soldiers, armed with muskets and pikes, to a peaceful Hackensack village.

"Young children, some of them snatched from their mothers," a witness wrote, "were cut in pieces before the eyes of their parents, and the pieces were thrown into the fire or into the water; other babes were bound on planks and then cut through, stabbed and miserably massacred so that it would break a heart of stone."

Nineteenth century historian John Romeyn Brodhead wrote: "Warrior and squaw, sachem [main chief] and child, mother and babe were alike massacred. Daybreak scarcely ended the furious slaughter. Mangled victims, seeking safety in the thickets, were driven into the river, and parents rushing to save their children, whom the soldiery had thrown into the stream, were driven back into the waters and drowned before the eyes of their unrelenting murderers."

The Dutch soldiers killed 120 men, women and children, and laid 80 bloodied Hackensack heads on the streets of New Amsterdam — now New York City — for public viewing. Kieft's mother kicked them around like soccer balls.

Soon after that, Kieft hired an English mercenary and veteran Indian fighter by the name of Captain John Underhill who commanded two companies of 120 to 150 volunteers and Mohican scouts. On their first outing, Underhill's army killed more than 120 men, women and children near today's town of Massapequa on the south shore of Long Island.

When the toll of dead on Long Island reached 500, Kieft declared a day of thanksgiving. Other attacks followed against the natives on the north shore of Long Island.

It's worth noting that there were an estimated 10,000 natives living on Long Island in 1600. Warfare and sickness reduced that number to 500 by 1659. On one day alone, Underhill upheld his reputation as "the scourge of the Indians" by attacking an encampment north of Stamford, Connecticut, and killing 700 men women and children.

Underhill was fond of expressing his deeply-held Christian conviction that the Bible commanded that "children must perish with their parents."

Champlain, on the other hand, saw the natives as equals whose support would be the determining factor in the survival of the French settlements he was establishing in the St. Lawrence River valley and in Acadia. He was a firm believer in cohabitation.

Here's how Professor Fischer of Brandeis University once put it: "In the region that began to be known as Canada, small colonies of Frenchmen and large Indian nations lived close to one another in a spirit of amity and concord. This successful partnership was made possible in large measure because of Champlain's dream of humanity."

The Ojibways frequently complained that the British treated them no better than they would slaves or dogs. British commanders were inclined to treat the Ojibways and other native people with contempt. The Ojibways, who had lived, traded, and intermarried with the French, became increasingly dissatisfied with the British occupation of their land and the new policies and attitudes that were being imposed upon them.

That contrasted sharply with their treatment under the French as once described by Sir William Johnson. "[The French] took care to cultivate a good understanding with the Western Indians, which the safety of their colony and their ambitious views of extending their boundaries, rendered indispensably necessary; to effect this, they were at an immense expense in buying the favour of the Indians."

According to Peter S. Schmalz's *The Ojibwa of Southern Ontario* which was published by University of Toronto Press in 1991: "French trade goods were diplomatic tools. British trade had exclusively one objective—to fill the pockets of a few mercenary merchants. Many Ojibwa saw the British traders as a necessary evil in their society, but did they have any choice?"

The Ojibways took particular exception to the decision by General Jeffrey Amherst, the British Commander-in-Chief of North America, to cut back on the French tradition of giving gifts of guns, knives, tobacco, clothing and other items to the village chiefs as part of their ongoing effort to build and maintain goodwill among the Indians.

This long-established practice enabled the village chiefs to gain stature among their people by redistributing some of the gifts. Everybody benefitted. However, General Amherst considered this to be a form of bribery that was no longer necessary. The Ojibways saw it differently and considered the withdrawal of gifts as an insult.

General Amherst also placed restrictions on the amount of ammunition and gunpowder that traders could sell to the natives. Again, a reversal of the French policy of making such supplies available to their native allies who relied on the guns in providing food for their families and skins for the fur trade.

Amherst, on the other hand, did not trust the natives, especially after armed Cherokee warriors in what is now the southeastern United States attacked the British during a failed uprising in 1758. In his opinion, the fewer guns and less ammunition the natives had at their disposal the better things would be for the British.

That's not the way the Ojibways and other tribes saw things. They were convinced the British were trying to disarm them as a prelude to making war. The Lake Superior Ojibways joined forces with other tribes in June, 1763, in an effort to drive British settlers and soldiers out of their territories.

In a book that he wrote in 1809, English trader Alexander Henry described the June 2, 1763, massacre at Fort Michilimackinac on the Straits that connect Lakes Huron and Michigan as follows: "I heard an Indian war-cry and a noise of general confusion. Going instantly to my window, I saw a crowd of [400] Indians within the fort, furiously cutting down and scalping every Englishman they found. In particular, I witnessed the fate of Lieutenant Jemette [who was killed along with many of his soldiers] ...

"In this dreadful interval, I saw several of my countrymen fall, and more than one struggling between the knees of an Indian, who, holding him in this manner, scalped him while yet living! ... Amid the slaughter which was raging, I observed many of the [almost 300] Canadian [French] inhabitants of the fort calmly looking on, neither opposing the Indians nor suffering injury. From this circumstance I conceived a hope of finding security in their houses."

A sympathetic native slave from one of the southern states took him to a garret in one of the houses for safety. "Through an aperture, which afforded me a view of the area of the fort, I beheld, in shapes the foulest and most terrible, the ferocious triumphs of barbarian conquerors.

"The dead were scalped and mangled; the dying were writhing and shrieking, under the unsatiated knife and tomahawk; and, from the bodies of some, ripped open, their butchers were drinking the blood, scooped up in the hollow of joined hands, and quaffed amid shouts of rage and victory. I was shaken, not only with horror, but with fear. The sufferings which I witnessed, I seemed on the point of experiencing. No long time elapsed, before every one being destroyed, who could be found, there was a general cry of 'All is finished!'"

Despite the loss of Fort Michilimackinac, the British eventually managed to turn things around. And it wasn't just British military muscle that won the day. In June, 1763, Field Marshall Jeffery Amherst, Commander-in-Chief of the British forces in North America, was reported to have asked the commanding officer at Fort Pitt (present-day Pittsburgh): "Could it not be contrived to send a Small Pox among those disaffected tribes of Indians? We must on this occasion use every stratagem in our power to reduce them."

According to Francis Parkman's 1851 *The Conspiracy of Pontiac and the Indian War after the Conquest of Canada, Volume 2,* Colonel Henry Bouquet replied: "I will try to inoculate ... some blankets that may fall into their hands, and take care not to get the disease myself. As it is a pity to expose good men [soldiers] against them, I wish we could make use of the Spanish method, to hunt them down with English dogs."

In *The Ojibwa of Southern Ontario*, Peter Schmalz writes: "A few months later, smallpox is known to have played havoc with the enemy groups." Two blankets and a handkerchief from the smallpox hospital had been presented to the some chiefs as presents.

"Although there are no complete statistics on Indian deaths by disease or in battle," Schmalz writes, "the colonial reports give the impression that more Ojibwa were killed by smallpox than by English bullets."

It's worth noting that, like most natives, the Lake Superior Ojibways were often devastated by smallpox and other deadly diseases the white men brought with them to the new land. An interpreter at Fort Michilimackinac received a message from Sault Ste. Marie on June 16, 1783, which said that "all the Indians from Fond du Lac, Rainy Lake, Sandy Lake and other places are dead of smallpox."

Almost one-half of the Blackfoot in what is now Alberta were wiped out by the great plague of 1781 and about one-third of those remaining died in a subsequent outbreak in 1837. About 30 years later, in 1869, the plains tribes were devastated by a major smallpox epidemic and the Sarcee on the eastern slopes of the Rocky Mountains, were almost completely exterminated.

To put things in perspective, an estimated 400,000 Europeans died annually of smallpox during the closing years of the 18th century. The disease was also said to be responsible for one-third of all cases of blindness. And, there were no exceptions. Among those who lost their lives to smallpox were: Peter II of Russia, King Louis XV of France, and Maxmilian III Joseph, Elector of Bavaria.

According to Alexander Henry, a party arrived at Sault Ste. Marie by canoe from Fort Niagara in 1764 with a message from Sir William Johnson. Henry quotes the messenger as telling the chiefs assembled in council: "My friends and brothers, I am come with this belt from our great father, Sir William Johnson. He desired me to come to you as his embassador [sic], and tell you that he is making a great feast at Fort Niagara, that his kettles are all ready and his fires lit. He invites you to partake of this feast, in common with your friends, the Six Nations [Iroquois], who have made peace with the English.

"He advises you to seize this opportunity of doing the same, as you cannot otherwise fail of being destroyed, for the English are on their march with a great many, which will be joined by different nations of Indians. In a word, before the fall of the leaf, they will be at Michilmackinac, and the Six Nations with them."

According to William Warren, "the tenor of this speech greatly alarmed" the bands throughout the Northwest and they sent delegates to meet with Johnson at Fort Niagara. He says the Sault Ste. Marie Ojibways sent 20 delegates who joined the representatives of 22 different tribes.

"Though they went in fear and trembling, [they] were well received at the hands of Sir William Johnson and they experienced the good consequences of having listened to the advice of their trader [Michel H. Cadotte]."

After the council, Colonel John Bradstreet led a large military force, including a battalion of native allies under the command of Alexander Henry, and marched to Fort Detroit. Eight French forts were destroyed and hundreds of settlers/colonists were killed or captured.

The Lake Superior Ojibways gradually shifted their allegiance to the English king, started trading with the British, and declared themselves ready to fight alongside the British soldiers. Many of their chiefs wore the badges and medals of the British king and flew the Union Jack outside their wigwams.

In no time at all, Ojibways from Rainy Lake, Red Lake, Pembina and other areas were doing a brisk trade with the Hudson's Bay Company and trekking hundreds of kilometres north once a year to trade their furs for guns and other goods.

On June 18, 1812, the United States declared war on Britain primarily because of four reasons: 1) the *Quebec Act* of 1774 asserting control of the territory lying between the Ohio and the Mississippi; 2) restrictions placed on American merchant ships on the high seas by the Royal

Navy, 3) a desire on the part of the Americans to invade and take over the poorly-defended British colonies in Canada; and 4) a strongly-held belief that the British were inciting the natives to attack U.S. settlements on the western frontier.

The first British attack in the War of 1812 was on Fort Mackinac on Mackinac Island, an important American trading post in the straits connecting Lake Michigan and Lake Huron. Captain Charles Roberts, commander of the British post at St. Joseph Island, about 64 kilometres southeast of Sault Ste. Marie, had assembled a small force of 50 British soldiers, 150 Métis fur traders and voyageurs (licensed adventurers from Montreal who travelled to and from the fur country by canoe), 300 Ojibways, and 110 Sioux, Menominee and Winnibego who had been at the island to trade their furs.

They set out for Mackinac Island on an armed schooner belonging to the North West Company accompanied by 70 war canoes and 10 flat-bottomed bateaux.

The American commander of Fort Mackinac was unaware that war had broken out between the Americans and the British—the American Secretary of War had sent the news by regular mail. Captain Roberts and his force of British soldiers, fur traders and native warriors, landed on the north end of the island early on the morning of July 17, 1812. After quietly removing the village residents from their homes, they dragged a six-pounder cannon through the woods to a ridge above the fort. They then fired a single round before sending a message, under a white flag of truce, demanding that the Americans surrender.

Three of the villagers had accompanied the flag of truce and they greatly exaggerated the number of natives who were poised ready to attack. Fearing that they would be massacred, the Americans surrendered without firing a single shot. The British and their Ojibway and other native allies then moved on to victories at Brownstown and Magauga and the capture of Detroit on August 16th.

Interpreter Jean-Baptiste Askin was quoted as saying at the time that "without the Indians we [British] never could keep this country, and that with them the Americans will never take the upper posts, for let them send forward as many men as they will, if we employ the ... Indians we can have equal number, which is more than is wanted, for in the woods where the Americans must pass one Indian is equal to three white men."

Some of the western natives who had participated in the capture of Fort Mackinac moved south to join Shawnee Chief Tecumseh and the other tribes at Fort Amherstburg, at the mouth of the Detroit River. As news of the American defeat at Fort Mackinac on July 17, 1812, spread, several tribes, including the Hurons near Detroit who had previously been friendly with the Americans, moved their allegiance to the British Crown.

With his military strength reinforced, Tecumseh conducted a series of coordinated attacks on American posts in Indian Territory. In their efforts to deal with these attacks, the Americans had to divert forces that would otherwise have been used in a concerted effort to invade and occupy Lower Canada (Quebec) which, with its control of the St. Lawrence River, was considered to be of great strategic importance.

It is believed that Tecumseh — Shooting Star — an Algonquin-speaking Shawnee chief from the Indiana Territory, was born in what is now Ohio on March, 9, 1768. Like the Ojibways who eventually wound up in the Lake Superior area, the Shawnee had been driven out of their ancestral homes by the Iroquois during the Beaver Wars of the 1600s. Tecumseh's father was a Shawnee chief and was killed in 1774 by white frontiersmen who violated a treaty and forced their way into Indian territory.

In 1808, Tecumseh established Prophetstown in the Indiana Territory with his younger brother Tenskwatawa (The Prophet), a reformed alcoholic and religious leader who was urging the Shawnee to reject the ways of the whites and stop surrendering their lands to the government of the United States.

Tecumseh believed that the only way to stop the rapid encroachment on their lands by the white settlers was for the many tribes to form a united nation and stake out a territory of their own between the Ohio River and the Mississippi.

"The whites have driven us from the sea [Atlantic] to the lakes," he said. "We can go no further ... unless every tribe unanimously combines to give a check to the ambition and avarice of the whites they will soon conquer us apart and disunited and we will be driven from our native country and scattered as autumn leaves before the wind."

Tecumseh was receptive to overtures that were being made at that time by the British in Upper Canada. His brother, whose fame overshadowed Tecumseh's at that time, declined an invitation to meet with the British at Fort Amherstburg in June, 1808, and sent Tecumseh in his place. In a report to Governor General James Henry Craig, Francis Gore, the Lieutenant-Governor of Upper Canada, described Tecumseh as "a very shrewd intelligent man."

Tecumseh told the British officials that he and his brother were trying to gather all of the American tribes into one confederacy in order to defend their lands. However, they had no interest at that time in taking part in any war between Britain and the United States. He did add, however, that "if their father the King should be in earnest and appear in sufficient force they would hold fast by him."

Tecumseh was strongly opposed to a treaty negotiated in September, 1809, under which a delegation of half-starved natives signed away 1,215,000 hectares of territory to the United States. He is reported to have said: "No tribe has the right to sell, even to each other, much less to strangers ... Sell a country? Why not sell the air, the great sea, as well as the earth? Didn't the Great Spirit make them all for the use of his children? ... The only way to stop this evil is for the red man to unite in claiming a common and equal right in the land, as it was first, and should be now, for it was never divided."

When Indian agent William Wells asked Tecumseh to come to Fort Wayne in present-day northeast Indiana for talks, he is reported to have replied: "The Great Spirit above has appointed this place for us on which to light our fires and here we will remain. As to boundaries, the Great Spirit above knows no boundaries, nor will his red people acknowledge any."

In August, 1810, Tecumseh and 400 armed warriors travelled down the Wabash River to meet with William Henry Harrison, Governor of the newly-formed Indiana Territory, and challenge the legitimacy of the treaty that had been signed the previous year.

He warned Harrison that settlers should not move onto the lands surrendered under the treaty and acknowledged that he had threatened to kill the chiefs who signed it. Before leaving, he warned that he would form an alliance with the British if the Americans did not nullify the treaty.

Harrison's father-in-law was active in developing and selling land, including much of the land Harrison had acquired through questionable treaties with the natives. While Tecumseh posed a direct threat to Harrison's plans to increase white settlement on native lands, he had a grudging respect for the Shawnee chief.

"The implicit obedience and respect which the followers of Tecumseh pay to him," he once said, "bespeaks him one of those uncommon geniuses which spring up occasionally to produce revolutions ... If it were not for the vicinity of the U.S. he would perhaps be the founder of an Empire that would rival in glory that of Mexico."

Tecumseh is reported to have said to Governor Harrison: "You have the liberty to return to your own country ... you wish to prevent the Indians from doing as we wish them, to unite and let them consider their lands as common property of the whole ... You never see an Indian endeavor to make the white people do this ... How can we have confidence in the white people?"

Tecumseh, accompanied by 300 warriors, met again with Harrison the following year and told him that he wanted peace but would have no option but to wage war if the whites insisted on encroaching on their territory. After the Americans spurned his entreaties, Tecumseh sought an alliance with the British in Upper Canada who quickly supplied him with guns and ammunition.

In rallying support for his cause as he travelled among tribes hundreds of miles away from Prophetstown, Tecumseh played up the fact that the British would support them in their fight to remove the American settlers from their lands. While speaking to the Osages in western Missouri, Tecumseh is reported to have said: "Brothers, our Great Father [King of England] over the great waters is angry with the white people, our enemies. He will send his brave warriors against them; he will send us rifles, and whatever else we want—he is our friend, and we are his children. Brothers, who are the white people that we should fear them? They cannot run fast, and are good marks to shoot at: they are only men; our fathers have killed many of them: we are not squaws, and we will stain the earth red with their blood.

"Brothers, the Great Spirit is angry with our enemies; he speaks in thunder, and the earth swallows up villages, and drinks up the Mississippi. The great waters will cover their lowlands; their corn cannot grow; and the Great Spirit will sweep those who escape to the hills from the earth with his terrible breath. Brothers, we must be united; we must smoke the same pipe; we must fight each other's battles; and, more than all, we must love the Great Spirit: he is for us; he will destroy our enemies, and make all his red children happy."

He is also reported to have said on that occasion: "The blood of many of our fathers and brothers has run like water on the ground, to satisfy the avarice of the white men. We, ourselves, are threatened with a great evil; nothing will pacify them but the destruction of all the red men. Brothers, when the white men first set foot on our grounds, they were hungry; they had no place on which to spread their blankets, or to kindle their fires. They were feeble; they could do nothing for themselves. Our fathers commiserated their distress, and shared freely with them whatever the Great Spirit had given his red children. They gave them food when hungry, medicine when sick, spread skins for them to sleep on, and gave them grounds, that they might hunt and raise corn.

"Brothers, the white people are like poisonous serpents: when chilled, they are feeble and harmless; but invigorate them with warmth, and they sting their benefactors to death. The white people came among us feeble; and now that we have made them strong, they wish to kill us, or drive us back, as they would wolves and panthers. The white men aren't friends to the Indians ... At first they only asked for land sufficient for a wigwam; now, nothing will satisfy them but the whole of our hunting grounds from the rising to the setting sun."

Despite the power of Tecumseh's oratory, most of the tribes he approached decided to remain at peace under the treaties they had entered into with the American government and spurned his appeals to fight alongside the British. Nevertheless, he decided to move forward with the considerable number of warriors he had rallied to his cause.

At a meeting at Fort Amherstburg in November of that year, Tecumseh astonished Lieutenant-Colonel Matthew Elliott by informing him that he was ready to go to war with the Americans. Elliott said that he would lay the matter before the British King. Elliott's letter worked its way through the system to the desk of Governor General James Henry Craig who, not wanting to create problems with the Americans at that particular time, promptly instructed the British chargé d'affaires in Washington to warn the Americans that Tecumseh might attack.

Concerned about reports that Tecumseh was planning an attack with the support of the British, Governor Harrison assembled an army of 1,000 army regulars, Indiana Rangers, volunteer militia and native warriors — at a time when Tecumseh was travelling in the American deep south on a mission to recruit allies — and marched north to Prophetstown with the aim of either reaching an accommodation with, or destroying. Tecumseh's people.

Despite having been ordered by Tecumseh not to do so, Tenskwatawa conducted two pre-dawn attacks on Harrison's forces on November 7, 1811. He claimed to have had a vision from the spirits and that the white men would not be able to kill them. Governor Harrison's army repelled both attacks, forced the Shawnee to flee and then burned Prophetstown to the ground — along with their cooking utensils and 5,000 bushels of corn and beans without which they would have difficulty surviving the winter.

Major American newspapers carried stories about the battle — including the fact that 37 of Governor Harrison's men were killed in action, 25 mortally wounded and about 126 less seriously injured — and public outrage toward the Shawnee quickly grew.

Many Americans blamed the British for inciting the tribes to violence and supplying them with arms and ammunition. Andrew Jackson, who would become the seventh President of the United States in 1829, charged that Tecumseh and his allies were "excited by secret British agents" and called for a declaration of war against Great Britain.

Governor William Blount of Tennessee called on the government to "purge the camps of Indians of every Englishmen to be found." Congress passed resolutions condemning the British for interfering in America's domestic affairs.

On August 5, 1812, Tecumseh and 24 warriors set upon 200 American soldiers attempting to ford Brownstown Creek, just south of Fort Detroit. Despite outnumbering the natives by a ratio of eight to one, the Americans scattered in a panic. Eighteen were killed, 12 wounded, and 70 went missing.

It was at that point that Tecumseh met Major-General Sir Isaac Brock, the Commander of all British Forces in Upper Canada at the British garrison at Fort Amherstburg.

Brock was born on the island of Guernsey, just off the coast of France, on October 6, 1769. He joined the British Army at the age of 15 and fought the French in Barbados and Jamaica, the Danes and Norwegians at the Battle of Copenhagen and arrived in Canada in 1802 in command of the 49th Regiment of Foot.

Brock developed considerable affection and respect for Tecumseh. He called him the "Wellington of the Indians" and, in a letter to British Prime Minister Lloyd Liverpool, Brock said "a more sagacious or a more gallant warrior does not I believe exist"

Here's how one of Brock's officers described Tecumseh at that time: "Tecumseh's appearance was very pre-possessing; his figure light and finely proportioned; his age I imagined to be about five and thirty; in height 5 feet nine or 10 inches; his complexion light copper; countenance, oval with bright hazle [sic] eyes, beaming cheerfulness, energy and decision.

"Three small silver crowns, or coronets, were suspended from the lower cartilage of his aquiline nose; and a large silver medallion of George the Third, which I believe his ancestor received from Lord Dorchester, when Governor General of Canada, was attached to a mixed coloured wampum string, and hung around his neck.

"His dress consisted of a plain, neat, uniform, tanned deer-skin jacket, with long trousers of the same material, the seams of both being covered with neatly cut fringe; and he had on his feet leather moccasins, much ornamented with work made from the dyed quills of the porcupine."

It was reported that Brock "quickly discovered the superior sagacity and intrepidity of Tecumseh." Canadian military historian Colonel C. P. Stacey once wrote: "A relationship of mutual confidence and regard had been established between Brock and the Shawnee chief Tecumseh, who was the effective leader of the Indians at Detroit; it was reflected in the fact that Brock is said to have presented to Tecumseh his sash (which Tecumseh modestly passed on to a senior chief), while Tecumseh gave Brock his sash in exchange. This story has been questioned, but the presence of an 'arrow' sash among the general's uniforms as received by his family seems to provide rather strong presumptive evidence for it."

According to the account of someone who was there, Brock told Tecumseh and the other chiefs that he had been "ordered by their great father to come to their assistance and, with their aid, drive the Americans from Fort Detroit."

Tecumseh "commenced with expressions of joy that their great father beyond the great salt lake [meaning the King of England] had at length awoke from his long sleep and allowed his warriors to come to the assistance of his red children who had never ceased to remain steady in their friendship and were now all ready to shed their last drop of blood in their great father's service."

About 600 warriors under the command of Major-General Colonel Matthew Elliott (more than half of which were Tecumseh's warriors) crossed the Detroit River during the night and were ordered to be in position to attack the enemy from the flank and rear if they fired on the British troops when they landed. The British marched towards the fort and the warriors moved through the skirts of the woods and covered the left flank. The right flank was protected by HMS *Queen Charlotte*, a 16-gun sloop on the Detroit River.

In a letter to the American commander of Fort Detroit dated August 15, 1812, Major-General Brock said, in part "The force at my disposal authorizes me to require of you the immediate surrender of Fort Detroit. It is far from my inclination to join in a war of extermination; but you must be aware that the numerous bodies of Indians who have attached themselves to my troops, will be beyond my control the moment the contest commences. "

The Americans surrendered on August 16th and Brock took possession of Fort Detroit. That wasn't the only time the threat of a gruesome death at the hands of the warriors had put fear into the hearts of American soldiers. Later that month, during the Battle of Queenston Heights, hundreds of American soldiers refused to cross the Niagara River on hearing the war whoops of the Mohawk and other warriors who were fighting alongside the British.

The key role played by the Mohawks of the Six Nations of the Grand River—who moved to Upper Canada from their homeland in what is now New York State after supporting the British during the American Revolutionary War—in the Battle of Queenston Heights was acknowledged by Sir George Prevost, the Governor-in-Chief of British North America.

On congratulating Mohawk Captain Joe Norton on his courage and perseverance, Prevost urged him to "keep up and increase the numbers of a description of Force so truly formidable to their Enemies and so capable of sustaining the good cause in which we are engaged."

Something similar happened in June of the following year when British troops supported by native allies ambushed the Americans near present-day Thorold, Ontario. At one point in the battle, the British officer in command approached his American counterpart under a flag of truce, pointed out that the Americans were greatly outnumbered and advised him that, if they did not surrender, he would be unable to restrain the natives from slaughtering every American in sight.

According to Captain Dominique Ducharme, the natives "fought savagely" and "their horrible yells" prompted the Americans to seek refuge in a hollow from which they quickly surrendered.

At the Battle of Butler's Farm in July, 1813, American General Peter Porter lamented the fact that "this army lies panic-struck, shut up and whipped in by a few hundred miserable savages" led by Ottawa Chief Blackbird.

American fear of death at the hands of the warriors also played a key role during the British siege of Fort Erie on September 17, 1814. Surgeon William Dunlop witnessed warriors in action and said "whenever they knocke a fellow over, their yelling was horrible."

The effectiveness of the native warriors in creating fear in the hearts of the American soldiers prompted Montreal philanthropist and fur trader James McGill to say: "The Indians are the only Allies who can aught avail in the defence of the Canadas."

Brock was, indeed, fortunate to have the support of Tecumseh and his ferocious warriors. In addition to fighting the Americans, he was also fighting a profound sense of indifference on the part of most residents of Upper Canada—a majority of whom were originally from the United States.

On August 29, 1812, Brock wrote to the adjutant general at the British headquarters in Montreal: "My situation is most critical, not from anything the enemy can do, but from the disposition of the people—the population, believe me is essentially bad—A full belief possesses them all that this Province must inevitably succumb—This prepossession is fatal to every exertion—Legislators, Magistrates, Militia Officers, all have imbibed the idea, and are so sluggish and indifferent in their respective offices that the artful and active [American] scoundrel is allowed to parade the Country without interruption, and commit all imaginable mischief ... What a change an additional regiment would make in this part of the province! Most of the people have lost all confidence—I however speak loud and look big."

Before dawn on the morning of October 13, 1812, a large American military force crossed the Niagara River at Queenston, Ontario. The first wave of American soldiers managed to land despite heavy fire from British artillery and took over the battery at the top of the heights.

The sound of the fighting awakened Brock from his sleep at nearby Fort George and he mounted his horse and galloped to the site of the attack. With the Americans in control of the battery at the top of the heights, it was only a matter of time before the rest of them would make it across to the Canadian side of the river.

When Brock gallantly led a charge on foot against the Americans, his height, bright red tunic with its gold lace and epaulettes—plus the colourful sash Tecumseh had given him—made him an easy target for the American marksman who shot him dead.

Tecumseh had remained with his warriors and their families at Fort Amherstburg and was not involved in the Battle of Queenston Heights. When British Major-General Henry Procter decided to abandon Fort Amherstburg the following year because American ships had cut off his supplies, Tecumseh wanted to stay and fight the Americans.

Tecumseh pleaded with Procter to, at the very least, leave behind guns and ammunition so his warriors would have a better chance against the Americans. This is how he put it. "Father, listen! The Americans have not yet defeated us by land. Neither are we sure that they have done so by water. We therefore wish to remain here, and fight our enemy, should they make their appearance …

"Father! You have got the arms and the ammunition which our great father sent for his red children. If you have an idea of going away, give them to us. Our lives are in the hands of the Great Spirit. We are determined to defend our lands, and if it be his will, we wish to leave our bones upon them."

When Procter turned a deaf ear to his impassioned plea, Tecumseh reluctantly followed him in a retreat up the Thames River with the Americans, under the command of the same William Henry Harrison who had burned Prophetstown, in hot pursuit.

Harrison had at least 3,500 infantry and cavalry. The British numbered approximately 800 and Tecumseh had about 500 warriors. Because the Americans had cut off the supply line to Fort Amherstburg, the British and the native warriors had been on half-rations for quite some time.

When Procter decided to take a stand near present-day Chatham, Ontario, Tecumseh's warriors took up positions in a black ash swamp on the right side of the British so as to flank the Americans. Before joining his men, Tecumseh rode along the British line and shook hands with each officer.

As Procter lacked the knowledge and military skills of Brock, he did not fortify his position, thus leaving his troops open to attack from the Americans. Seeing how exposed the British troops were, Harrison had his cavalry launch a frontal attack. Despite the flanking fire from Tecumseh's warriors, they broke through the line—partly because the British cannon failed to fire.

The exhausted, underfed and thoroughly demoralized British troops fired only one ragged fusillade before giving way. Procter fled with 250 of his men. The rest of his troops surrendered.

Despite being outnumbered six to one, Tecumseh and his warriors stood their ground and kept fighting. When about 20 American cavalry charged into their position, they responded with a volley of musket fire and killed or wounded 15 of them. The main force of Americans continued to push forward and Tecumseh was killed in that encounter. He was 44. News of his death spread quickly and his remaining warriors withdrew from the battlefield.

Harrison, who would be elected President of the United States in 1840, took 601 prisoners and set fire to a nearby village occupied by Delawares who were accused of aiding and abetting the British.

In a short biography of Tecumseh in the Dictionary of Canadian Biography Online, Herbert C. W. Goltz, Associate professor of history at St Thomas University in Fredericton, wrote: "With his death, effective Indian resistance south of the [Great] lakes practically ceased. Little more than a week later some of the tribes represented at the battle signed a truce with the Americans. Various efforts by the British to re-enlist them failed. By July 1814, months before the end of the war, Harrison met with more than 3,000 Indians to outline his conditions for peace. Neither those talks nor the Treaty of Spring Wells (1815) demanded new land cessions.

"By 1817, however, the Americans had returned to their old policy. In that year, except for a few left on small reserves, the Indians were removed from Ohio. By 1821 the native inhabitants of Indiana, Illinois, and Michigan had met the same fate. A small number of the displaced came to Upper Canada but most were gradually pushed westward. Of Tecumseh's confederacy nothing remained. Ottawa chief Naywash (Neywash) pronounced its epitaph in 1814 when he said, "Since our Great Chief Tecumtha has been killed we do not listen to one another, we do not rise together. We hurt ourselves by it ..."

Professor Goltz also wrote: "It was and is impossible to cast Tecumseh as a Canadian patriot first and an Indian second. His loyalty was never to Canada or even to the British in Canada. It was to a dream of a pan-Indian movement that would secure for his people the land necessary for them to continue their way of life. The few months he spent fighting with the British forces were in service of that vision. In his failure and death the cynical British and Canadians were only slightly less his enemies than the Americans."

A British war schooner, H.M.S. *Tecumseh*, was built in 1814 and based at the Royal Naval Establishment at Penetanguishene on Georgian Bay to help protect the upper Great Lakes from any future attack by the Americans.

One hundred years after Tecumseh's death, the name of Ryegate Postal Station—on the south shore of Lake St. Clair just east of Windsor and Detroit—was changed to Tecumseh in honor of the Shawnee war chief. Tecumseh is now a town of approximately 24,000 with a large Franco-Ontarian population, many of who are descendants of the French who settled on the banks of the Detroit River in the 1700s.

Chapter 5

The Canadian government was particularly concerned about feelings of resentment and hostility that had built up among the Blackfoot, Blood, Sarcee and Peigan tribes who occupied the unceded territory between the Saskatchewan River and the Rocky Mountains.

In his report for the year 1877, Hon. David Mills, the Minister for the Interior, wrote: "This portion of the North-West [stretching east from the slopes of the Rocky Mountains] is occupied by the Blackfeet, Blood and Sarcees or Piegan Indians, some of the most warlike and intelligent but intractable bands of the North-West. These bands have for years past been anxiously expecting to be treated with, and have been much disappointed at the delay of negotiations.

"In last year's report, I stated that His Honour Lieut.-Gov. [Alexander] Morris, very strongly recommended that no further delay should take place in entering into negotiations with these Indians. His Honour reported, in effect, 'that there was a general consent of opinion amongst the missionaries settled in that territory, and others who are acquainted with these Indians, as to the desirableness of having such a treaty made at the earliest possible date, with a view to preserving the present friendly disposition of these tribes, which might easily give place to feelings of an unfriendly or hostile nature, should the treaty negotiations much longer be delayed.'"

Father Constantine Scollen wrote a letter to Lieut.-Gov. Morris on September 8, 1876, in which he said: "The Blackfeet are extremely jealous of what they consider their coun-try, and never allowed any white men, Half-breeds, or Crees to remain in it for any length of time. The only reason they never drove the Amer-icans off, apart from their love for whiskey, was their dread of the Henri rifle [a .44 calibre, rimfire, lever-action, breech-loading repeater rifle introduced in the late 1850s which could fire at a rate of 28 rounds a minute]."

He also said that the settlers were anxious that a treaty be made as soon as possible "so that they may know what portions of land they can hold without fear of being molested." In a postscript to his letter, Father Scollen said: "The Sioux Indians, now at war with the Americans, have sent a message to the Blackfeet tribes, asking them to make an alliance offensive and defensive against all white people in the country."

When war broke out between the Sioux and the American Gov-ernment in 1876, Lieut.-Gov. Morris wrote in his 1880 book, "the American Sioux endeavoured to induce those in Canadian territory to join them, but they refused. Precautionary measures were however taken, and messengers sent to them, by the Lieutenant-Governor, to warn them against taking any part. They disclaimed all intention to do so, and said they meant to live peacefully, being grateful for the kindness with which they had been treated."

He also said: "The Sioux in the Dominion [of Canada] are refugees from the United States, the first body having come over some 14 years ago. A large influx of similar refugees have recently fled to the Do-minion from the same country as the issue of the recent war between the United States and the Sioux ...

"Much interest has been awakened with regard to this warlike race, owing to recent events; namely, the war between them and the United States, the destruction by them of Captain [sic] George Armstrong] Custer's command [at the Battle of the Little Bighorn] and their sub-sequent flight into British territory [Saskatchewan], and now prolonged sojourn there."

On June 25, 1876, Lieutenant-Colonel George Custer — who had become a household name because of his exploits as a Union officer in the American Civil war and for leading a series of controversial battles and early-dawn attacks against native camps — led his 7th Cavalry Regiment in an attack against a Sioux village on the Little Bighorn River in southeastern Montana. Custer expected a quick victory. However, he did not know that, several weeks earlier, more than 2,000 Sioux had left their reservations to follow Chief Sitting Bull — who had estab-lished quite a name for himself by attacking wagon trains, small forts, and outposts.

Sitting Bull's warriors outnumbered Custer's forces by a wide margin and Custer lost ground quickly and was forced to retreat. The jubilant Sioux moved in for the kill and annihilated Custer and his soldiers

News of Custer's defeat and death led to public outrage and demands for more soldiers to deal with the militant Sioux warriors. Beefed-up American Army forces moved into the area over the next year and forced many of the Sioux to surrender. Sitting Bull refused and, in May, 1877, he moved his people to Saskatchewan.

Here's how the Deputy Superintendent General of Indian Affairs put it in his report in 1877: "The presence of Sitting Bull and his warriors in Canada is a source of anxiety, both to the government of Canada and the United States. These Indians harbour feelings of fierce hostility towards, and thorough distrust of, the United States people and government.

"These feelings may be traced to two principal causes, the dishonesty of Indian agents and the failure of the federal authorities to protect the Indian reservations from being taken possession of by an adventurous and somewhat lawless white population.

"The officers of the North-West Mounted Police have been instructed to impress upon Sitting Bull and his warriors the necessity of keeping the peace towards the people of the United States, and there is no reason for supposing they will not heed the warnings which have been given them.

"It is not, however, desirable to encourage them to remain on Canadian territory, and Col. [James] McLeod [sic] has been accordingly instructed to impress upon them their probable future hardships after the failure of the buffalo, should they elect to remain in Canada; that the President of the United States and his Cabinet are upright men, willing and anxious to do justice to the Indians; and should they return peacefully they will be properly cared for, and any treaty made with them will be honestly fulfilled.

"It is desirable that as wards of the United States, they should return to that country upon the government of which morally evolves the burden and the responsibility of their civilization."

However, most of the Sioux decided to stay in Canada and established good relations with the white settlers on the prairies and with the Canadian authorities. In fact, on the day after the Blackfeet Treaty was signed in September, 1877, Lieut.-Gov. David Laird and the other Commissioners left for Fort Walsh in the Cypress Hills, about 170 kilometres southwest of Swift Current, Saskatchewan, to attend a meeting with Sitting Bull.

In his report about the Sioux living in Canada in 1877, the Deputy Superintendent-General of Indian Affairs said: "Upon the whole, they appear to have made fair progress in cultivating the land, and their prospects for the future, had they the advice and assistance of some good farmers, for a few years, would be encouraging. Indeed, the Sioux generally, who are resident in Canada, appear to be more intelligent, industrious, and self-reliant, than the other Indian bands in the North-West."

Sir John A. Macdonald, Canada's first Prime Minister, reported in 1878 that: "It is only just to them [Sioux] to say, that they have behaved remarkably well ever since they crossed into Canada."

In writing about the Blackfeet Treaty, a report in the Toronto *Globe* said: "On Wednesday, the Commissioners met the Chiefs at the great Council House. A guard of honor of fifty mounted men accompanied them, commanded by Major Irvine. The Police band received them and at one o'clock the guns fired a salute as the Governor [David Laird] and Col. [James] McLeod [sic] took their seats."

During his stay at Fort Macleod, Lieutenant-Governor Laird reviewed the garrison which consisted of Troops C and D and two divisions of artillery. According to the *Globe*: "They deployed past at a walk, trot and gallop, and His Honor expressed his unqualified admiration of the splendid form of the men. He was especially pleased with the artillery, whose horses and equipments were in beautiful condition, and requested Col. McLeod [sic] to convey to the officers and men his surprise and pleasure at finding the force at this post so perfectly drilled and acquainted with their duties.

"On the 12th the two troops and the artillery, accompanied by a baggage train of six light wagons, left Fort McLeod [sic] en route for the scene of the treaty. The Commissioner took command of the detachment, and the Assistant Commissioner remained behind to accompany the Governor on the 14th.

"The force accomplished the march in three days and pitched the tents on ground previously laid out for the encampment by Inspector Crozier at the head of a magnificently wooded valley of about a mile in width and extending for several miles along the Big Bow. It is a lovely spot, this 'Ridge under the Water', and has always been a favorite ground of the Blackfeet nation."

Before describing the first day of the negotiations, it is worth noting something Lieut.-Gov. Laird wrote in his report about what happened when the chiefs first arrived. "The Stoneys and one Blood chief applied for flour, tea, sugar and tobacco, but said they were not then in need of beef. Crowfoot and some other chiefs under his influence would not accept any rations until they would hear what terms the commissioners were prepared to offer them.

"He appeared to be under the impression that if the Indians were fed by the bounty of the government, they would be committed to the proposals of the commissioners whatever might be their nature. Though I feared this refusal did not auger well for the final success of negotiations, yet I could not help wishing that other Indians whom I have seen had a little of the spirit in regard to dependence upon the government exhibited on this occasion by the great chief of the Blackfeet."

Here's how Lieut.-Gov. Laird described the Blackfoot Crossing on the Bow River: "At this crossing, where the Indians had latterly been notified to assemble for the treaty, there is a beautiful river bottom on the south side of the river. It extended about one mile back from the river and is some three miles in length. The river, as far as the eye can reach, is skirted close to the water by a narrow belt of cotton-wood and other trees.

"When I surveyed the clear waters of the stream, the fuel and shelter which the wood afforded, the excellent herbage on the hill and dale, and the Indians camped in the vicinity crossing and re-crossing the river on the 'ridge' with ease and safety, I was not surprised that the Blackfeet were attached to the locality and desired that such an important event in their history as concluding a treaty with Her Majesty's Commissioners should take place at this spot."

Here's how the reporter from the *Globe* described the first day: "Nearly all of the Chiefs and minor Chiefs of the Blackfeet, Blood, Piegan, Stony, and Sarcee tribes were seated directly in front of the Council House; and forming a semicircle of about one-third of a mile beyond the Chiefs, about four thousand men, women and children were squatted on the grass, watching with keen interest the commencement of the proceedings."

Here is Lieut.-Gov. Laird's main message to the natives assembled there that day:

"The Great Spirit has made all things—the sun, the moon, and the stars, and the swift running rivers. It is by the Great Spirit that the Queen rules over this great country and other great countries. The Great Spirit has made the white man and the red man brothers, and we should take each other by the hand.

"The Great Mother loves all her children, white man and red man alike. She wishes to do them all good. The bad white man and the bad Indian she alone does not love, and them she punishes for their wickedness. The good Indian has nothing to fear from the Queen or her officers. You Indians know this to be true.

"When bad white men brought you whiskey, robbed you, and made you poor, and, through whiskey, quarrel amongst yourselves, she sent the [North-West Mounted] Police to put an end to it. You know how they stopped this and punished the offenders, and how much good this has done.

"I have to tell you how much pleased the Queen is that you have taken the police by the hands and helped them, and obeyed her laws since the arrival of the Police. She hopes that you will continue to do so, and you will always find the police on your side if you keep the Queen's laws.

"The Great Mother heard that the buffalo were being killed very fast, and to prevent them from being destroyed her Councillors have made a law to protect them. This law is for your good. It says that the calves are not to be killed, so that they may grow up and increase; that the cows are not to be killed in winter or spring, excepting by the Indians when they are in need of them as food. This will save the buffalo, and provide you with food for many years yet, and it shows you that the Queen and her Councillors wish you well.

"Many years ago our Great Mother made a treaty with the Indians far away by the great waters of the east. A few years ago she made a treaty with those beyond Touchwood Hills and the Woody Mountains. Last year a treaty was made with the Crees along the Saskatchewan, and now the Queen has sent Col. Macleod and myself to ask you to make a treaty. But in a very few years the buffalo will probably all be destroyed, and for this reason the Queen wishes to help you live in the future in some other way. She wishes you to allow her white children to come and live on your land and raise cattle and grain, and should you agree to do this she will assist you to raise cattle and grain, and thus give you the means of living when the buffalo are no more. She will also pay you and your children money every year, which you can spend as you please. By being paid in money you cannot be cheated, as with it you can buy what you may think proper.

"The Queen wishes us to offer you the same as was accepted by the Crees. I do not mean exactly the same terms, but equivalent terms, that will cost the Queen the same amount of money. Some of the other Indians wanted farming implements, but those you do not require, as your lands are more adapted to raising cattle, and cattle, perhaps, would be better for you.

"The Commissioners will give you your choice, whether cattle or farming implements. I have already said we will give you money, I will now tell you how much. If you sign the treaty every man, woman and child will get twelve dollars each. The money will be paid to the head of each family for himself, women and children. Every year, forever, you, your women and your children will get five dollars. This year Chiefs and Councillors will be paid a larger sum than this. Chiefs will get a suit of clothes, a silver medal, and flag, and every third year will get another suit.

"A reserve of land will be set apart for yourselves and your cattle, upon which none others will be permitted to encroach. For every five persons one square mile will be allotted on this reserve, on which they can cut the trees and brush for firewood and other purposes. The Queen's officers will permit no white man or Half-breed to build or cut the timber on your reserves. If required roads will be cut through them. Cattle will be given to you, and potatoes, the same as are grown at Fort Macleod. The Commissioners would strongly advise the Indians to take cattle, as you understand cattle better than you will farming for some time, at least as long as you continue to move about in lodges.

"Ammunition will be issued to you each year, and as soon as you sign the treaty one thousand five hundred dollars' worth will be distributed amongst the tribes, and as soon as you settle, teachers will be sent to you to instruct your children to read books like this one [the Governor held up a Bible] which is impossible so long as you continue to move from place to place. I have now spoken. I have made you acquainted with the principal terms contained in the treaty which you are asked to sign.

"You may wish time to talk it over in your council lodges. You may not know what to do before you speak your thoughts in council. Go, therefore, to your councils, and I hope you may be able to give us an answer tomorrow. Before you leave I will hear your questions and explain any matter that may not appear clear to you."

A few questions asked by the chiefs were answered, and the council was closed for the day. In a report that he wrote at the time, Lieut.-Gov. Laird said: "On Saturday, 22nd September, we met the Indians to conclude the treaty. Mekasto, or Red Crow, the great Chief of the South Bloods, had arrived the previous evening, or morning, on the ground, and being present, came forward to be introduced to the Commissioners.

"The assemblage of Indians was large. All the head Chiefs of the several tribes were now present. Only two Blackfeet and two Blood minor Chiefs were absent. The representation was all that could be expected.

"The Commissioners had previously informed the Indians that they would accept the Chiefs whom they acknowledged, and now close in front of the tent sat those who had been presented to the Commissioners as the recognized Chiefs of the respective bands.

"The conditions of the treaty having been interpreted to the Indians, some of the Blood Chiefs, who had said very little on the previous day, owing to Red Crow's absence, now spoke, he himself in a few kind words agreeing to accept the treaty. The Commissioners having first signed it, Mr. L'Heureux, being familiar with the Blackfoot language, attached the Chiefs' names to the document at their request and witnessed to their marks.

"While the signing was being proceeded with a salute was fired from the field guns in honor of the successful conclusion of the negotiations."

Chief Crowfoot rose during the negotiation of the Blackfeet Treaty and said: "While I speak, be kind and patient. I have to speak for my people, who are numerous, and who rely upon me to follow that course which in the future will tend to their good. The plains are large and wide. We are the children of the plains, it is our home, and the buffalo has been our food always. I hope you look upon the Blackfeet, Bloods and Sarcees as your children now, and that you will be indulgent and charitable to them.

"They all expect me to speak now for them, and I trust the Great Spirit will put into their hearts to be a good people — into the minds of the men, women and children, and their future generations. The advice given me and my people has proved to be very good. If the Police had not come to the country, where would be all now? Bad men and whiskey were killing us so fast that very few, indeed, of us would have been left today. The Police have protected us as the feathers of the bird protect it from the frosts of winter. I wish them all good, and trust that all our hearts will increase in goodness from this time forward. I am satisfied. I will sign the treaty."

After Crowfoot spoke, Red Crow, principal chief of the Blood tribe, said: "Three years ago, when the police first came to the country, I met and shook hands with Stamixotokon [Colonel James. F. Macleod] at Pelly River. Since that time, he made me many promises.

He kept them all. Not one of them was ever broken. Everything the police have done has been good. I entirely trust Stamixotokon and will leave everything to him. I will sign with Crowfoot."

Father of Many Children then said: "I have come a long way, and far behind the rest of the bands. I have travelled with these travois [see book cover] that you now see out there with my women and children. I cannot speak much now, but I agree with Crowfoot and will sign."

Old Sun was next to speak: "Crowfoot speaks well. We were summoned to meet the Great Mother's Chiefs here and we would not disappoint them. We have come and will sign the treaty. During the past Crowfoot has been called by us our Great father. The Great Mother's Chief [Lieutenant-Governor Laird] will now be our Great Father. Everything you say appears to me to be very good and I hope that you will give us all we ask—cattle, money, tobacco, guns, and axes—and that you will not let the white man use poison [strychnine] on the prairies. It kills horses and buffalo as well as wolves and it may kill men. We can ourselves kill the wolves and set traps for them. We all agree with Crowfoot."

Col. Macleod thanked the chiefs for their kind words and said: "The Chiefs all here know what I said to them three years ago, when the Police first came to the country—that nothing would be taken away from them without their own consent. You all see today that what I told you then was true. I also told you that the Mounted Police will continue to be your friends, and be always glad to see you.

"On your part you must keep the Queen's laws, and give every information to them in order that they may see the laws obeyed and offenders punished. You may still look to me as your friend, and at any time when I can do anything for your welfare, I shall only be too happy to do so."

Part of the text of the Blackfeet Treaty says: "And whereas the said Indians have been informed by Her Majesty's Commissioners that it is the desire of Her Majesty to open up for settlement, and such other purposes as to Her Majesty may seem meet, a tract of country, bounded and described as hereinafter mentioned, and to obtain the consent thereto of her Indian subjects inhabiting the said tract, and to make a treaty, and arrange with them, so that there may be peace and good will between them and Her Majesty, and between them and Her Majesty's other subjects; and that her Indian people may know and feel assured of what allowances they are to count on and receive from Her Majesty's bounty and benevolence ...

"In view of the satisfaction of Her Majesty with the recent general good conduct of her said Indians, and in extinguishment of all their past claims, she hereby, through her Commissioners, agrees to make them a present payment of twelve dollars each in cash to each man, woman, and child of the families here represented."

In its account of the treaty-making proceedings, the *Globe* said: "On Wednesday the Chiefs presented an address to the Commissioners expressing their entire satisfaction of the whole nation with the treaty and to the way in which the terms had been carried out. They tendered their good wishes to the Queen, the Governor, Col. McLeod [sic], and the Police Force. They spoke in the most flattering and enthusiastic manner of the Commissioner, Assistant-Commissioner, officers, and the Force in general and said that it was their firm determination to adhere to the terms of the treaty and abide by the laws of the Great Mother. Potts, the interpreter at Fort McLeod [sic], said he never heard Indians speak out their minds so freely in his life before."

According to the *Globe*, "All were glad to get back to the headquarters [Fort Macleod] as the weather had been for some days intensely cold and the prairies covered with snow." In a report that he wrote after the treaty was concluded, Lieut.-Gov. Laird said: "After ten years it is feared the buffalo will have become nearly extinct, and that further protection will be needless. At any rate by that time the Indians hope to have herds of domestic cattle. The country on the upper part of the Bow River is better adapted for settlement than most of that included in the Blackfeet reserve, consequently the Commissioners deemed it advisable to agree that a belt on the south side of the river should be exempt from general occupation for ten years, particularly as the Indians set great value on the concession ...

"The land around the fort and indeed for almost the whole distance between the Bow and Old Man's Rivers is well adapted for grazing; and where cultivation has been fairly attempted this season grain and vegetables have been a success. In short, I have very little doubt that this portion of the territories, before many years, will abound in herds of cattle and be dotted with a few comfortable homesteads."

In writing about the Blackfeet Treaty in his book, Lieut.-Gov. Morris said: "The Commissioners met the Indians on that day and after five days of tedious negotiations, the treaty was satisfactorily concluded, and signed by the Chiefs and head men present.

"The total number of Indians, represented at the making of the treaty, and who were paid the gratuity under it, was four thousand three hundred and ninety-two. The terms of the treaty were substantially the same as those contained in the North-West Angle [Treaty #3] and Qu'Appelle treaties, except that as some of the bands were disposed to engage in pastoral pursuits, it was arranged to give them cattle instead of agricultural implements.

"The Minister of the Interior well observes in his report 'that the conclusion of this treaty with these warlike and intractable tribes, at a time when the Indian tribes, immediately across the border, were engaged in open hostilities with the United States troops, is certainly conclusive proof of the just policy of the Government of Canada toward the aboriginal population,' and, I add, of the confidence of the Indians in the promises and just dealing of the servants of the British Crown, in Canada; a confidence that can only be kept up by the strictest observance of the stipulations of the treaties."

Chapter 6

There's not so much as a hint in the official record that the commissioners appointed by the Canadian government—not by the Queen—to negotiate treaties with the scattered bands living between Thunder Bay and the eastern slopes of the Rocky Mountains considered these to be "nation-to-nation" negotiations or that the various tribes constituted sovereign nations.

Politicians like Scottish-born Prime Minister Sir John A. Macdonald who were familiar with the United Kingdom's centuries-old heritage of kings and queens, lords and ladies, silver cutlery and fine bone china, castles, palaces and cathedrals, highways, railways and bridges, hotels, concert halls, universities and libraries, and monuments to the thousands who bled and died on land and sea in service to the British Empire, certainly didn't consider the nomadic, tent-dwelling, tribes to be nations.

The total population of Canada when the first of the seven numbered treaties was negotiated in the summer of 1871 was approximately 3.8 million of which, according to the official census, only a little more than 100,000 of those who were referred to as Indian at that time lived in Ontario and Quebec.

The total number of Ojibways, Crees, Blackfoot and other tribes living on the newly-acquired HBC territory between Thunder Bay and the eastern slopes of the Rocky Mountains was less than 50,000.

Lieut.-Gov. Alexander Morris and the other commissioners operated on the premise that they were dealing with British Indians on British soil each and every one of whom was a subject of the British Queen and required to obey her laws. During the negotiations at Lower Fort Garry in July, 1871, for example, the Cree negotiators demanded that four Swampy Cree boatmen who had been employed by the Hudson's Bay Company be released from jail. They had been found guilty of deserting their post along with several other Swampy Cree and given the option of paying a fine or going to jail for 40 days. While some had paid the fine, four were still in jail at the start of the negotiations for the Stone Fort and Manitoba Post Treaties.

Here's what Lieutenant-Governor Adams G. Archibald wrote in a report dated July 29, 1871. "On learning the facts, I told the Indians that I could not listen to them if they made a demand for the release of the Indians as a matter of right; that every subject of the Queen, whether Indian, half-breed or white, was equal in the eye of the law; that every offender against the law must be punished, whatever race he belonged to; but I said that on the opening of negotiations with them the Queen would like to see all her Indians taking part in them, and if the whole body present were to ask as a matter of grace and favor, under the circumstances, that their brethren should be released, Her Majesty would be willing to consent to their discharge; she would grant as a favor what she must refuse if asked on any other ground.

"They replied by saying that they begged it as a matter of favor only. Thereupon I acceded to their request, and directed the discharge of the four Indians. This was received with great satisfaction. I explained again, that there might be no misunderstanding about it, that henceforth every offender against the law must be punished. They all expressed their acquiescence in what I said. The discharge of the prisoners had an excellent effect."

There was most certainly no indication of "nation-to-nation" negotiations or agreement to share the land as equals in that exchange.

At one point during the negotiations at the Northwest Angle of the Lake of the Woods leading up to the signing of Treaty #3, the chiefs asked if some of their children living in the United States would be allowed to return to Canada and live on the land that was being reserved for the Ojibways.

"I told them that the treaty was not for American Indians," Lieut.-Gov. Alexander Morris said later, "but any *bona fide British Indians* of the class they mentioned who should *within two years* be found *resident* on British soil would be recognized."

At the time the numbered treaties of 1871–77 were negotiated, the United Kingdom of Great Britain and Ireland was the most powerful nation on earth. The British Queen ruled over England, Scotland, Ireland and Wales and, also, India, Burma, Australia, New Zealand, Malaya, the British West Indies, Singapore, Ceylon, Java, Gibraltar, Malta, parts of Africa and China and, of course, her Dominion of Canada. In India alone, she ruled over 200 million souls and did not hesitate to deal harshly with anyone who questioned her right to rule.

If any nation had dared challenge the British Queen's sovereignty over the Canadian land mass and all of the inhabitants therein, its ships would have been sunk on the high seas by Her Majesty's Royal Navy, the most formidable military force on earth.

The government of the United States most definitely recognized that everything north of the border was British territory. In September, 1862, for example, about two hundred Sioux sought refuge in what later would become the province of Manitoba after an estimated 500 white settlers and soldiers were killed in southwestern Minnesota in an effort to drive the whites out of the territory.

According to a Mrs. Justina Krieger, who witnessed the massacre and survived: "Mr. Massipost had two daughters, young ladies, intelligent and accomplished. These the savages murdered most brutally. The head of one of them was afterward found, severed from the body, attached to a fish-hook, and hung upon a nail. His son, a young man of twenty-four years, was also killed. Mr. Massipost and a son of eight years escaped to New Ulm.

"The daughter of Mr. Schwandt, enceinte [pregnant], was cut open, as was learned afterward, the child taken alive from the mother, and nailed to a tree. The son of Mr. Schwandt, aged thirteen years, who had been beaten by the Indians, until dead, as was supposed, was present, and saw the entire tragedy. He saw the child taken alive from the body of his sister, Mrs. Waltz, and nailed to a tree in the yard. It struggled some time after the nails were driven through it! This occurred in the forenoon of Monday, 18th of August, 1862."

The main body of about 500 Sioux men, women and children, sought refuge in what is now Manitoba and set up camp at Sturgeon Creek—about six miles from Fort Garry—and the others pitched their tents at Poplar Point and Turtle Mountain.

They left behind 303 Sioux prisoners who were later sentenced to death for the crime of murder and rape against civilians by a military tribunal. President Abraham Lincoln commuted the death sentence of 264 and the other 39 were condemned to a mass hanging before the public on December 26, 1862, in Mankato, Minnesota.

In the book that he wrote in 1879, Lieut.-Gov. Morris said the arrival of several hundred Sioux at the Red River settlement "caused great consternation." U.S. military authorities sent an envoy to the Governor-in-Chief of Rupert's Land and the North-West Territories with a view to having the Sioux ordered back to the United States. They assured the Governor-in-Chief that, while they would punish any warriors who had been involved in the massacre, those who were found to be innocent would be provided with supplies and clothing for the winter if they surrendered peacefully.

Despite repeated attempts by the American military authorities, through the good offices of the British Queen's representatives in Canada, to get the Sioux to return to the United States—including an offer four years later of "entire absolution for all past offences"—they preferred instead to remain in the British territory.

Not once, at any time, did the U.S. military authorities make any attempt to cross over the border and hunt them down. They accepted, 100%, that the Sioux were now living under the protection of the British Crown.

There was very little in the way of two-way negotiation in the treaty-making process. The terms were pretty much what the representatives of the Government of Canada had decided in advance that they should be. Very little, if anything, that the chiefs of the bands asked for was granted.

Here's what Lieut.-Gov. Morris told the chiefs and headmen during the discussions leading up to the signing of Treaty #6 at Fort Carlton, Saskatchewan: "We are not here as traders. I do not come as to buy or sell horses or goods. I come to you, children of the Queen, to try to help you. When I say yes, I mean it and when I say no, I mean it too."

During the negotiations at Fort Ellice, Manitoba, Lieut.-Gov. Morris said: "We are not traders. I have told you all we can do and all we will do. It is for you to say whether you will accept my hand or not. I cannot wait long. I think you are not wiser than your brothers [who had already signed a treaty]. Our ears are open, you can speak to us. Later on, he told them: "You must be good subjects to the Queen and obey her laws."

In reporting on his negotiations at the Stone Fort (Lower Fort Garry) in Manitoba, Lieut.-Gov. Archibald said: "In defining the limits of their reserves, so far as we could see, they wished to have two-thirds of the Province. We heard them out, and then told them it was quite clear that they had entirely misunderstood the meaning and intention of reserves.

"We explained the object of these is something like the language of the memorandum enclosed, and then told them it was of no use for them to entertain any such ideas, which were entirely out of the question."

During the negotiations near Fort Qu'Appelle, Lieut.-Gov. Morris said: "The Queen's High Councillor here from Ottawa, and I, her Governor, are not traders. We do not come here in the spirit of traders. We come here to tell you openly, without hiding anything, just what the Queen will do for you, just what she thinks is good for you, and I want you to look me in the face, eye to eye, and open your heart to me as children would to a father, as children ought to do to a father, and as you ought to the servants of the great mother of us all ...

"It is for you to say. Not for us. We have done all that men who love their red brothers can do. It is for you now to act. On you rests the duty of saying whether you believe our message or not, whether you want the Queen to help you or not, whether you will go away and let the days and the years go on, and let the food grow scarcer, and let your children grow up and do nothing to keep off the hunger and the cold that is before them. It is for you to say that, not for us. If we had not your good at heart we would not have been here, we would not have labored all these many days, if our hearts were not warm towards you, and if we did not believe what we are doing would be for your good as children of our Queen. I have said all."

In a letter to the Secretary of State for the Provinces dated November 3, 1871, Indian Commissioner Wymess McKenzie Simpson said: "When their [Chiefs'] answer came back it proved to contain demands of such an exorbitant nature, that much time was spent in reducing their terms to a basis upon which an arrangement could be made."

In a report Lieut.-Gov. Morris wrote to the Minister of the Interior on October 11, 1876, describing negotiations with the Ojibways and Swampy Crees north of Lake Winnipeg, he said: "They then claimed a reserve on both sides of the river of large extent and extending up to the head of the Great Rapids, but this we declined to accede to.

"Eventually, as the locality they had hitherto occupied is so important a point, controlling as it does the means of communication between the mouth of the river and the head of the rapids, and where a 'tram-way' will no doubt ere long require to be constructed, presenting also deep-water navigation and excellent wharfage, and evidently being moreover the site where a town will spring up, we offered them reserve on the south side of the river.

"They objected, that they had their houses and gardens on the north side of the river, but said that as the Queen's Government were treating them so kindly, that they would go to the south side of the river, if a small sum [They were paid $500 — the cost of about 20 to 25 cows.] was given to them to assist in removing their houses or building others, and this as will be seen by the terms of the treaty, we agreed to do, believing it to be alike in the interests of the Government to have control of so important a point as the mouth of the great internal river of the Saskatchewan, and yet only just to the Indians who were making what was to them so large a concession to the wishes of the Commissioners."

In a report to the Minister of the Interior about revisions to Treaty #1 and #2 dated October 5, 1876, Lieut.-Gov. Morris wrote: "We then brought before them your request that the portion of the reserve embraced in the proposed new town near the Pacific Railway crossing should be sold for their benefit, to which they agreed, and the formal instrument of surrender will be enclosed to you by the Indian Commissioner."

At one point in the negotiations with the Ojibway chiefs and headmen at the Northwest Angle of the Lake of the Woods, Lieut.-Gov. Morris told them: "This is the best I can do for you. I wish you to understand we do not come here as traders, but as representing the Crown, and to do what we believe is just and right. We have asked in that spirit, and I hope you will meet me in that spirit and shake hands with me today and make a treaty forever. I have no more to say."

The assistance that was to be provided to the bands west of Thunder Bay by the Canadian government under the terms of the treaties that were negotiated between 1871 and 1877 was intended to be a short-term measure—sort of a bridge over troubled waters—to help them make the difficult transition from their nomadic lifestyle of hunting, fishing and gathering to supporting themselves by farming and/or raising cattle.

The goal was that they would become a self-supporting population able to take care of themselves in the same manner as the white settlers without further assistance from the Canadian government.

A review of the negotiations that took place at Fort Carlton, Saskatchewan, in August, 1876, demonstrates the manner in which the representatives of the Government of Canada emphasized, time and time again, that—other than the annual treaty payments of $5 for every man woman and child, and money each year for ammunition and twine for their nets—the assistance that was to be provided was going to be a one-shot deal.

At one point in the negotiations, Lieut.-Gov. Morris said: "In order to encourage the keeping of cattle we would give each band a bull and four cows. Having all these things we would give each band enough potatoes, oats, barley and wheat for seed to plant the land actually broken. This would be done **once for all** [emphasis added] to encourage them to grow for themselves."

Oo-pee-too-kerah-han-ap-ee-wee-yin said: "We have heard your words that you had to say to us as the representative of the Queen.

We were glad to hear what you had to say, and have gathered together in council and thought the words over amongst us. We were glad to hear you tell us how we might live by our own work.

"When I commence to settle on the lands to make a living for myself and my children, I beg of you to assist me in every way possible. When I am at a loss how to proceed I want the advice and assistance of the Government. The children yet unborn, I wish you to treat them in like manner as they advance in civilization like the white man. This is all I have been told to say now. If I have not said anything in a right manner I wish to be excused. This is the voice of the people."

In reply, Lieut.-Gov. Morris said: "I cannot promise, however, that the government will feed and support all the Indians. You are many, and if we were to try to do it, it would take a great deal of money, and some of you would never do anything for yourselves. What I have offered does not take away your living. You will have it then as you have now, and what I offer now is put on top of it. This I can tell you, the Queen's Government will always take a deep interest in your living."

The Badger said: "We want to think of our children. We do not want to be too greedy. When we commence to settle down on the reserves that we select, it is there we want your aid, when we cannot help ourselves and in case of troubles seen and unforeseen in the future."

Sak-ah-moos and several others in order repeated what The Badger had said. In response, Lieut.-Gov. Morris said: "I have told you that the money I have offered you would be paid to you and to your children's children. I know that the sympathy of the Queen, and her assistance, would be given you in any unforeseen circumstances. You must trust to her generosity.

"Last winter when some Indians wanted food because the crops had been destroyed by grasshoppers, although it was not promised in the treaty, nevertheless the Government sent money to buy them food, and in the spring when many of them were sick a man was sent to try and help them.

"We cannot foresee these things, and all I can promise is that you will be treated kindly, and in that extraordinary circumstances you must trust the generosity of the Queen …

"I have another word to say to the Indians on this matter. Last year an unforeseen calamity came upon the [white] people of Red River. The grasshoppers came and ate all their crops. There is no treaty between the people of Red River and the Queen, except that they are her subjects. There was no promise to help them, but I sent down and said that unless help came some of the people would die from want of food, and that they had nothing wherewith to plant.

"The Queen's Councillors [in Ottawa] at once gave money to feed the people, and seed that they might plant the ground. But that was something out of and beyond everyday life and therefore I say that some great sickness or famine stands as a special case. You may rest assured that when you go to your reserves you will be followed by the watchful eye and sympathetic hand of the Queen's Councillors."

The Badger then said: "I do not want you to feed me every day. You must not understand that from what I have said. When we commence to settle down on the ground to make there our own living, it is then we want your help, and that is the only way that I can see how the poor can get along."

Lieut.-Gov. Morris said: "You will remember the promises which I have already made. I said you would get seed. You need not concern yourselves so much about what your grand-children are going to eat. Your children will be taught, and then they will be as well able to take care of themselves as the whites around them."

Mis-tah-wah-sis, one of the leading chiefs, said: "It is well known that if we had plenty to live on from our gardens [farms] we would not still insist on getting more provision. But it is in case of any extremity, and from the ignorance of the Indians in commencing to settle that we thus speak. We are as yet in the dark. This is not a trivial matter for us.

"We were glad to hear what the Governor was saying to us and we understood it. But we are not understood. We do not mean to ask for food for every day but only when we commence and in case of famine or calamity. What we speak of and do now will last as long as the sun shines and the river runs. We are looking forward to our children's children, for we are old and have but few days to live."

Ah-tahk-ah-coop, the other leading chief, said: "I have heard the good things you promise us. You have told us of the white man's way of living and mentioned some of the animals by which he gets his living, others you did not.

"We want food in the spring when we commence to farm. According as the Indian settles down on his reserves, and in proportion as he advances, his wants will increase."

The interpreter read a list of demands from the chiefs and headmen, including: "To make some provision for the poor, unfortunate, blind and lame" and "That we be supplied with medicines free of cost."

After the list was read, Tee-tee-quay-say said: "When we look back to the past we do not see where the Cree nation has ever watered the ground with the white man's blood, he has always been our friend and we his. Trusting to the Giver of all good, to the generosity of the Queen, and to the Governor and his councillors, we hope you will grant us this request."

Lieut.-Gov. Morris said in reply: "I told you yesterday that if any great sickness or general famine overtook you, that on the Queen being informed of it by her Indian agent, she in her goodness would give such help as she thought the Indians needed. You asked for help when you settled on your reserves during the time you were planting. You asked very broadly at first. I think the request you make now is reasonable to a certain extent. But help should be given after you settle on the reserve **for three years only**, [emphasis added] or after that time you should have food of your own raising, besides all the things that are given to you. This assistance would only be given to those actually cultivating the soil.

"Therefore, I would agree to give every spring, **for three years**, [emphasis added] the sum of one thousand dollars to assist you in buying provisions while planting the ground. I do this because you seem anxious to make a living for yourselves. It is more than has been done anywhere else. I must do it on my own responsibility and trust to the other Queen's councillors to ratify it …

"I cannot undertake the responsibility of promising provision for the poor, blind and lame. In all parts of the Queen's dominions we have them. The poor whites have as much reason to be helped as the poor Indian. They must be left to the charity and kind hearts of the people. If you are prosperous yourselves you can help your unfortunate brothers …

"A medicine chest will be kept at the house of each Indian agent, in case of sickness amongst you ... At first we heard of only two chiefs. Now they are becoming many. You ask for a cooking stove for each. This we cannot give. He must find a way of cooking for himself."

At that point, Ah-tuck-ah-coop said: "I never sent a letter to the Governor. I was waiting to meet him and that we have asked we considered would be for the benefit of our children ... Now I ask my people, those that are in favour of the offer, to say so."

All of the Cree chiefs and headmen assembled there that day signalled their approval by holding up their hands and shouting. A short time later, Oo-pee-too-korah-hair-ap-ee-wee-yin (The Pond-maker) said: "I do not differ from my people, but I want more explanation. I heard what you said yesterday, and I thought that when the law was established in this country it would be for our good. From what I can hear and see now, I cannot understand that I shall be able to clothe my children and feed them as long as sun shines and water runs.

"With regard to the different Chiefs who are to occupy the reserves, I expected they would receive sufficient for their support, this is why I speak. In the presence of God and the Queen's representative I say this, because I do not know how to build a house for myself. You see how naked I am, and if I tried to do it my naked body would suffer. Again, I do not know how to cultivate the ground for myself. At the same time I quite understand what you have offered to assist us in this."

There is no record of any response from Lieut.-Gov. Morris to what The Pond-maker said. However, at a later stage in the proceedings, he said: "I want the Indians to fully understand that all that has been offered is a gift and they still have the same mode of living as before."

Later on he said: "I will speak to you in regard to food as I have spoken to the other Indians. We cannot support or feed the Indians every day, further than to help them to find the means of doing it for themselves by cultivating the soil. If you were to be regularly fed some of you would do nothing at all for your own support. In this matter we will do as we have agreed with the other Indians, and no more ... In a national famine or general sickness, not what happens in everyday life, but if a great blow comes on the Indians, they would not be allowed to die like dogs."

In addressing the Cree chiefs and headmen at Fort Pitt on September 13, 1876, Lieut.-Gov. Morris said: "The Government will not interfere with the Indian's daily life. They will not bind him. They will only help him to make a living on the reserve by giving him the means of growing from the soil his food. The only occasion when help would be given would be if Providence should send a great famine or pestilence upon the whole Indian people included in the treaty. We only looked at something unforeseen and not at hard winters or the hardships of single bands and this, both you and I, fully understand."

In a report that he wrote at that time, Lieut.-Gov. Morris said that he had told the Cree chiefs that "they had their own means of living and that we would not feed the Indians, but only assist them to settle down. The Badger, Soh-ah-moos and several other Indians all asked help when they settled, and also in case of troubles unforeseen in the future. I explained that we could not assume the charge of their everyday life, but in a time of great national calamity they could trust to the generosity of the Queen."

After agreeing to a modest increase in cattle and farm equipment that would be provided after the treaty was signed, Lieut.-Gov. Morris re-emphasized that, after three years, the Crees would be entirely on their own. "I closed by stating that, after they settled on the reserves, we would give them provisions to aid them while cultivating, to the extent of one thousand dollars per annum, **but for three years only,** [emphasis added] as after that time they should be able to support themselves ... We told them that they must help their own poor, and that if they prospered they could do so."

In response to the concern expressed by the Cree chiefs about the need of assistance in the time of pestilence, famine or other calamity, the text of Treaty #6 states: "That in the event hereafter of the Indians comprised within this treaty being overtaken by any pestilence or by a general famine, the Queen, on being satisfied and certified thereof, by her Indian Agent or Agents, will grant to the Indians, assistance of such character and to such an extent as her chief Superintendent of Indian affairs shall deem necessary and sufficient to relieve the Indians from the calamity that shall have befallen them."

There is no reference to pestilence, famine or other calamity, in any of the other treaties that were negotiated between 1871 and 1877.

With respect to the promise to provide a medicine chest at the house of the Indian agent, the actual handwritten text of Treaty #6 states: "That a medicine chest shall be kept at the house of each Indian agent for the use and benefit of the Indians, at the **discretion** [emphasis added] of such agent."

That paragraph of the treaty, as shown on the website of Indigenous and Northern Affairs Canada, has been changed to read: "That a medicine chest shall be kept at the house of each Indian Agent for the use and benefit of the Indians at the **direction** [emphasis added] of such agent."

There is a significant difference between the word "discretion" as found in the original text and the word "direction" that appears on the government website.

The 1969 annual report of the Department of Health and Welfare said: "Despite popular misconceptions of the situation and vigorous assertions to the contrary, neither the federal nor any other government has any formal obligation to provide Indians or anyone else with free medical services."

In the 1971 case of *Regina vs. Swimmer*, the Saskatchewan Court of Appeal held that the reference to a "medicine chest" in a treaty does not impose upon the Government of Canada any obligation to provide free medicine and hospital services to all those covered by the treaty.

Treaty #6 is the only treaty containing a reference to a medicine chest. The issue was not raised by any of the bands covered by the other six treaties that were negotiated between 1871 and 1877.

There is no mention in any of the treaties of the Canadian government being under any obligation of any kind whatsoever to provide the bands with housing, doctors and/or nurses, hospitals, water, sewers, social assistance, or funds for economic development.

Under the terms of the seven treaties that were signed between 1871 and 1877, the chiefs and councillors of the bands covered by each treaty became officers of the British Queen and were subject to her laws and command. Here is how Lieut.-Gov. Alexander Morris put it to the Cree chiefs when he was negotiating Treaty #6 at Fort Carlton, Saskatchewan, in August, 1876. "Chiefs ought to be respected, they ought to be looked up to by their people. They ought to have good Councillors. The Chiefs and Councillors should consult for the good of the people. The Queen expects Indians and whites to obey her laws. She expects them to live at peace with other Indians and with the white men.

"The Chiefs and Councillors should teach their people so, and once the Queen approves a Chief or Councillor he cannot be removed unless he behaves badly. The Chiefs and head men are not to be lightly put aside. When a treaty is made they become servants of the Queen. They are to try and keep order amongst their people. We will try to keep order in the whole country ...

"I have said a Chief was to be respected. I wear a uniform because I am an officer of the Queen. The officers of the [North-West Mounted] Police wear uniforms as servants of the Queen. So we give to the Chiefs and Councillors good and suitable uniform indicating their office, to wear on these and other great days ... In addition [to a uniform and silver medal] each Chief will be given a [British] flag to put over his lodge to show that he is a Chief ... The chiefs' and headmen's coats will wear out. They are meant to be worn when it is necessary to show that they are officers of the Queen and every third year, they will be replaced by new ones."

In the book that he wrote about the treaty-making process, Lieut.-Gov. Morris said: "The Indians of Canada have, owing to the manner in which they were dealt with for generations by the Hudson's Bay Company, the former rulers of these vast territories [from 1670 until 1870], an abiding confidence in the Government of the Queen, or the Great Mother, as they style her. This must not, at all hazards, be shaken."

In a letter dated November 3, 1871, Indian Commissioner Wemyss McKenzie Simpson said: "The Indians of both parts [Stone Fort and Manitoba Post] have a firm belief in the honour and integrity of Her Majesty's representatives, and are fully impressed with the idea that the amelioration of their present condition is one of the objects of Her Majesty in making these treaties ...

"Although serious trouble has from time to time occurred across the [American] boundary line, with Indians of the same tribes, and indeed of the same bands as those in Manitoba, there is no reason to fear any trouble with those who regard themselves as subjects of Her Majesty.

"Their desire is to live at peace with the white man, to trade with him, and, when they are disposed, to work for him; and I believe that nothing but gross injustice or oppression will induce them either to forget the allegiance which they now claim with pride, or molest the white subjects of the sovereign whom they now regard as their Supreme Chief."

Here's what Commissioner J. Lestock Reid wrote in a letter to Lieut.-Gov. Morris dated October 14, 1876: "I would here mention that previous to my departure from Norway House [a settlement on the Nelson River 30 kilometres northeast of Lake Winnipeg] there was a very hearty and apparently sincere expression of gratitude, on the part of all the Indians present, for the liberality extended to them, and a general and spoken wish that their thanks be conveyed to the Queen's Representative in this Province [Manitoba] for his kind interest in their welfare."

At the conclusion of the negotiations for Treaty #6, Lieut.-Gov. Morris later reported: "I then presented Sweet Grass his medal, uniform, and flag, the band playing 'God Save the Queen' and all the Indians rising to their feet. The rest of the medals, flags, and uniforms, were distributed, as soon as possible, and Mr. [W. J.] Christie made the payments."

Thomas Howard, a commissioner involved in negotiating an adhesion to the Winnipeg Treaty, said that he read the adhesion to The Pas and Cumberland House chiefs and they signed. "I then presented the medals and clothing to the Chiefs and Councillors, with which they were greatly pleased, and having congratulated them upon wearing the Queen's uniform, and having in turn been heartily thanked by them for what had been done, I proceeded to pay them."

One of the chiefs at Fort Carlton said he wanted to have a blue uniform, just like the one worn by Lieut.-Gov. Morris. "I wear this [blue] coat," Lieut.-Gov. Morris told him, "but it is only worn by those who stand as the Queen's Councillors. Her soldiers and her officers wear red, and all the other Chiefs of the Queen wear the [red] coats we have brought, and the good of this is that when the Chief is seen with his uniform and medal everyone knows he is an officer of hers."

Most of the treaties contained language along the line of the following from the text of Treaty #3: "They [chiefs] promise and engage that they will, in all respects, obey and abide by the law; that they will maintain peace and good order between each other, and between themselves and other tribes of Indians, and between themselves and others of Her Majesty's subjects, whether Indian, Half-breeds or whites, now inhabiting, or hereafter to inhabit, any part of the said ceded tract; and that they will not molest the person or property of any inhabitant of such ceded tract, or the property of Her Majesty the Queen, or interfere with or trouble any person passing or traveling through the said tract, or any part thereof; and they will assist the officers of Her Majesty in bringing to justice and punishment any Indian offending against the stipulations of this treaty, or infringing the laws in force in the country so ceded."

The Treaty #3 text also said that the chiefs would be "responsible to Her Majesty for the faithful performance by their respective bands of such obligations as shall be assumed by them [under the terms of the treaty]."

Each chief (as an officer of the Queen) was to receive an annual salary of $25 — cows were being sold at that time for $20 to $25 a head and pork was $50 a barrel — and the headmen were to receive $15. "Such Chief and subordinate officer as aforesaid shall also receive once in every three years a suitable suit of clothing; and each Chief shall receive, in recognition of the closing of the treaty, a suitable flag and medal."

In the book he wrote about the treaty-making process, Lieut.-Gov. Morris said that the chiefs "should be strongly impressed with the belief that they are officers of the Crown, and that it is their duty to see that the Indians of their tribes obey the provisions of the treaties."

He referred to the "advantage it is to the Crown to possess so large a number of Indian officials, duly recognized as such, and who can be inspired with a proper sense of their responsibilities to the Government and to their bands, as well as to others.

"In all the negotiations for treaties, the Chiefs took a controlling part, and generally exhibited great common sense and excellent judgment. It is therefore of the utmost importance to retain their confidence and cause their office to be recognized and respected by both whites and Indians."

Large numbers of Aboriginals covered by the treaties the newly-formed Dominion of Canada entered into with the scattered bands living between Thunder Bay and the eastern slopes of the Rocky Mountains had converted to Christianity long before Confederation. Many of their children were attending boarding schools established by the different churches. When Ojibway Chief Peguis—who had extended a helping hand to the first settlers at the Red River Colony—was baptized into the Anglican Church in 1840, he gave up three of his four wives and changed his name to William King. His children took the surname Prince.

Evidence of how strongly many Aboriginals valued their Christian faith can be found as far back as 1760 when the primarily-Catholic Mohawk, Huron and Abenaki—who had fought alongside the French—were guaranteed the right to practice their Catholic religion. Article 40 of the Capitulation of Montreal states "they shall have, as well as the French, liberty of religion, **and shall keep their missionaries** [emphasis added]."

The first Anglican church in Ontario was built on the Six Nations of the Grand River in 1785—82 years before Confederation—by the British Crown to show gratitude for the important role the Mohawks had played under the leadership of Chief Joseph Brant in support of the British during the American Revolutionary War. Her Majesty's Chapel of the Mohawks had a bible, prayer books and a silver communion service given to the Mohawks by Queen Anne when they were still living in the Mohawk Valley down in what is now the state of New York.

During negotiations at Fort Carlton, Saskatchewan, in 1876, the chiefs requested that a minister be sent to their camp to conduct a service. About 200 adult Crees attended the service conducted by an Anglican minister. The nomadic Crees, who were still living in tents, wanted to learn how to farm and asked for missionaries and teachers.

In *The Treaties of Canada with the Indians*, Lieut.-Gov. Alexander Morris said: "The treaties provide for the establishment of schools, on the reserves, for the instruction of the Indian children. This is a very important feature, and is deserving of being pressed with the utmost energy. The new generation can be trained in the habits and ways of civilized life—prepared to encounter the difficulties with which they will be surrounded, by the influx of settlers, and fitted to maintaining themselves as tillers of the soil. The erection of a school-house on a reserve will be attended to with slight expense, and the Indians would often give their labour towards its construction."

Because the buffalo herds were almost extinct, the nomadic bands' ability to support themselves had been greatly diminished. Lieut.-Gov. Morris said providing farmers and carpenters to instruct them in farming and building houses would assist them to become "self-supporting". He also said the "universal demand for teachers, and for some of the Indians for missionaries, is also encouraging. The former, the Government can supply; for the latter they must rely on the churches, and I trust these will continue and extend their operations amongst them. The field is wide enough for all, and the cry of the Indian for help is a clamant one." Among a list of items the chiefs had presented to Lieut.-Gov. Morris was: "To supply us with a minister and a school teacher of whatever denomination we belong to."

In describing negotiations with the bands in the Athabasca region in June, 1899, the treaty commissioners' report said: "All the Indians we met were with rare exceptions professing Christians; and showed evidences of the work which missionaries have carried on among them for many years. A few of them have had their children avail themselves of the advantages afforded by boarding schools established at different missions."

The report said the bands wanted education for their children "but stipulated that in the matter of schools there should be no interference with their religious [Catholic or Protestant] beliefs." During treaty negotiations in northern Saskatchewan in August, 1906, the chief of the English River band "insisted that in the carrying out of the government's Indian educational policy among them there should be no interference with the system of religious schools now conducted by the mission, but that public aid should be given for improvement and extension along the lines already followed."

The Ojibways in the Manitoba Superintendency in 1877 wanted to be taught farming and construction. Some in the Fort Frances area were making progress in cultivating the soil. The Ojibways at Lac Seul had built two villages in order to have the benefit of schools. The Indian agent in the Lake Manitoba district said one band had built a good school, 19 new houses, and had 140 acres under cultivation.

There were two Christian missions at Fort Albany — one Roman Catholic and one Anglican. A large boarding school operated by the Grey Nuns from the parent house at Ottawa accommodated 20 Aboriginal pupils. Assistance was provided for the sick in the hospital ward and a number of elderly people unable to hunt with their relatives were supported every winter. The celebration of mass on Sunday was well attended.

The Church of England mission was said to be "in a flourishing condition". The large church was filled for all Sunday services and the worshippers participated in their own language. A feast was held after the treaty was signed at which the Anglican Bishop of Moosonee "began with a prayer in Cree, the Indians making their responses and singing their hymns in the same language." The church at Moose Factory established by the Church Missionary Society "was crowded every evening by interested Indians."

A mission at Isle à la Crosse in northern Saskatchewan established around 1844 was showing signs of age and was being replaced. The treaty commissioner said the school "is cosy within, and the children whom I had the pleasure of meeting there, evidenced the kindly care and careful training of the devoted women who have gone out from the comforts of civilization to work for the betterment of the natives of the north." A two-storey school had been built about 48 kilometres south of the mission and the children were moving into it.

None of the bands received title to the lands that were set aside for their use and the Government of Canada reserved the right to use the lands for other purposes. The Fort Qu'Appelle treaty, for example, states that "in no wise shall the said Indians, or any of them, be entitled to sell or otherwise allocate any of the lands allotted to them as reserves."

And, according to the adhesion to Treaties #1 and #2, the natives didn't own the animals either. "These animals and their issue to be Government property, but to be allowed for the use of the Indians, under the superintendence and control of the Indian Commissioner."

In the book that he wrote about the treaty-making process in 1879, Alexander Morris said: "It will be found desirable, to assign to each family parts of the reserve for their own use, so as to give them a sense of property in it, but all power of sale or alienation of such lands should be rigidly prohibited.

"Any premature enfranchisement [right to vote] of the Indians, or power given to them to part with their lands, would inevitably lead to the speedy breaking up of the reserves, and the return of the Indians to their wandering mode of life, and thereby to the re-creation of a difficulty which the assignment of reserves was calculated to obviate."

The text of Treaty #3 clearly states that: "It is further agreed between Her Majesty and her said Indian subjects that such sections of the reserve above indicated as may at any time be required for public works or buildings, of whatever nature, may be appropriated for that purpose by Her Majesty's Government of the Dominion of Canada, due compensation being made to the Indians for the value of any improvements thereon, and an equivalent in land or money for the area of the reserve so appropriated."

Consider this exchange between one of the Treaty #3 chiefs and an Indian Commissioner on the question of the Ojibways giving up reserve land to make way for public works or buildings:

CHIEF — Of course, if there is any particular part wanted by the public works they can shift us. I understand that. But if we have any gardens [farms] throughout the country, do you wish that the poor man should throw it right away?

COMMISSIONER — Of course not.

It was also clearly stated in the treaties that the natives would have the right to hunt and fish in the traditional territories outside the actual reserves that had been set aside for their use—but only until such time as the lands were needed for settlement or other purposes—and that they would have to obey all laws and regulations related to hunting and fishing.

During the negotiations at Fort Carlton, for example, Lieut.-Gov. Morris said: "The North-West Council is considering the framing of a law to protect the buffaloes, and when they make it, they will expect the Indians to obey it."

While negotiating with the Ojibway chiefs at the Northwest Angle of the Lake of the Woods, he said: "I will give you lands for farms, and also reserves for your own use. I have authority to make reserves such as I have described, not exceeding in all a square mile for every family of five or thereabouts. It may be a long time before the other lands [outside of the reserve] are wanted and in the meantime you will be permitted to hunt and fish over them."

In a letter to the Secretary of State for the Provinces dated July 27, 1871, Lieutenant-Governor Adams G. Archibald said: "Furthermore, the Indians seem to have false ideas about the meaning of a reserve. They have been led to suppose that large tracts of ground were to be set aside for them as hunting grounds, including timber lands, of which they might sell the wood as if they were proprietors of the soil. I wished to correct this idea at the outset."

While negotiating the Stone Fort and Manitoba Post treaties, Lieut.-Gov. Archibald said: "Till these lands are needed for use you will be free to hunt over them, and make all the use of them which you have made in the past. But when lands are needed to be tilled or occupied, you must not go on them anymore."

During the negotiations near Fort Qu'Appelle, Lieut.-Gov. Morris said: "We have come through the country for many days and we have seen hills and but little wood and in many places little water, and it may be a long time before there are many white men settled upon this land, and you will have the right of hunting and fishing, just as you have now until the land is actually taken up."

The actual text of Treaty #3 states: "Her Majesty further agrees with her said Indians, that they, the said Indians, shall have the right to pursue their avocation of hunting and fishing throughout the tract as hereinbefore described, subject to such regulations as may from time to time be made by her Government of her Dominion of Canada, and saving and excepting such tracts as may from time to time be required to be taken up for settlement, mining, lumbering or other purposes, by her said Government of the Dominion of Canada, or by any of the subjects thereof duly authorized by the said Government."

While addressing the chiefs at Fort Carlton, Lieut.-Gov. Morris said: "There is one thing I would say about the reserves. The land I name is much more than you will ever be able to farm, and it may be that you would like to do as your brothers where I came from [Ontario] did. They, [at the Six Nations of the Grand River] when they found they had too much land, asked the Queen to sell it for them. They kept as much as they could want, and the price for which the remainder was sold was put away to increase for them, and many bands now have a yearly income from the land. But understand me, once the reserve is set aside, it could not be sold unless with the consent of the Queen and the Indians. As long as the Indians wish, it will stand there for their good. No one can take their houses."

In *The Treaties of Canada With the Indians,* Lieut.-Gov. Alexander Morris said: "To carry them out, the treaty area has been divided into two Superintendencies, that of Manitoba, including Treaties Numbers One, Two Three and Four; and that of the North-West Territories, including Treaties Numbers Five, Six and Seven.

"Mr. Dewdney, late a Member of the House of Commons from British Columbia, has recently been appointed to the latter Superintendency as Chief Superintendent, and has spent the summer among the Indian tribes. He has had large experience among Indians, and will prove, I have no doubt, an efficient and able officer. His residence will be in his Superintendency, and he will be able to meet the Indians and supervise his deputies.

"Under the Superintendents are agents having charge of particular districts and the bands within them, who reside among them. The

Chief Superintendents and agents are officers of the Department of the Interior, and are directed by and report to the Deputy Superintendent of Indian Affairs at Ottawa, Lawrence Vankoughnet, Esq., who has long experience of Indian management in the older Provinces [Ontario and Quebec], and his superior, Col. Dennis, Deputy Minister of the Interior, who had a large practical acquaintance with the North-West, and the head of the Department, now the Premier of the Dominion, the Right Hon. Sir John Macdonald.

"The system of management is thus a complete one, and doubtless, day by day, its mode of management, will be perfected and adapted to the growing exigencies and wants of the native population."

At the conclusion of his book, Lieut.-Gov. Morris said: "I have every confidence in the desire and ability of the present administration, as of any preceding one, to carry out the provisions of the treaties and to extend a helping hand to this helpless population ... I look forward to seeing the Indians faithful allies of the Crown while they can gradually be made an increasing and self-supporting population. They are wards of Canada, let us do our duty by them and repeat in the North-west the success which has attended our dealing with them in old Canada for the last hundred years ...

"Let us have Christianity and civilization to leaven the mass of heathenism among the Indian tribes. Let us have a wise and paternal government faithfully carrying out the provisions of our treaties and doing its utmost to help and elevate the Indian population who have been cast upon our care, and we will have peace, progress, and concord among them in the North-West; and instead of the Indian melting away, as one of them in older Canada tersely put it, 'as snow before the sun,' we will see our Indian population, loyal subjects of the Crown, happy, prosperous and self-sustaining, and Canada will be enabled to feel, that in a truly patriotic spirit, our country has done its duty by the red men of the North-West, and thereby to herself. So may it be."

Lieut.-Gov. Morris said he wrote the book: "As an aid to the other and equally important duty — that of carrying out, in their integrity, the obligations of these treaties, and devising means whereby the Indian population of the Fertile Belt can be rescued from the hard fate which otherwise awaits them, owing to the speedy destruction of the buffalo, hitherto the principal food supply of the Plain Indians, and that they may be induced to become, by the adoption of agricultural and pastoral pursuits, **a self-supporting community** [emphasis added]."

In order to ensure that all of the treaties that were negotiated at that time were administered in a proper manner, the government of Canada brought in the Indian Act in 1876. Under that act, complete control of all lands reserved for bands and the people living on them was exercised by white Indian Agents appointed by the government. It is clear from the language and tone of the legislation that the government of the day did not have much faith in the ability of the natives to think for themselves and/or handle their own affairs.

The lawmakers were most likely not aware of the business acumen exhibited by the Ojibways of Treaty #3 who, rather than spending the $12 a head that was provided to them after the treaty was signed on the spot, decided instead to take most of it home with them or to entrust it to, as the article in the *Manitoban* reported "white men and Half-breeds upon whose honor they could depend, to be called for and spent at Fort Garry when 'the ground froze'."

Chapter 7

In a letter dated November 3, 1871, Indian Commissioner Wymess McKenzie Simpson said: "Although many years will elapse before they can be regarded as a settled population — settled in the sense of following agricultural pursuits — the Indians have already shown a disposition to provide against the vicissitudes of the chase by cultivating small patches of corn and potatoes.

"Moreover, in the Province of Manitoba, where labor is scarce, Indians give great assistance in gathering the crops. At Portage la Prairie, both Chippewas and Sioux were largely employed in the grain field; and in other parishes I found many farmers whose employees were nearly all Indian."

In a report to his superiors dated December 4, 1876, Lieutenant-Governor Alexander Morris said: "It is unnecessary to multiply instances of the aptitude the Indians are exhibiting, within so recent a period after the completion of the treaties, to avail themselves of obtaining their subsistence from the soil. Their desire to do so, should be cultivated to the fullest extent."

Lieutenant-Governor David Laird reported in 1877 that some of the bands in Treaty #4 and Treaty #6 had harvested grain and potatoes with good results that year. One band had about 40 hectares under cultivation. The band at Whitefish Lake had raised enough that year to maintain themselves without going out to hunt.

Commissioner Thomas Howard reported on October 10, 1877, that the bands in the Lake Winnipeg region had started "to farm and settle down, and we heard that a number of houses had been built at Poplar River, and considerable clearing done there since the treaty was made with last year. The implements and tools we brought them were therefore most acceptable."

The Indian district agent for the Qu'Appelle region reported in November, 1878, that of the 24 bands in the treaty, 11 were "gradually turning their attention to farming." Chief Cote of Swan River was the most advanced. He had harvested 280 bushels of barley, more than 3,000 bushels of potatoes, and a large quantity of other vegetables. The four cows he had received four years ago had produced 11 calves.

In the Manitoba superintendency, it was reported that "a general desire to be taught farming, building and other civilized arts exists, and some of the Indians in Treaty Number Three, living in the vicinity of Fort Francis [sic], are said to evince enterprise and progress in their farming operations."

At the time that Treaty #3 was being negotiated at the Northwest Angle of the Lake of the Woods in 1873, the Lac Seul band northeast of Sioux Lookout was growing potatoes and Indian corn and wanted other grains for seed and some implements and cattle. By 1877, the band had established two villages in order to have the benefit of schools.

One band in the Lake Manitoba district had 18 small farms of 40 hectares each on which they raised potatoes, Indian corn and garden vegetables. They had 29 houses, 24 horses, and 36 head of cattle.

Another band in that district built a good school-house and 19 houses in 1877 and had 50 hectares under cultivation. Another band that had just started farming built six houses, two stables and a barn and had seven head of cattle. Yet another band had 23 houses and 60 hectares under cultivation and was growing barley, wheat, potatoes and vegetables. They also had 36 head of cattle.

The Whitemud River band on the southwest shore of Lake Manitoba had houses and farms. The Sioux at Bird Tail Creek, northwest of Brandon, had broken ground for cultivation and were cutting hay for their own use and for sale.

Evidence of how determined some Aboriginals were to support

themselves by farming can be found in the case of James Seenum, chief of the Whitefish Lake Crees. When he first started tilling the fields northeast of Edmonton in 1864, the chief factor at the Hudson's Bay Company gave him a plow that eventually broke. As they had no horses or oxen, Chief Seenum and his brothers had been dragging the plow through the soil by themselves and pulling up tree roots to use as hoes.

"I feel my heart sore in the spring," he said during the negotiations at Fort Pitt, "when my children want to plow—when they have no implements to use. That is why I am asking them [government officials] to send them as soon as possible. By following what I have been taught I find it helps me a great deal. Surely, when the Great Mother hears of our needs, she will come to our help."

In a paper published by the Manitoba Historical Society in 1989, Sarah Carter of St. John's College, University of Manitoba, said many Aboriginal families "were reported to be enterprising, industrious and anxious to farm in the early years of reserve life. This was clearly exemplified in their willingness to hitch themselves to the ploughs or harrows through the ingenious use of ropes or portage straps, and some efforts were made to have dog trains do the work of oxen.

"At Norway House, Cross Lake, Grand Rapids and Beren's River in the late 1870s it was reported that ploughs were worked by manpower, and at Crane River in 1881 there were still no oxen but 'to prove their anxiety four of them at a time got into harness and ploughed about twenty acres.' Efforts were made in some places to break land with pointed sticks, and crops of wheat and other grain were raised with no other implements than grub hoes."

However, while most Aboriginals were committed to doing all that they could to become self-supporting by transitioning to farming, they were often not provided with the tools that had been promised to accomplish that task.

In his 1878 annual report, Ebenezer McColl, the Inspector of Indian agencies, complained that supplies were often inferior and would not be accepted at any price by the white farmers. The bands had been given wild or worn out cattle that could not be used for plowing or dairying. The seed and grain they received arrived too late. Garden hoes had been provided instead of grub hoes needed to break up the scrubby land.

This failure on the part of the Canadian government to meet its responsibilities under the terms of the treaties is also highlighted in a paper Cree lawyer Delia Opekokew prepared for the Federation of Saskatchewan Indians in 1980. Here's what she wrote: "In early 1885, more than eight years after the signing of the [#6] treaty, and more than six years after many of the bands in the eastern region of Treaty 6 had settled on their reserves, the Indians were insisting that they had not received the implements and livestock that they had been promised.

"Assistant Indian Commissioner Hayter Reed investigated and found that for ten bands in the Fort Carlton district alone ... the Crown had failed to deliver 872 hoes, 439 spades, 54 ploughs, 61 harrows, 434 scythes, 200 whetstones, 401 hayforks, 408 reaping hooks, 1 auger, 3 tool chests, 5 handmills, 1 harness, 20 sows, and 10 boars.

"What was more, Reed found that some of the goods that were delivered were defective. For example, many of the cattle given to the bands were too wild to be controlled, and had to be shot before any herds could be built up. It is worthy of note that Reed's investigation only covered ten bands in Treaty 6. No similar investigation was carried out for the remaining fifteen Saskatchewan bands who were then in Treaty 6, or for any of the bands in the other treaties.

"Furthermore, the Department failed to keep good records from which it could be ascertained whether or not the promised implements and livestock had been delivered. Nevertheless, upon the receipt of Reed's report the Deputy Superintendent General of Indian Affairs (i.e. the Deputy Minister) cheerfully declared that he believed that the Indians had no real grounds for complaint at the way in which the treaties were being fulfilled."

The federal government was required under the treaties to provide farm implements, livestock, seed and other agricultural aids. However, as we have seen, a corrupt administration at the local level often short-changed the bands.

Notwithstanding the abject failure of the Department of Indian Affairs to live up to the terms of the treaties, many Aboriginals pushed on against great odds. However, all too often, their fertile lands were taken away from them by greedy land speculators aided and abetted by corrupt government officials.

Consider, for example, the case of the St. Peter's band, at Selkirk, Manitoba, which was hailed as the most advanced of all the bands. Indian Affairs pointed to it as proof positive that the government was on the right track. By the late 1870s, more than 808,000 hectares was under cultivation. The Ojibway residents of St. Peter's lived in comfortable, whitewashed, log homes and had cattle, sheep, pigs and modern farm machinery.

In 1885, the Indian agent responsible for St. Peter's said the community would compare favorably with most settlements in the area. In fact, he wrote, the people at St. Peter's were "more prosperous and make more money in a year than thousands of people living in the older provinces [Ontario and Quebec]."

St. Peter's wasn't the only success story. During the 1870s and 1880s many Aboriginal farmers extended their acreage, increased their herds, and acquired the machinery necessary to cultivate their fields.

Perhaps because of the success the Ojibways at St. Peter's had made of their reserve and their new way of life, white citizens called on the federal government to move them out of the area and sell the land that had been reserved for them—and upon which they had carved out a good living for themselves.

James Colcleugh, one of the leading citizens of the Selkirk area, said the Ojibways' occupation of the land was a "drawback to our growth and prosperity." He told the local Member of Parliament that if he could "devise some means of busting the reserve ... your name will be immortalized!"

In the paper that was published by the Manitoba Historical Society in the fall of 1989, Sarah Carter says the story of St. Peter's should be told as a reminder of a time "when government and many non-Natives shared the attitude that reserves should not be in neighborhoods of fine agricultural land, when there was potential for white settlement and profit ... Such sentiments were widespread in the West among townspeople and homesteaders near Indian reserves. It was felt that Indians held land far out of proportion to their needs, that they did not effectively use this land, and that their presence inhibited the growth and progress of a district.

"Prime agricultural land especially was thought to be wasted in the hands of Indian bands, even when these people farmed with success, as in the case of St. Peter's and many other bands across the West. Beginning in the 1880s such arguments were used throughout Manitoba and the North West in letters, petitions and deputations to federal members of Parliament."

As a result of pressure from the white citizens—who, unlike the Ojibways, had the right to vote—thousands of hectares of land reserved for the bands were "surrendered". St. Peter's was one of the main casualties.

"As land prices in the Selkirk district steadily rose after 1896," Ms. Carter wrote, "people active in politics and commerce in the community, especially the Selkirk Board of Trade, began to promote the idea that the reserve should be opened up for sale."

In 1906, Chief Justice Hector Howell of the Manitoba Court of Appeal issued a report in which he said that it was in the interests of both the neighborhood and the band that the Ojibways "get off that reserve" which, in his opinion, was "a black spot" and altogether too close to "civilization."

Justice Howell said the only reason the St. Peter's band members objected to surrendering their land was because "the Indian loves his reserve just as people are patriotic, not so much for love of country but because of the graves. Their graves were there and that is what held them to the place just as it holds us."

In response to public pressure, the Department of Indian Affairs started the process of having the Ojibways surrender their productive farmland. Only one day's notice was given for the meeting at which the surrender of the reserve lands was to be voted on and most people were out fishing on Lake Winnipeg. Many residents didn't even know the meeting had been called.

At the meeting, which was held in a small school house where only half of the people could get in, the surrender agreement was not properly explained and was read in English only. When it came time to vote, those in favor of the surrender were asked to line up on one side of the room and those opposed on the other. In the middle of the proceedings, the Indian agent, who was also a shareholder in the Selkirk Land and Investment Company, pointed to the Yes line and called out in Cree: "Which of you want $90 go over there."

The Deputy Superintendent General of Indian Affairs had $5,000 in a satchel and made it clear that the money would be distributed if the vote was Yes. If the vote was No, the money would go back with him to Ottawa.

A Commission of Inquiry subsequently found that there was "clear evidence that up to the time of the 'parading the satchel' before them," Sara Carter wrote, "the band was not favourable to the surrender and had not asked for it. When the vote was taken it was found that 107 were standing in favour and 98 against, but no record of the vote was taken as was customary in elections for chief and councillors.

"There could well have been people there who had no right to vote as no attempt was made to authenticate band membership. Certain additions to the surrender document were made after the vote and were never voted on or ratified by the band, so that the surrender submitted to the vote was not the same as the one signed."

The Department started to close the St. Peter's reserve in 1907 and move the Ojibway families about 120 kilometres north to a new reserve on the Fisher River. There were no houses, schools, churches or roads. None of the land had been broken. The only store was 12 kilometres away and the nearest town was 120 kilometres away.

Despite the Commission of Inquiry's finding that the surrender was not conducted in a proper manner and was illegal, Parliament passed The St. Peter's Reserve Act in 1916 confirming the surrender of the Ojibways' land.

"As this land was no longer part of a reserve," Ms. Carter wrote, "it could be mortgaged, or seized for debt. Alcohol became an effective tool for land buyers who offered to pay fines for drunkenness in exchange for title to the allotments."

The new reserve was named after Ojibway Chief Peguis without whose help the first settlers at the Red River Colony would most likely have starved to death. One of the signatories to the Stone Fort and Manitoba Post Treaties of August, 1871, was Peguis's son whose English name was Henry Prince but was also known by his Ojibway name of Mis-koo-ke-new.

Peguis's grandson, William Prince, a chief of the St. Peter's Reserve, was one of the first Canadians to serve in an overseas military expedition. He was recruited, along with about fifty voyageurs, to serve under General Garnet Joseph Wolseley in an unsuccessful attempt in 1885 to sail up the Nile and rescue General Charles George "Chinese" Gordon who was under siege by Sudanese rebels at the British garrison in Khartoum.

General Wolseley had first met Prince in 1870 when he led the Red River Expedition through the Treaty #3 territory. Prince served as the steersman for the canoe that took him through the Lake of the Woods and down the Winnipeg River to Fort Garry.

Gen. Wolseley remembered the prowess Prince had shown as a voyageur and wanted him to lead the group of Canadians he was relying upon to get the British forces through the rapids on the Nile.

The expedition reached Khartoum on January 28, 1885—two days after the entire garrison had been slaughtered and General Gordon beheaded. Gen. Wolseley wrote a letter to the Governor General of Canada praising the Canadian rivermen for their efforts and the British Parliament passed a motion of thanks.

However, the Ojibway chief's service to the British by sailing up the Nile in an unsuccessful effort to save General Gordon did not deter the citizens of Selkirk and the government agents from stealing his land.

Even at the new reserve, white settlers started to complain that the presence of the Ojibways would make white people less inclined to settle in the area.

"With increased immigration after 1896, a rise in wheat prices and land values," Ms. Carter wrote, "non-Natives began to cast jealous eyes on reserve land that was in prime agricultural zones. The arguments used throughout the West in support of surrender were that the land was not effectively used, that the presence of Native people was a drawback to the prosperity of a district, and that reserves close to towns was damaging to the morals of all."

It would be a mistake to think that the manner in which the enterprising Ojibways at St. Peter's were dealt with was the exception that proved the rule. According to an 1828 report prepared by Lt.-Col. H. C. Darling, Ojibways in the Orillia area of Ontario presented a petition in which they complained that "white men seize on our furs, and take them from us by force, they abuse our women and violently beat our people. We are poor in lands and have few places for hunting, much of our hunting grounds are covered by white settlements."

Here's something Peter S. Schmalz wrote about the Ojibways in the Lake Simcoe area in *The Ojibwa of Southern Ontario*. "The Lake Simcoe Ojibwa were doing extremely well in their transition from food gatherers to sedentary farmers, according to [Captain T. G.] Anderson, who certainly had a wealth of experience in his half-century contact with them. In his report, however, he noted threatening signs for this budding farm community, particularly from the nearby Europeans."

The Ojibways were forced to abandon their farms and move away. "Progress for the whites took precedence over progress for the Ojibways. The bands scattered to more isolated areas in the Saugeen territory — Rama, Beausoleil Island, and Snake Island."

A considerable number of them re-established themselves at Colpoy's Bay on the western shore of Georgian Bay near Wiarton. They cleared the land, built barns and houses and established a saw mill. And then, once more, they were found to be in the way.

"In 1861, when the Colpoy's Bay Band were forced from their frame houses, barns, cleared fields, and saw mill, no European was prepared to protest," Schmalz writes. "Many Ojibwa felt that their European friends had abandoned them, and that cooperation in the civilization scheme had come to an end."

After describing how Ojibways were moved off a successful settlement in order to appease the increasing number of townspeople in Owen Sound, Schmalz says: "Such a removal was diametrically opposed to the Indian Department's stated policy of 'civilizing' the natives and to the attempts by some of the more 'progressive' Indians to assimilate into white society."

In 1836, Francis Bond Head, the Lieutenant-Governor of Upper Canada, justified the forced surrender of 600,000 hectares of "the very richest land in Upper Canada" south of Owen Sound by saying the Newash and Saugeen bands needed to be protected from the "white man's vices". Lieut.-Gov. Head said they would be better able to preserve their traditions and way of life if they were relocated to an isolated area on the Bruce Peninsula far removed from the influence of the ever-increasing number of white settlers.

Lieut.-Gov. Head promised to build houses for the relocated bands and that they would be protected from any further encroachment. Ten years later, many of them were in debt to traders and on the verge of starvation because commercial fishing by whites had depleted the fish stocks they relied on for food. Twenty years later, the relocated Newash band was forced to surrender its new village and 4,000 hectares of land to clear the way for the expansion of Owen Sound.

Between 1851 and 1861, the Ojibways were forced to surrender an additional 20,800 hectares to satisfy the white settlers' insatiable demand for good land. The land base that they were reduced to at Cape Croker was said to be "unfit for cultivation."

The displacement of Aboriginal farmers continued at a brisk pace after the British government transferred control of Indian affairs to the Province of Canada in 1860.

"Hundreds of acres [of lands reserved for Aboriginals] continued to be carved off the Ojibwa reserves in southern Ontario, not only for farm land but also for the expansion of towns and cities as well as roads," Peter Schmalz wrote. "Several bands tenaciously and successfully held on to at least a small portion of their ancestral holdings ...

"As the Ojibwa relinquished their millions of acres in southern Ontario, they either retained small areas, usually on rivers and lakes which had traditionally been their summer camps, or purchased or were permitted to settle on small tracts isolated from the more populated European settlements."

Consider the case of the seven Ojibway bands living along the Rainy River in northwestern Ontario who were removed from their fertile lands in 1915 to make way for white settlers.

The Government of Ontario wanted the land that had been reserved for them under the terms of Treaty #3 opened up for the white settlers. As far as it was concerned, the federal government had no right to set aside reserves on lands that had belonged to the province prior to Confederation.

That position was supported by the courts and the provincial government made it a condition of its agreement to enact legislation confirming all of the reserves established under Treaty #3 that 17,105 hectares of the most fertile land in the region be surrendered so it could be used by white farmers.

The seven Rainy River bands lost almost 90% of their lands and were reduced to one small reserve at Manitou Rapids which covered approximately 15 square kilometres—4.8 kilometres north from the Rainy River, and about 2.4 to 3.2 kilometres to the east and west.

The unscrupulous acquisition of land that had been reserved for Aboriginals was still going on in the 1920s. In 1927, for example, a land developer purchased 83 acres of land from the Chippewas of Kettle and Stony Points on the eastern shore of Lake Huron for $83 an acre and sold half of the land two months later for $300 an acre. The purchaser was present while the surrender of the reserve land was being voted on and gave each person voting in favor $5 with the promise of another $15 at a later date.

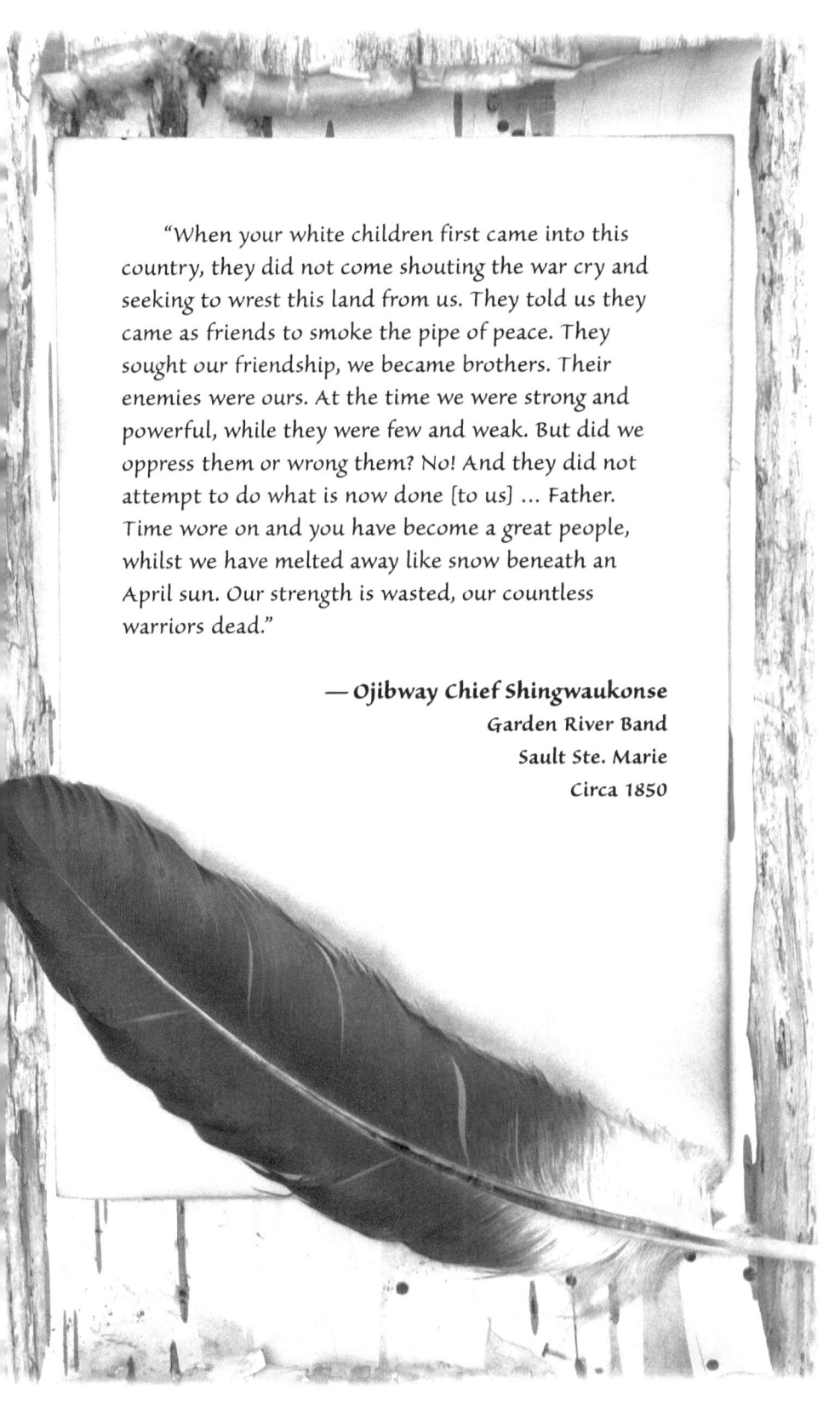

"When your white children first came into this country, they did not come shouting the war cry and seeking to wrest this land from us. They told us they came as friends to smoke the pipe of peace. They sought our friendship, we became brothers. Their enemies were ours. At the time we were strong and powerful, while they were few and weak. But did we oppress them or wrong them? No! And they did not attempt to do what is now done [to us] ... Father. Time wore on and you have become a great people, whilst we have melted away like snow beneath an April sun. Our strength is wasted, our countless warriors dead."

— **Ojibway Chief Shingwaukonse**
Garden River Band
Sault Ste. Marie
Circa 1850

Chapter 8

While the lives of the Crees near Battleford, Saskatchewan, had not been impacted to the same devastating extent as the Blackfoot, they were still much poorer when Treaty #6 was being negotiated in August, 1876, than they had been before the arrival of the white man. And, in addition to the never-ending state of hostilities with the Blackfoot, they were constantly being encroached upon by white settlers.

A few days after the treaty was signed, Chief Wah-ta-nee and his younger brother, Red Pheasant, met with Lieutenant-Governor Alexander Morris at the Battle River. Red Pheasant said: "I do not wish to turn out any white man. But I wish to return to my former mode of life. Ever since my grandfather lived at Battle River, it has been my home. Our houses were swept off by a flood two years ago, and after that we repaired some old houses that were built by outsiders and we had fenced in the buildings. But a short time ago some Canadians arrived, knocked down the fences, and built inside the enclosure."

Chief Wah-ta-nee picked up the story at that point and informed the Lieutenant-Governor that they had selected a point about a mile from where they were now speaking and cut logs for fences and houses. "When we returned from the plains, we found they had all been taken away. There are now twenty families, and ten more to come in from the plains.

"We wish to be remembered to the Queen, and we are thankful to see the Queen's soldiers coming to make their homes on the land that we have been brought up on. I hope that the Queen will look upon our poverty when she hears that we are poor Indians and have welcomed her people to live amongst us.

"This is my country where I have lived. I want to make way for the Queen's men, and I ask her in return to keep me from want. Next spring, I want to plant here wherever I can get a piece of ground. By that time, I may have selected a spot for my reserve. The reason I want to select my reserve is that I do not want to be cramped up by settlers. In the meantime, I do not want any white men to settle on the Eagle Hills."

Chief Wah-ta-nee asked Lieut.-Gov. Morris to give him some advice he could ponder on over the winter months. "I will speak to you frankly," Lieut.-Gov. Morris (who was only 50 at the time) said, "as if I was talking to my own children. The sooner you select a place for your reserve the better, so that you can have the animals and agricultural instruments promised to you, and so that you may have the increase from the animals, and the tools to help you build the houses, etc.

"When you are away hunting and fishing, the best of the sun and the rain is making your crops to grow. I think you are showing wisdom in taking a place away from here, although it has been your home. It is better for the Indians to be away a little piece from the white man. You will be near enough to bring your furs to a good market, and by and by I hope you will have more potatoes than you require, and have some to dispose of. I am very anxious that you should think over this, and be able to tell the Commissioners next year where you want your reserve."

Lieut.-Gov. Morris said that, in the meantime, he had arranged for a local farmer to provide Chief Wah-ta-nee's band with 1.2 hectares of land so that they could plant potatoes the following spring. The farmer had also agreed to plow the land for them.

"I am much pleased with the conduct of the Battle River Crees, and will report it to the Queen's Councillors," Lieut.-Gov. Morris said in ending the meeting. "I hope you will be prosperous and happy."

Seventy-eight years later, Chief Wah-ta-nee's grandson, William (Bill) I.C. Wuttunee, — about whom I told you in Chapter 1 — became the first Aboriginal lawyer in western Canada.

Bill Wuttunee was invited to speak at a conference organized by the Welfare Council of Greater Winnipeg in February, 1961. At that time, he was a liaison officer with the Department of Citizenship and Immigration.

The suggestion was put forward by Marion Ironquill Meadmore who was born on the Peepeekisis reserve, about 90 kilometres northeast of Regina, and had been living in Winnipeg for eight years.

Marion had attended quite a few of these conferences over the years and had grown a bit tired of listening to white people discussing problems faced by the Aboriginal people and what should be done about them.

"I had this strong feeling that I did not like white people talking about us because all they talked about was our 'problems'," she told me during an interview in 1996. "I never felt we were problems. I really never did. My family was not dysfunctional. My father was a great leader. My mother was a great mother and we never had violence in our family."

Marion's father, Joe Ironquill, graduated from the University of Manitoba with a diploma in agriculture in 1919 and went on to become a very successful farmer. "My Dad became chief of the reserve and in that capacity he often took in whole families who stayed at our house until he could get them readjusted back into the community," Marion recalled. "Chiefs were elected because they were in a position to help people. Of course there was no payment to the chief. My Dad put the idea in my head that I was expected to go to university."

Marion had attended grade school at the File Hills Indian Residential School which served four bands of Plains Cree and was operated by the United Church of Canada. It was located approximately 20 kilometres northwest of her home.

Like many of the Indian residential schools of that era, File Hills had a rather sorry history. Consider this from the official website of the United Church of Canada.

> "For much of its history, the school was plagued with high levels of sickness, buildings in poor condition, overcrowding, and a shortage of staff. In 1922, Medical Inspector H.P. Bryce reported in *The Story of a National Crime: Being an Appeal for Justice to the Indians of Canada*, that 24 per cent of all children who had attended residential schools in Canada had died. At File Hills, '75 per cent were dead at the end of the 16 years since the school opened.'
>
> "When Principal Gillespie reported the death of two girls under treatment at the school for tuberculosis in the winter of 1908, she blamed their dormitory, which was later condemned: 'We fear the girls' dormitory is largely responsible for disease among the girls. The boys, as a rule, are healthy.' Between 1907 and 1910, the boys slept, summer and winter, in a tent on the school grounds.
>
> "By 1948, File Hills IRS was overcrowded and the building was considered a fire hazard. An inspection of the school's plumbing revealed unsanitary bathrooms, contaminated milk, a laundry that was 'a first class germ trap,' and a kitchen, dangerous to the health. 'A complete medical check up should be made of all inmates of the institution, and if repairs are not carried out, it would be criminal neglect,' reported the inspector.
>
> "The Indian Department recommended closing the school and establishing a day school on the site. United Church officials reluctantly agreed and on June 30, 1949, the school was closed. Children from the File Hills communities within walking distance attended the day school. Other students were sent to the United Church residential schools at Brandon [abut 280 kilometres away] or Portage la Prairie [360 kilometres away from home]. In 1953, the school buildings were dismantled and the land sold, with the exception of 101.93 acres that were added to the Okanese Indian Reserve."

Despite that unpleasant history, Marion survived the residential school experience with no major regrets. "The school did not have a serious negative effect on me although I had problems in that I was confined, like everybody else. My Mom and Dad used to come and visit often. We missed each other terribly, but I could always count on them coming so I was able to survive. I became part of a large family of friends. We joked a lot and pulled some funny stunts on each other just for laughs. I did not encounter dysfunctional staff so did not notice any assaults of any kind. My dad was the chief at that time so he made sure we were OK at the school. I never saw any of those things [that are often associated with the Indian residential school experience]."

Although the Indian residential high school at Lebret was only about 60 kilometres west of Marion's home, she was moved about 180 kilometres east to attend the high school at Birtle, Manitoba. "I went to Birtle because it was a Protestant school. Lebret was Catholic."

Marion stayed at the residential school, which was on the top of a hill, and went to the high school in town. "The only thing that was a bit of a challenge was the mile and a half we had to walk down hill to the high school and the return trip uphill every day. It was only a challenge on really cold days. Again, we made many life-long friends at this school."

She enrolled at the University of Winnipeg in 1953, despite the fact she was now almost 500 kilometres away from home. "I was destined to go to a Manitoba university because the high school I graduated from was in Manitoba." Soon after arriving in Winnipeg, Marion and some friends formed a lobby group to promote adult education for Ojibway people living in Winnipeg. She then helped establish the first Indian friendship centre to help the increasing number of Ojibways moving to the north end of Winnipeg from the outlying reserves make the transition to life in the city.

However, during the first 10 years or so, the friendship centre was very much in the control of white people. "We had a lot of non-native people involved in the friendship centre and it was, in my opinion, a rug that they were trying to establish to hide a lot of the things that they had identified as 'problems'. I was very inhibited by the non-native people that were there. But, as I attended these things, I just got stronger and stronger and started to speak up to the point where, about 10 years later, we took it over."

Marion Meadmore wasn't the sort of person who sat around hoping things would get better. From advocating for adult education programs for Ojibway people to taking over the Indian friendship centre with some of her colleagues, she has always been at the forefront of social change.

In 1970, she helped establish Kinew Housing Corporation — the first non-profit urban corporation in Canada sponsored, owned, and managed by native people. "That was one of the offshoots of the friendship centre," she told me in 1996. "We wanted to get into our own housing. It's now a $50 million housing project. We have about four or five hundred homes. I was busy in those days managing that housing corporation." They would buy older homes and repair/renovate them and rent them to low-income Aboriginal families.

Marion Meadmore lived a full and adventurous life. "I toured the Amazon in a plane with a pilot and visited Indigenous people up and down the river. That's when I was still buying and fixing houses and managing the corporation."

At 39, she decided it was time to go back to university and study law. She graduated in 1977 and became the first Aboriginal woman in Canada to practise law. "When I finished, I went into criminal law and ended up in corporate law. I love corporate law."

When I interviewed her in 1996, she was running a very successful business called Arrowfax. "My interest in life is economic development, creating wealth and power. Without those two things you're going to have a hard time. I saw fax machines as a way to do it. When I started in 1988, there was hardly any faxes at all, just a very few. And almost 100% of the ones that had them were the Inuit, way up north. They were really ahead."

Why would the Inuit be so much farther ahead than other Aboriginal people? "Because they needed it the most. They're isolated and they saw this as a good deal so almost all of them had fax machines. If you go to our first directory and look to see who had the faxes, you'll see that almost all of them, almost 100 per cent of the Inuit had faxes."

By getting as many bands as possible on a fax directory she believed that they could eventually have a central order desk. "Then we could just fax orders and get really good deals because we'd be able to save a lot of money. We could save up to 50% for each item that the reserve buys. Then we would have enough clout so that we could go ahead and manufacture these things. Find somebody to manufacture them and create a lot of wealth and employment. That was the level I was on."

Within a matter of years, Marion was publishing 13 fax directories. "We've been in the United States now for four years," she told me in 1996. "We're doing Mexico in January and February of this year. Then we're going to Central and South America. That's still the dream. My greater dream is that we now put this whole database into a big international trade centre because I've gone to trade shows and I've really liked them.

"We're reawakening ancestral trade links and they're fun. Everybody that goes keeps coming back. We're starting to become traders again and we're having fun doing that and it feels good. Only we can understand ourselves and it feels good when you trade with another native person because you've got something that they like."

Looking back in 1996 to the time when she first arrived in Winnipeg, Marion said life had changed for the worse for the Ojibways. "We never had drunks sleeping under the bridges in those days or the problems that occur today. We didn't have those kinds of really serious problems in those days. It was just merely a lot of us arriving in town here. We started to come in large numbers and we didn't quite measure up.

"There were a lot of people in poverty as a result. There were a lot of people starting to suffer from alcoholism. They were feeling pretty hopeless. But there wasn't a lot of people living here because there was no other place to go to. There were people here that were training, that had moved into the city for whatever reason, for marrying and those are the type of people that were here. Our problems were not so much poverty, but social. People needed to get together to socialize."

That didn't stop the white people from highlighting problems within the Aboriginal community. "White people were classifying us as problems and I started to resent it. I think what was happening then is that they were starting to sow the seeds of what is now happening," she said in 1996. "No matter where you turned in the city of Winnipeg, we were always seen as a problem. You can go back in the newspapers for the last 40 years and you will not find anything good on the front pages or the back pages about native people. Instead of throwing a positive slant on things, it was always a negative thing.

"If native people needed some money for, let's say, to fight diabetes, therefore, they had to do studies that would show how native people, because of poverty or whatever reason, came down with diabetes. It was always a negative slant. And then you talk about suicides and then you keep on talking about whatever. There's so many negative things, drunkenness, everything to do with our stereotype. You couldn't find a good thing. It was always the negative. You've heard about the self-fulfilling prophecy, well that was a big contributor to it.

"What's happening now in Winnipeg is two things. One, they're just reaping the seeds of what was sown all those years ago. Nobody would jump on the bandwagon and give us any credit for anything. It was negative, negative, negative. That's what's happening in the city of Winnipeg right now. That's going to happen until somebody figures out what's good about being native, and there's so many good things about it.

"The Indian people are a new form of manpower. Indian people are being educated. There's training and there's a lot more people in the city now. Most of them are not the problems. There are very few who cause problems.

"I'm really positive about things. I see a great future for us. But unless people like myself can get off our rear ends and start talking positive about being native or finding something good about it, then we're always going to be spiralling downward, even though we're trying hard and lots of money is being spent in trying to get us out of this thing that we're into.

"Take the police, for example. There's these Indian gangs and they think they've got a handle on things. They've got curfews going. They're really picking on the Indian gangs. Why don't they pick on the bikers? They leave the bikers alone but they pick on the Indian gangs. That's really cheesing me off."

What concerned her most back in the late 1950s was that white people involved in the Indian friendship centre and in the conferences where the situation of the native people was discussed seemed overly inclined to do things FOR them rather than WITH them.

"What really irritated us is we were listening to our problems being discussed in a whole new context. White people talking about us and we didn't recognize that and I didn't like it. These are white people doing things for us. These are not the issues that we would be interested in talking about. Why are we letting them do this? That's what motivated me to get out and do some organizing."

She had attended several conferences sponsored by the Welfare Council of Greater Winnipeg where the Aboriginal experience was discussed. "We weren't doing any of this ourselves. The conferences weren't put on by us or even for us. It was a big event of the year and they had a big speaker come from somewhere that everybody heard of and everybody went there. It brought a few of us together."

Marion decided it would be a good idea to have someone who had actually lived the Aboriginal experience be the main speaker at one of the conferences. She recommended that Bill Wuttunee be invited to speak at the conference that was slated for February, 1961.

"Bill was known as a lawyer, first Indian lawyer in Canada. He'd had a lot of publicity and I suggested that they bring him in as a speaker because we needed to have some native people speaking about our issues."

While Bill Wuttunee was in Winnipeg, he got into a discussion with Marion and Jean Cuthand, a registered nurse by training who was then working at the Indian Affairs Branch of Secretary of State in Ottawa, about forming a national organization.

Jean was born on the Little Pine reserve about 70 kilometres west of North Battleford. Her father, John Tootoosis, was a well-regarded leader of the native movement. He was a long-time associate of Bill Wuttunee's father and Bill had recommended him as the first president of the Federation of Saskatchewan Indians.

Jean recalled, back when she was growing up at Little Pine, how her family would cross the river in a wagon pulled by a team of horses to perform the sun dance—which had been banned by the Canadian government at the request of the churches—with other families in the bush.

"We'd go right in the bush somewhere by the hills, they call it Blue Hill, where no car would ever get to. The sun dance has never been left, never been forgotten. After that was over, there'd be a pow wow, a social function," she recalled when I interviewed her in 1996.

"The churches were in the process of trying to convert us. They were busy doing their thing in residential schools and on reserves. And then they found out every summer people were going to ceremonies, having ceremonies like sun dances here on the prairies, which is one of the most important functions of every year plus the pow wows, the social functions. And their objective was, 'well if they're going to do that, they're not going to go to church, they're not going to work', and so on and the whole concept was to change us into something that we weren't. But they never succeeded."

In fact, she told me, she never stopped going to sun dances and had participated in one in British Columbia just a year before I interviewed her. "It's a very religious ceremony. If something happens to you, like you've been sick or whatever or you want to make a vow, you start the year before the sun dance. The dance consists of fasting for four days and dancing and sometimes people make a vow to do that every year for the rest of their lives. There was no way that the churches or the government were going to stop that because that promise that we've made is a commitment to the Creator. When an elder is chosen or happens to be the one that has to put on this function, he has to do it four years at a time. He can't stop, otherwise it's devastation to him.

"I had spent a lot of time with my grandparents. Saw a lot of their tradition, their songs and their ceremonies and things. It just became part of my life. Dancing and celebration is so much a part of our lives. It's something you do and enjoy. Often, depending on the songs and when I'm sitting there at a pow wow, if I hear a song that's sort of familiar, I think of the spiritual aspect of it. All those people that have gone to the spirit world are there to be with us and to help us celebrate.

We have certain feasts for the spirits that have gone. We know they're around,. They're with us and I think this is why we don't have churches because you can pray anywhere.

"Indian people moving to the city needed a place [friendship centre] to go. We had two women who were counsellors. It was an all-Indian staff. And it was another long-hours job, but totally different from what I'd been doing as a nurse. I met people there, like Marion Ironquill Meadmore."

Despite the fact the Standing Buffalo reserve is only about 320 kilometres from Little Pine, Jean experienced a pronounced degree of culture shock when she moved there in 1966 after marrying Ken Goodwill, a Santee Sioux who was working for the federal government in Ottawa.

The Standing Buffalo people are descendants of Sisseton-Santee-Dakotas (Sioux) who were allotted reservations along the upper Minnesota River under an 1851 treaty with the United States government. The fertile land that they were allotted attracted the attention of white settlers and they were forced to move to Canada as refugees in 1878 and establish the reserve near Fort Qu'Appelle.

Several Dakota chiefs had received King George III silver medals in recognition of the assistance they provided to the British during the American Revolutionary War. They also claimed to have aided the British in the War of 1812.

Not being able to speak Sioux was a problem for Jean. She couldn't speak Sioux and they didn't understand Cree. "It's as different as English and German or French. Nothing similar. That's the other thing, that misconception that the Canadian people have of Indian people. They think we're all the same. We're different cultures right down to the ceremonies. We have basic beliefs mind you, the basis of our beliefs are the same, but our customs and our value systems and rituals are different as is the language. Language to me is very very important."

In addition to the language barrier, there were several cultural differences. "For example, when we have a sweat lodge ceremony at my home at Little Pine, men and women and children can go into these ceremonies. The Sioux people have certain lodges just before their sun dance and the men and women are separate. There's still things like that that are vastly different.

"I'm still continuing to attend healing ceremonies and hope to be attending some this summer in my part of the country—with the Crees. I've learned a lot from the Sioux. I go to their ceremonies. When we have ceremonies we always say a prayer. When they say a prayer in Sioux, I say mine in Cree. I really appreciate the fact that I've been able to develop a good knowledge about their culture too, besides mine. There's some similarities. I really respect and appreciate what they believe."

Bill Wuttunee, Marion Meadmore and Jean Cuthand decided that the first organizing meeting of the National Indian Council they were establishing would be held in Regina. Letters were sent out to the chiefs of various bands and to the presidents of native organizations across Canada.

"Guy Williams came from B.C.," Bill recalled. "Guy was president of the native fishermen's union in B.C. It's pretty powerful. It was the main native organization in B.C. at that time. And John Tootoosis came as well and all the leaders from western Canada, from Alberta and Saskatchewan and Manitoba and Ontario. We didn't have anybody from Quebec. We didn't have anybody east of that and that was it. But it was a good turnout."

Chapter 9

Andrew Delisle, chief of the primarily Catholic Mohawk community of Caughnawaga—now known as Kahnawake—across the river from Montreal, was invited to attend the second meeting of the newly-formed National Indian Council.

When a railway bridge was built across the St. Lawrence River to provide a rail link between Montreal and the south shore, men from Kahnawake worked as bridgemen and ironworkers and demonstrated an unusual ability to work without fear hundreds of feet above the ground.

Their high-level skills as ironworkers were quickly recognized and got them well-paying work in New York building the Empire State Building and other skyscrapers. Riveting gangs from Kahnawake also worked on the George Washington Bridge, the Daily News Building, the Bank of the Manhattan Company Building and the Hudson Bridge. Many of them brought their families with them and, pretty soon, there was an area in Brooklyn known as "Little Caughnawaga" (the English name for Kahnawake).

They were still at it in 1971 building the World Trade Centre. And, on August 30, 2012, they helped install the last beam for the steel structure of the 104-storey One World Trade Centre which replaced the twin towers that had been destroyed during the terrorist attacks of September, 11, 2001.

As a result of the income they earned as rivermen, ironworkers and at other trades, the Mohawks of Kahnawake have always enjoyed a very good standard of living. Pictures from the early 1900s showed them living in 1½ storey stone houses just like any other small community in Quebec. Men women and children were dressed like all other families in Quebec.

As you will recall, the French had an altogether different relationship with their Aboriginal allies than did the Dutch and the English. They treated them as equals and promoted cohabitation rather than conquest. That helps explain why the people of Kahnawake have surnames like Beauvais, D'Ailleboust, de La Ronde, Thibaudière, Delisle, Lafleur, Delormier, Lefebvre, Giasson, Mailloux, Leclaire and Montour.

At the time that Chief Delisle was invited to the second organizing meeting of the National Indian Council, the Mohawk community of Kahnawake — a 20-minute drive from downtown Montreal — was one of the most advanced reserves in Canada.

Andrew's great-grandfather was a chief and so was his grandfather and father. He learned early on not to put too much trust in the white people. He recalls a story from when his father was selling coal.

"My father couldn't read and they'd give him a paper upside down and laugh," he told me in 1996. "But he knew how to count. They'd try to trick him on the figures and he'd always catch them. That made me a little aggressive in my dealings with government."

People would often come knocking on the door of the Delisle home looking for food or help. As was the case with Marion Ironquill Meadmore's father at the Peepeekisis reserve in Saskatchewan, that was part of the job of being chief.

During the time when it was illegal for natives to purchase liquor, the Quebec police came down hard on the Mohawk drinkers rather than on the suppliers. "I saw the way the police treated the people because of the liquor laws. The police would come and beat up these guys for drinking when, in fact, the law was made for them [to prevent people from selling liquor to natives]. The guy that was selling the liquor shouldn't be selling. I saw all this. It's what makes me the way I am."

When Andrew became chief in 1959, there was only one Mohawk

attending high school. "That was one other thing I wanted to improve. I got together with the other people and said 'let's try to improve the situation'."

Councillor Gene Lahache was also invited to attend the meeting in Winnipeg. "I wanted to know what was going on," he told me when I interviewed him in 1996. "I was curious but, also, I wanted something to happen that all the Indians in Canada should join together and have a voice. We didn't have any kind of voice. Like, in the [band] council, we passed a resolution and then the Indian agent would say 'hey you can't do that.' I didn't want that anymore.

"There were a lot of old people in the town council here. A lot of old men in their 70s that couldn't be changed. They were stuck to the old ways and they would say 'well the Indian agent won't like this if we do this.' We were outspoken, the young guys that were in there. There was three of us then, Andrew [Delisle], Ronnie [Kirby] and myself.

"We started to talk to the people at the meetings and said we need younger people to change the way of thinking. So that's when the council changed here and then it was more than likely the youngest council in Canada. It was all young guys and that's when they started to champion the organization of the reserve and, at the same time, going and talking to everybody else in Canada, seeing what's going on."

"They [Bill Wuttunee and Marion Meadmore] called me up and they asked me to collect all the chiefs in Quebec," Andrew recalled when I interviewed him in 1996. "I had a little Volkswagen at that time and I went to as many reserves as possible. I went to Seven Islands [Sept-Iles], quite a way [at the mouth of the St. Lawrence River more than 800 kilometres east of Montreal]. I had the opportunity to see the condition of the people.

"They were living in ramshackle houses. They were in a bad situation. I remember going over there and the first person I met to let me know where the chief lived was an RCMP [Royal Canadian Mounted Police] officer. It was the only building I could see. I went in and he's sitting back in his chair with his feet on the desk and his shirt unbuttoned. When I introduced myself, he jumped up, buttoned his shirt and took me to the chief's house. I saw some pretty sorry situations. For instance, they had a TV, but they were using it as a heater also. The kids were leaning against it to keep warm."

I asked how a TV could keep them warm. "They thought it would, I guess. They were leaning against it. At that point in time, you have to remember, the Indian people in Quebec were still in the forest hunting. They were still living in tents. There were no settlements, especially in the Cree areas. There were no settlements at all. They had tents and lean-tos and the only houses were the schools and the government houses and trading posts.

"When you went to Restigouche [about 750 kilometres northeast of Montreal] they had a lot of houses. They were more modern. But they were still living off the land, fishing and so forth."

I asked what sort of reaction he received from the local people about having a national association. "Well, at that time, when I introduced the subject to the chiefs, they were interested. Keep in mind that at that time the average age of the chiefs was about 62, 63. I learned there was only one place where there was a fairly young chief and that was Restigouche. I think he was only 23."

Andrew believed that most of the chiefs he spoke to about forming a national organization to speak out on behalf of Aboriginal people "wanted a big change." However, while the interest was strong, not many of them could afford to travel to Winnipeg for the meeting.

"They reacted positively, of course, but they couldn't all come. They had heard of the organization because there had been people around before talking about it. They had informal organizations so they became interested but, like I said, not that many came. They were isolated. They didn't have any money at all. They couldn't come.

"I remember the guy from Restigouche came down and they got a discount for the rail fare from Restigouche to Montreal. But then, in the Montreal to Toronto corridor there's no discount. But from Toronto to Winnipeg there was. That's the first experience that I had with people that had not travelled far out of their community. So I had to show them all how to do these things. I had to take them step by step how to do it. That was an experience."

When they arrived in Winnipeg, they found that most of those at the second meeting of the National Indian Council were from western Canada. "They had been organized much more than we had because they had that North American Indian Brotherhood from B.C.," Andrew said. "And then they had the other brotherhood with Walter Dieter [Federation of Saskatchewan Indians] around the Fort Qu'Appelle area."

I asked Andrew what was going through his mind on the way to Winnipeg. "We didn't know what to expect," he recalled. "We just said 'well we're going to meet other Indian people'. When we got there, we were glad to see so many people. There must have been about 300."

That second meeting of the newly-formed National Indian Council was held at Winnipeg's Royal Alexandra Hotel. When it was opened by the Canadian Pacific Railway Company in 1906, the "Royal Alex" was one of the finest hotels in western Canada and quickly became the centre of Winnipeg society.

Marion Ironquill Meadmore and Jean Cuthand were the principal organizers of that second meeting. "When we got there," Andrew said, "they were pushing a lot of stuff that was happening, like the agendas and taking care of people and all that kind of thing. They played a big part."

What benefit did he expect to receive from attending the meeting? "There was a lot of expectation on our part because we were learning a lot of things. I think most of our people at that point in time were living in their own little communities and weren't aware of what was happening."

The young chief from Restigouche, Quebec, played a fiddle and guitar and created a bond among the natives from different parts of Canada. "We were taken in right away because all Indian people play fiddle and guitar music and sing western songs and that was something that brought everybody together."

Marion and Jean encouraged everyone to speak about their concerns and aspirations. "Everybody had a chance to speak," Andrew recalled. "We brought forward all those things that we were dissatisfied with and we had some discussions."

"It just put a whole bunch of strangers in a room together and the only thing we had in common is we were all Indian and now we had to figure out what that meant and that's what that conference did," Marion recalled.

They deliberated on what would be the next best step and where was the best place to get the information they would need to build a truly national organization. Follow-up meetings were organized across the country.

"A lot of other small meetings took place which I attended as a representative of the group in the east," Andrew recalled. "We were trying to develop a cross-section."

"We didn't get an office right away because we had no money," Bill Wuttunee recalled. "We wouldn't accept [government] money. I said to them 'so long as we depend on the government for money, we'll always be dependent on them'. I said we have to be independent and we agreed that we would not accept any money. And so we were kind of distant with the government. But we worked hard trying to organize people and people were really keen.

"Those were times when there was still a lot of discrimination and people were not anxious to admit they were native people and so a lot of work had to be done. We have to go ahead with the business of surviving, of trying to get along with Canadians. You have to put out and do something."

The National Indian Council did accept a small government grant to organize the Indians of Canada Pavilion at Expo 67 in Montreal—the focal point of which was a 100-foot high teepee made of metal and wood.

The wooden walls of the building featured bold, colorful, murals painted by native artists. A 65-foot Kwakiuti totem pole with a Thunderbird on top stood near the entrance. There was also a carved cedar figure of a warrior in full battledress standing guard.

The Canadian government had appointed Chief Andrew Delisle

commissioner general of the pavilion and he escorted Queen Elizabeth II when she attended. It is said that the Queen was quite taken aback — "ashen faced" as one account described it — when she read some of the provocative messages posted throughout the Indians of Canada Pavilion.

Here's a sample of what was in store for the Queen and any of the more than 50 million people from Canada and around the world who attended Expo 67 and decided to visit the pavilion.

> *"You have stolen our native land, our culture, our soul ... and yet, our traditions deserve to be appreciated, and those derived from an age-old harmony with nature even merited being adopted by you."*
>
> *"Wars and peace treaties deprived us of our land."*
>
> *"The White Man fought each other for our land and we were embroiled in the White Man's wars. The wars ended in treaties and our lands passed into the White Man's hands. Many Indians feel our fathers were betrayed."*
>
> *"We wanted to live our own life on our own land."*
>
> *"The white man's school, an alien land for an Indian child."*

Next to a picture of Aboriginal children lined up in their winter clothes before boarding a school bus outside an Indian residential school, there was a statement saying:

> *"Dick and Jane in the storybook are strangers to an Indian boy. An Indian child begins school by learning a foreign tongue. The sun and the moon mark passing time in the Indian home. At school, minutes are important and we jump to the beat. Many precious childhood hours are spent in a bus going to a distant school and coming home again."*

Another statement pointed out that *"the great discoverers of Canada traveled in Indian canoes, wore Indian snowshoes, ate Indian food, lived in Indian cabins. Without their Indian friends, not one of them could have survived or made their travels."*

"We sheltered him, fed him, led him through the forest."

There was also a message for the Christian missionaries and their churches.

"The early missionaries thought us pagans. They imposed upon us their own stories of God, or Heaven and Hell, of sin and salvation. But we spoke with God—the Great Spirit—in our own way. We lived with each other in love and honored the holy spirit in all living things.

"Long before they came, we had already talked with God, whom we called the Great Spirit, after our fashion. We lived together as brothers and we saw the Spirit present in every living thing."

"The reserve is the home of our spirits."

Next to a mural showing a moose, a stag and bloody hands, a message said: "To still our hunger, we killed an animal, and after eating our fill, we gave thanks to the Great Spirit who had sent it to us."

At the end of the tour, visitors descended from the upper level and sat around an artificial campfire and read the last message. "And now, my brother, sit down by the fire. Let us talk about the times which are coming. You have traveled over the long footpaths along which your forefathers trudged ... In a moment we shall take to the trail again. But during this stop, let us search in the flames for visions of the future."

When word about the provocative statements got out a few days before Expo 67 opened, pressure was put on the Liberal government of Prime Minister Lester B. Pearson to have them toned down. However, Pearson—whose Ontario riding of Algoma East included a large number of Ojibway bands—was firmly of the view that the Aboriginal people were entitled to have their say.

Despite the enthusiasm with which the idea of forming a national voice for all of the Aboriginal people of Canada had been received, the

National Indian Council ran into a problem at the outset that could not be resolved.

The natives from western Canada, whose bands had entered into treaties with the government of Canada between 1871 and 1877, made it known during the early meetings that they didn't consider the natives from Quebec to be "real Indians".

"I remember at those meetings that they considered us as not being Indian because we had no treaties and some of us were French-speaking so that made it doubly worse," Andrew Delisle recalled. "But the basic thing that they said was 'no you're not Indian because you have no treaties. Only people with treaties can be Indian.'

"That was strong in their thinking. They had been organized much more than we had. So, consequently, there was a division right there. East and the West and then B.C. B.C. was on their own. We were alone. The western provinces were alone. And that was quite a burden for the new organization. They could never resolve that problem for years and years and years."

Andrew said the attitude of those from the west came as quite a shock. "It was really something of a surprise to us. There was this division as to who should be the rightful spokesmen for the native people and who shouldn't be. Eventually we did overcome all that and started to work together, but it lasted for many years. I even think at the time of the 1969 White Paper, even after that, there was still some feeling that people with treaties are the people that have rights as native people and those that don't have any treaties were not considered as Indians. I think some of the people still feel that way to this day [1996]."

Jean Cuthand picked up on the cultural divide right away. Her dad told her he was going to write to all of the chiefs in western Canada and tell them the National Indian Council was a bad idea,

"I heard my dad [John Tootoosis who had been recommended by Bill Wuttunee in 1958 as the first president of the Federation of Saskatchewan Indians] speaking and he told me privately that he was going to write to all the chiefs. I believed him because, when he said he was going to do something, he'd do it. And I knew then this was the beginning of the end.

"He told me that it's not going to work because of the presence of the non-treaty Indians and the Métis and non-status Indians. He ex-plained it to me and I understood and I believed him. But I didn't say anything to my colleagues.

"Even though at the time I agreed with the concept of the National Indian Council, I knew in the back of my mind, just by talking to him, that it was going to disintegrate. That it wasn't going to work because of the different legislation in the provinces and the situation with the federal government and the treaties. The treaties were the number one priority to my dad and the others and that's the way it turned out."

"It was more culture than anything else," Andrew Delisle recalled. "The people that were involved meant to do good, but it just wouldn't work because there were status Indians, non-status Indians, treaty Indians, non-treaty Indians and everybody had their own thing. I wasn't happy with that for a long time."

When he was first approached about becoming part of the National Indian Council, Andrew had hoped that it would have become the national voice of independent organizations. "I was always promoting that it should have been a confederation of Indians in the real sense of the word. Like independent organizations coming to trade with each other in the earlier days. A confederation to deal with things at the national level.

"I always tried to push that but people, at that point in time, didn't understand it at all. They really didn't understand it simply because of that fact that there were Indians and non-Indians, treaty and non-treaty. 'He's got a treaty. We don't have'. So that's why we changed. Now [1996] it's the Assembly of First Nations. It's getting more to that confederacy kind of thing."

Bill Wuttunee didn't put nearly as much stock in the treaties. "The reason I had a different approach was that I read the treaties, that I studied law, and to me there was nothing in those treaties," he told me during one of our many interviews. "It was a bit dead. There wasn't much in those treaties. And people asked me and said to me would you change your opinion and I'd have to say no because the treaties were a special time in the late 1800s when the buffalo had been wiped out. If the buffalo had not been wiped out, there would have been no treaties because my people would have been independent. They would have said 'to hell with you we can survive on our own we don't need you at all.'

"The Indians were in a bind, especially on the plains, because the buffalo had been wiped out. Just imagine what would happen with the white people if the gas and all the oil evaporated. They would absolutely come to a dead halt, right? They wouldn't be able to do very much.

Nevertheless, he was unable to convince his fellow natives in western Canada that it was time to move beyond the treaties.

Sol Sanderson, who would later become president of the Federation of Saskatchewan Indians, was still a student when he attended a meeting in Regina where it was clearly evident that the differences between the treaty and non-treaty natives had reached the point of no return.

"We didn't have much money," he told me during an interview in 1996. "When we arrived there, we didn't have any place to stay. Andrew Delisle had rented a suite and in the suite was a piano and the late David Knight could play organ and piano so the people wanted to have a party. Andy invited us over to his suite and that's basically where Dave and I spent the nights.

"Expectations were high in terms of forming some type of a national organization and the debate at that time was pretty emotional. I can recall the Bill Wuttunees and Delisles getting into a fairly emotional debate. The older leaders like John Tootoosis were pro-treaty and that was a shock to the eastern people in non-treaty areas to realize as far as many of our elders in the treaty areas were concerned you have nothing unless you have a treaty. That was a very real debate because they didn't want to have any Indian get involved in violating the treaty arrangements as we understood them from here.

"In terms of looking at organizing nationally, it wasn't just a cultural issue that had to be addressed in terms of the many First Nations that exist in Canada like the Sioux, the Iroquois, the Cree and so on. Around that time, you were coming out of a stage of political development where, if you were a Cree, there were the Crees and those who want to be and, if you were an Iroquois, there was an Iroquois and those who want to be. Our people, generally I found, tended to want to continue to isolate themselves from the influence of other First Nations. I think it was largely because of the experience we had with non-Indians leading up to that time. Those of us from treaty areas, like the late John Tootoosis and others, they would start from treaty rights and the treaties.

"The debate was on about the need to set up a new forum. We couldn't carry on with the National Indian Council formally. There were debates being held about expanding the movement nationally and there were similar issues that you hear being discussed today. Taxation was an issue back then. Social issues like health, education, housing were on the agenda and we didn't have the formal organization, the structures that you see today. Nevertheless, the issues debated during those three days were much the same and the urban issue was new. We were organizing what we called urban Indians and we were forming the Urban Indian Association of Saskatchewan and we had Indians from Regina, Saskatoon, Prince Albert, North Battleford and so on, organizing to assist the leadership to deal with the social issues, economic issues, In terms of the National Indian Council, it sort of, for some reason, lost momentum."

Gene Lahache was chief of the Kahnawake Mohawks during the last days of the National Indian Council. When I interviewed him in 1996, he described the tension that developed between the treaty and non-treaty natives.

"The Indians that live on the reserves say 'hey we're Indians with numbers, you guys don't have numbers. You can't decide what we should do in our land. It's not yours. If you want to have something to do, organize your own groups and we'll organize ours'.

"There was six linguistic groups in Canada and about 400 different bands, none of which relate to each other. You can't get an Indian from the east coast to live with an Indian from northern Saskatchewan. You can't get an Indian from the west coast to come and live with an Indian on the east coast even though they're both societies living by the ocean. They don't get along.

"I remember when I was younger they said if you're not a Mohawk, you're not an Indian. They had the word for it in Mohawk that means somebody from somewhere else who's a different kind of person from us. They're Indian, but they're not real Indian because they're not Mohawk. It's like those other ones that say that without a treaty you're not an Indian.

"The National Indian Council idea worked pretty good in the prairies, but not in the east and not in B.C. In Quebec, everyone was interested. They wanted to know what was going on, didn't want to be left out, but they weren't ready to organize. The Iroquois and eastern Indians were really over organized and if another organization was coming in they would have had to split the people that belonged to all the existing organizations. But we kept going. We went to every meeting that there was, but I wasn't really satisfied because of the way that it was operating. It was more social than anything that would benefit the people as a whole.

"Then we had this meeting in Toronto and by then I was the chief and decided that we should separate. The registered Indians and the non-registered Indians should have their own organization. The Métis and the non-registered could go out together, but the registered Indians should have their own. They should conduct their own business. It's not related. Two different groups of people. On-reserve people are not the same as people who live off the reserve even if they live right next door to the reserve. They're not the same."

Marion Meadmore recalls that meeting at the Indian Friendship Centre in Toronto sometime in 1968 which was attended by, among others, Walter Dieter of the Federation of Saskatchewan Indians, Andrew Delisle and Gene Lahache of Kahnawake.

"They started to talk about the polarizing so, right about that time, it just made all the sense in the world to separate into two national organizations. And that's what was done at the NIC's last meeting. It was done on purpose because of the polarizing."

The status Indians formed the National Indian Brotherhood—

which later became the Assembly of First Nations. The non-status Indians and the Métis formed the Native Council of Canada — which later became today's Congress of Aboriginal Peoples.

Years later, at a meeting Andrew Delisle attended in Vancouver in 1972, the debate over treaty versus non-treaty was still raging on. "We started promoting aboriginal rights and we were opposed because they said there was no such thing as aboriginal rights. There were treaty rights and that was it. We made a long spiel about aboriginal rights being the basic rights and the treaty people said 'no, no, we got treaties and that's what they are, treaties with the Queen and that's what supersedes everything else'. The difference in thinking in so far as one group or the other was concerned was still there.

"Of course we had treaties. The Iroquois people had pre-Confederation treaties with the French, the Dutch, the English, but nobody respected them except the native people themselves. I guess, at that point in time, people in the west were ignorant of these treaties so they said well you don't have any treaties, therefore, you're not considered Indian and yet we did have treaties."

Another reason for the profound differences of opinion, Andrew suggested, was the fact that the treaties the western natives held so precious and dear were not entered into until the 1870s. "I guess the difference was that we were more affected by the colonial system. We'd been with the colonialists for 300 years and, at that point in time when we met the western people, it had only been 75 years or 200 years when they had real contact. That was a big difference because we had some thinking that was basically indoctrination and they were just new at it.

"What we tried to do at that point in time was warn them. I remember many times we said watch out for this and watch out for that because what happened to us is what's going to happen to you, Surprisingly enough, in the later years, you find out that the real application of those treaties was the Indian Act. I know that act was created for that. That was a tool of the government to fulfill the terms of the treaties. I remember how often myself and other people went over there and said, watch out because this is what's going to happen because it's happening to us and we've experienced it for 300 years. So that was the difference between the two groups. They're just two altogether different ways of looking at the relations between the whites and the Indians."

Even in 1996, when I first interviewed him for this book, Andrew Delisle said there were profound differences of opinion between the natives in the prairie provinces and those living in the east. "A lot of people out there still base everything on the treaties. That's where their rights are in the west. Here in the east we sort of disregard that type of thing and go back to a basic argument of aboriginal and inherent rights more so than they would. That was where our rights really came from and they were never abolished. That's what we believe in."

Another problem he saw in 1996 between the Aboriginals of the west and the east was the manner in which the National Chief of the Assembly of First Nations (AFN) was elected by chiefs from across Canada. "They have more reservations in the west than we have in the east and I think politically there's a problem there," he said. "Through the years of Indian organization nationally you only had one chief for a short period of time from the east as being president because they had more people."

In fact, in the 2014 AFN election, the chiefs of British Columbia, Alberta, Saskatchewan and Manitoba had 388 votes among them—B.C. cast 57% of those votes. The bands from Ontario to Newfoundland and Labrador had 209. Of the 12 individuals who served as National Chief of the National Indian Brotherhood/Assembly of First Nations between 1968 and 2015, only two came from east of Manitoba.

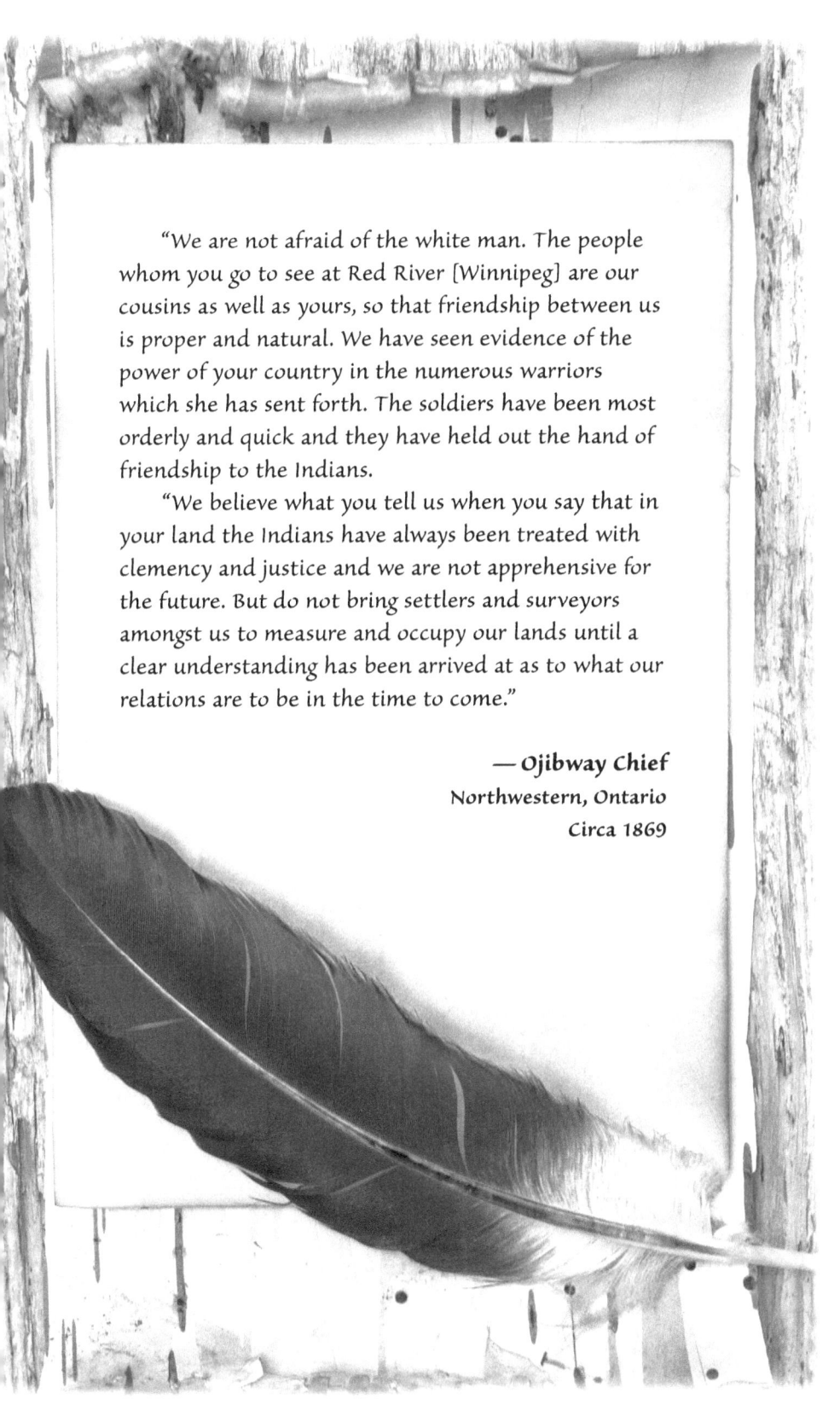

"We are not afraid of the white man. The people whom you go to see at Red River [Winnipeg] are our cousins as well as yours, so that friendship between us is proper and natural. We have seen evidence of the power of your country in the numerous warriors which she has sent forth. The soldiers have been most orderly and quick and they have held out the hand of friendship to the Indians.

"We believe what you tell us when you say that in your land the Indians have always been treated with clemency and justice and we are not apprehensive for the future. But do not bring settlers and surveyors amongst us to measure and occupy our lands until a clear understanding has been arrived at as to what our relations are to be in the time to come."

— **Ojibway Chief**
Northwestern, Ontario
Circa 1869

Chapter 10

On New Year's Day 1996 the residents of the isolated Ojibway community of Whitedog in northwestern Ontario were in the grips of a major crisis. There had been more suicides in 1995 than there had been in the last ten years. More and more young Ojibways had given up hope of having any reason to live. They wanted out. Permanently.

Over the last eleven months, there had been eight suicides and two unresolved deaths that appeared to have been the result of crime. Prior to this suicide cluster, there had been seven suicides over a ten-year period.

Between March 18 and April 22, 1995, for example, two brothers, a cousin and a close friend—all between the ages of 20 and 30—committed suicide at Whitedog. Autopsies revealed high levels of alcohol and paint lacquer (fast-drying varnish) in their blood.

An article in the May 4, 1995, issue of *Wawatay News* said that Nodin Counselling Services of Sioux Lookout, Ojibway Tribal Family Services and Community Counselling of Kenora, and Wabaseemoong (Whitedog) Family Services had provided counsellors and crisis teams to help those who were grieving or having trouble coping.

Band member Louie Cameron and social services director Ron P. McDonald had spearheaded a project to pull the community of approximately 900 on the banks of the Winnipeg River about 95 kilometres northwest of Kenora together.

They had opened a 24-hour crisis intervention and counselling centre and were coordinating a volunteer foot patrol 24 hours a day to keep an eye on popular lacquer sniffing and drinking haunts and to search the community for anyone at risk of committing suicide.

Elders and school staff were holding suicide prevention workshops and talking about the dangers of alcohol and solvent abuse. The crisis centre had become a safe place for young people or anyone else in the community who needed to talk. It was the focal point of the Ojibway community's effort to save lives.

Louie Cameron was quoted as saying: "It's a hopeful sign that people are taking the responsibility of looking after each other. People have put aside their individual differences and their religious beliefs and come together. Saving the lives of our young people has become more important ... We have to deal with the issues of self-respect, self-esteem and feeling good about the future to eradicate alcohol and solvent abuse." In an interview with the *Winnipeg Free Press* at that time, he said: "From the time we are born, we are always mourning."

During an interview at Whitedog in 1996, Ron Roy McDonald, chief of the Islington Band of Saulteaux (the French name for the Ojibways), told me: "Lacquer is killing our young people and it's also affecting the community as a whole. What's happening right now as we speak, there is a sub-culture of lacquer sniffers, we call them sniffers. This is what I'm trying to target. I'm trying to eliminate that problem, people sniffing.

"It's impacting my community, this lacquer, and I mean it's total, what the government has done to our people here in Whitedog. It's forced them to live this way. It's forced them. It's like a genocide. It *is* a genocide. This is what they've done to our people."

Chief McDonald said approximately 80% of the people at Whitedog in 1996 were unemployed and relied on welfare assistance. "Some of these [small] homes [lining both sides of the gravel road running parallel with the shoreline] have two or three families in there and that can cause chaos, if it's compounded with drinking, dependency on welfare, no jobs.

"And it's also affecting the community as a whole. For example, we had one incident about four or five years ago. One of our band members was high on this lacquer stuff and he went into the town of Keewatin and killed a female merchant. In our neighbouring community, Grassy Narrows, we believe the guy that shot the OPP [Ontario Provincial Police] officer in Grassy was under the influence of some form of lacquer or some form of substance.

"Right now, in fact, yesterday about this time, a man came in here [to the Band Council office]. I mean my office was just full of fumes in here, just by his presence. This is a full-grown man. He had lacquer breath on him. He wanted money. He said, 'I need food. I need to buy stuff for my kids.' Then, after the meeting, after he left, his uncle came by and said 'I hope you didn't give him any money.' He'd go and buy some more lacquer. That's why he wanted the money."

Chief McDonald estimated that 10 to 20 per cent of the community —at the end of a dead-end gravel road that ran off the paved road to Kenora—were using solvents and other means of getting high. They ranged in age from 10-year-olds to people in their mid-30s.

He tried to deal with the problem by having the Ontario Provincial Police lay charges against the substance abusers. "They said, 'no'. There is no law against lacquer. There is nothing criminal about having lacquer in your possession or even sniffing it for that matter. There's nothing. There's no criminal offence there so that's the problem we're having. Right now I'm trying to take steps with the court system in Kenora, with the authorities in Kenora, to help us combat the lacquer problem, to try and say to them, 'OK, treat it as though it's a liquor offence'. We want to eliminate the lacquer substance abuse problem in the community. That's the main cause of trouble right now in the community is lacquer."

He said the substance abuse problem at Whitedog started in the early 1970s—soon after they learned that their lakes and rivers had been poisoned with methylmercury.

Between 1962 and 1970, the pulp and paper mill operated by British-owned Reed International Ltd. at Dryden, about 170 kilometres directly southeast of Whitedog, dumped more than ten tons of raw mercury into the English-Wabigoon river system. Fish in the rivers had 33 to 50 times the accepted level of methylmercury, a highly toxic form of mercury. The fish were unsafe to eat by humans or animals.

In March, 1970, the government of Ontario ordered the company to stop dumping mercury into the river system and banned all commercial and sports fishing. Overnight, the people of Whitedog and the nearby Grassy Narrows reserve lost their two main sources of employment—guiding and commercial fishing—and their confidence in the safety of their food and water. More than 480 kilometres of a productive river ecosystem was expected to remain contaminated for 50 to 100 years.

Commercial fishermen at Whitedog and Grassy Narrows who had been making enough to pay their own way and have cash in their pockets lost their only source of livelihood and had to turn to welfare. The residents were forced to rely on fish trucked in from outside.

"We weren't informed," Josephine Mandamin, one of the elders at Whitedog, told me in 1996. "We didn't hear. We didn't see. It was instantaneous, instant type of thing with us. It just hit us one day. It must've been happening for years back before the government chose to let us know. I don't believe that they weren't aware of it, what the progress of the mercury was doing to the environment in our river system.

"I think they were quite aware of it but, from way back, we've always been looked at as second-class citizens, 'the Indian people. Put them in their reservations and box them in and they won't cause no problem.' We never caused them any problem."

There were signs of mercury poisoning early on. Diseased fish were found in the rivers and on the shores. Diseased cats and other fish-eating animals were also found. However, no one paid much attention to it at the time. The government officials certainly didn't say or do anything about it.

"Now we're trying to cope with the backlash of those doings by the governments," Josephine said. "To this day, 1996, we're still coping with the circumstances, the negative circumstances that arose from the doings of people who were careless with our livelihood, careless with our gifts from the Creator. The river, the water, is very sacred to us people. The trees. The rocks."

How did she react when she first learned that the rivers and lakes had been poisoned? "I suppose my first reaction was anger and then it turned into sadness and then it sort of worked itself out to acceptance because I had to accept what things I couldn't turn around. Pollution is a big thing once it works itself out. You almost never heal from it. The Japanese people got the worst end of it, the mercury poisoning in their country, and they came to share their circumstances with us."

Josephine was referring to people from Minamata, Japan, who travelled all the way to Whitedog to share their experience with mercury poisoning and offer support and advice. From 1932 to 1968, a chemical company dumped an estimated 27 tons of mercury compounds into Minamata Bay which is located on the island of Kyushu at the southwest corner of Japan. Thousands of people whose normal diet included fish from the bay unexpectedly developed symptoms of methylmercury poisoning. The illness became known as the "Minamata Disease".

A doctor from the Chisso Corporation Hospital reported as early as May 1, 1956, that "an unclarified disease of the central nervous system has broken out." He linked the disease to the fish the people of Minamata depended on for their daily food.

Victims were diagnosed as having a degeneration of the nervous system. Numbness occurred in their limbs and lips. Their speech became slurred, and their vision constricted. Some people had serious brain damage. Others lapsed into unconsciousness or suffered from involuntary movements. Some victims were thought to be insane when they began to shout uncontrollably.

From around 1950 onwards, cats had been seen to have convulsions, go mad and die. As the mercury destroyed their brains, they passed through a stage of crazed spinning and whirling. Locals called it the "cat dancing disease", owing to their erratic movement. Finally, birds were strangely dropping from the sky. These unexplainable occurrences brought panic to Minamata.

Josephine Mandamin really appreciated the fact that the people from Minamata took time out from their devastated lives to travel to Whitedog and Grassy Narrows to show support and offer advice to the Ojibway people.

"They felt a kindness to share their circumstances with us. Most of the governmental bureaucrats at that time, I remember, were making fun of them. In fact, one MPP [Member of Provincial Parliament], Leo Bernier, who always had a problem with native people as far as trying to understand them, called them 'the singing troubadours', the Japanese people.

"And then we had a provincial health minister in those days, Dennis Timbrell, who made a comment: 'Oh those people in Wabaseemong [Whitedog] and Grassy won't die from pollution, from mercury poisoning. They'll die from VD [venereal disease].' A minister talking like that, it's appalling. A health minister!"

The Japanese visitors informed them that mercury poisoning was an "invisible type of festering" that could take up to 35 years to surface. "They said by that time you'll probably have a high percentage of diabetes and problems with alcohol and the government 'll love that much more because they'll be able to blame that rather than the mercury poisoning," Josephine told me. "Nevertheless, it will be mercury poisoning in the physical sense of it 26 years later or 36, or generations, future generations will be affected in the genes."

Josephine's husband Isaac, a former chief of the Islington Band of Saulteaux, told me the Japanese people strongly advised them that it would be better to enter into negotiations with the government rather than trying to take the government or the British pulp and paper company to court.

"When the Japanese people were here," Isaac said, "they said the only way you could prove that you've lost something over this contamination is through the mediation process because right now the government won't move, you won't get nothing if you have to take it to court. But, if you go through mediation, that's the only way you'll get something, some benefits out of it because right now at that time they said, nothing will really show up in the system until 20, 25 years, 30 years down the road. Then the symptoms will show up in the people and now that's exactly what's happening right now. Everything is coming up to the surface."

By 1977, several residents of Whitedog were showing symptoms of the Minamata Disease—numbness in the limbs, trembling, inability to control their movements, hearing loss and tunnel vision. Asked to what extent the problems the community was dealing with in 1996 were a direct result of the poisoning of their lakes and rivers with mercury from the British pulp and paper mill at Dryden, Isaac said: "If you look at it before the mercury contamination here, well I'd say maybe two per cent of the people in the whole community were diabetics at that time. Now about 50 per cent of the whole community, all diabetic, whether it's directly affected by the mercury we don't know, but nobody won't say.

"No, nobody's going to say a word. Because that's a true fact of the way the society operates. The government was trying to get all the tax money he can get from that giant paper company [in Dryden]. If you put a little pressure on that outfit, they pull out. Happens in every country. Then you're sitting there with an empty bag. So this all had a lot to do with economics at the same time."

There was no doubt in Isaac's mind that the poisoning of their lakes and rivers was having a devastating effect. "My wife and I were having children during the discovery of mercury," Isaac said, "and our kids and their kids, those are the ones that are really having a hard time because you can see the stages where the symptoms will have shown up and this is exactly where the teenage population right now is. It's hit right now."

People sniffed gasoline in the 1970s in order to get high. And then, in the mid 1980s, they started sniffing paint thinner.

In the interview she gave me at her spacious log home at Whitedog in 1996, Josephine Mandamin said she was highly suspicious of the white government and its white bureaucracy and had a lifetime of good reasons to feel that way.

"We see what's happening to the community at large," she said. "Alcohol abuse, the sniffing abuse, the solvent abuse, the violence against women and children. We are aware of it. We recognize it so we want to do things about it. So we [Band Council] make by-laws and resolutions and it gets bumped into the [Indian Affairs] agency. It can't get over that brick wall to get to the people that could do something about it, the Solicitor-General, the Premier, the Prime Minister, the ministers and that's how it is. We're concerned about the suppliers of, sellers of, lacquer and solvent abuse and alcohol, bootlegging."

However, because of the almost iron-clad control the white bureaucrats at both the federal and provincial level exercised over the community, the people of Whitedog were often stymied in their efforts to deal with the problems.

"People who have control over other human beings want to keep that control and that's where bureaucracy comes in," Josephine said. "Bureaucracy, to me, is something I want to do without in the near future for the next generation of my people. I hate dealing with bureaucracy, the middleman. I think it would be more beneficial to everyone in this country if they had a government-to-government wheeling and dealing take place instead of always being consumed by paper work, by bureaucracy practices."

Isaac cut in at that point. "You could have a minister wanting to do right but there's always somebody there behind him giving him ideas. 'No, no, no, you can't do that.' And this basically is what's happening. It's unfortunate, but that's the name of the game. It is very hard for a lot of the people, the public, to know what's going on. I've seen it happen. I've been inside the bureaucracy and I've been outside and I've been the chief and so on, so you get to know exactly where everything sits. It's really hard for the public trying to find out whether it was right or not."

"We always had the capacity of dealing with things," Josephine said. "Cutting off the bud of a problem. But the allowance of trying to deal with it has never been allowed in Whitedog. We have so much resources that are not recognized. The elders, the family unit itself could be very helpful in prevention of the negativeness of alcohol abuse and sniffing, but it has never been allowed. When a crisis happens in Whitedog, oh gosh the resources people are there flying in soup, kicking up a lot of dust and then they blow away. There's no follow. We're still left holding this problem. We bump into so many negative walls and that's where bureaucracy is, local ministries are at fault.

"There's so many brick walls that we just find too defeating. We have to break those or go around them, find a way. We have to go around them and just keep on striving for what we envision. Reality has to kick in, acceptance has to kick in, hope has to kick in, respect, a lot of those things have to. Tolerance has to be there too because that's the only way I can see.

"The boundaries that I love to talk about were not there in my day. The restrictions were not in my day, but they are now in reality so you have to find the capacity to work with those realities in order to accept and, from what little you have left, make it into a positive goal and vision and hope."

Despite dropping out of school after Grade 3, Isaac Mandamin went on to become chief of the Islington Band of Saulteaux. He ran a successful transportation business and politicians — including future Ontario Premier David Peterson — sought out his counsel and support.

"We had what you call the medical transportation business for 25 years," Josephine said, "and, through our enterprise in the family, we managed to make a good living by tying up the whole caboodle of things, not allowing outsiders to tap into the business of doing field trips for the school and medical clients and other resources, agency, courts, driving them back and forth [to Kenora]. Yes we did make a good living

"Isaac's been chief off and on. In fact, when he first became chief he looked like he was still wet behind the ears, that's how young he was, but very responsible. His background consists of good training. It may be so that his ancestors didn't speak a word of English, but they were good trainers in life, perspective of things. So he's been chief off and on quite a number of years."

"I have an academic training," Josephine told me. "I don't think I'm past Grade 2. I went to a residential school. I'm a product of a residential school syndrome. I went to school in Kenora in a Catholic school called St. Mary's [Indian Residential School]. I was sent there by the Indian agent and the RCMP [Royal Canadian Mounted Police] by bush plane from Whitedog where we were gathered in the fall.

"Four generations of my family went there, my grandfather, my mother, myself and my kids in a residential setting. In those days residential schools weren't very hyper about academic training because I perceive that, again, dominant captivity was very much the fad. Just to teach the native people domestic skills. Not that I'm putting it down. It became quite helpful for me later on."

Before being transferred to St. Mary's, Josephine spent a year at the Cecilia Jeffrey Indian Residential School which was Protestant. Both schools, by the way, were huge multi-storey institutions. "We were abused there, my siblings and I either by the older kids or the staff and I made the mistake of telling my mother when she came to visit us and she had a terrific physical fight with the principal in those days. They got a hold of the Indian agent in the Kenora office to come and intervene and my mother was very strong willed too so they negotiated and that's how we came to St. Mary's school."

When I asked her if the experience at St. Mary's was any better, she said: "No, but it was more peaceful because I used to love playing with the beads on the nun's habit and, to me, playing with those huge beads and the long habits of the nun reminded me somewhat of the long dresses of my grandmother back home where they had long dresses."

She only spent one year at St. Mary's and then she had to return to Whitedog. "Our circumstances has a way of intervening. My siblings got stuck in the residential school setting. I had to go home because of the breakup of my parents' union and from there I had the responsibility of raising my younger brothers. I had an older sister who died in infancy so I'm the oldest."

When I suggested that some of the people at the Indian Affairs office or at the residential schools must have meant well and done their best to improve the lives of the children and, while they might have wound up doing the wrong thing, some of them really did try, she said: "Let me phrase you, something. Good intentions pave their way to hell. You have to be careful. Good intentions are acknowledged and appreciated but, if you take them literally as the gospel truth then these things could lead you to hell."

Considering the fact that she dropped out of school after Grade 2,

Josephine Mandamin was remarkably knowledgeable and astute. She also had a delightful sense of herself. "You know, Robert," she once said with a mischievous smile. "Isaac and I are a very strange, unique couple. He's strange and I'm unique."

As far as Josephine was concerned, too many things were happening to create grief and hardships for native people in general and that had "created a lot of dissension, divisions in the community because of being afraid, scared.

"It's not as if we're united in this community. We're not and I'm not blaming everything on the white people. I think it was way back allowing too much, having too much, trust and faith in very bad people who tend to be expert at obscuring truths. I think Indian Affairs has a lot to answer for, to correct some of the devious, conniving, undermining that went on because my people couldn't speak English.

"We are at fault too because stupidity had a lot to do with it. That the great white father would take care of us. Never did. He never did. I don't feel that I have any pride in the great Canadian standard. That's why I feel that sometimes when they sing the national anthem I don't want to stand up. What's so glorious and free with the situation? Canada itself is glorious, but attitudes of Canada towards native people is something else.

"I don't feel free in Canada. I have to abide to the piper and the piper comes in the shape and form of agency persons, bureaucrats, civil servants. I resent being used as a scapegoat by those very people to make taxpayers angry that we are draining their tax dollars. That's bullshit. That's the public service that's doing that with great expertise and I mean that and I won't retract my opinion.

"When I heard about this [recent] visit of our Foreign Affairs Minister to Cuba to go and talk to Fidel Castro about human rights I started laughing my head off at the irony of it. 'Why you obviously bald-faced hypocrite, sanctimonious asshole,' I said. I wouldn't have the nerve to do that. I'd be ashamed and I was ashamed of him, Lloyd Axworthy, going to talk to Fidel Castro. If Fidel Castro were to come here under an invitation of a Canadian native, in spite of what he did, dictatorship, he was blunt about it. He didn't try and hide what he was. He never did. There's honesty in there. But our own politicians are dictators of great skill, ministers, program heads and they hide it, camouflage into another way. I think I would tend to put the halo on Fidel Castro, anoint him as a saint compared to what our people are basically, especially those who control Canadians."

Josephine believed too many decisions were being made by the white bureaucrats and that the Ojibway people should have been allowed to take more responsibility for their own lives.

"The white man's perception of solutions for native people can backlash in a negative way," she said. "Take vandalism. Instead of trying to work out something with the community and the family, they immediately apprehended those kids and sent them to training school. That's where they got sniffing solvent abuse and more tricks on how to vandalize or steal. They brought that back with them and it had a very negative impact on native children.

"I'm paying a big price. I'm losing my future because of bureaucracy. I want to retain and I want to be allowed to be responsible for my own generation, next generation of the future, which is my kids, young people in Whitedog. I want to be allowed that, to be responsible, be allowed to make my mistakes and learn from it instead of rewinding itself time, time and again, revictimizing the young people in Whitedog and retraumatizing them over and over again for the sake of 'I know best.'

"They're taking responsibility away from the people in Whitedog and promoting alcoholism, alcohol abuse and sniffing abuse when they do that. We have to be allowed to handle or be given back our responsibility as far as where our grassroots or reservations are concerned. I don't like local ministries for one thing. They have the gift of lying, fictions, not telling the truth. 'Oh, everything is fine in Whitedog. Everything is going well, we're on top of it.' Bullshit! They've never been on top of anything except taking control of other people's lives. Bureaucracy intervenes and prevents First Nations [the term applied to each of the more than 600 bands scattered across Canada] being heard by the very people that could do something about it. We're just doing things from crisis to crisis to satisfy the bureaucrats and to make the general public not aware of what's really happening in First Nations."

Josephine mourned the loss of the past, the rich traditions through which the Ojibways celebrated their spirituality, lived off the land and survived the bitter cold of winter. "Most of those things are gone by the great knowledge of the great white man knows what's best for everybody and these are gone now. But sometimes you have to face reality and learn to manoeuvre yourself and how to adapt to these changes and accept them and just integrate yourself and find ways of how to loop around negative surroundings."

Josephine said the Ojibway people themselves have the capacity to deal with many of the problems in their communities but are often sidelined by the white bureaucracy. "We have a problem in most communities with alcohol, with solvent abuse, but like hell will we be allowed to work on those problems ourselves. There's too many false prophets, false messiahs, saviours that come in wolf's clothing. I think the survival of the native people should be allowance, tolerance from a dominant society. We can never, I guess, we'll have to try and seek that in ways we can co-manage, because basically everyone doesn't live in a rose garden.

"Everyone has problems, basically all cultures, but it's more pronounced in the Indian lives and I always thought that governments in general towards native people were very thoughtless, not understanding, not trying to understand."

While she had harsh words for the bureaucrats at Indian Affairs and the provincial ministries, she was also quite critical of the Ojibways employed at the local band office. "They only do enough to justify a pay cheque. That's what it's all about. It has nothing to do with intervention, prevention. I think that's why we in Whitedog have 80 per cent of diabetes which is mostly because there's no education about it."

She also lamented the lack of regular police presence in the community. "Justice is another thing that I'm really disappointed in. Trying to believe that we have 24 hours police service here. We don't. But, when something happens in the community, oh gosh they're here like the Fifth Cavalry in the boring Hollywood movie. That's the only time you'll see a uniform here."

While the Ontario Provincial Police employed some native officers, Josephine did not consider them to be effective. "These are not recognized as policemen. Our own boys. They're more messengers. It all pertains to attitude. Sometimes I think the 1965 march we had in Kenora [more about this later] did improve and change a lot of things within the past years. It seems the general public in Kenora want to understand and apply some kindness, but it's the agencies that will never change. We're still having some hardship coming in from the court house, through the social services, from the police because of attitude. See that's what I mean. It's an attitude.

"And that's why I said we're a very enterprising commodity. We got to keep those white people working in the jails. If it starts to empty out alarmingly, then they'll go after the alcohol-related warrants to fill that jail up. Nothing ever kicks in in the support system pertaining to child and family services, pertaining to police, court or any social service. Nothing ever kicks in to support in the way of intervention and prevention.

"We're losing our future, how we envision it. We're losing the language. We're losing the right to connect with what the Creator gave us in the way of environment. We can't seem to have the right to protect it. Bell Canada comes any time they want to spray [pesticides]. The Ontario Hydro comes along any time they wish."

Josephine expressed deep concern about the increasing number of Ojibway children and young people who were being taken away from their families and placed in white foster homes or training schools.

"We, especially here in Whitedog, are losing our grip on the future and the way it's being done is by taking our future [children and youth] away from this community and I think the worst crime that could be mentioned is taking the future from any community. The youth and the kids are supposed to have rights to safety and protection and bonding to their culture and language and they take them away.

"They abuse that right in the name of protection. They're not protecting anybody, much less our kids. The child services people, CAS [Children's Aid Society] or what have you, just come any time into the reserve with assistance of the provincial police and, in a very intimidating way, just take our children off the community to go to more confusion and hurt. In that way, we're losing the grip to retain that control of our future because the [Ojibway] language is not going to be there when they come back.

"I don't know how many lies have been written in the paper trail. Everything is so much justified on paper trails and most of them are pure fictional lies. Truths can be hidden by paper trails and there's so much of that happening here in Whitedog pertaining to our kids being taken away from this community.

"We have people saying that Whitedog is not a safe place to live and is dangerous. Then what I am doing here? I, Josephine Mandamin, who has always looked at Wabaseemoong as a place of magic and mystery and beauty and a good place to live. If allowed. See, I'm not absent from the intimidation of everything that's negative here, but I try to skirt around it. I have to live with it and I don't mind so much of that from my own people that I share this community with. What I mind is the undermining, the negative attitude of those that are supposed to provide services for the people here in this community. The attitude of negativeness that comes from the justice system, the social services. That's what I don't like.

"At least in the [Indian] residential school setting we looked out for each other but, in the social services component, those kids are not having that protection. I'm always apprehensive about what's happening to my future. They're not here in this community. They're away in a very negative environment.

"Nobody's taking care of the children. Nobody cares. I hope someday the government will see and try to understand and be tolerant to the people, especially here in Wabaseemoong, that they should stop somewhere. They've already taken our land, poisoned our water, and now they're taking our children."

Chief Ron McDonald was just a young boy living at One Man Lake when Ontario Hydro flooded their homes in 1958. He has fond memories of the good life the Ojibways enjoyed before being forced to leave their homes and move to Whitedog.

"My dad used to get up at six, seven in the morning," he once told me. "I remember that. I remember the nice fire he made every morning. I remember him going outside and sometimes the ducks would swim by, mallards would swim by, and he would shoot it and he'd be laughing and very happy about it and he'd tell my mom to have it ready for dinner.

"By that time, it was around eight o'clock, he'd be on the boat, gas tanks down the hill, wide open. The gas tanks hadn't been touched. Nothing is hidden. Everything's out in the open. He'd go out and do his business, come back, eat his meal with the family.

"Everybody's happy, everybody's talking, everybody's been well fed and we start to wind down from the day's work, washing dishes and all that. Everybody just talking and helping each other and getting ready for bed. There was no neighbour telling me to shut up or coming over to ask for a fight or to bother us.

"And then, all of a sudden, when we were forced to move to Whitedog, there's a neighbour in every direction you look within ten, maybe 30 feet from us. We couldn't put our boat down the hill, gas tanks wide open. Our gas tank would be gone, maybe even our motor. Somebody would've stolen it.

"My dad couldn't shoot that duck if there was a duck landing outside. Couldn't shoot him because we can't fire a gun in public. We couldn't sit down together as a family without a drunk pounding on our door or some guy, sniffed out [from inhaling gasoline or paint lacquer], bothering our family. Things like that. That's the kind of way of life we had, the way of life that changed.

"Now it's even gone worse. We have political interference now. We're trying to live with the religious groups right now within the community, the Baptists, the Christians, the Evangelists or what have you. Our own people fighting amongst each other just because of religion. Yeah, and this is the way of life that was taken away. The feeling that we had out in One Man Lake is not here anymore.

"What they did to the Indians is criminal. It was a criminal offence to do that, forcibly move somebody out like that. It's almost like a war crime to me. It was totally unrealistic, unreasonable to move the people when they were already self-sufficient, when they were off their asses so to say. They were supporting themselves. They were self-reliant. They didn't need welfare. They didn't need grants.

"Before we moved here, we never had problems with lacquer. We never had problems with alcoholism and I don't remember my friends ever being drunk up in One Man Lake. They never drank. We had a livelihood depending on commercial fishing. I remember even though I was only two, three years old. I remember the way we lived."

What would the advantage have been if they had not been forced out of One Man Lake? "The advantage? I believe it would be self-sufficiency, independence, living again the way we did before."

Josephine Mandamin shared Ron McDonald's sense of loss. "One Man Lake was very beautiful, beaches everywhere, a sustainable lifestyle was there," she told me during the interview in 1996. "And then it got flooded in the name of progress. Here, no matter who was born in One Man Lake ended up being a Whitedog person."

Josephine had fond memories of the early days out in the bush where she and Isaac used to trap beavers, pick blueberries and harvest the wild rice. It was a good life. "We followed the nomads' life in the fishing, the blueberry picking, the rice picking and the trapping. It was a beautiful way of life. When I say nomads, we were very traditional then. We survived, me and Isaac, when we first got married. We still practised the nomad life in trapping because he trapped for a living. In the summer, he guided in the tourist camps and that's how we survived. We had settlements where we stayed, like our log houses in Whitedog. Living like nomads, moving around, the freedom to move. There was always a learning experience in every place you went to.

"We had blueberries and chokecherries, all the berries and rabbits and birds that you could eat, partridge and all that. The bounty in those days was terrific. Nobody sprayed our bounty with pesticides.

"Life had its own lessons and the connection we had with our environment, the thanksgiving we practised, often to give thanks to the Creator for what he provided, plenty of fish, no pollution and no restrictions."

The Ojibway people would gather together during the summer blueberry season and exchange gifts to symbolize the bounty that the Creator had provided. There would be people from Shoal Lake, Grassy

Narrows, Kenora, Swan Lake, Whitedog, One Man Lake and other communities. There were no boundaries, no segregation. Everybody was there for a reason, to pick blueberries during the day and enjoy poker, square dancing and good stuff like that after the sun went down.

What was life like in the harsh, biting, cold of Canada's long winters? "The winter?" Josephine asked. "Remember, I'm talking about days when surviving was a way of life for the Indian people. Welfare wasn't there as yet, but, just on the basis of survival, we were more healthy in mind, spirit and body because we had to move to survive the winter, the trapping, the cleaning of pelts [furs], putting in the wood. So, in that way, I never considered it as a hard life. In fact, it was beneficial to the mind, spirit and the body.

"You didn't have time to get fat for one thing. So, in that way, you had a much better life. Diabetes was unheard of. Substance abuse was unheard of. In those days, you could leave your things on the shoreline and nobody would touch them."

They travelled by canoes, boats, horses, dog sleds and, sometimes, by bush plane. They would go to nearby white communities to buy things like sugar, lard, salt, flour, baking powder, and clothing.

"That's all you needed in those days because we provided everything else ourselves," Josephine said with a sense of nostalgia. "Life was more meaningful because we were living off the land for one thing. Welfare wasn't as important because you had your pride, you had your integrity. You were proud that you were capable of living off the land and had the freedom to do so. It was a good life, yeah, but you got to face reality now. People still, young people especially, want to hurt themselves or go on sniffing [paint lacquer]. We have a community-based concern. Let's put that fact on the table right now."

Isaac Mandamin told me Ontario Hydro didn't warn the people that their homes were about to be flooded in 1958. "They didn't even prepare anything, nothing was prepared at all. The people from the One Man Lake community were either out blueberry picking or [wild] rice picking. When they came back, all their stuff was floating around, coffins were floating around. Today [1996], we still haven't got a complete restored graveyard in One Man Lake. Partially it's done, but partially it's not there. We're still waiting to have that completed."

Chief McDonald recalled that, at the time of the flooding of 1,600 hectares which raised the level of One Man Lake by three metres, the pulp and paper company in Dryden—the same company that poisoned the lakes and rivers with mercury—wanted to expand its logging operations in the area. "We were in the way and Ontario Hydro was the other company that wanted us out of there. Ontario Hydro, of course, as you know, wanted to build two dams in that area so we were in the way."

Both Josephine and Isaac Mandamin were critical of the government's decision to dump strangers from three different communities into one isolated spot and expect them to live together in harmony. When they were living at One Man Lake, the families of the different clans lived separate from one another. The McDonalds would be in one spot and, an appropriate distance away, the Fishers would have their homes. The Henry and Land families would also have separate areas.

However, when the families from One Man Lake and Swan Lake were moved to Whitedog, they were all bunched together in cookie-cutter houses that followed the straight line of the newly-laid water and sewer pipes. The close living arrangement led to tension, conflict and violence.

"Why couldn't they have compensated us with land instead of boxing us in, boxing us in here [Whitedog]?" Josephine asked. "They must have been very sure that it would create a lot of tension, jealousy, competitiveness. They should have looked better at other alternatives because we used to get along better even then as neighbours.

"It seems like distance makes the heart fonder. You're not supposed to live together like the beavers in a beaver house [a cone-shaped lodge made of branches and mud with an underwater entrance]. You've got to have space to breathe and space to survive as best as you can and it was there [One Man Lake]. But when it came time to unite, if there was death or danger or an issue that had to be dealt with, we came together. It was there. Now, it's not here."

Isaac Mandamin agreed. "Those communities were put together all in one so there was a lot of things that took place there. It's hard to put people together and expect them to get along right away. It's taken all this time. We still have differences today."

Isaac was still quite young when Ontario Hydro flooded the homes and built the two hydro electric generating stations. "The community didn't have no input in the whole process in the beginning because Indian agents did everything.," he said, "and now Indian Affairs are saying that they haven't got nothing to do with it.

"But, actually, they're the people that negotiated on behalf of the community. There was no referendum whatsoever to see how we were doing, surviving, after the dams were put in and before that, when Hydro was forcing the people to move into the Whitedog community.

"Nobody, with the exception of about two families, was on welfare. Everybody was standing on their own. Everybody had a log house. The only thing that was given to them was the roof and the flooring, but they had to build everything by logs so that's how they were surviving and everybody looked after themselves."

"Our water used to be crystal clear in Whitedog and One Man Lake before Hydro came and we didn't benefit from Ontario Hydro. I'd like to make that clear," Josephine said. "While they were selling kilowatts to the general public, it was ten years after that we actually got electricity. Now we're trying to survive, striving to make things better for our future and it's a losing game now.

"You've heard recently, maybe in the media, we're losing our kids to suicide and their addiction to solvent abuse and our people's addiction to alcohol abuse. We recognize those things. But I would have much preferred if Ontario Hydro had treated us with more respect in a human approach type of courtesy or respect or caring, to compensate us more in a long-term economic development type of thing."

Josephine worried about the possibility that their homes might be flooded again. "I strongly believe it could happen because it's right there. I live with it all the time and the potential of something happening with the technology. Something could happen. We could all drown in hours. There's no provisions of insurance that that's not going to happen.

"We've got hydro dams situated on either side of us. They're treating us like animals when they have a reservoir right in the middle of the community. If we don't dance to their tune, they could easily flood Whitedog again with all of us in it."

Chief McDonald told me there was still a lot of resentment over the flooding of their homes and the forced relocation. "Ever since they've been forced to move together, there's always been this political rivalry, social unrest, instability, rampant drug abuse, substance abuse, alcohol abuse, suicides ever since."

I suggested that asking the police or the courts to do something about the problem did not explain why so many people were getting lost in lacquer in the first place. "We were forced to be on welfare," he replied. "And along with that came a lifestyle that wasn't conducive to the kind of lifestyle that we had before. Like, before we were forced to move [from One Man Lake and Swan Lake], we had our livelihood. We had a way of life which was fishing, trapping and seasonal work. What I mean by that, seasonal work, a lot of our people worked in [tourist] camps, as guides, different types of guiding like fish guiding or hunting guiding, hunting trips and all that.

"We survived through what I call an Indian or aboriginal diet. It's also interesting to note, at that time, they didn't have any diseases. I shouldn't say any disease. I'm saying like the kind of diseases we have today like, for example, diabetes. Here it's very, very, high right now in this community. Diabetes has just shot right up, right up through the roof and statistics show that this community is suffering another form of destruction, of genocide, whereby diabetes is widespread within our community now. We never had diabetes in those days. Maybe there was the odd case, but I'm saying not on a large scale where it affects the whole community.

"In those days, our diet was meats, wild meat, fresh meat, fish, berries, wild rice and that was our bread and butter. Now we're forced to eat a certain type of food. We're more sedentary. We're more, like, we're just like sitting ducks. We're asking for it sort of speak. Like we're just saying 'OK, we're going to sit back and enjoy this free handout [welfare] and we're just going to sit tight and hopefully somebody will look after us.' This is what the mentality is. Welfare has a lot to do with that.

"When they killed a moose back in One Man Lake, they used to share. They used to share the moose with the community. Now you can't do that. You can't go to every house and share the moose. You can't do that. There's just too many people, you see, because there's three different communities, three different groups. There's bound to be conflict.

"Maybe the aggression that we're doing today is because we're sniffing out and we're showing violence and waste. Maybe that's our way of rebelling, like we don't agree with what they did to us. We don't agree with what the government did to us. The genocide.

"I believe they owe us. And it's not the money that's going to resolve a lot of the problems here. It's not the money. They can pump billions of dollars into this community and it's still not going to be the answer. What's going to be the answer is if we change the life and lives of each of the community members, to change their way of life.

"What we gave up at One Man Lake and Swan Lake we'll never replace. We'll never replace that with money, OK? Never. No matter how much they try to give us, whether it's $50,000 for a baseball field or $50 million for a land settlement, it's not going to do it. That's not the question. That's not the problem. What we gave up is the problem. What we gave up, what we're still giving up right now—our lives, our kids' lives. Yesterday, for example, somebody died because of complications from diabetes.

"There's the billions of dollars that they're making from our lands. This is what we gave up. The two hydro dams that sit between my communities. They're making billions of dollars profit. There's a difference here, millions and billions. So this is what I mean by money. Like the money part is nothing. This is what I'm saying, they'll never replace that and what they have to provide us is something that will impact our way of life for my community. For example, why couldn't they give us funding for education, more funding for education, specialized education? A lot of our children are special education needs students. They need that, remedial opportunities.

"When they took away our livelihood, fishing, commercial fishing [because of the mercury poisoning], I think they also took with them a way of life. Our main staple was fish and they took that away from us and we have to find alternative ways of surviving now and the only way would be education. That's the only way out of the whole mess, is to provide the education opportunities for our children. Get them to become what they want to be. We need lawyers, doctors, etc. etc.

"That's the only way and we have to educate our adults too, our adult population. They have to go back to school. To become self-reliant you got to have the education background to try and survive in the white man's world. This is a white man's world and we have to use their tools and I believe their tools is education.

"I want to use education as a stepping stone, a starting point to where I want to get. I'm including all band members, not just students. I'm including those dropouts and I'm including those girls who got pregnant when they were in high school. They had to quit to take care of the baby, those kind of people and I believe they have to be included in the movement.

"This is what I'm trying to start: a movement where education is a vehicle for us to get back on our feet again. It's not going to happen overnight. At least we got to have a plan, a five-year plan, maybe even a ten-year plan, 20-year plan. What are we going to do for an education system here? This is where I'm trying to get our kids moving, start thinking that way."

Ron McDonald is a strong believer in the traditional culture and beliefs of the Ojibway people.

"To this day, my tradition, my constitution, my way of thinking in terms of religion is governed by the drum. I follow the tradition of my culture. I'm an Ojibwa traditionalist. That's my way of thinking. I don't believe in culture, meaning the Anglicans, for example, or any other across-the-ocean religion. A religion that promotes their God to be punishing if you don't follow their rules. I don't believe in religion that hung, nailed their God to a cross. How can they do that to a God, a person of authority like that? How can they do that to a person, nailing their God, their Saviour to the cross? That's what I felt and I still feel that today. What kind of God is that?

"In our culture we don't do that. We don't do that to our Creator. We don't punish. In fact he's in equal balance with us. The religion that I follow is based on the medicine wheel. Everything comes in fours. The mind, spirit, the physical and emotional parts. The four colours, black, white, yellow and red. The four cardinal points of direction. The earth and the circle of life, the circle of the sun, the circle of years, the moon. Things go in cycles, the four seasons. That's what I believe. Ojibwa people are in harmony with nature. That's what I believe in.

"I tried the residential school preaching and teaching of religion. I tried that. It didn't work for me. In fact, look at what's happened with the residential school settlement where priests have abused their authority of trust to the children. For God sake, they abused the children that they had power over. They sexually abused them. They physically abused them, emotionally and all that. These people of that so-called religion of theirs, look what they've done. I mean it's a criminal act to humanity and they're getting away with it. I still think they're getting away with it."

His name, by the way, Ron Roy McDonald, has nothing to do with any Scottish ancestry. "It's a historical thing," Ron told me. "We had a traditional [Ojibway] name. For that matter, our family drum which is from One Man Lake is a traditional name. When I asked my dad about that, he felt that there was some connection with the treaty agent that came around to reserves in that era. They had created names for some of us and that's how we got the last name McDonald. It's an adopted name."

Ron had a pretty rough time of it when he attended Beaver Brae Secondary School where he encountered racism and bullying by the white students. The attitude towards native people in Kenora was difficult for a teenage Ojibway boy to deal with.

"I saw visibly firsthand what was going on outside the restaurants, turning us away. Telling us to get out, 'don't even have pop in my restaurant' when I was a kid. Like 'don't hang around my restaurant. Get out of here'. After dismissal from high school every day, I had to walk through some people's lawns to get home and they'd come running out with Labs [Labrador Retrievers] and stuff, chasing me out of their yard.

"I became frustrated as well when I was a teenager, having gone through Kenora residential school, going through high school, etc. etc. and seeing firsthand the racism problems that we had in the early times."

I asked Ron to what extent the government was prepared to accept responsibility for allowing the mercury from the paper mill to poison their rivers and lakes. "Well, that's the other part of my argument," he replied. "I believe the government is all a big cover up. I sincerely believe that. I have community members in Whitedog right now that are suffering mercury-related diseases and the government is covering it up by saying 'Oh he or she is suffering from Lorenzo's Oil.' [a genetic disease that destroys the brain] Lorenzo's Oil? To me, it has to be proven that it is Lorenzo's Oil first. I want to see a Japanese doctor say that. I want to see a Japanese doctor come over to my community and confirm that this is Lorenzo's Oil."

Five residents of Whitedog were taken to a Winnipeg hospital in March, 1977, after becoming intoxicated sniffing gasoline at a party. They died in the hospital shortly after arrival and autopsies were performed to determine the cause of death.

All five were known to eat fish from the poisoned river system on a regular basis and brain tissue samples were taken to determine if the methylmercury had affected their brains.

Area residents said it was essential that the tissue samples be tested to confirm their contention that mercury poisoning was a very real and present danger for the people living in Whitedog and Grassy Narrows. The tests showed that damage had, indeed, been done to the brains.

According to a May 6, 1977, article in *The Winnipeg Free Press*, several residents at Whitedog were known to have the telltale signs of mercury poisoning—"numbness in the limbs, trembling, inability to control their movements and tunnel vision."

The article went on to say: "The federal and Ontario governments have been testing people but have yet to confirm one official case of the disease named after the Japanese chemical town where hundreds have died and thousands have been horribly crippled. In Minamata an industry dumped mercury into the sea from which the city took much of its food."

Not surprisingly, the article said: "Government officials have indicated the problem is not as serious as the Indians seem to think it is."

Dr Brian Wheatley of the federal health department appeared on a Global Television Network program around that time and said extensive tests were carried out on almost 100 Ojibways on the reserve in April and May of 1976 and 31 individuals exhibited symptoms which could be caused by mercury pollution. He said more extensive tests would have to be carried out to confirm it.

"I have a strong feeling that this is mercury related and all these diseases that's cropping up right now, for example, diabetes, lacquer sniffing and all these things, social problems," Chief McDonald told me. "It's all related to mercury [poisoning], the mercury issue. We've got a historical problem with the mercury and I'm also speaking for the Indians that are now affected by the mercury and why it is a problem. They [government officials] do a report on our students, like our school kids. They tell us the problems, the behaviour problems, the academic shortcomings are not related to mercury at all.

"Why do they keep saying that? Every second page, 'mercury is not related to the issue here.' They're trying to escape their responsibilities. They're trying to run away from their responsibilities. They're trying to deny. They're denying what the problem is and, of course, when you deny something, it builds up. It comes out the wrong way and this is what we think."

"It sounds like a very sick recording," Josephine Mandamin told me. "What are they [government people] trying to say? Why keep repeating it? We know it has <u>everything</u> to do with the mercury, the sniffing, the alcohol. It has everything to do with it."

"They're giving us wrong information," Chief McDonald said. "They're giving us lies and they're giving us more ways of hurting ourselves. For example, the sniffing, the drinking, lack of housing, the water quality. We've been addressing that just about every day, trying to tell Medical Services [in Ottawa], 'Hey, the water.' We gotta keep it at a certain level for safe drinking.

"This is what I mean by money will not replace what we're suffering right now. Money's not going to be the answer compared to what they're profiting. We've given up a lot for those things that they have so what we have to do is provide as much as we can to try and change the lives of our people, our young people particularly, and give them the opportunities, the learning experiences of education.

"Education is the key to turning this community around. Educating our young people, who they are, what they are, what they want to become, how they want to see the community change. That's the key — the school system. If we don't, we're just gonna have one vicious cycle of this lacquer sniffing and alcoholism.

"Right now, I'm just scratching the surface, see, right now, trying to change these people that are sniffing. Trying to change these people who are drinking their lives away. Trying to change these people of welfare mentality, the people who are saying to me, 'oh welfare will look after me'. We gotta change that frame of mind, that mentality."

He paused for a moment, scratched his head, and tried to figure out why the federal government was shipping fish into Whitedog from thousands of kilometres away in the Northwest Territories. "Why is Medical Services [federal government] paying thousands of dollars for trout to send them over here all the way from the Northwest Territories? Why couldn't we do the same thing with land-locked lakes that are not affected with mercury? We're thinking about stocking lakes that aren't mercury infected. There are lakes close by.

"Why couldn't they provide our people with jobs to go into these lakes and grow fish farms and then, in turn, these fish farms could feed our people to supplement their diet? Why couldn't they do that rather than, like today, as we speak, our frozen trout comes from the Northwest Territories. By the time it gets here, by the time it hits the frying pans, it's freeze-dried. It's not fresh. The fish has been frozen as long as six months sometimes. We all know that if you try to cook something that's been frozen for a long time it doesn't have the natural taste and the proteins. The vitamins have all evaporated. Their kind of trout is a little bit different from our trout. Their kind of trout is much, much, bigger.

"The kind of trout that we're so used to living with is the smaller medium-sized trout so it makes more sense that we provide from our own local area. That's the kind of stuff I'd like to see our people in the future taking over. Why couldn't they pay us? And this is the thing I was getting at with the fish farm idea. We're kind of brought up with fish. Our diet and our way of life is with fish. We're sort of connected and so that's why I say fish farming would be feasible, reasonable economic development."

Chapter 11

The attitude of most of the white citizens of Kenora towards the Ojibways living on the surrounding reserves in 1965 was quite similar to the attitude of whites in the segregationist states of the southern United States towards the black descendants of the millions of slaves who had been forcibly snatched from their villages in Africa.

Most restaurants in Kenora would not serve Aboriginals. Restrictions were placed on them that were not placed on the whites. Seven out of ten of the inmates at the local jail at any one time were Aboriginal.

Fred Kelly, a former chief of the band at Sabaskong, more than half way between Kenora and the American border, told me during an interview in 1996 what it was like: "For instance, you could go into the bus depot and you could see a bunch of people looking at the magazine rack. But, if you were Indian, you were told to leave. You couldn't do that. You weren't served properly at restaurants. There were certain places that you were made to feel you couldn't go and, in fact, there were places where you could not go. Things like, for instance, the beer par-lours where we weren't allowed to drink after eight o'clock at night."

Fred recalled going to a bar in Kenora and asking for a drink. The time was 8:10 p.m. "I can't serve you," the bartender said. "Why not?" Fred asked. "Because it's after eight o'clock."

Fred Kelly wasn't the type of person to simply accept that sort of restriction without a challenge. He asked to see the manager. "Why am I being cut off at eight o'clock when I haven't even had a drink? Why?" he asked the manager. "We can't serve Indians after eight o'clock," the manager replied. "We find that they get too rowdy. They can't hold their drink."

"And I said 'so what's so magical about 8 o'clock?' So I'm an Indian and I can see it's 8 o'clock now because it's 8 o'clock, albeit Central Standard Time and not Eastern Standard Time [one hour ahead] which presumes that, according to Eastern Standard Time, those Indians in Toronto, Thunder Bay, what not, would now be incapacitated by alcohol.'

"I was tired of being very sarcastic and tearing holes into this kind of theory. What is magical about 8 o'clock? Anyway, they apologized and they served me drinks and what not but I'm still not satisfied with that."

Andy White, a former chief of the Whitefish Bay reserve, about 95 kilometres southeast of Kenora, remembers what it was like at that time. "It was pretty rough," he told me. "There was a lot of racism. At that time you couldn't go in the bars — most of us that were trying to make something out of ourselves, working people in real life."

Andy recalled going into an optician's store and asking to have his glasses repaired. He was told that they couldn't fix them right away and he should come back a few days later. He then went outside and gave the glasses to a human rights worker who had been waiting outside. "He was a white guy from Toronto. I would give him my same glasses and he would walk in and ask if they could be fixed. 'Sure, right away,' the guy said.

"I walked in and said 'how come you're fixing up these glasses and you weren't going to fix mine?' And then they would say 'well he had an appointment' or 'he asked to come at this certain time.' 'But they're the same glasses I just gave you about two minutes ago.' They look surprised. 'Calm down', stuff like this.

"Same thing with the hotels. I walk into the hotel and say can I have a room? They say 'no'. Same [white] guy walks in there, 'can I have a room?' They said 'yeah'. So I go in and ask how come they wouldn't give me a room? 'Well, he had a reservation', they'd say. Bullshit. He <u>didn't</u> have a reservation. But that's how it was."

Fred Kelly went into a bar in Sioux Narrows, about 80 kilometres southeast of Kenora, with some friends on July 1st, Canada Day, and ordered a gin and tonic. His friends ordered beer. The manager came over to Fred's table and said: "How do you rate?" Fred asked: "What do you mean?" And the manager said: "Look what you're having." Fred didn't have to look because he knew he was drinking gin and tonic. At that point, the manager took the drink away and told Fred he couldn't have it. "Why not?" Fred asked. "We find our Indians behave better if they stick to beer," the manager replied.

A couple of years later, Fred was on national television with Justice Minister Pierre Elliott Trudeau, who later went on to become Prime Minister of Canada, and he told the story about the gin and tonic.

"So everybody got alerted," Fred recalled. "'Watch out for Fred Kelly because, if he comes into your establishment, he's here looking for trouble.'" Fred became known as a troublemaker because he was always out talking with the Ojibway people and identifying problems that had to be addressed.

"It became to me very painfully obvious, the mistreatment, not so much over liquor, but in all other areas," he recalled. "Then, our people, when I met with them, they would talk to me about some of their needs and some of the things that I could maybe deal with. But then it got to be spread out in terms of the kinds of things that were going on, with the children [who were being forcibly removed from their parents], the things that were going on with all aspects of their livelihood. I felt that something here was happening, that I had to do something about it and not me alone, personally, but something to do with the people.

"I became a little more outspoken and I started speaking out against the plight of our people in terms of attitudes, in terms of the racist prejudice, the mistreatment, incarceration, alcoholism, the whole range of issues, social issues. That was our situation and I wanted to attempt to bring to light the situation as we had it here in northwestern Ontario.

"The objective at that point was to talk about, and stress the need for, this conviction of self-determination and why our people couldn't have that despite the treaty of 1873 and if that was the relationship that was intended, then why was the Indian Act [of 1876] still there and why were we restricted and constrained to our reservation?

"The history of the Indian Act, which is a history in terms of the oppression that our people had received, but not only that, the reinforcement of the attitudes of society that we were second-class citizens and that we didn't belong any place. We were 'unemployed', we were 'drunk', we were 'sickly', we were 'starving' and a 'drain on the taxpayers' and so on and so forth."

There was more to it than the treatment Ojibway people received at the restaurants and bars. A lot more. For three years in a row, flooding from dams built by Ontario Hydro had wiped out their wild rice crops. The financial loss was severe.

Then there were the arbitrary rules about when you could, or could not, trap. If a beaver was on the north side of the Canadian National Railways tracks at a certain time of the year, you could trap it. If it was on the south side, you couldn't.

Fred remembered that problem well: "The Ministry of Natural Resources in Ontario, which was one of the most bigoted ministries that ever existed in terms of subjugating our freedom as traditional [Ojibway] people, proclaimed that the fur trapping season ends south of the CN line on March 30, I believe it was, something like that. North of the CN line it's extended to April 15th.

"Then again, I took off in my little tirade and asked, 'how does the beaver know that it is midnight March 30th? What is magical about his fur or her fur that at midnight it all of a sudden becomes not any good and the two weeks extra allows your [Ojibway] people north of the CN line and, which reminds me, how does the beaver know that he is south or north of the CN line?' My purpose was to tear holes at the logic, the supposed logic, that was there. Now that issue is very dear to our people in terms of their relationship with the land."

The main problem was that many Ojibway men made their income trapping in the winter and guiding at the tourist camps in the summer. However, as the fishing season didn't start until the middle of May, arbitrarily ending the trapping season on March 30 and April 15 left them without any source of income for several weeks.

"It was pretty frustrating because no matter where you looked, you're pretty powerless," Fred recalled. "There was no jobs. There was sickness. There was no movement. We were at the mercy of the Department of Indian Affairs and, to some extent, the [provincial] Department of Public Welfare. It was a real mess." In fact, some Ojibway families were squatting on the outskirts of Kenora and picking garbage in order to survive.

An Indian-White Committee had been formed in Kenora to explore possible ways of improving relations between the native minority on the surrounding reserves and the white majority. Fred Kelly was invited to attend and subsequently became co-chairman. At about the same time, he was invited to speak at the Kenora Chamber of Commerce about the ongoing problems between the whites and the Ojibways.

"I guess, for them, it was sort of like a sincere effort to bridge the gap," Fred said. "But to me, if there was such a thing as an Indian problem, I didn't refer to it as an Indian 'problem'. I dealt with it as an Indian 'fact', the way things are. And so I became outspoken and then I was invited by people here and there, several groups, I was invited here and there."

Fred, who was 23 at the time, was working for the provincial Department of Public Welfare as a case officer and he had an insider's view of some things that he found to be quite disturbing.

"There were many things that were very discomforting," he told me. "I'll give you a case in point. I was administering welfare programs from Sioux Lookout [north] to Upsala [east] to the Manitoba border [west] and just north of Sioux Narrows. I was administering about six different social assistance programs from the Province of Ontario, including general welfare, disabled person's allowance, blind person's allowance, mother's allowance, deserted fathers, deserted mothers and so on, so forth.

"We were told at that time, in our orientation course in Toronto, that you do not publicize [among the Ojibway population] what is available from the Department of Public Welfare. However, if asked about specific questions, you were obligated to tell.

"People would have to know what the buttons were and how it was working so that they could ask questions. But most people who are down and out simply do not know. I could not go and tell them what was available and yet I may know of some certain circumstances that might address a need, but I was directly told that I could not tell them. But, if they asked, I had an obligation to tell them about a specific program. Now that's a sort of Catch-22. You gotta know about a blind person's allowance before I could tell you the full story of a blind person's allowance. But, if you don't know anything about the blind person's allowance, then you're still in the dark.

"The Ontario Department of Public Welfare's rationale, of course, has always been cost cutting under the guise of preventing people from fraudulently obtaining programs and so on, so forth. It was a very, very discomforting position.

"I should point out that I was not hired to deal with the Indian needs as such. I was hired to do the work of a welfare field worker as any other welfare field worker would do. I was always very, very much aware, not that I was looking for anything in particular, but I was always very much aware of the differences in approaches taken [to whites and Aboriginals]."

Working for the provincial government meant that Fred had to wear a suit and tie on the job and carry a briefcase. "People started looking at me as, within the town of Kenora, as almost like 'our Indian success story.' It was only a dictate of the job that I had to dress this way. I would have preferred not to have to wear these things, but that was the way it was."

About twelve years before Fred was walking down Main Street with his suit, tie and briefcase, he was a young Ojibway boy squatting on the outskirts of Kenora and picking garbage in order to survive. "A lot of people were homeless. There's no decent housing and there still isn't and where are they going to move? So many lived along the shores, many lived along wherever they could to gain access such as they could and social services were not available to our people.

"What were we living on? I'll give you an example. I'm not going to name names here as to who I saw doing whom, but I can tell you that I myself was squatting in and around Kenora when I was 11 years old. I was living off the garbage, the best in the garbage that was left over. That's what was available."

On finishing Grade 8 at St. Mary's Indian Residential School in Kenora, Fred Kelly was shipped several hundred kilometres away from home to the St. Paul's High School at the former Catholic mission of Lebret, Saskatchewan, which was operated by the Oblate Fathers. Lebret is a tiny community at the eastern end of Mission Lake, about 70 kilometres northeast of Regina.

Why go several hundred kilometres west to Saskatchewan in order to get your high school education? "Apparently, it was just simply unthinkable for us to go to a public school and the rationale being, as far as the churches were concerned, they wanted to see our [Catholic] religion intact and to keep me from falling prey to the evils of society, whatever the hell that was.

"My continuous rebellion [to the officials at Indian Affairs] was, 'explain to me why I cannot go to any of these high schools in town [Kenora]?' It was never discussed. It was just because you cannot. Simply the answer was because you cannot go and we're going to send you where we think is best for you. So I went to Lebret."

All of the letters Fred sent home and all of the letters that were sent from home were censored by the school authorities. In its 1889 Rules and Regulations for Industrial Schools, the Department of Indian Affairs directed that, while children were to be allowed to write to their parents twice a year, their letters as well as all incoming mail "must be scrutinized by the Principal before transmission or delivery."

"I would imagine it was to keep out outside influences," Fred suggested. "Don't forget that when residential schools were set up, and I didn't know about this until later on when I found out some of the policies, the residential schools were based on total assimilation.

"Duncan Campbell Scott, [the Deputy Superintendent General of Indian Affairs from 1913 to 1932] said in the House of Commons when he announced the residential school system something to the effect of this is the best system that's going to be there and it is going to be implemented until not one body, until not one Indian, remains that has not been absorbed into the Canadian polity. So it was based on assimilation, obviously.

"And that's putting it kindly. I'm talking about cultural genocide here because you were talking about a system of the Indian Act that was so oppressive that forced the kids to be taken into school. The [white] Indian agent was the person who was in charge of enforcing the Indian Act. You needed permission to leave the reservation and he could enforce the law in that way, so he was also judge and jury and also the enforcer. Check these out in the Indian Act and it's quite clear the powers that he had and that was the judicial system on reserve, remnants of which we still see and so to that extent, by going at the parents, if you were not in school, they could go after the parents and literally force them by law.

"When the family allowances [a monthly payment to Canadian families with children regardless of income] were later to be instituted [in 1945] and being applicable as universal, then the Indian Act was also amended so that people could not receive family allowances if their kids were not in school. So they used that Indian Act and coercion among the parents to force their kids into school. Those that defied that were, in fact, jailed or charged.

"Such was the power of the Indian agent, such was the power of the Department of Indian Affairs who then worked in co-operation with the churches to carry out this policy and thus the residential school system. Most of them were established somewhere around the turn of the century and I believe St. Mary's [in Kenora] was established in 1902, 1903, somewhere in there."

Fred said the British Government had a "detribalization policy" in Canada and in Africa and that the whole purpose of that policy was to wipe out the tribal system. Stop it dead in its tracks. "When we say it kindly, we say assimilation. But the downright policy was extermination which is cultural genocide, by extermination. Let me give you an example. One of the Indian agents at the time, Duncan Campbell Scott, speaking in support of this residential school policy said, the best thing that we can do for these Indian people is to educate the savagery out of them, therefore, we must take them away from their parents, isolate them."

Fred quoted Scott as saying. "Secondly, they must not speak their language. If we wish to remove them from their culture, we must remove them from their language." That's why he couldn't speak Ojibway in the school system, Fred said. "Remove them from their culture, remove them from our customs and our traditions and our own sacred beliefs."

Despite the unrelenting efforts of the Sisters and Fathers to drum it out of him, Fred held on to his own language during the unhappy days he spent in the Indian residential school system. "I've never lost my language and that was a struggle," he said rather proudly.

Nevertheless, he did suffer the emotional and physical abuse that was so often an inescapable part of attending one of the Indian residential schools. "The indoctrination of the residential school system did not suit me well, did not suit me. I didn't like the indoctrination, the regimentation, the brainwashing. I got beaten up, my head bashed, kicked, beaten up time and again, physically, emotionally and all the time I felt that, and the outcome was, I was stuttering at the time and I didn't know why and I didn't even know what it was called.

"The emotional turmoil of being in a residential school had to come out in some way or another in what is, might be known as, aberrations of behaviour. Some would wet the bed, some would be reticent, some would just withdraw. I would stutter. Other people would just outright be defiant and cause greater abuse to themselves. It's an emotional release and, in my case it was an emotional result, because I obviously don't stutter now and shortly after I left, I didn't stutter anymore."

Being able to speak Ojibway was a big help when Fred Kelly was out in the bush in 1965 talking to the Ojibways in the Kenora area and identifying issues that had to be addressed.

However, because he was employed by the government of Ontario, he always had to preface his remarks when he was talking outside the reserves about the conditions the Ojibways were living in with a disclaimer. "I always had to preface my remarks by saying I'm speaking personally, not as a member of the Ontario Civil Service. I prefaced my remarks that way. People started noticing that I had to speak with a preemptive disclaimer and so I didn't feel free."

Nevertheless, he continued meeting with people in an effort to determine the most effective way of bringing about positive change in the lives of the Ojibways. "I went to each reserve to the extent that I could. I had no car so sometimes I'd take the bus or hitch a ride with somebody. I'd go and talk with people, see what's happening, trying to find a commonality, not so much on blood. I knew all the issues.

"I was looking for more of a commonality of action, what they were feeling. And then, I said, 'I think probably what we need to do is call attention to our situation and that we want some say in how to deal with these things. Do you agree?' They said, 'OK. Yeah. We agree.' It was then I started talking about the idea of a demonstration.

"I was 23 at the time and the people more or less went about in such a way that they were not being extremely vociferous about their situation. We have to deal with it, but no one's going to listen and so we had to do certain things ourselves. We had to agree between ourselves if we had to do something ourselves.

"We didn't preconceive. The ideas had to come from the people. Like I didn't go on a rhetorical binge. If it's going to mean something to you, it's got to have something that touches your heart.

"Things started to pick up. There was momentum. There was all kinds of controversy like blowing up the Trans-Canada Highway, the railways, the river dams. There were all kinds of things happening."

The Ojibways had decided that they had suffered more than enough discrimination and abuse. Something, something dramatic, had to be done to draw attention to the conditions they were being forced to live in.

Some of the more militant leaders wanted to blow up the Trans-Canada Highway at Kenora. Others suggested dynamiting the railway tracks or one of the big dams Ontario Hydro had built across their rivers to generate electricity for people living in white communities.

The more peaceful among them suggested that it would be better to adopt non-violent means of attracting attention to their situation. They leaned toward holding a conference on the issues they were confronted with and a peaceful march through the streets of Kenora.

Everyone agreed that something had to be done to make the federal government in Ottawa and the provincial government in Toronto sit up and listen. They were tired of being treated as second-class citizens.

And then, of course, there was the inevitable tie-in to the growing civil rights movement in the United States.

At the time that some Ojibways were talking about blowing up the Trans-Canada Highway at Kenora, America was still reeling from the psychological shock of riots that broke out in the crowded black neighborhoods of Rochester, Philadelphia and New York in 1964 and continued on into the black neighborhood of Watts, South Central Los Angeles, in August 1965.

Sixteen thousand soldiers from the 160th Infantry, the 1st Reconnaissance Squadron, the 18th Armoured Cavalry, and the 40th Armoured Division were sent into the riot area in Los Angeles.

By the time the six days of rioting came to an end, 34 people had been killed, 1,072 were injured, and 4,000 had been arrested. Almost 1,000 buildings were damaged or destroyed and the damage was estimated at US$40 million.

"A lot of people in Canada who'd seen that [riots] would say: 'Look at the situation down in the United States, isn't it terrible? Isn't it too bad? Isn't it too bad if we would let it get that way here? Aren't we lucky we don't have a problem?', Fred said. "And then, when in fact it turned out that Canada did have a problem, it became an 'Indian problem'.

"We were not in contact with any of the black people. We didn't know the ideology, the motivations and what not, except that the Americans were racist and racism was widespread as well in Canada."

A commission set up by the Governor of California later identified the cause of the riots as high unemployment, poor schools, and inferior living conditions. One year after the Watts Riot, the militant Black Panther Party of Self-Defense was formed in Oakland, California. It advocated armed self-defence to protect people living in black neighborhoods from the widespread police brutality that existed at that time.

A perceived connection between Fred Kelly and the militant black civil rights leaders in the United States became a major problem. "I went to Grassy Narrows [about 85 kilometres northeast of Kenora] and met with the pulp cutters up in their community and they said, yeah, they were supportive of us in our efforts. It would be a peaceful demonstration. Then I got a phone call that night from the chief who wanted to know what was this mad idea of Fred Kelly and why he wants to be like the black leaders. The pulp cutters had changed their minds but they asked if I could come back and see them. I had no car but I said that I would try and get up there."

He hitched a ride on one of the pulp trucks and went back up to Grassy Narrows to see the workers. "And I told them, I said 'no, this is yours, your march', I said, 'I'm not even sure if I'm going to be speaking. You guys will have to determine what is going to be said and done.' So they felt better and said they would be at the march."

There was no doubt that the white establishment in Kenora and some of the more docile Ojibways were opposed to what Fred was doing. "I was being labelled as a radical, irrational radical, out for self-promotion, and what not. There was talk about Stokely Carmichael and Rap Brown [two of the more militant leaders of the black civil rights movement in the United States] and 'the mindless militants in the States.' All of these adjectives were being thrown, bandied about."

In other words, 23-year-old Fred Kelly was fast becoming a threat to the established order of things. "I got actively involved in the Indian movement when I was 14," he told me. "I was swimming with the rest of the kids in the summer time when my own chief and council came and got me. I was in grade eight at the time and they said 'we would like you to write a letter on our behalf about timber rights.' Well I don't know a thing about timber rights. 'We'll tell you,' they said. 'All you gotta do is write.' So that's how I got involved.

"And then, after that, whenever they were at a council meeting, sometimes, now that I had started to get to know things and being brash and what not, I would say, 'well look I have an opinion here to offer and I got something to say' and I would raise my hand and they wouldn't let me speak. I got a little turned off by that and the chief got me outside afterwards and said 'don't feel bad about what's happening.

Your time will come when you are going to be looked upon by people too, say what it is what you have to say. But in the meantime, listen well.' So, by the time I was 23, I'd already been involved in the Indian movement for some nine years."

Fred Kelly's superiors at the provincial Department of Public Welfare started expressing concern about his public campaign to draw attention to the plight of the Ojibways and asked him to tone it down. So he quit the department and went to work for the Kenora Children's Aid Society.

Harold Treen, the director of the Children's Aid Society, was sympathetic to what Fred was attempting to accomplish for his people. "He said, 'I would like to hire you to do some studies within the native, within these Indian communities and look at the situation of what gives rise to the situation that causes children to be taken into care and what can be done by way of preventive measures. You dealt with the problem when it happened. Now we're dealing with the symptoms.'

"And so he hired me and then he also said this which was really remarkable, an obvious time to stick his neck out because he was going against the establishment back then. And he said, 'Fred', he said, 'when you speak, I want you to speak as Fred Kelly and as a member of the Children's Aid Society. I want you to have no qualms about that because I'm getting sick and tired of hearing who you're not representing but you're speaking as an individual. A lot of people agree with your views.'"

Fred took immediate advantage of the freedom to speak his mind that had been given to him. "I had laid the groundwork of getting the people together and now we had to go and see them and it was not a situation where you bring them in, into a group, and tell them what you want to do. You had to go out there and find out what it is they want. If they're still supportive, what they want to do and what it is they want to say. That was the trick."

And that's why he trudged for mile upon mile in the forests tracking down Ojibway pulpwood cutters and talking to them about the upcoming march. "Hopefully if you can meet with them during their lunch break then they would go home and they would talk about it so it became a community point of discussion. Then we'd move to another community like Whitefish Bay, Shoal Lake, Whitedog and other places.

"The issues that came out very clearly were these: the drunkenness and the incarceration in the Kenora jails. So what's happening? What can be done that is being done elsewhere or isn't being done? The incarceration, the violence, all those things had something to do with how you feel about alcohol and the treatment of alcoholism. Because at that time, amongst our people, it was treated as a behavioural aberration rather than a disease requiring sophisticated treatment in Toronto and in other areas.

"You couldn't get any welfare. You couldn't get anything so you just lived as close as you could to whatever was available. And so it was a pretty discouraging state of affairs amongst our people and that's why they were talking to me as though they saw at least somebody who could probably articulate, rather than being able to do something about, the situation and I certainly did not offer any solutions.

"There were all sorts of other things going on, There were all kinds of stories happening around, at about the same time. One judge, I forget his name, referred to a 'suicide cult' where [Ojibway] people were laying in front of the railway tracks and what not. I have no way of disputing that to say whether that was true or not."

In getting people ready for the big march in Kenora, Fed Kelly emphasized over and over again that they had to show initiative. It had to be their cause. Their march. "It was a time when our people decided for themselves that this is the time we had to take matters into our own hands, which was, in my opinion, the rising of the point of self-determination. Self-determination then had taken on different meanings. They are not different meanings in the sense of different aspects of self-determination. Economic self-sufficiency, better housing, better living conditions, treaties, the right to self-government, the right to a nation, the right to your own language, the right to your own culture.

"It wasn't until 1958 when our people could go into liquor stores. I'm not making a value judgment as to whether that was good or right, take a drink of rye and you're a criminal. I'm not saying that that's good or bad. I'm saying it's your right. If you want to exercise it, that's your prerogative. All of these things that are supposed to be otherwise available to you and me were denied for so long to our people. Why? Because of the Indian Act and because of the Department of Indian Affairs."

Fred started working on a conference that was to be held in Kenora in November, 1965, to focus attention on the appalling conditions the Ojibways were living in. He thought that might be the best time for them to stage some sort of demonstration or march.

"I ran into the Quakers [a pacifist group formally known as the Religious Society of Friends]. I was introduced to them. They were very supportive and the Student Union for Peace Action [Canadian university students actively opposed to poverty, nuclear armament and the war in Vietnam] who were at the time marching all over the place and they're all willing to come en masse to hold a demonstration."

Ron McDonald's father Roy was chief of the Whitedog band at that time. "He was very supportive of going either way," Ron told me in 1996. "Going all the way with guns or going through civil disobedience type of action, marching, rallying, using non-violence as a way of doing it."

And that reminds me of something Fred Kelly once said during one of our interviews. "How long can you subjugate a person?" he asked. "The most timid of animals, the rabbit, you corner a rabbit in the forest, there's no way out, that rabbit will fight. It will try to fight. So you got to leave it some way out. The woodchuck, the groundhog, they chatter their teeth."

Ron emphasized that his father was not a violent person. "He didn't believe in guns, using guns to get what you want or blowing up bridges. But he did believe in marching and doing other ways of drawing attention from the government. So this is the way he tried to influence everybody at that time. He tried to tell the Kellys, the Whitefish Bay people, the other tribes to try and do something more civil, using different tactics to get our way like marches. He was a very, very, prominent person in the 1965 march when they marched through Kenora. He was there and I believe that I carry some of that as well."

After considerable discussion among the Ojibway leadership, a consensus emerged that blowing up bridges or highways was not the best answer to drawing attention to their plight. "That was seen as a very destructive, negative kind of talk and a very provocative kind of approach," Fred recalled. "What we had to do was respect the style of our people, the way of doing things which is a peaceful way, a collective way. We had to respect the traditions and our values."

The offers of support from the Quakers and the Student Union for Peace Action were very much appreciated but Fred felt it would be better for the Ojibways to do something on their own. "Somehow it didn't seem to me the logistics were quite right and secondly I thought that our message would probably get lost in the whole mass of a massive demonstration."

So then, rather than involving the Student Union for Peace Action and other outside groups, they decided on a march through the streets of Kenora by Ojibway people from the reserves in the surrounding area and a few local supporters from the white community.

Allan White, Andy White's cousin and also a former chief of the Whitefish Bay band, is proud of the fact that he took part in the big march in Kenora in November, 1965. "We were young and ambitious and whether we were stupid or crazy, we were part of that march. We just went there to support something that we wanted to be part of."

Allan was a youth of about 20 at the time and did not play a key role in organizing the march. "My father [who was the chief at that time] was one of the people that orchestrated that march in Kenora and this was specifically what they were after—control—not being controlled [by the bureaucrats at Indian Affairs].

"They were trying very hard to get attention by the federal government and they were trying to find different avenues of getting their attention because of the environment that they were starting to realize that was being created.

"When my father talks about that, he says that Jim Davidson was the mayor in Kenora at that time and Jim Davidson wanted to help in the way of communication, to communicate the real needs of the Anishinaabe [Ojibway] people because he was witnessing things that was happening in First Nations in the area.

"So they were trying to find a place where it would be suitable for a march like that and I guess Kenora was chosen probably because of the mayor and because Rat Portage [Kenora's original name] has a very unique history as a town itself."

The name Rat Portage was derived from the English translation of the Ojibway name for the "portage to the country of the muskrat." The community changed its name to Kenora in 1905, primarily because a potential new industry — Maple Leaf Flour Company — understandably balked at the thought of having the word "Rat" displayed on its flour bags.

"So there is a lot of history in there and also this was the central gathering area for all Lake of the Woods peoples, First Nations like Big Island, Grassy, Whitefish, Shoal Lake and all the First Nations. That was their place where they went once every year in the summer."

Allan believed that many of the residents of Kenora were actually of mixed blood. "An elder from Shoal Lake told me that the majority of Kenora, the town of Kenora, back then had Indian blood in them. A lot of them are Métis [half native, half French] that he knew as a young man back, probably at the first world war. So that's how the town was built by them. A lot of them don't want anything to do with who they are, he used to tell me."

Josephine Mandamin had heard the same story. "It [inter-marriage] was there precisely," she said. "It was there from the landing of Columbus. It's always been there. But it wasn't until it became a monetary thing, a money thing. How you could have access to free this and money for that through the Bill C-31 [an Act that became law in June, 1985, to restore status and membership rights to native women who had lost their rights by having married white men], that it became popular to claim that you had Indian blood. Before that you hid it with a passion."

Did she ever deny her Ojibway heritage? "I never did. I never did," she answered emphatically.

In an article that was published in the *Kenora Daily Miner and News* on October 29, 1965, Fred Kelly wrote about the big conference that was going to be held to address the problems Ojibways faced that had been planned for November 13 and 14 under the sponsorship of the Indian-White Committee.

"As an Indian, this writer wishes the reader to realize that we urgently require your help if we are to be successful and if we are to quicken our social transition and evolution," he wrote. "Unless a meaningful 'dialogue' is created in the community between the Indian people and the whites — between the economically depressed and the affluent, between Indian Society and Culture and the rapidly changing white community, then we cannot expect true progress."

There was a picture of Fred on the front page of the next day's *Kenora Daily Miner and News* in a suit, white shirt and classy tie. He was on the front page again on Wednesday, November 17, 1965. The headline read:

**Indians are Frustrated;
Uprisings Sure to Follow**

An angry Fred Kelly was quoted as telling white citizens of Kenora: "We go from crisis to crisis, but what about in between?"

The meeting had been called to discuss the fallout of a negative article published on July 31, 1965, in the *Weekend Magazine* with the headline — "The Indian: an Abandoned and Dispossessed People." The article claimed Ojibway children in the Kenora area were being taught to hate white people.

"The Indian is at the point of frustration ... is at the point of violence," Fred was quoted as saying at the meeting called to discuss the magazine article. "If you don't see it in Town, then you just don't want to see it. Why are Indians wrecking property? Why are there night riders along Golf Course Road? The Indian-White Committee was given the ball ... we wanted an audience to hear grievances, but no one was there ... God curse the day when the Indian will have to take to violence. The Indian is a peace-loving man, but he is a human being ... he has been forsaken while the white man has gone ahead ... I put it to you in no uncertain terms, the Indians will rise."

Bishop H. E. Hives, who had spent 40 years working with and among Ojibway people, said too much media attention was being paid to everything that was wrong in the Ojibway communities and not enough to such things as the success he and his colleagues had had in establishing co-ops in northern reserves.

The article in the *Kenora Daily Miner and News* quoted him as saying responsibility on the part of the Ojibway is the one ingredient which can change his life from what it is to what it might be.

He made reference to new houses the government had recently built at Whitedog which were now in no better condition than the rundown shacks they had replaced a month earlier. Houses worth $4,500 were being sold to the Ojibways for $50.

"Liquor is a curse, changing Indians from quiet, gentle and dignified people," he said, "degrading them to the point where they lose their self-respect."

He was quoted as saying: "We have all made mistakes, unintentionally. We have been too kind and have destroyed the thing, initiative and human dignity, which all men must have."

An Ojibway by the name of Paul Bruyere was quoted as saying: "The white man is always up here and the Indian is way down there. The whites don't come down and the Indians can't come up."

Bruyere, who had worked hard all his life to support his large family, was quoted as saying that dignity and self-respect had been taken away from the Ojibways because they have been controlled. As an illustration, he told of how, when he bought and sold cattle, he had to seek permission from the Indian agent. The fact that he could not control his own possessions robbed him of a sense of dignity.

Hundreds of Ojibways marched down the main street of Kenora on a snowy November 21, 1965. The march was a terrific success and generated headlines in newspapers across Canada. Ojibway people were brought in by buses from all of the reserves in the Kenora area.

"I, myself, went down to my own community [Sabaskong] with the bus to pick up the people," Fred said, "and we didn't tell them, 'get on that damned bus' or anything like that. 'Who else wants to come?' We had to order a second bus. I phoned Whitefish Bay and they also wanted another bus. Grassy Narrows wanted another bus. We had about 400 people, maybe 500."

Up until that time, the Aboriginal people of Canada had not participated in demonstrations to draw attention to their situation and speak for themselves. "It was an accomplishment," Fred said. "After that march we went back to the church basement where we had started from and everybody felt good, everybody felt empowered. It was an extreme culmination of organizational and tactical activities that we had to go through, but not extremely difficult in convincing our people that they wanted to do something, that they had to do something. So this was a grassroots movement, a community movement and I did not march up to the front of the podium and say, 'well here's what we've got to say.'

"We had a prepared text and they, the people and the chiefs, not all chiefs, it was community people who were there and they said, 'well, Peter Seymour and Fred Kelly should make the presentation on your behalf' so I ran the first part and Peter Seymour ran the other and then people went home thinking well, we've done something for ourselves."

Allan White was convinced that the march—and the front-page headlines it generated across Canada—was a turning point in the history of the Ojibway people of the Kenora area.

The headline in the *Winnipeg Tribune* said: "400 march for equality." The subhead said: "Kenora Indians air grievances."

"This had an impact on First Nations people," Allan told me in 1966. "They were successful in terms of that march. That was the turning point of the Anishinaabe people.

"That was the turning point that the federal government and the provincial government finally opened their eyes in terms of political —not in terms of business and not in terms of the social fabric of life—but in terms of politics. That was the turning point.

"That was the awakening for Canada, for the world, that the Anishinaabe people were the victims. Whether it's genocide or something like that, it's in the eyes of the individual people themselves as far as I'm concerned."

After the march, the Ojibway people crowded into an auditorium to make a presentation to the Kenora Town Council.

"Contrary to many rumors," a brief read alternately by Fred Kelly and the Grand Chief of Grand Council Treaty #3 said, "we are here not to beat the drums of war, but rather to smoke the pipe of peace. But the peace we seek, unlike the peace we have, is a peace based upon dignity, equality, and justice for the Indian people."

The brief went on to say that "poverty ravages our people" and the "greatest majority of our people exist on seasonal jobs and welfare cheques ... Many of our people have complained bitterly of discrimination in Kenora business establishments. In a number of cases they have pointed out that regardless of proper conduct and decorum, they were either denied service or they were given insolent treatment. Even though we depend so much upon the Town of Kenora we protest being subjected to such indignities in the pursuit of the necessities of life."

The brief held out hope that a reasonable accommodation could be reached between the approximately 3,000 Ojibways living on reserves in the Kenora area and the white citizens of the town.

"In spite of the many grievances listed here, we believe that the great majority of Kenora citizens are sympathetic and responsive to our problems. What we need is an official instrument to activate this public sympathy."

The brief called for the establishment of a special mayor's committee on Indian/white relations "to act as a medium for the adjustment of grievances between Indian and Non Indian people, and to promote greater long range inter-racial cooperation and understanding in this area...

"Such an initiative undertaken by the Town of Kenora would give our people more hope than they have experienced in generations. It would mark the beginning of a new and vital relationship between the Indian and non-Indian people of this area. We cannot and do not expect miracles overnight. But in the words of the late U.S. President, John F. Kennedy: 'LET US BEGIN'".

During our interview in 1996, Fred Kelly told me they asked the Town Council to support their request for an extension of the fur trapping season. "We weren't talking about the unfettered right to trap on Crown land and all this kind of stuff. We were simply talking about the extension of the fur trapping season, but it did have those ramifications which are close to you as a person, as a trapper, as an Indian living in a community because that's your source of livelihood, your relationship with the land, which brought in all that.

"The other issue that we talked about was the alcoholism. We simply asked that the Alcoholism Research Foundation be sent to Northwestern Ontario and start having a presence. Why? With their expertise and their knowledge of alcoholism, what could be done to look at developing a strategy with, by and for our people? That was the idea. Again, not an unreasonable request. It's available to citizens. It's an Ontario agency.

"Another one that we asked for is radio telephones be established in the isolated communities. Why? We documented cases, for instance, where the closest ambulance and the closest police detachment was some 25 miles away.

"The fourth thing that we asked for was that there be a Mayor's committee on race relations to deal with ongoing race relations. So, when you look back at the time, these were not outrageous demands."

They got everything they had asked for.

Fred Kelly put a rather interesting slant on the negotiations between the Canadian government and the Ojibways and the frustration Lieutenant-Governor Alexander Morris and other representatives of the Canadian government had expressed during the treaty-making process of 1871–77 about the fact that the many tribes were "not of one mind."

"Imagine," Fred said, "if I had the audacity or the capability to go to Europe and, say that we're back in 1492, and say: 'All you people seem to be white, get together and come to me with a common voice and tell me what it is that you want, then we can talk.'"

As Fred so aptly pointed out, the Germans, French, English, and the Scots were most definitely not of one mind—despite the fact that they were all white.

"You transpose that [European reality] to the situation as what happened which is the same colonial attitude that has progressed up to now and say: 'You may be Algonquin, you may be Ojibwa, you may be Cree, but you're all under Section 35 [of the Canadian Constitution] as Aboriginal People. And you're one and the same so come, get together, have one common voice. You must be united.'

"So many times your [white] people fall for that fallacy that you must be united. How can I be united with other people who are of a different nation? That's another form of assimilation. We are as diverse as the Canadian mosaic is.

"The best that you could really go for is a uniformity of cause, because the same oppression, the same situations are what confront us. But you must do it as an Ojibwa Nation, you must do it as a Mohawk Nation or you must do it as a Cree Nation and in doing that, you must do it as a community. Within the community you must do it as a family. Within the family you must do it as individuals.

"If you want unanimity, that translates into uniformity of cause. We agree to pursue our treaty rights for instance. That's about as unified as you can get. But to be unified and to speak with one voice forever and a day is just simply impractical, impossible and not necessarily desirable.

"A case in point. Our Anishinaabe [Ojibway] traditional system is a patriarchal system. The Haudenosaunee, commonly called the Iroquois, is matriarchal. Now what is the commonality there?

"What has become known as the Indian culture, if there is such a thing, is a commonality towards the amalgamation of what appears to be common and sociologists, anthropologists and archeologists reinforce this concept. So we fall for this concept that we must be united."

Chapter 12

Thirty years after Allan White took part in the big march down the main street of Kenora in November, 1965, most of the people at his home community of Whitefish Bay were dependent on welfare—despite several attempts at developing a degree of economic self-sufficiency.

The Whitefish Bay reserve is about 15 kilometres south of Sioux Narrows, a small summer tourist village half way between Kenora and Fort Frances. The village sits on both sides of a narrow channel that separates Whitefish Bay from Regina Bay. It got its name from a legendary altercation between the Ojibways and a war party of Sioux that had come up from the south.

According to a short history put together by the Township of Sioux Narrows and Nestor Falls, the warlike Sioux lived well to the south and delighted in raiding the more peaceful Cree and Ojibway villages to the north and east. They would sweep up Whitefish Bay in their canoes and cross east through the Sioux narrows into Regina Bay. From there they continued north through Lobstick Bay and on toward the plentiful game lands almost as far north as Sioux Lookout. When the raids became more frequent and the Cree and Ojibway losses reached the breaking point, both tribes joined forces in an effort to beat back the invaders.

At sunset one evening, they spotted a large Sioux war party coming up Whitefish Bay. The Sioux warriors camped for the night on a point that was later called Sioux Point, where a beautiful sand beach provided an ideal landing place for the canoes. After a bout of boasting and story telling the tired Sioux war party turned in for the night.

Meanwhile, the Ojibway and Cree warriors, who had concealed themselves among the rocks and bushes high up on the sides of the narrows, stayed awake all night and kept an eye on them.

When the Sioux war flotilla got well into the channel early the next morning, there was a single fierce yell and a cloud of arrows flew from both sides of the narrows. And then rocks were hurled down at the flimsy birchbark canoes. Next thing you know, any Sioux who had survived the arrows were struggling in the water and, when they tried to climb the slippery rocks on the shoreline, the Cree and Ojibway warriors attacked them with knives and tomahawks.

There were no survivors. The big Sioux raid had failed. The jubilant Crees and Ojibways lived peacefully after that for a great many years. That's the way the story is told on the township's website.

The big hope at the Whitefish Bay reserve in the early 1970s was a fur factory the Department of Indian Affairs had established to provide immediate employment and pave the way to a better way of life for the residents.

The idea behind the project was that fur scraps would be shipped to the Ojibways at Whitefish Bay from the markets in Montreal, New York and Chicago where they would be sorted and sewn and turned into fur plates which would be sold to manufacturers of fur coats. Like most projects of its kind at the time, the Ojibways had very little input into the planning of the operation. As Josephine Mandamin so often said, it was a case of the white man always knows best.

"The chief at that time and the council they didn't ask for that," Allan White said when I interviewed him in 1996. "They just wanted something [in the way of economic development], but somebody in Ottawa had a brilliant, whether it's brilliant or not, idea that the Indians are trappers, they get all kinds of fur, why don't we get an industry of something like that? So they hired Rosengarden [an expert in the fur industry]. I don't know where they picked him up."

Despite their lack of input into the development of the project, the Ojibways welcomed the opportunity to earn immediate income and establish a base for a better economic future. They also proved quite adept at mastering the skills necessary to produce the fur plates, most of which were mink. Husbands and wives worked side by side in the factory and pulled in about $400 a week (good money in the early '70s) between them.

The fur factory started in the basement of a building on the reserve and the Department of Indian Affairs provided one year of training for about 15 people.

"They took us to Montreal, all 15 of us, for ten days," Allan White recalled. "We visited the furriers in Montreal and most of them were Greeks, a lot of them were Greeks, a majority of them were Greeks, and we were escorted by departmental officials. We visited all the factories in Montreal."

Allan was on the band council at that time and he had a pretty good understanding of politics — and of people. "I overheard some of the workers in their own funny way of English language saying that these people [Ojibways] are going to take our jobs. I never said nothing and I told that to the group, I said, 'what the hell are we doing here? These people don't want us here, they're double-faced people.' I was talking in our language so we came back home.

"We weren't disillusioned or anything like that, because the elders had told us to go as far as we can, see what happens. The department was just pushing us to have a factory and the people said that we could go in."

However, in the back of his mind, he kept wondering about what the Greek workers had said in Montreal. What he was hearing from the Department of Indian Affairs was quite different from what he had overheard in Montreal. He told the Department official in charge of the project about his concerns and misgivings "but he wouldn't listen.

"I said OK, the people said OK let's go for it, see what happens and the elders here they would advise us because it's a whole new gamut, it's a whole new thing that you don't understand because it comes from another part of the world and because we're going to have to live in it, our children are going to have to live in it, so let's go for it. Let's find out exactly what will happen. If you don't get into it, we'll never know, so let's find out and we'll learn from that. If we're successful, the better for our community. If not, then we'll find the answer why it won't be successful. And that's when we started talking about that economic value."

Allan White became the first president of the company that operated the factory. "It was running all right. It was a very hard labour but it was still income for families, the man and wife working together, so there was finally steady income being around for a lot of us. But there was a lot of turnaround of employees. We kept training people and bringing new people and people going out."

They moved out of the basement and into a factory that had been built with funds provided by the Department of Indian Affairs. "The factory provided us with home industry," Allan said. "Like there was three or four women that were doing their own work at their home, at their houses because they couldn't handle working in the factory like that. So they took the sewing machines home and they worked at home and they created their own environment. Indian women needle and do the chores that they want.

"In between that time, they start sewing. And there was women working for them and I think they call it piece work, the thing that they call it. So it created a lot of different things. It created a sort of support in the community. It supported our kids, our families."

And then trouble landed at their front door. "I hung around there for nearly three years and then this Kastoria thing came in," Allan White recalled rather ruefully.

It turned out that the people of Kastoria in northern Greece had been in the fur business for a couple of hundred years and, because their labor costs were considerably lower than those at Whitefish Bay, they were able to pay a higher price at the fur scrap auctions in Montreal, New York and Chicago. The fur factory was in deep trouble. They couldn't bid high enough at the auctions in order to get the scraps.

"When George Giroux [a Montrealer the Department had hired to train them] came in, we learned from him that they were doing this in Greece at the very, very, low wage rate and here I'm making this kind of money. Hey, that's what I was talking about. Somewhere in this world somebody's doing this. I was talking about that back when we first started.

"We knew that the mink plate factory was doomed to failure. Certainly, Indian Affairs didn't want to take the heat or the responsibility and certainly we didn't want to take the heat or the responsibility so we had to change. And we did change. We went to making coats, fashion coats, designs with our labels."

At one point in the interview, I suggested that getting into the fur fashion business is even more competitive than the fur plate business. "Yeah, we'll find that out too," Allan said, with a mischievous smile on his face.

"So what happened is that, yes, that we were successful in making fashionable coats, beautiful design, really beautiful. As a matter of fact, I see that skater, the world famous skater back in 1970s, Canadian, he's still around."

Did he mean Toller Cranston, the Canadian national figure skating champion from 1971 to 1976? The 1976 Olympic bronze medalist? "Yeah, Toller Cranston. He bought one of those coats from our chief when we were in New York. We were there to visit the industry, the fashion industry in New York, and we met Toller Cranston there and he ordered a coat. So, we manufactured a beautiful, beautiful, mink coat for him. Three thousand, he paid for it, but it's probably worth about $10,000.

"Part of the deal was for him to wear it in different public places in the world and he agreed to that. We had no contract, just like a verbal thing. Became good friends. So we started getting some business. People wanted to handle our merchandise.

"People in St. Louis, Chicago, New York, Vancouver wanted to handle our merchandise but no one in Montreal or Toronto would touch us. We sold a lot of coats locally to Winnipeg, Thunder Bay, a lot of them. People used to come in here to order coats and I still see a lot of these wolf fur coats. People are still wearing a lot of those in Kenora. I go to Winnipeg in the winter and I see someone wearing one and I recognize them."

Word of the success of the fur coats from Whitefish Bay soon spread around and that caused a problem. "When they woke up what they said was, 'hey, that's our tax dollar.'"

The argument was that the Ojibways were making fur coats and taxpayer's dollars were being used to finance the operation. "So they killed it and we told the department and our chief told the Department of Indian Affairs, we don't blame us and we don't blame you. But we didn't recognize the business world and understand the business world between two peoples. So yes we accepted that and we have to live on, we have to start learning, but anyway, a lot of us learned a lot from this experience.

"Twenty-eight of us took that training so, after the place was shut down, several of our people went to work in Winnipeg. But, again, that's a different environment because it's a big city and people couldn't cope. So they came home."

He said it wasn't a lack of skills that resulted in them coming back to the reserve. "That [Winnipeg] was a different pace, a kind of work. It's not necessarily lack of skills, it was the living conditions in the city. Once here [at Whitefish], you got a little factory here, you're more or less in a different environment like and it's pure air you're breathing and in the city all you smell is the restaurant smell coming out of the restaurants."

I asked Allan what impact the factory had on the whole community. Like, what was the reaction when it was operating? "Well, like I said, it was a change. It was a change for the working man, for all the people that were involved in it and certainly the people themselves were very proud to be a community member, a part of the factory. The reason for that was that they weren't so much gung ho on the plating. But once we started making coats, that's when the people really started, because they were opening up something.

"People, even in the streets of Kenora, there's people wearing those wolf jackets and fox jackets, these raccoon jackets that were made in our own community and that was a beautiful thing for our people, still is. It still is."

It also resulted in them getting their first professionally-run day care centre. The people who were going to work at the factory had children that had to be cared for while they were at work.

"They have to talk to the elders about this. 'What about my children? I have little ones, everyone has little ones.' I said, build something for them, babysitting service. Go ahead. Rosengarden [the person from

Indian Affairs supervising the project] went to look into it and, next thing you know, there was a babysitting service. I think it was one of the elderly women that used to look after these children and the day care came in. That day care took off just like that. We went after the Ontario government and we said we need help with this.

"So we let [rented] the building across here [from the former factory] and that became our day care so we had to train people and we brought in some women that took training in early childhood education from Thunder Bay and come and teach our women how to run a day care. People were saying that was a good babysitting service, but we never looked at it that way because they were experienced and we started talking to people about that. We said, this is not a babysitting service, this is early childhood education for our children. We're preparing them to kindergarten.

"This is how we're going to operate and they're going to learn both languages [English and Ojibway] so, because it's going to be a lot of work for our women, certainly that's how it happened. So in the meantime, while all this movement is going on and maybe that's why the factory was successful in those five years because the man and wife were working together and the children were safe in that and also they were being fed well and also they were being trained well like both languages and they were being prepared to go to the big school and a lot of these children that you see here in Whitefish, a lot of these children that were there are now our leaders, are now our educators and are working here in the [band administration] office. That makes me sort of thinking that I'm getting old." He was 51 in 1996.

At one point, when I was providing public relations counsel and service to the Department of Indian Affairs, I arranged a fashion show at Whitefish Bay as a means of promoting the enterprise. Some of the women went to Sioux Narrows to get their hair done and then returned to the reserve to model some of the beautiful coats that they had made at the fur factory.

They looked sensational in their high-fashion fur coats and were excited about wearing them because they hadn't expected to ever be wearing them in the first place. It was a very exciting experience. "Hey, we did this. This is an accomplishment. <u>Our</u> accomplishment."

Ron R. McDonald's father Roy was chief of the Islington Band of Saulteaux at the time that the Whitefish Bay people ran into trouble acquiring the fur scraps because of the competition from Kastoria and he came up with a good idea. His community was still reeling from the loss of the commercial fishery resulting from the discovery of the poisonous mercury in the river system and desperately needed to find some other source of income.

Why couldn't the people at Whitedog raise mink and then ship them down to Whitefish Bay so they could make fur coats out of real mink pelts instead of working with scraps? "We can't eat the fish," Chief Roy McDonald said at the time, "but we can feed the fish to the mink and then we can make a living."

He put the idea to the Indian Affairs officials from Toronto during one of their visits to Whitedog. They said they would consider it and get back to him. A couple of months later, during their next visit to Whitedog, they said pregnant mink miscarry if there is too much noise and there was too much noise at Whitedog.

On their next visit to the reserve, Chief McDonald, who was a very resourceful and persistent fellow, told them he had some good news. There was a very quiet spot down by the Ontario Hydro right-of-way and they could raise the mink there. The Indian Affairs officials said they would get back to him.

A couple of months later they told him that idea wouldn't work either. The Health Department officials had told them that, because of the mercury in the water, the mink couldn't eat the fish either.

When I told Chief Andy White during one of my visits to Whitefish Bay as as consultant to the Department of Indian Affairs that the department wouldn't let Whitedog raise mink because of the mercury problem, he said: "Well, there's nothing wrong with the water here. Why can't we send fish from here so they can feed them to the mink at Whitedog?"

The officials at the Department of Indian Affairs didn't like that idea either and said that the Ojibways should stick to traditional forms of employment like cutting pulpwood for the white-owned lumber companies.

"Roy McDonald was very much in tune of trying to get a mink farm going in Whitedog and we tried to help as much as we could," Allan White recalled in 1996. "Of course, the department won't understand, wouldn't go for it because it wasn't their idea. See, that's the key at that time. If it's their idea, then they'll go for it. If it's your idea, they won't go for it because they want the credit. So that's why they didn't go for it and also there was a [white-owned] mink farm just outside of Kenora, just east of Kenora.

"It's not the Ministers, it's the bureaucracy that want to control the poor Indian. The Ministers have good intentions, but the bureaucracy warps the whole process and they make bullshit liars of their own political leaders. This is not the way Indian people operate. That's the difference."

That wasn't the first time the officials at Indian Affairs rejected sound business ideas the Ojibway people came up with on their own. Back when Andy White was the chief in 1970, he started to explore the possibility of purchasing pontoon houseboats the band could rent out to tourists in the Lake of the Woods area.

"First thing I asked when I came in," he recalled, "was I want you guys to do a feasibility study for me. I want some houseboats up on the lake. I want you guys to build them because there's nothing here. I'm positive we can kind of develop some kind of a business in boat houses. So they went out and did a research. They came back. 'It's not feasible.' That's what they told me and I told them, it is feasible. People like to do that. Even me like to do it. I'd like to get in a boat and just go by the lake for a couple of days and you can rent those. At that time you could rent those for 100 bucks a day. So they came back again, 'Indian Affairs says it's not feasible. We can't do that. It's too expensive.'

"Just a couple of years later, you see a whole bunch of houseboats and they're doing extremely well. Really extremely well. We could've had, ten years before that, we could've had a whole bunch of houseboats, a whole fleet of houseboats out there. We could've been probably the only ones dominating the lake on this [east] side. There's nothing on this side. This is a good lake here. Really good lake for trout and everything. We would've had at least ten houseboats, but that kind of advice was kind of bad.

"We tried, did a quite extensive research kind of study but it never went through. Just everything fell through. 'It doesn't work.' Same thing with that fur factory, I think, when I have these flashbacks. I feel kind of, sometimes, disappointed in terms of when I was a chief, in terms of my advisers for instance Indian Affairs and also my economic development adviser here at the office."

"How did we know about pontoon houseboats?" Allan White once asked me. "One of our friends from here in Whitefish drove to Florida with his family and one of the [tourist] camp operators in Sioux Narrows, Bill Salvador, and his son owned a pontoon houseboat in Florida and this guy went and visited. So he brought that idea back here. He took pictures of pontoon houseboats and then we applied [to Indian Affairs] if we could have one, if we could have that kind of business in Lake of the Woods.

"Like everything else, guys like [district manager] Dick Persian who was here in the district office, the one who says no it was no. They never heard about it and it's never heard of in Ottawa. We didn't even know Toronto [the headquarters of the Ontario region of the Department of Indian Affairs] existed so our government was in Kenora and if Dick Persian said no, it was no. One of the secretaries said no, it was no at that time. So that's where it got sort of stalled. It wasn't approved. Within about two years, we started seeing one houseboat, second year, about five. We missed the boat."

White entrepreneurs were doing a good business renting out houseboats to the summer tourists—just like the Ojibways at Whitefish Bay had wanted to do.

At one point in the interview I suggested to Allan White that, since most of the people at Whitefish Bay were getting welfare cheques from the government, there really wouldn't have been much of an advantage in working at the fur factory.

"Let's put it this way," he said. "The people of this reserve are very, very, technical and very highly motivated by the seasons. I don't know about others, but this reserve, since existence, since I know personally, we look at the seasons and what we're going to do.

"Like in the 1960s, in the summertime, from May to October, you do your guiding. That's four and a half months doing guiding. In the fall you do the commercial fishing and from October to practically the third week of November commercial fish, whitefish and they're spawned and in the winter you either have enough UIC [unemployment insurance] to survive or you do pulp cutting, wood cutting, for UIC and fishing and trapping. In the spring we go out trapping the beaver.

"We did that cycle over and over so the people that weren't involved in the fur industry, they were out doing other things. They weren't on welfare. Now, (1996) all we have is welfare."

I told Allan White about an Ojibway teenager I had picked up at Shoal Lake one day when I was driving to Winnipeg to catch a plane back to Toronto. We started talking and it became readily apparent that the boy was totally lost.

He was part of a native street gang in Winnipeg called the Scammers, one of several gangs in Winnipeg's north end where young native prostitutes ply their wares at street corners on Main Street and destitute natives line up at the Salvation Army outlet near the Canadian Pacific Railway station in the harsh cold of winter for a warm cup of soup. As part of the initiation to the gang, he had to steal something from a store and not get caught.

The boy had gone to school at Whitefish Bay and, when he moved to Winnipeg, he found that the education he had received was far behind what he would have received in Winnipeg.

Allan told me that the boy I had described was his nephew and that, yes, the educational standards at the Ojibway-run school at Whitefish Bay were not on a par with the standards in Winnipeg. "It's still like that," he said. "We still have that and the reason for that is that the administration of education it's still over at the [Indian Affairs] administration. Once we have that jurisdiction, it'll be different."

Police ConstableTara Kelly, about whom I will tell you later, had a similar experience. When Tara left the Sabaskong reserve down the highway from Whitefish Bay and went to a high school in the predominantly-white community of Fort Frances, the white students would talk about having read school books about which she hadn't even heard.

"'How come you don't read those books?' they'd ask. 'You're supposed to have that.' And that's when you just know that your teachers weren't interested in teaching you."

She said they didn't have enough money to hire experienced teachers at Sabaskong so they wound up with recent graduates from Teachers' College.

"They only have enough money to afford new teachers. While they're trying to learn [how to be teachers], you're trying to learn and they try and teach you at the same time. That's all you get and then the longer they stay, they're not getting a raise or anything, they leave. By the time they get to know us they're gone and it's always like that."

I asked Tara how that affected the quality of education at the school on the reserve. "From what I was seeing a couple of times, they're [teachers] just there. They're making the money, they're getting the years in but they're not really providing good teaching skills. They're not doing the right education, like the level they should be at. They're just there. I remember sitting in English class and getting answers to the test coming up."

Part of the problem, Tara said, was that many of the students were not motivated to learn. "A lot of it has to do with the students' own interest in school. Like a lot of them are just going, not really trying to accomplish something for themselves because, if you look at their parents, none of them have gone to high school. They went up to grade nine, grade 10, that's it. They want to start teaching them their language, trapping and stuff like hunting."

Herb Hoffman, a former accountant from Minneapolis, Minnesota, operated the Red Indian Lodge at Sioux Narrows. I suggested that some politically correct people would have a problem with the name Red Indian Lodge. Why not call it White Man's Camp or something like that?

"I had a guy who was a real [native] militant down in Minneapolis come by," he recalled when I interviewed him in 1997, "and he said 'Why are you calling that Red Indian Lodge?' I says 'because I got mostly

Indians [from Whitefish Bay] work here and they're very, very, proud of the name and if I ever change it, they'd probably scalp me' and the guy walked right away. He went to jail, this guy from the States. He went to jail for something. I think he killed some people or something out in Pine Ridge in South Dakota or something like that.

"Anyway, we joke about the name of the lodge with my [Ojibway] employees all the time. It's all in the mind. If I talk to my own people that work here they would be very, very, upset if I changed it. They're pretty proud of it. It's all in perception."

I asked Andy White if he found the name offensive. "No, we don't find it offensive," he said. "I don't think it's ever really occurred to anybody in the community. Like I said, I think if there was some kind of problem they had to deal with that's the first guy they're going to be talking to, Mr. Hoffman."

Herb told me about a meeting of the Kenora District Camp Owners Association where they were trying to get the area Ojibways more involved in the tourism industry. An Ojibway woman objected to a lawyer at the meeting referring to the people from the reserves as "Indians".

"She got up and just really brought him down. Really took him down. 'Well', he said, 'what would you like to have me call you?' She said 'you got to call us Anishinaabes [Ojibways].'

"Well if you got to group somebody, every place you go you're going to have to call somebody a different name. You don't know what tribe they are. So, isn't that crazy? For a person to say we're not Indians anymore? One of the chiefs there in Kenora used to stop here once a year because he used to work here before I bought the place and he always stopped in. They were kind of proud of the word Indian and so why would a guy want to say, 'don't say Indian' or like 'Red Indian Lodge'? I think a guy should be proud of the name."

Herb Hoffman was born on a farm near Bellingham, Minnesota, and his family moved to Minneapolis when he was 17. He worked as a punch press operator at Honeywell and joined the army at 19. Because he spoke fluent German, he often surprised German locals in Europe when he would say something in German after listening quietly to their conversations about the American soldiers.

When his tour of duty was over, he went to night school to learn accounting, got a job with a local accounting firm and then set up his own practice in partnership with his brother.

Part of his success in building Red Indian Lodge into a world-class resort was his personal touch in all aspects of the renovations. He even made his own lumber, from skidder to sawmill.

Most of the clientele were well-heeled tourists from the United States who enjoyed fishing among the 14,542 islands of the Lake of the Woods. Most of the employees were Ojibway.

"They make pretty good money with the tips and everything," Herb said. "Like tomorrow I'll use 22 of their people as guides. So that's 22 families that are going to make well in excess of $100 a piece. With all the fringe benefits and what not they average about 125 bucks a day and that's not too bad. It's easy work and they like to do that.

"A lot of the times the tip is in U.S. funds. [The U.S. dollar was worth $1.38 Canadian at the time.] They kind of like that idea. With the three-day party they'll probably get 50 bucks U.S. That's not too bad. So they're making pretty good money at that, but it doesn't last that long. Ninety days. That's nothing."

I asked Herb, a short little 63-year-old with a crewcut, how he got along with the Ojibways he had worked with for more than 25 years. He said they got along very well together and, in fact, after the first year, they told him that they had decided to honour him with an Ojibway name. They told him what the name was in Ojibway.

"Gee, that's great," he said, "but what does that mean in English?"

They told him that the English translation of his new name was Eagle That Walks.

"Hey, that's great," he said. And then he thought about it for a moment.

"What does Eagle That Walks actually mean?"

"Herb," they told him, "It means that eagle is so full of shit it can't fly."

Next morning, I was down by the dock as the American tourists were getting ready to go out for a day's fishing with their Ojibway guides. Herb called over to one of the guides and asked him to tell me what his Ojibway name was. Without missing a beat, the guide said: "Eagle That Walks." And that's what they called him.

Herb told me he enjoyed a very good rapport with the people of Whitefish Bay over the years. "I've made probably a little extra effort a lot of times. In the winter time, Christmas time or something or somebody's destitute or somebody dies, you give them 600 bucks, an advance. I'm in the hole with some of these people like five, six hundred bucks in the winter time before they start [guiding], but I've lost very little over the time. Pretty loyal that way. They pay it back and I figure well if they don't pay it back, that's the bonus to the happy hunting ground. I mean that's about the only way I don't get paid back is if somebody dies."

Having lived in the Kenora area for more than 25 years, Herb Hoffman was convinced that the reserve system did not work, never had worked, and never would work. He saw the reserves as something akin to the black townships that were created in South Africa under the racist apartheid system.

"I really question the idea of building even a school on the reservation because that just sort of segregates you more. All you got is, like inside of New York you got Harlem. And that's what I look at that as. We got a Harlem community, within a Harlem community almost like there. They have to get out somehow. Education is the answer to getting out or off the reserve and if you're going to have a reserve, then the next thing is that you have to have some economic reason to be there.

"There has to be some economic base in any community, otherwise it's just not going to grow. Every community is there for an economic reason. What happens to the gold mining town when the gold runs out? It collapses. Agriculture. If you don't have agriculture up in Manitoba, the town collapses. Indian reserves are there for no reason whatsoever except for the brown envelopes [welfare cheques].

"There's two things that you can do here in northwestern Ontario and that's all you can do. Tourism and trees. There's a little bit of mining but, really, when you get down to it, that's what this whole area is all about. Tourism and trees.

"Let's look at the forestry side. They could replant a lot of acreage of trees. Put everybody out there, have big nurseries, do this and do that. I'm sure there is enough stuff to do that would employ everybody gainfully, but some of the stuff is hard work and the discipline has been lacking. I was in the army and I keep telling people in my staff room what the army was like. I mean, you're on your hands and knees picking up cigarette butts and the sergeant says 'all I want to see is assholes and elbows.' The discipline is unbelievable.

"The Whitefish people don't have any of that there and they can't handle working at any job, like even guiding. By the time two or three months goes by, they've about had it. They're not used to discipline. They like that seasonal stuff. 'Let's pick rice.' That's easy. 'Let's pick rice for a couple of weeks and make a few hundred bucks there and let's shoot a couple of beaver and then let's do this and do that.' They like to look at the next season and it's very difficult for those people to work in a fur factory 12 months out of the year and run a sewing machine for the rest of their life because the discipline isn't there."

Herb recalled being at Whitefish Bay shortly after taking over the Red Indian Lodge and asking one of the leaders what they had in the way of a long-term plan for the community. "'Yeah, what's your long-term range plan?' I asked. And he said, 'we don't have any.' I was here for one year and driven out to the reserve and picked up guides and said 'geez, there's got to be something done because this isn't going to go anywhere and I could predict,' I said, 'I can predict that this is leading you into a real crunch. At some future date, somebody's going to have to address it and it has to be addressed rather quickly.'

"Well, this is 27 years ago and it still hasn't been addressed and it's the same as it was then. When you go out to Whitefish now the only outside source of income is in the tourist industry, that's the guiding and we got a couple of cabin girls and so everything else you see, every house, every car, every television set, everything you see comes from government money.

"That's got to be a pretty damn big burden. Double that every ten years. I don't think that people [Canadian taxpayers] can handle that much longer and it's going to get worse because like when 13-year-olds don't have the responsibility not to get pregnant and all of a sudden they got a bunch of kids by the time they're 20. They've never had a job, never will have a job and now they're single parents and you got to have housing for them. Well I got a [white] manager that works for me and he still doesn't own a house and these guys have brand new houses and we're going to build more of those and there's no economic base outside of the tourism industry which isn't enough. Isn't enough.

"It starts right with the kids. I can drive out there at 11 o'clock at night. There'll be little kids that are six, seven years old. They're all running around in the streets and they don't go to bed. Some of the older Indians over there, they joke about it. They say 'well when they run around all night they sleep all day.' That's all they do."

Herb had some real concerns about some of the things that were going on in the Ojibway community of Whitefish Bay in 1997. "Right now I talked to a couple of my guides that are kind of in the know and they say there's 13-year-olds getting pregnant." I asked Andy White, who was acting as a family counsellor at that time, if teenage pregnancies were a problem on the reserve. "It's not too bad," he replied. "It's not too much. There's a few. That's how it is here. I think that's why you still have young girls getting pregnant because they're living together. I suppose they're all married, marriage in the traditional [Ojibway] way, as long as the parents approve their living together, the arrangements."

But, what if a girl is pregnant at 13 and she's living openly with a guy? "I can't even think of any young girl that's been pregnant without living with a guy and the parents had their approval," Andy replied. "But still I think that's wrong because I see a lot of young marriages breaking apart after five, six years. So what happens they already got one or two children. It's the children that suffer. A lot of times the children will end up in our office to try and protect them so they don't go to the provincial CAS [Children's Aid Society] society."

Herb Hoffman knew a lot about what went on in Whitefish Bay.

"I hear a lot of stories. I got a couple of them [employees] that are quite well educated and we'll talk exactly like I do just about. 'We're going nowhere and the hierarchy in the reserve gets all the money,' one of them said. 'Why do they need to have a brand new boat and a brand new car and everything the minute they become a councillor or get on the payroll?' There's a few rich people. He said 'I have to work for it. I've got a pickup truck here and it works. It's good enough. Why can't they drive used? But everything is brand new or leased vehicles, three or four hundred dollars a month. They have to need this, right?' he said. This is him talking. 'They have to have everything right now and the best of everything right now right here and now.'

"I got an '87 Escort, Ford Escort, '87. That's my best car and then my van is an '85. These guys laugh at me when I take them back and forth. The road is pretty rough. I'm using the older van this [that we're in] is a 1980, but it does the job. It goes back and forth.

"Things are just going to keep on going the way it is unless somebody takes the bull by the horns and really does something, but I don't know what. There are opportunities in this area. Let's say you wanted to cut off the [government] funds a little bit more and get the people going. I think that there's enough economic base here in the resource, especially if you get into the trees section of it, between trees and tourism. That's all you have. I mean, everything that they have should be forestry or related. In other words, if you're going to do anything and have an industry. I think they had a shoe factory one time up in Shoal Lake [a reserve southwest of Kenora] that bombed."

He recalled how the attempt at running the fur factory in the early 1970s ended in failure. "Yeah, everything has folded pretty well. I think that if I had the power I would definitely lean towards tourism. They're good at tourism really. The people like them. They're a likeable bunch of people. They're jolly and what not and so they do well in tourism, particularly as guides. Even we've got a couple of girls that work here in the housekeeping part of it. Nice people."

But a troubled people. At the time that they started the fur factory, for example, they did not give sufficient consideration to the social problems that might result from the sudden influx of new money into the reserve.

"My father keeps coming, telling me that you figure out something when you're developing," Allan White recalled. "'When you guys were developing something, you forgot something,' he said, 'a very key component.' How stupid we were not to realize that. We created a new environment and the whites created a new environment. A man and wife working together, which had never happened before.

"So the whole new gamut of things started to change and the whole social fabric of our community started to fall apart because of that. There was no counsel or anything like that because of the humongous amount of money that was coming here, which was a lot at that time. Man and wife making $800 in two weeks. That's a lot of money at that time. Man and wife working together, that was a new thing. The whole social fabric started to fall apart because there was a lot of drinking, a lot of abuse came in, man and wife and children and that's one thing he [father] keeps telling me, kept telling us that when you create something, make sure that you think it out."

Herb objected to the way some Ojibways made an issue of the fact that they lived in the area long before the Europeans arrived. "When somebody tells me 'we were here first', I tell these guys, 'listen, I think it was a tribe that started with a T or something like that and they got pushed off by the Cree and then the Ojibwa pushed the Cree out into Manitoba and it's all because of resource. Because there's only so many deer, so many moose and so many fish and beaver pelts and what not that they have.

"This area had about three different tribes and the battles that they had were fierce. They fought each other and when the white man came they said 'this is the end of our battles, this is it. All we need is to be able to survive now.' There was no more Indian battles after that. But before that, it was unbelievable."

Herb Hoffman scoffs when he hears the Ojibways claiming they have an inherent right to the land and should be able to govern themselves as a sovereign people. "My generation came from Germany. My mother was born in a little piece between Germany and Poland. They gave it away during the Potsdam agreement after the First World War and now it belongs to Poland and the Russians were in there and I know exactly what they would've said if I would've gone over there and said 'give me my land back.' They'd 've taken a bayonet and shoved it up about this far up my rear end and said 'get out of here'."

Herb also expressed concern about the enormous amounts of money the government was spending on the mostly-unemployed people of Whitefish Bay and other reserves across Canada. "You take an organization like Indian Affairs for instance. That's the tip of the iceberg. There are so much other costs involved. If you look at the jail in Kenora. Who's in the jail? [Ojibway prisoners] That is under Correctional Services. Then you look at the OPP, why do we have nine OPP here when you got a population of 350 [at Whitefish Bay] when there used to be only one person without a uniform and we had no crime? Now we got all kinds of crime and they can't keep up. There's nine policemen here and all they do is drive up and down the road. Why would there be nine policemen with a population of 350?

"Then you go into the medical part and you see every time there's a snivelly nose or whatever, they're in Kenora. My kids never went to a doctor until they were about half dead. That's the way Germans are. They got to be nearly dead before they see a doctor. Well here they pick them up with helicopters and what not. What I'm saying is the cost that you see when you look at Indian Affairs that's just the tip of the iceberg of all the other costs. I mean there's stuff run through the education department, there's stuff run through housing. CMHC [Central Mortgage and Housing Corporation], for instance. They built all the houses and they're [Whitefish Bay people] supposed to pay rent. They're never going to get all their rent money or, if they do, it's just recycled money [paid from the welfare cheques]."

That brings to mind a conversation I had with Chief Ron McDonald in April, 1997. He said the Whitedog band had fallen $2.1 million behind in arrears—primarily because of people not paying the rent on their homes—and the Department of Indian Affairs covered the deficit. "So now I'm sitting here wondering how it's going to impact our funding now for fiscal year 97/98 and the following years. How is that going to impact us? Are we going to be penalized? By the way, we're under co-management."

When I asked what that meant, he said Indian Affairs was now overseeing all of the band's spending. "Whatever we decide, they have to agree. If we want to spend a dollar, that dollar has to be agreed upon and that's because of the CMHC problem that we have, the $2.1 million arrears and also apparently our spending practices weren't satisfactory. They told us that we were overspending, etc. etc. Now we got to keep an eye on this which we agree. They [Indian Affairs] should be paying that [deficit] anyway. We don't see no problem. The deficits, they call it a deficit. We don't. We call it prepaid advance for being an Indian. I'm a status Indian."

The way the system worked was that CMHC would build the houses and the Ojibways would then pay rent. Chief McDonald said he had always paid the approximately $453 monthly for his house on time. However, as 80% of the residents were on welfare, they were either unable to, or not willing to, pay the rent on their homes.

"If you put a family in there that's on welfare, some of these homes have two or three families in there, and if it's compounded with drinking, dependency on welfare, no jobs, it creates chaos. At least 80 per cent of the members don't have jobs, right, so they can't pay."

In their 2011 book *Beyond the Indian Act,* authors Tom Flanagan, Christopher Alcantara and Andre Le Dressay noted that 97% of the Piikani band in southern Alberta living in rental housing in 2002 were not paying their rent. The Cowichan Tribes on Vancouver Island were losing an estimated $600,000 a year because of non-payment. The Blood Tribe in southern Alberta had to close its housing department for a year because of lack of revenue from people not paying their rent.

Herb Hoffman recalled having a shore lunch on one of the islands in the middle of the Lake of the Woods with an official from Indian Affairs who told him it would cost less to house every Aboriginal person in Canada in a nice hotel than to pay for their upkeep on the reserves.

"In other words, put them in the best hotel, feed them, eat, sleep there and it would be cheap compared to what our cost is now in housing and so forth. He said the problem is the politicians don't want to bite the bullet and, when the Indians came in, he said, at the Parliament with all their drums and what not everybody just kind of knelt down and listened. They wouldn't really sit down and say 'here's what ought to be done.'

"It's a dead end situation and it just really frustrates me when I see that as a compassionate person. I think that they've been wronged in a different way than a bleeding heart thinks that they've been wronged. Completely. Because I think the whole approach was wrong to start off with. It's flawed. I mean, everything about the [reserve] system was flawed. Total assimilation is the answer, was the answer. Now it's getting tougher and tougher.

"Someday, somebody's going to have to bite the bullet and come along and say 'hey, enough is enough. Let's do something.' I really don't know the answer of what to do. It's gone so far now that if you, let's say, you hear [white] people around here say well let's just cut off the funds. Well you can't, I mean you can't do that right now because you'd have war. I mean there'd be bloodshed right away. So you got to ease it in somehow because it's gone too far. You could've done that maybe 25, 30 years ago—cut off the funds. [Prime Minister Pierre] Trudeau's White Paper of 1969 was probably a good time to do it, but now ...

"I can understand why the chiefs don't want it [funding cuts] and why the councillors don't want it. No one wants to lose their power structure. Whoever is in control they get the money. I mean the chiefs and the councillors are driving brand new cars and brand new boats and motors and the rest of them are suffering and that's the way it is. It's a very socialistic type of way they do things. It's almost like Russian socialism in that the leadership is up here and they can go to the commissary and get all the goodies and everybody else used to have to stand in line for a long period of time to get their butter and milk and so forth and Indian reserves are exactly the same way. Very socialistic government except it isn't pure socialism. They have the leadership on top and then everybody else is equal after that. I don't know if you've noticed that."

Herb said he did whatever he could to help the Ojibways of Whitefish Bay provide for their families. "I'm not a bleeding heart, but yet I have compassion and a lot of compassion in a way and that's why I hired as many as I do because I could hire a lot more white guides and so forth. I think this is a selfish reason as well because it's good for me and it's good for them. They're always here. If you hire a bunch of whites, let's say some white students or something, they're going to be here three or four years and then they're going to be a doctor, a lawyer, whatever they went to school for and it takes about three or four years to really train people. This way it's a two-way street. It's good for me and it's good for them [Ojibways], but it's probably more good for them than it is for me, I don't know."

As good as it was for the Ojibway guides in 1997, it was not as good as it had been 10 years earlier. "In the last ten years you would probably see maybe a 60, 70 per cent cut in guiding," Andy White said. "Back in the old days, a couple of Americans would come from down in the United States to come fish up in northwestern Ontario so they're fairly new and they don't know the lake so what they would do is they would take a guide. But then they started bringing their own boats. They started bringing their own boats and they pick them up themselves and they didn't bother with guides. That's one of the reasons why there's a lot of [job] cuts." In fact, there were twelve fewer tourist camps in Sioux Narrows in 1997 than there were when Herb bought the Red Indian Lodge.

"When I first got here in '71 I mean the road was full. I mean all the gift shops were busy and now they're, the last few years, they kept boarding up more and more and more. Except for a few, two resorts, Totem Lodge and us, are the only ones that have increased in size and we are tough marketers."

Chapter 13

There was a big snow storm at the end of March, 1996, when Ron Irwin, Canada's Minister of Indian Affairs, met with the Grand Council of Treaty #3 which represented 25 widely-scattered bands of Ojibways living in the heavily-wooded area between Thunder Bay and the Manitoba border.

The Minister flew in on a government jet, accompanied by a full entourage, and arrived at Kenora's Best Western Lakeside Inn quite a bit behind schedule. Before entering the hotel, he put on the buckskin jacket he usually slipped into before meeting with Aboriginal people. Then he was escorted to the ballroom where about 300 members of Treaty #3 were waiting for him.

Josephine Mandamin was seated in the place of honour reserved for elders on an elevated platform. The Grand Chief was seated at the head table wearing an eagle feather headdress and red traditional shawl. The chiefs of several of the bands, including Chief Ron Roy McDonald of Whitedog, were seated at tables set up in a horseshoe fashion. Drums were beating. The air was filled with the scent of burning sage.

The Minister peppered his opening remarks with several jokes —including one about the spiralling increase in the Aboriginal population across Canada indicating that they must really enjoy sex. He referred to the assembled chiefs as "you guys" despite the fact three of them were women, Pacing back and forth with a hand-held microphone, he outlined several steps his department was planning to take in an effort to improve things for native people.

Chief Ron McDonald rose and read a letter urging the Minister to do something about "the current state of crisis that grips my community." Here's part of what his letter said:

> "The devastation resulting from the multiple suicides is being exacerbated by numerous copy-cat suicide attempts. Solvent inhalation by 80 to 90, mostly young, residents appears to be a major factor underlying the attempted and completed suicides. We, as Chief and Council, are taking steps to deal with our community's solvent abuse and suicide epidemic.
>
> "The current overcrowded housing contributes to the suicide and solvent abuse crisis in that many sniffers returning home after treatment have no home to return to that is sniff-free. Additionally, the lack of private space for recovering solvent abusers and alcoholics, in effect, a bed and space in a bedroom, contributes to feelings of not belonging and not feeling supported in staying straight or sober. The result is that sniffers form peer groups that take control of houses which become sniff houses. I feel that the lack of sufficient adequate housing is contributing to the death toll."

In concluding his letter to the minister, Chief McDonald wrote: "You are invited to our community to meet with the Chief and Council for a tour. We would appreciate the opportunity to talk with you about our situation and assist us in our problem solving process." The Minister said he would take the letter under advisement.

Chief McDonald was hoping for support for his community in the form of funding to address the suicides. He was afraid that things were going to escalate, that the community was going to have another rash of suicides.

Towards the end of the meeting, the minister joined the chiefs and the others as they shuffled around the room to the beat of the ceremonial drums during the traditional Ojibway Giveaway. Presents of socks, gloves and other items were presented to everyone in attendance.

Watching Ron Irwin, all decked out in his buckskin jacket, Josephine Mandamin wondered how much longer they would have to listen to platitudinous speeches like his before something meaningful was done to improve the lives of the Ojibways of Treaty #3.

Towards the end of the meeting, she rose from her seat in the place of honour reserved for elders and addressed some remarks to the minister. She told him a long list of ministers had said that things were going to get better, but they never did. Words are just words, she said, and the people of Treaty #3 wanted him to actually <u>do</u> something concrete to help resolve their problems.

And then she pointed her index finger at him and said, in a somewhat threatening tone: "We will be watching you."

When I met with her after the meeting, I asked if she had always been that strong and self-assured. "No. I wasn't," she said. "I was more like the traditional sense of a good wife, very obeying, very submissive and duty of the macho type of chauvinistic pig thing."

Did she mean by that that, in the earlier days, she fashioned herself after the men's idea of what a good woman should be? "Yeah, a good woman. It can do all sorts of things and you just accept it. I suppose I went along with it to a certain time. My kids were small. I have eight children. But I was not absent from the role of a strong woman in a traditional sense before, with my grandmother. She ruled the household with an iron hand and I was more keen to that type of role where you should have the freedom and will to be involved in discussion and decision making in your role in being a woman, because to me being a woman warrants more respect from your unit in the family, from your peers.

"After all, in the old days, and this is getting back to a long time ago in the Celtic age, women were powerful as healers. And in the traditional old days, in the buffalo days, when the buffalo was there, women were seen as and respected as the same as the warriors in the old days. They were allowed to sit on council.

"It goes way back because in the Celtic age it caused some concern with the state heads of the men. They wouldn't allow woman's power to happen so I assume the Church took the first steps to persecute women in those days and classified them as witches. They felt sort of threatened by the powerful healing methods that the women had so, in that way, the persecution, they warned them."

Does that mean that the male power structure in those early days sensed the power that the Celtic women had and considered it a threat? "Yes, it was a threat and now in this modern time and age, you're going towards, finishing the 1900s, to some extent it still exists. But I wish to see a turnaround soon where the women will be seen as equal partners with the men and other women and other types of things because we have a lot to offer as far as surviving is concerned and in the workplace and the family unit and the political field and the life skills mandate.

"I wish to see more women in the policing. I wish to see more women doctors. I wish to see more lawyers, women lawyers. In that way, we can balance out the negativism of how women are looked at today because we have a right to our place in this society and anywhere else as women to be involved in what takes place, what's happening in our environment."

How much of what Josephine Mandamin was thinking and saying in 1996 would have been in her head back 30 years before? "Thirty years ago is not a fair question where I'm concerned. I've always thought that I was born old. That's my conception of myself, that I was born old. I don't know why I feel that way. Maybe it was because my roots back then were always with the older people, grandparents and uncles. I got along really well with older people."

How did that affect her relationship with people her own age? "I never had any problems getting along with any age group. I feel very comfortable with infancy, adolescents and the middle age and the older. I have no problem with that."

I suggested that was a gift. "Yeah, we are, maybe some of us are privileged with certain gifts, but the thing is it's not a right, it's a gift, no matter how you look at it and sometimes gifts can be abused. You have to be careful when you acknowledge it, respect it and feel humbled by it. Sometimes it makes me real sad when I see people that have charisma that could do so much when they turn it into abuse, their gift into profit, monetary, utilize it that way. That makes me sad. Even the Bible is abused. The Bible is there for information, direction to sort of get directions from it or even legends, fairy tales.

"Scriptures are, they're very small, but you can run with a three-word scripture. You can run a mile, expand it and through your own methods of how you interpret. Sometimes you get confused by the way scriptures are contradicted by the clergy in their interpretation of the good word, because, as far as I'm concerned, it's there for your benefit. The Bible was written for the benefit of mankind, but it's not working that way. It's being utilized, abused in a negative way and in some certain cases I've seen it abused.

"It makes me sad, especially in courts, in the legal system. Why put on the walls of the courthouse a creed, 'You shall not discriminate against race, culture, religion'? Bullshit. These are just words. They do it every day. I feel so sorry for the Bible sometimes, being abused the way it is being abused."

I asked if she was more in touch with the Ojibway traditions in 1996 than she had been 20 or 30 years earlier. "It's always been there. Maybe, in the intervening years, it has laid dormant, shelved, but it's always been there and, of course, I'm very proud of what I have. I think I have a very, in my opinion, a very magnificent connection to what was planned for me as an Indian by the Creator. If I had been allowed to be a traditional [Ojibway] culturally, maybe things wouldn't be the way they are now."

A lifetime of experience had taught Josephine not to place too much trust in the opinion of experts. "There's what I call 'the expert opinion syndrome.' Let's take, for example, nutrition. This nutritionist says one thing, 'this is the answer to all your fat syndrome problems, how you can deal with it' and then you get another conflicting opinion from another expert. So I hold no faith in those opinions anymore. I just do what I have to do for myself in order to care for myself because they're so contradicting.

"They contradict each other and it's the same way with bureaucracy. One will make a tentative, helpful, approach and then you have another bunch of bureaucrats who have been there for so long they're ready to fall off their bureaucratic chairs and die sitting up in their bureaucratic chairs. So I don't see any great breaking ground. But I see hope in trying to persuade the women to be more involved where our future's concerned."

How much of a difference would the women make? What would they bring to the table that wasn't already there? "We have a lot to offer. We got to be allowed to say our piece in order for the man to ponder and think 'oh, there must be something there.' After all, we don't break that easily. Remember that. Women are strong when you come right down to it. You [males] may be the symbol of a strong tree. Maybe you've taken for granted that you are that symbol, the strong tree. But strong trees wilt. Women, on the other hand, are like willows. They bend. You have to do a lot of bashing and cutting to make it fall. So you got to give the respect to women to allow them the courtesy of their opinions."

But, wouldn't it be fair to say that there are a lot of chiefs out there who would take quite some time to really understand and appreciate that? "Yeah. If you allow time to work for you, as we've done through ages past, we too will come, never doubt that."

Did she believe that that was more likely to happen in 1996 than in years past? "Yes. After all, we had the first Prime Minister for a few months, woman Prime Minister in Canada, and that's a break." She was talking about Avril Phaedra Douglas "Kim" Campbell who was Prime Minister from June 25 to November 4, 1993.

I asked Josephine to look ahead 10 or 15 years and describe the future she saw for her daughters. "The future I want to see for my daughters and granddaughters is more involvement in the state of affairs. That's what my vision for my women is, women in general. They can become corporate directors, business-minded, running airlines, running corporations. That's what I envision for my women in Canada, especially for my daughters and granddaughters. Maybe for my granddaughters to be more specific. I would say in everything to be allowed the courtesy of being seen as who they are, women with power, women with intelligence, women with great potential. Positive things happening. That's what I want to see."

But, let's say her granddaughter becomes the president of a major airline. She wouldn't be doing that in Whitedog. "That's where the integration comes in, to take all education has to offer, all the good things that the university, colleges, degrees, have to kick in for that to happen. Segregation shouldn't be there any more for those young girls. Prejudice should be balanced out, racism should be balanced out."

Let's say granddaughter A is President of an airline and granddaughter B is a judge on the Supreme Court, who's in Whitedog? What happens to Whitedog 30 years from now? "Hopefully the ties to the magic and magnificence of Whitedog will stay with them. The negative things with time they'll sort of go away but the good things will stay there."

This might be a good time to take a look at what Melvin H. Smith, British Columbia's leading adviser on constitutional law between 1967 and 1987, had to say about government spending in his 1996 book, *Our Home OR Native Land?*

Here's the breakdown he provided of the approximately $3.3 billion the federal government spent on Aboriginal people in 1993–94.

Band government support $271.0 million.

Elementary and secondary education $695.5 million.

Post-secondary education $212.2 million for approximately 22,000 students.

Social services $267.3 million—including $184.9 million for child and family services. Approximately 4,900 children in care.

Social assistance $557.9 million. Approximately 145,000 on-reserve residents receiving welfare.

Construction and maintenance of schools, roads, bridges, sewers and other community facilities $566.2 million.

Housing $132.8 million. The government built 4,365 new units and renovated 3,916.

Health services $896 million.

After examining the $557 million the government spent on the social assistance program in 1993–94, Auditor General Denis Desautel said the government had no legislative authority to deliver social assistance and the administration of the program was "complex, cumbersome and difficult to manage." He added that the government did not monitor the program.

The Auditor General's report said that the Canadian Aboriginal Economic Development Strategy was a black hole into which the Canadian government had poured more than $1 billion since 1989. According to his report, the departments implementing the program had little concern for the viability of the economic projects that were being proposed. Again, only a few of the projects were monitored for success.

The Auditor General noted that the Department of Health's Aboriginal programs had no statutory basis, the mandate was unclear, expenditure control processes were deficient; and the cost of the entire program was buried because "there is no 'distinct expenditure component'."

In his 1996 book, Melvin Smith said: "Much of the Department of Health's Indian programs are targeted to public health problems endemic in some native communities: drug and alcohol abuse, child mortality, family violence and diseases associated with poor living conditions such as tuberculosis. Indian and Northern Health Services is the focal point for the delivery of public health in these communities, amounting to $896 million in 1994–95, 11% of Health Canada's entire budget."

He said the federal government provided "dental costs, vision care, drugs and medical transportation ($508 million); public health services ($224 million); and the native component of the Department's Child Development Initiative which focuses on mental health, solvent abuse, child development and parenting skills."

The federal government was operating six general hospitals, numerous clinics and providing medical staff for all of the facilities.

"Twenty-seven Health Transfer Agreements have now been signed with 82 bands," Smith wrote, "allowing them to exercise control over the delivery of their own health services. $27.5 million is transferred annually. Another 77 transfers are in the planning stage involving 213 bands."

In 1994-95, the Department of Canadian Heritage spent $38.6 million to "define and participate in the resolution of the social, cultural, political and economic issues affecting their [Aboriginals'] lives in Canadian society."

The Canadian Identity Program offered an Aboriginal Friendship Centre Program to "improve the quality of life for Aboriginal peoples residing in or travelling through urban communities." The centres offered referral services and support programs and employed 1,800 people. Budget? $18.1 million.

The Northern Native Broadcast Access Program received $10.1 million.

The Aboriginal Womens' Program received $2.3 million in 1994–95.

The Native Social and Cultural Development Program received $900,000.

The Aboriginal Representative Organizations Program provided $5.8 million to native advocacy groups that "enable Aboriginal people to participate in the political, social and economic life of Canada."

And the Aboriginal Constitutional Review Program provided $27.6 million over two years to cover legal fees and other costs.

Speaking about lawyers, Smith said information obtained under the Access To Information Act showed the federal government paid more than $12 million to lawyers acting for native bands involved in law suits of various kinds against the government of British Columbia between 1980 and 1982.

"Of this," he wrote, "it appears that over $8 million was paid to counsel representing the natives in this [Delamuukw] case. This, of course, does not include the fees of those lawyers on the government side (both federal and provincial)—also paid by the taxpayer—which could well be of equal amount or more. That is just legal and expert witness fees. It does not include the untold cost of bureaucrats' time at both the federal and provincial levels in researching archival and other material nor the cost of official reporters and court personnel engaged in administrative support of all kinds."

In *Our Home OR Native Land?*, Smith also had something to say about an audit released in January, 1995, which showed that between 1988 and 1993 one-third of the country's bands ran up deficits totalling $537 million.

"The Manitoba bands were deepest in the hole having tripled their debt over the period to $54 million. These are the ones that the DIAND [Department of Indian Affairs and Northern Development] Minister is in the process of handing over programs to administer themselves under his much ballyhooed DIAND dismantling project."

The 1985 Ministerial Task Force on Program Review [led by Deputy Prime Minister Eric Nielsen] rejected the claim put forward by Indian Affairs' officials that much of the spending was mandated by treaty obligations that the Government of Canada was obligated to fulfil. Here's what the Nielsen report said:

> "The large proportion [of Aboriginal] spending] devoted to status Indians and Inuit is commonly attributed to federal obligations under the treaties or the Indian Act. In fact, only 25 per cent of these expenditures can be directly attributed to these obligations. The remainder go largely to services of a provincial and municipal nature and stem from decades of policy decision designed to fill this void which have, by convention, come to be considered as though they were rights."

The report concluded that 37% of federal spending on Aboriginals fell into the category of "discretionary."

The Nielsen report criticized the government's efforts to create modern urban suburbs in remote areas with "no consideration of the communities' long-term economic capacity to pay for the maintenance and replacement of this level of service."

The report said the government's approach had created an "artificial world on Indian reserves where reliance on government is almost total.

"In effect, the government has created communities in which housing and other services are often far better than those in surrounding communities ... In so doing it has also unwittingly created a disincentive to move to areas of economic opportunity.

"This has only been accomplished at great cost to the federal government. As notable, however, is the incalculable human cost in lost pride, purpose, independence and self-motivation."

Most of the houses I saw at Whitedog, Whitefish Bay, Sabaskong and Manitou Rapids between 1996 and 2013 were of good quality and in good repair. Many were new or recently-built. Satellite dishes brought in news and entertainment from the TV networks.

The cars and pick-ups were new or less than five years old. Many lawns were littered with children's toys and some had inflatable pools.

And most of the people, with the exception of Manitou Rapids, were on welfare and without hope of finding employment.

The six years Allan White spent as chief of the Whitefish Bay band—flying back and forth to meetings, dealing with the Indian Affairs bureaucracy, and trying to make life better for the people of Whitefish Bay—took an enormous toll on his life and health.

"I was sick all the last year of my term, the third term," he told me. "I became sick and I didn't know what was causing that and I couldn't focus very well. I didn't want to run for a fourth term, but people kept pushing me. Another guy came in and he became the chief. He won the election and then I fell flat on my face and had to see a doctor and then I lay in bed for about six months.

"I was down to 165 pounds from 240 pounds. I lost it in about four months. No energy. I had to be driven. I was able to walk, but I was just staggering or walking with a cane. I was eating, but not normal, three meals a day. I wasn't eating right. Something was wrong."

During the time he was in politics, as a councillor and then as chief for six years, he experienced visions from the spirit world. "They never, every time they came and visited me, they never ever told me those things that they wanted me to do and why they wanted me to do this stuff. They'd just come and talk to me and then they'd leave, but I didn't know who they were.

"At first, they scared me, but then I started getting used to them so when I was talking to this elder in town [after Allan became deathly sick] about the dreams that I have and the visitations that I was having, he said, 'you have to change. You're an Indian. You're Anishinaabe. You're not a white man. You don't belong in that field [politics]. You're finished with it.'

"So he took me to a ceremony and then he told me that I have to go to four sweat lodges [a dome-shaped structure in which people sit in a circle around a fire pit where water is thrown on hot rocks] and after the fourth sweat lodge, that's when I will be given the responsibility to make my own decision in terms of what kind of life I'm going to have. If I'm going to go with the way I've been going for the last 30 years, then I'm dead. But if I'm going to change, and start carrying the responsibilities of the Anishinaabe person, then I have a future in life because this is totally different, different field of education that I was going to go through.

"But still I was very weak and I came home and I tell about those things, but I kept going to the sweat lodges. Every week I went to a sweat lodge, different sweat lodge, kept going, making that effort and finally I started to, this is now in February, I started getting stronger.

"I started getting my energy back. I got a call from Shoal Lake, from one of my friends there, and he told me to come down to Shoal Lake and have a sweat. I was getting my energy back and I wanted to drive myself and I knew then that I was going to be all right.

"So I was there, that's the spring of 1990, and we had that sweat and this elder from Saskatchewan, we were finished and he said, 'Allan stay a minute, I want to talk to you' and this is the first time I ever spoke to this old man. He said, 'how can people allot for many, many, years, all your life?' And I looked at him and I said, 'yeah' and we were talking about these things 'and you're paying the price.' I said, 'what do you mean?' 'You're sick.' I'm just getting on my feet now because I've been in bed for five months and I've been going to sweats the last three months and finally getting back my energy. He looked at me and he talked to me he said, 'you never ever go back to the ways of the way you used to make your living, being a chief, being councillor, being a leader in that fashion. They [spirits] don't want you there, they want you here.

"'There's a whole new way of things that is being set up, developed for you. It's being set up right now, as a matter of fact, you're in it right now and this whole new environment will enable you to understand the things that you learn from politics and the things that you don't know about the way of Indians, Anishinaabe people.

"'And, when you understand that, then you will understand both of them and that's how you're going to help your people and you're going to bring these two together and this is what's going to happen because this is what's being planned for you by the spirits.'

"I was amazed and I was really, really, amazed that this old man knew my name. I come out of that sweat lodge and I said, 'someone talked to my friend? How does he know me?' I said, 'did you mention anything about me?' He said, 'no' and that became my spiritual adviser, that old man from Saskatchewan.

"So that changed my way of life, but in general, he advised me that this isn't going to happen overnight, this isn't going to happen in a period of six months. This isn't going to happen in a period of one year, but it's going to happen in a period of years 'because everything that you did back in those 30 years of your life, alcohol took over your life and you're going to have to clean that out and, Allan, you're starting fresh.'

"I didn't get involved in politics [after that] and I was accused by the people that I wasn't responsible because I wasn't involved in helping with certain things and what was happening here in front of me, but little did they realize that this is the way that I have to be. It took me about three years before I could be able to face the people here in Whitefish and tell them exactly why I can't be involved with those things. But they still tried to get me to run for chief or council.

"'What are you trying to do to me, trying to kill me?' That's what I told them and so I started seeing things different and I started getting involved right away as soon as I got on my two feet again and had my strength and I was back to 190 pounds, 185 pounds. I was trying to work for [Ojibway] Tribal Family Services in Kenora in their summer project. This is a project involving the elders and the youth and we made a film about suicide. I helped coordinate that, developing that film, along with the company in Winnipeg or Toronto that made films.

"I travelled to fourteen First Nations all that summer getting information and help, mostly from elders, and that's when I started to feel the environment, the right environment that elder was talking about. I was talking with the elders and it started getting as if I knew them, as if I've known those elders all my life, from Sioux Lookout, from Grassy Narrows, Whitedog, Shoal Lake, like I'd known them. I became very close and started to understand why I was created and finally the whole new purpose of way of life opened up on me and the whole thing I was blocking from my vision and when the elders were talking to me dating back to 1873, the treaty making process, all that history was just opened up because I took the oath of the elder. This is the way that I'm going to be. This is the way I have to be and the whole focus of the politics of Canada, the politics of the western world started to look different and the bureaucracy started to look dirty and here I was dealing with these guys all the time and I was friendly to them and the worst enemy that I had was the politician, but the bureaucracy was even worse.

"After I completed our project with Tribal Family Services, I went to work for Treaty Three and I went to work with them to work with the elders and I stayed with them for four years.

"I was gathering information from the elders, talking to the elders, holding elders' conferences. The reason for these elders' conferences was that the whole structure of Anishinaabe, the way of, the old traditional structure of Anishinaabe way of life wasn't there. But the vision of bureaucratic structure was there, which was created by the Department of Indian Affairs. But the whole structure of, the spiritual structure of, Anishinaabe way of life wasn't there.

"When I was working for OTFS [Ojibway Tribal Family Services], that's what I was learning from the elders, when I was there with the OTFS and they were giving me all this information about the things, how they used to be and that's so, because of that knowledge that I had and because of the whole new thing that I had, new perspective in myself, the Grand Chief asked me if I could come and help out for 25 First Nations in Treaty Three territory. I travelled all over. I said 'OK, I'll help you' so that's what I did and I compiled all that information, put it in my notes, every community, compiled everything and sort of put everything together and finally the elders are being heard. A lot of people don't want to talk about this.

"As I was growing up in politics, we used to be told that there were certain things that we're not supposed to do. Certain things that the elders can't talk about. It almost took my life, because of my neglect, how close I came. I had to communicate this with the young people, not necessarily the youth, but the young people that are just behind me, like, five, six, ten years behind me. I had to communicate this with them and my experience."

He told them how close he had come to death and how the elder from Saskatchewan put him on the right track, the Anishinaabe track, and how they could avoid the mistakes he had made with his life.

"I started asking the elders about certain things and things that they used to be told that they're not to talk about these things because they believe that there would be a repercussion from the spirits. At least, we started talking about these things because it's paranormal. They can talk about these things among themselves, but they can't talk about these things outside.

"So I told the elders that, because I came so close [to death], that I'm no longer afraid. If I have to go tomorrow, I'll go, but before I go I wanted to communicate this with the children. This is what the elders used to tell us in Whitefish and this is what probably caused me almost losing my life because of that and I'm responsible and I want to talk about this with the children.

"So I started working with the elders and even started focusing on a lot of things that can help the young people today and also I'm putting together a piece, a structure of Anishinaabe people, the way they used to live, the way that they structured themselves in terms of internal politics and in terms of bureaucracy. This thing exists and I'm just determined to find it. The role of the money now is a thing that really offsets this thing, but it was always there and I arranged from putting all that information together and I started developing this thing. I'm doing this, I'm doing that, I'm doing this and so I started sort of my journey, my journey was going on and then I knew where I was going. I knew I had to get to a certain, the big lodge, the Anishinaabe people, that was my journey, that was the destiny that I was supposed to have done back in 1970.

"It was the destiny. I really came close in realizing that and this is what they [spirits] wanted me to do so during the journey I had a lot of different experiences, a lot of teachers and elders, from the spirits. I'm going to the psychologic and a lot of experiences, the good experiences so I guess with that, with the elders giving me the green light to talk about a lot of things. That's sort of opened a whole new door, relationship between the elders, the chiefs, the structure of what traditional government is all about, of the women council which is now known as a women council, but they are in our terminology and the youth, they're all in there and that sort of opened up a whole new area of what Indian government is all about and I was a big part of it and I'm still a big part of it.

"I'm very grateful for the role of the elders and the component of Treaty Three organization, the territorial organization. They're proud of that, to have been part of that and we're still being part of it as the process goes on. I'm going on 52 years old and I'm hoping that my role is filled and it's theirs for the next ten years. The whole gamut of things that changed in terms of my view, in terms of the Canadians and Anishinaabe politics and also starting back from the treaty [of 1873], the way I understand the treaty, the whole and completed treaty back then. But now today, since 1970, here in our community, I don't know what the percentage is that are here in Whitefish that are graduates. We have graduates here in the school, graduated from grade 12. The whole new environment of life which wasn't here."

Back when Allan White was a chief attending meetings in Ottawa with other chiefs and officials from the Department of Indian Affairs, he noticed that the bureaucrats at Indian Affairs had a habit of providing a reception on the night before the meeting and plying the chiefs with Scotch and other intoxicating spirits.

All too often, at the meeting early the next morning, some of the chiefs would be hung over from drinking too much the night before and the department officials would be bright eyed and bushy tailed and ready to negotiate the fine points of agreements affecting the lives of thousands of Aboriginal people.

Ron McDonald recalled his father coming home from a meeting with some of the other chiefs and officials from Indian Affairs saying: "We didn't achieve anything at that meeting. There was nobody around. We didn't have a quorum, no chiefs were around."

"It's because they were drinking," Ron said. "They couldn't get up in the morning. They were busy drinking all night at these conventions in Toronto, Ottawa. But, nowadays, you should see them. You should see the chiefs' attendance now. Although it may be not as it should be like 100 per cent, but you definitely see more."

That's the way Allan White saw things. "The biggest achievement I see as I sit here since 1970," he recalled, "let's go back to 1965. The biggest achievement that I have seen in my time in leadership are our chiefs and councillors. They just love going to a chiefs' meeting where it's so different an environment. You don't see anybody with a hangover. That's the most beautiful thing that I see, with their opening prayers and their remarks. It's the most beautiful thing. I've seen change in my time."

Chapter 14

Annie Wilson, an elder from the Rainy River First Nations reserve at Manitou Rapids—about 220 kilometres southeast of Kenora on the border between Canada and the United States—sat beside Josephine Mandamin when the Minister of Indian Affairs met with the Grand Council of Treaty #3 in March, 1996.

Annie held on to her native language despite the efforts of the white nuns to erase it from her memory. During the five years she attended St. Margaret's Indian Residential School in Fort Frances she, along with the other native students, was forbidden to speak Ojibway.

"The nun would make me stand up and say 'I'll not speak my language again' if I got caught speaking my language," Annie told me during an interview in 1997. "That's what she would make me do. 'I'll not speak my language', from nine o'clock till midnight at night I had to repeat that. From nine in the evening till midnight, I had to repeat that for a whole month. That was my punishment for speaking my language. And, at the back of my mind, I said 'No. It's going to stay there.'

"So I got out of the boarding school just in time. I was only there for about five years. It didn't take anything away from me, but I knew I would've lost my language if I would've stayed a little longer. I got out just to keep my language at that time. I almost was forgetting the things that I was taught, the things that I was told by my grandparents. Yeah, they taught me a lot, a lot of things because they took me all over. They took me to all those rituals. I understood everything.

"Everywhere you went, there was a sweat lodge because the sweat lodge was your teacher of all the environment, the nature, and you learnt a lot of this and because you were cleaning yourself as you were learning from the sweat.

"Your sweat helped you remember things, remember everything, how it feels to go through a learning, like sort of like wisdom. You have to say a few things when you were in there. People had to hear you talk about your spirituality or whatever, whatever you were comfortable with you had to talk about. You didn't go in there just because you were to get clean or whatever. You had to go in there and say something."

Annie wished that the young people of today could have had a taste of the good life that was lost. "My grandparents made their own butter as I remember doing this with cream and stuff like that and us kids used to do that and then we'd weed the gardens in the summer time as kids. Kids were told to do things at that time. I don't know today, it's so hard for a child to do anything for nothing. It's not like a long time ago. To me, a long time ago, when you were being taught, you felt that you were being loved.

"Today it's not like that. The loving is misunderstood I think. That's the way I feel sometimes is a misunderstanding. How do you love what's conditional? When I was growing up as a child, when I seen people working at home, like my grandfather, my grandmother working together, I thought well this felt like I was loved because I was being taught something that I was going to be able to do something with. The way I used to hear it when I was younger, it was a beautiful life before they were disturbed by any people, like the white people."

While she believed it was important to get back to the old ways, the traditional ways of the Ojibway, she said that could not be done if people couldn't speak the language. "I think if we get back on our own it will be a better way, but the language has to come in also. The language has to be understood by the younger people so they'll all carry on the traditions of how life was supposed to be."

Annie was emphatic about the benefits she enjoyed as a result of being able to speak Ojibway, as a child and as an adult. "The way I felt when I was a child there was a lot of sharing. Today there's no sharing. The kids don't understand what you're saying because we have to speak in English. They don't know the language. If they knew that language, honest to God, those people would be very smart. They don't know what they're missing. I really feel sorry for them. That's what I tell them in schools when I talk to kids. You missed what I went through when I was a child. I seen love, I seen caring, I seen how things grow.

"You will never see that. You will never be taught the things that I was taught. That will never be in the school neither. But what I went through, when I come out of that boarding school, I was taught to have a garden, taught to go trapping, understand the animals, oodles of stuff. That's when my education started—when I came back out of the crazy school."

Annie told me about the times in the early 1990s when she would travel long distances to counsel suicidal young Ojibways, one of whom had made three attempts at taking his own life. "It's not tradition to kill anybody or commit suicide. You never reach your grandmother when you commit suicide. No. Because it's not a natural death. A natural death is better than taking your own life. You're disobeying the Creator so you don't get there.

"That's how I teach the kids when they're suicidal. That you're not going to see your mother. Your mother died a year ago and you want to commit suicide because you don't have a mother. 'Why die,' I said, 'why kill yourself when you're not going to see her anyway?'

"The Creator didn't say to take your life. Keep it to help somebody and then go when you're finished. That's what the teachings are. You don't take your own life, I say, and think that you're going to go to a good place. You'll never get there. You'll just go. You're just out of this world, but your spirit doesn't have a home. You suffer."

Annie told the young people that everyone has to suffer a bit in life. "That's why the Creator gives us those trials, to see how strong we are. And we can get stronger because of death, because of grief and the grief is not supposed to last a year. It's only supposed to last a few days, till the body goes in the ground and is covered." In a traditional

Ojibway burial, a hole is drilled in the lid of the coffin just by the head so that, after four days, the spirit can leave the body.

"You live and you never forget that, but still you live," Annie told me. "You have to live a different life. You got to take what is good. You don't take the bad at all. Got to have a real mind, good mind."

Like Josephine Mandamin, Annie Wilson was highly suspicious of the white bureaucrats and their political masters. "We don't want to do what our ancestors did, just sign things [treaties] before they knew what they were giving you. There was so much promises but they never understood when they broke it. All those people are gone. All those promises to them was broken. But, then the education got in and that's when we started to see what actually happened with the abuse of the promises.

"This has been going on for years that I know of, like ever since I could understand my grandfather when he was the chief. There was all this negotiating over their rights, whatever, the promises were given. They were not met because some of the things that happened in my family, the stories that I've heard in my family, was how they got here [Manitou Rapids] at a certain time after the Treaty #3 thing was signed in 1873, whatever, and then, all of a sudden, we have to move from our reserves in 1915, '17."

After the government forced the Ojibways off the fertile land that had been reserved for them under Treaty #3, most of them moved to Manitou Rapids and some moved to Big Grassy River, about 45 kilometres north of the U.S. border. "They sort of scattered." Annie said. "Scattered all over the place. There was relatives all over."

Annie's grandfather moved his family to Manitou Rapids and they had to live in a tent for the first year. That's when her first grandmother passed away. "I was kind of young at that time, but I still wondered why they kept having meetings and I was kind of curious because I understood the [Ojibway] language. They were always speaking in that language, talking about what is happening to them, what is happening all the time in Indian Affairs or whatever. So I often wondered what are they talking about? Then pretty soon I started getting involved with all these meetings.

"Yeah. They're having all these meetings all the time. That's in the olden days for me, like, I'll be 72 in November and I remember lots from the things I heard, from the things that happened and how they done things like getting into different things. Like, when they wanted to fish, they would ask [Indian Affairs] for their nets and when they wanted to hunt, they would ask for ammunition."

The approximately 200 Ojibways at Annie Wilson's home reserve of Manitou Rapids had succeeded in making a much better life for themselves than the people at Whitefish Bay—about 1.5 hours north on Highway 71.

They had a large modern computerized sawmill, a windows factory and a fish hatchery where they were raising sturgeon. They also had part ownership of a 70-room motel in Fort Frances and a shopping mall. Every Ojibway at Manitou Rapids who was able to work could work. They were even providing employment for natives from surrounding reserves—and for some white people from the nearby villages. They had a gymnasium and, right next to it, a medical clinic. They grew hay for their own use and for sale to local farmers.

Chief Jim Leonard told me in an interview in 1997 that much of the band's success was due to the fact that they had always been on the Rainy River, that there were villages nearby and Fort Frances—with its big pulp and paper mill—was less than an hour's drive east.

"We had people just abutting our boundary, our farms, and we went to work for those people. We helped them in logging in the spring and went out and helped them in the fields, haying and things like that. We traded with them even though we weren't supposed to trade with them, but we traded with them," he said.

"We've had a lot of involvement through our history with the white people. We've always been very good friends with them in this area anyway, being on the river here and the river boats. Some of our people worked on the river boats and helped with the river trade so it was quite normal for us to, I guess, 'socialize' and that became a part of our culture, along with the more traditional aspects like feasts and pow wows. We did all those. We were quite comfortable doing those and we enjoyed doing those and our elders today have expressed a willingness to get back to those types of things. As a matter of fact, we've had a couple of square dances here during these last few months."

Jim Leonard, who has a degree in psychology, was very self-motivated and determined to build a better life for his children. "I grew up in a family that was very, very, poor. I come from a large family and I can recall being six, seven, eight years old, getting off the school bus at 4:30 when it's dark and going to check my rabbit snares to see if there was any rabbits so we would have some meat on the table for supper for the next day. I can remember having to go through four feet of snow to haul wood home so that we could have heat and I can recall very, very, clearly telling myself when I was pulling that log through the forest and the snow saying, my children will never ever go through what I'm going through."

Little did he know he'd be operating a sophisticated fish hatchery in 1997 funded 100% by the band. "The hatchery is doing very, very, well," he told me. "We're currently raising sturgeon. It's a prehistoric fish. It's 150 million years old and they haven't changed in 150 million years. There's nothing really close to it. We have three different classes. The year before we did some experimentation with lake sturgeon and charlenots [shovelnose sturgeon] and we've successfully bred a hybrid. We're using those technologies for growth rates and things like that. Just lately we've got some Russian sturgeon in there. We're looking at how fast they grow. Maybe, sometime down the road, we'll look at seeing if we can breed those type as a fish. It's all research. It's all geared towards research because the sturgeon is such a slow-growing fish, we've got to try and speed up the growth of it."

I asked how slow the process was. "Well it takes about twenty years to mature. In order to make the sturgeon economic for us, we've got to speed that up. We're also looking at raising other alternative species like trout, white perch, yellow perch, those things, because we've got to start making some money to recover our investment. Right now we're funding at 100 per cent, the band, and we're using money from our other enterprises."

How do you make money from raising sturgeon? Where's the profit? "The profit there could be in meat production. If we can speed the growth up so in three years we can have a five or six pound fish that we can sell to say the restaurant trade. We could sell the fingerlings to other hatcheries. There's a market in Eastern Europe for that and in Japan."

What are fingerlings? "Fingerlings are sort of the small three or four inch fish and right now it's being currently used in the aquarium business. There's a big business in the oriental countries because they like their fish ponds and their aquariums and things like that. In Europe, that's the same thing and also they're growing them for food."

So would you sort of try to market it as a "Rainy River" sturgeon, as a unique product? "Not necessarily. Because the species is in trouble right now. There's very little sturgeon in the market right now and because we have the capabilities to raise sturgeon and if we can grow them quicker, so to speak, then we'll obviously have a market advantage here. So as far as other people getting into the market, we have no concerns of that right now."

He then talked with pride about the success that they were having with their other enterprises. "We're selling a lot of windows locally. The First Nations communities in the area are starting to buy, but it's a growing process, like any business. It takes a few years to become established. We're trying to work with the Treaty Nine [James Bay area] bands. We've had people from northern Manitoba come and look at our windows and hopefully we'll do business with them.

"We've got to start utilizing the poplar and the hardwood species [at the sawmill], but at the same time we've got to become more efficient with the material that we're using. We've got to add more value to it in terms of manufacturing it down to the more valuable components. No longer that we're just selling eight by eights. We're actually making panelling and things like that, furniture components and stuff."

"They make a good product," Herb Hoffman of the Red Indian Lodge told me. "I've used it. I've used their panelling. Cabin 4, the long one, that's theirs. That whole inside came from Manitou and they did a nice job. Very nice quality stuff, good work. That's the right answer see. Anything that's highly labour intensive."

Back in 1972, when I first visited Manitou Rapids as a consultant for the Department of Indian Affairs, they were making boxcar doors for the railway and were in the process of expanding their sawmill.

The first thing you noticed, after crossing the railway tracks running parallel with the highway, was the wooden platforms they had built at the curb outside each house to keep the dogs from getting at the household garbage.

Harvesting wild rice by hand was an important cash crop for the Ojibways but they were having trouble competing with the rice farmers in Manitoba and Minnesota who used combines to harvest thousands of hectares at a time.

General Mills, at Minneapolis, Minnesota, set the price for the rice on the basis of supply. That meant that a price that was right for the farmers in Manitoba and Minnesota did not work for the Ojibways who harvested the wild rice by hand from canoes.

Willie Wilson, a leader with a special interest in promoting economic development who had been chief of the band at Manitou Rapids for 17 years, decided that their best hope was to get into the business of seeding large sections of the reserve and harvesting the rice paddies with combines.

He was outlining the new idea at a public meeting one night attended by about 100 Ojibways. At one point, he asked if there were any questions. A wise old Ojibway at the back of the room put up his hand and then rose and said: "For two hundred years now, they've been trying to turn us into brown white men. Now, you come along, and you want to turn us into Chinamen."

The elders had had so many proposals, so many half-baked ideas, coming at them over the years. This old guy's sitting there at the back of the room saying to himself "OK now what is it this time?" He's trying to figure it out, because it can't be what Willie is saying it is. "Oh, my God, I've got it! They want us to become Chinamen."

Jim Leonard told me the farmers in Manitoba and Minnesota had flooded the rice market and driven the price down. "And consequently today [1997] the wild rice industry is still trying to recover from that. May never recover. You can't afford to go out and pick it anymore because you don't get anything for it so I go out now and pick it for our own use. It sells for $8 a pound whereas you can buy it in Minnesota, the paddy rice, for 99 cents a pound. People that know the difference want the traditional rice, but a large percentage of the people don't know the difference so they buy the 99 cent rice. The paddy rice killed the market. Producers [from Minnesota and Manitoba] were dumping rice on the market."

Despite the financial success of the band at Manitou Rapids, Jim Leonard shared the criticism of the white bureaucracy voiced by Josephine and Isaac Mandamin at Whitedog and Andy and Allan White at Whitefish Bay. "In terms of the difference between now [1997] and 15 years ago, there's a massive difference, just the level of bureaucracy that the governments demand. Fifteen years ago you could go and talk to the governments without any paper and sit across from each other. Now you need massive files of paper to even get through the door."

Willie Wilson shared that view. "We still have those conditions. We still have the stigma of the federal government because of the Indian Act and because of the federal government's intervention. The communities can administer themselves but also there's a stumbling block for them to become more economically sustainable. It's the old story again where one of the communities decides to take advantage of methods of being able to generate its own revenues so that it can make its own decisions and govern itself accordingly.

"The Department of Indian Affairs in its own wisdom will say 'well, under the Indian Act, we have this traditional responsibility'. Indian Affairs wants to have control, wants to know exactly where money's coming from and how money's coming from. Chiefs and councils are very much controlled by the Indian Act, very much controlled by the government of the day."

He gave the example of what happens when the bands show some initiative and develop something that will generate revenue—like the Red Dog Inn they owned in Fort Frances and the shopping centre. "Every time you generate revenue, whatever you generate the next fiscal year the government will say, 'wrong, you've generated $50,000. That's $50,000 we're going to give you less this year'. There's no incentive. Under the new arrangements, for example, there's five communities that want a little shopping centre. They own the Red Dog, there's three communities that own the shopping mall, whatever they make the government wants to know how much you're makin'. How much revenue have you generated. Then they'll take it off the top. They want you to zero balance all the time. So there's no incentive to be economically viable where you can generate your own sources of revenue, etc. And there's no incentive there for us to educate our people to become self-sufficient."

Jim Leonard agreed with Isaac Mandamin and others who said the 1965 General Welfare Agreement making native people eligible for social assistance from the provincial government had a negative impact.

"In 1965 when the GWA Act came in, for the first time in our history we were given money if we didn't work in terms of welfare payments and I think that began almost immediately to create a dependency," he said. "People looked at material things. There was more of an emphasis on that want for more material goods. There was an immediate need for economic development and job creation so that you could keep up with the Joneses. If the Joneses bought a television set, you wanted a television set and vice-versa, whereas prior to that, we didn't have those. Nobody had those. We were very poor, but we were also very happy and very self-sustaining.

"In those days we didn't get very much help from the federal government. They kind of left us on our own for us to survive on our own and we did that and I think we were quite successful at doing that, even though we didn't have any money or some of the other material goods. We only had ourselves. We were like a family at that time and we functioned like a family.

"We had quite a self-contained community here prior to that. Our economy here was a communal farming type economy. Everybody had their own gardens [farms], social structure in the community was very tight and close-knit. If people were hungry, we shared. There was square dances. There was a lot of social activities and we were a happy tight-knit community.

"So that [1965] was a time of change for us, not good and not bad. I guess it's good from the sense that people began to have more money, having more material things, but bad from a sense of the social structure broke down almost immediately, overnight. That's where I'm coming from on that."

He spoke with bitterness about the government's decision, back in 1915, to move several separate bands off the fertile land Treaty #3 had reserved for them. "They were part of the seven communities and the settlers came in and they wanted the land for settlement and we were removed from the land. They [government] bundled us up and dropped us off in Manitou. It's the community's goal to get some of that land back and, if it's in private ownership, then we're not going to force anybody off. We'll work with the person. It will be a cooperative thing, not an adversarial thing."

He mentioned a white farmer who was occupying land that had been taken from the Ojibways. "His family's been here for 100 years. This is his home and we respect that. We want, when all the dust is settled and the claim is settled, we have to live together. Why not live together in a mutually beneficial environment? No adversary. It's our neighbours and we respect that and vice-versa."

While the relocation of the Rainy River bands was a lot more complicated than the amalgamation of the three bands at Whitedog, they managed to make a success of it. "We had seven chiefs, up until 1959, living in Manitou and so having that experience, that historical past of getting along with each other, of having seven different councils in one, it must've been a massive job in trying to run this place, but they did it. So we see that as part of our history, being able to get along with each other here and being able to progress. We've made use to the best of our ability of the resources that we have."

He emphasized time and again that they have always enjoyed good relations with the white people living in the surrounding communities. "We've always recognized that aspect of it and I think a lot of the reason for that relationship is because our people worked in the past for those logging companies, worked off the reserves for, at various times, for all these people" he said. "I think that's because of our history, our history of being on the river and trading with the white traders and integrating with those structures and becoming aware of those structures.

"We've traded with those people and built very, very, strong relationships with the people of Emo [a small village east of the reserve] and the people of Barwick [an even smaller village to the west] to the extent where we still have those relationships. Those family ties go back a long ways. Take, for example, the Tomkins family. My grandfather traded with old man Charlie and was very, very, good friends with him. I'm very good friends with his family now and continue to be. My sons are still very good friends with the Tomkins family so it's almost like, we lived side by side for the last 150 years or so and we've come to be very good friends and we'll continue to do that.

"Even with our land claims, we're working with community groups and trying to educate them that we're not here to take the land. We're here to come to a settlement that we were wronged in the 1900s [when the government moved them off the land that had been reserved for them under the treaty they entered into in 1873 in order to make way for the settlers] and we want to work with anyone to come to a point where everyone's satisfied. There's no winners or losers in a land claim. I think everybody has to be satisfied. That's the goal."

Another reason for the success at Manitou Rapids was the cooperative relationship they had developed with the Northwest Bay Band — about half way between Manitou Rapids and Fort Frances — and the Couchiching band on the eastern border of Fort Frances.

"I talk to those communities on a regular basis regarding opportunities," Jim said. "We're always talking about where we can jointly participate in economic ventures. Almost at every meeting we talk about this so it's continuing. There's jokes around the table, maybe we'll own the town of Fort Frances some day. It's something to look forward to. Probably never happen, but that's the attitude of First Nations because we all realize that we're not large enough, we don't have the resources to do things by ourselves. We have to join our resources together."

That cooperation extended to the policing of the three communities. "We have three [police officers] here and we have three in Couchiching and we also work with Northwest Bay and they have a couple. So, there's eight officers and they jointly patrol the three communities. There's various things we do, very informally. I talk to the chiefs of Northwest Bay and Couchiching on a regular basis, at least once a week, to talk about issues on all things. We're not isolated here. We consult fairly regularly."

Despite the economic progress the Rainy River Ojibways had made over the years, Jim Leonard agreed 100% with Annie Wilson that there was a need to get back to the old ways—to the true ways of the Ojibway people.

"Well, the way I like to put it is that we survived prior to getting the funding from Indian Affairs which started in the late '60s. We had our own close-knit family. We were poor. We had a lot of leadership there, but we survived and a lot of people were very happy the way we lived.

"That's why I say there's good and there's bad about it and there's a desire from our elders to return to that type of a life, to try to get some of them back, take the good things and incorporate them into today's lifestyle. Like, we can't go back and live in teepees and hunt by the river. We all got responsibilities. That can never happen, but there's certain aspects that we can try to bring those social pleasures, I guess if you want to call them, back and incorporate them today.

"There's a movement today of trying to get back those [spiritual and cultural] things that we lost. I can recall being in about grade three or so [at a public school] and the teacher got up and said to the class 'I want each of you to get up and say where you're from' and you had kids getting up and saying 'I'm from Italy, I'm from Germany and my parents are British' or whatever and, when we got to me, I didn't know what to say. You can understand how I felt. I felt very, very, inferior because I didn't know where I was <u>from</u>. So when you say that we were brought up to believe from society that we were inferior, at times, I think we did believe we were inferior."

Did the manner in which they were perceived by the overall white society become somewhat of a self-fulfilling prophecy? "Self-fulfilling prophecy, yes. You begin to have all these social ills and that was about like, in the early '70s. There was an obvious declaration in those communities that we would start to provide jobs and give our people that opportunity and we went overboard. So that, in the mid '80s, early '80s, there was a gradual reversal to learning about the more traditional aspects and that's where we're still going. But, at the same time, we all realize that we have to live and we have to live with the outside world. So we've got to find that happy medium. I'm very proud to be a Canadian, but I'm also very proud to be an Indian. Maybe 15 years ago, I wouldn't 've said that."

What about the language in his community? Did most of the children speak Ojibway? "I would say that the language is in trouble here, even though we've taught it in the schools for the last 20 years or so. It's been taught in the schools but it's still not being picked up. I'm sorry to say that that's happening. I myself, I don't speak the language. I can understand it and I could probably pick it up very quickly if I was immersed in it. I grew up until I was about five years old speaking the language and using the language, but, when I hit school, I lost it."

Despite having lost his language, Jim Leonard is very proud of his Ojibway heritage and would not consider living anywhere else other than Manitou Rapids. "This is my home. I was born here and I will die here. I lived off the community at various times. I've been away, going to school and I think I could survive, but I don't want to be any place else. This is a part of me, good or bad, I'll be here."

Jim Leonard was very enthusiastic about an interpretive centre that was being built at The Place of the Long Rapids (Kay-Nah-Chi-Wah-Nung) farther west on the bank of the Rainy River. "Well I guess, personally, the significance is that's where my family came from," he told me during a visit to the site of the interpretive centre. "We lived here for generations, forever. This was our home, this site where we're at today. My grandfather was born here and it was his dream that he would some day come back here. It was his dream to some day have something here that we could share with the rest of the world and I still carry that same dream. I guess no matter what the physical structure, what we put there, it has that spiritual significance and that's the greatest thing, that significance, the history that's there."

Also known as the Manitou Mounds, The Place of the Long Rapids was once at the centre of a continent-wide aboriginal trading network and is regarded by the Ojibway people as a sacred place. It contains the largest group of burial mounds and associated village sites in Canada and has a history that can be traced back 8,000 years.

"All the rivers from the north end up there and all the river streams that come from the south end up there so it used to be the largest trading area in North America," Willie Wilson told me. "You will see evidence of artifacts from Florida, from California, from both oceans. People used to trade with them."

The burial mounds are located on terraces along the bank of the Rainy River. They range in size from 18 to 24 metres in diameter and up to 7 metres in height. The original mounds were made by digging a shallow pit, placing the dead person in the pit and filling the pit with earth. The next person to die would be placed on top and covered with earth. Hundreds of years later, this layering process had created the mounds that are there today.

In order to prepare the deceased for life after death, medicine bags, pipes, food, clay pots, and tools and other items were often placed in the grave. The roundhouse, which was designed using traditional architecture under the guidance of the elders, has nine sides embodying clans, families and community. Its round appearance was designed to represent the Ojibways' belief that all that is circular is good. The four cedar poles in the centre of the roundhouse represent the four directions — east, west, north and south. The round earthen floor was designed so dancers could touch Mother Earth. A sculpture of the sacred eagle in the centre represented a vision that came to one of the elders from the Creator.

Jim Leonard envisioned the interpretive centre as a place where the Ojibways could rediscover their culture and learn and share something of their heritage with people from the outside. Part of that heritage is the annual practice of burning the prairie grass, as has been done every spring for generations, in order to facilitate the growth of prairie plants and inhibit the encroachment of invasive species.

The comparative lack of progress up the road at Whitefish Bay, which has about five times more people than Manitou Rapids, was not for any lack of ideas. Recall the fur factory, the houseboat rental plan and other projects.

Despite the fact he dropped out of school after Grade 2, Andy White was a very astute person and he had a good mind for business.

At one point, he decided to run for election as Grand Chief of the Grand Council of Treaty #3.

"I had this idea that I'm not very smart but at least, I told them, somebody can translate for me, if I want to meet the government official, I can talk to him in my own language. I'm not very good in terms of a real good dialogue, where it just goes back and forth in argument, but, if I can do that, my whole idea was all those years and I still think it's a very good idea and I think it could be done if only somebody were to listen. There's 25 reserves in Treaty Three and we all buy from Winnipeg. We all buy from Safeway.

"And I was saying, telling people, 'for Christ sakes look at us. Look what we're doing to ourselves. Let's stop blaming the government. Let's compete with the people for Christ sakes,' I said. Let's build a big lumber company let's say in Manitou. Everybody goes buying there. It's a big co-op for all Treaty Three. OK? Let's build another big shop, grocery shop in Kenora. Everybody goes shopping, even put one in Fort Frances and even one in Dryden. You got three of them. All Indian people go shopping. Start working as one, like a big co-op as one and make sure our chiefs support that, but it's not working like that. That was my whole idea and I still think that's a good idea."

The problem, he said, was that there were too many divisions in Whitefish Bay. Nobody had any interest in pulling together to build a better future for their kids. "There's a lot of divisions within the [Whitefish Bay] family," so nobody wants to do anything opposed to the other one and I think that's the trend that we are in right now. There's a lot of hatred in this community. There's literally hatred in this community. Division. You just have to pretend that everything's OK when you walk in here, but you know damn well there is division. There's four or five divisions so nobody just doesn't want to do anything. One group starts something on their own, another group starts something. They don't even go and help each other.

"Nobody wants to work without getting paid. That's just the way it is. There's no more what you call the quality of service. That was always the thing a long time ago, quality. Somebody starts something, everybody goes, women go, they cook, men eat in one place, they finish whatever they're doing. It's not like that now. It's a sad situation."

Andy's brother Clarence was chief of the Whitefish Bay band when I interviewed him in 1997. "I try to tell him, reason with him, but he's never here. He's never here. He's never around to look at his community, what's happened to his community."

I asked if it wouldn't it be better if all of the chiefs, not just his brother, but all of them spent more time at home. "It would be yeah and that's what I try to tell him. He's away right now and he's not going to be back until I don't know when. He's off to B.C. [British Columbia] next week, I suppose for the election of the national chief [of the Assembly of First Nations]. So we're lost. The community is in financial chaos. We're almost $2 million in debt from what I heard.

"The whole community, the whole band, is in chaos, simply because there's no control. Who's going to control it? Chief and council? We have a band administrator, maybe sometimes the chief tries to control, too. Band council meeting comes along. They set up committees and the committee's going to decide. Chief and council turns them off so what happens is committee lays it down and says 'if you guys have the power, then you do it' That's just the way it is.

"I'm sad. I'm sad what I see. Like I tell my wife 'let's just try and survive. Let's try and get our kids off to university' because my wife and I think the same. We think of the future, our children. That's how we talk all the time and we should have, but there's nothing we can do because our hands are tied. You can't even go to a council meeting.

"Like sometimes I ask what time for the council to go and discuss with them about situations in the community. About drugs coming in. Band employees are sometimes the suppliers and they work for the band. Can't we do something? Why can't the community say 'you're suppliers, you're using children and we want you either straighten around or go find something else', but they can't do that because our political people, I suppose, to protect themselves for the next election, but that's not the point. It's hurting our children. It's really hurting our children and I was, my wife and I, kind of sometimes I suppose put your children between and try and go along and let's just get our children to go and finish their university and we'll support them and then after that maybe we'll retire. We can just live. I think we'll build someplace. I think there's a little land out there someplace.

"Unless this community comes to a stop. I always tell my brothers, stop this community where it's going now, stop it. Stop right there and bring in all the good people, bring in those old chiefs that have been there and talk to them. Look at the future.

"They can't even do that. That's one of the big arguments we have. My brother said, 'I let my council decide. They're my advisers.' I said 'for Christ sakes they're only human beings. They're only people that were walking around the road here before elections and all of a sudden they become councillors and they think they're experts. I don't think so,' I said. The experts are the guys that have been in this organization, that were in the organization as chief and council. That's the one you should be dealing with. But they just won't do it.

"A lot of people on the reserve thought they owned chief and council. That chief and council are accountable to the people. A lot of people were very surprised that this isn't the case. The accountability is directed right straight to a minister and to the bureaucracy of Indian Affairs by way of accountability. I know some First Nations that are in serious deficits and there's nothing that First Nations can do with the people because they don't even know what the hell it [deficit] is."

As far as Herb Hoffman of the Red Indian Lodge was concerned, the best bet for the people of Whitefish Bay was to stick to tourism and forestry, with the main emphasis on forestry. "I think that's the answer, the forestry industry," he told me. "Now, if you're going to do forestry, then let's finish the product a little bit more. Don't sell the logs type of thing like they do in B.C., sell it to the Japanese and the Japanese manufacture everything and so on and so forth. So what you need to do is to manufacture that wood here a little bit.

"I think they might be better off with having their own municipal-type government than with Indian Affairs. This Indian Affairs thing is not working, the way I look at it. I mean look at the past 40, 50 years. It hasn't worked. So, if it hasn't worked, let's change it. Anything, but let's not put it in on the same level as the nation to nation. I mean, we're talking about a good municipal government and then run your affairs that way and then have your own destiny to a certain degree. I don't see anything wrong with that at all. That's fine. I'd go for that any day."

Chapter 15

Police Constable Tara Kelly, a very attractive young woman in a navy blue uniform with a radio phone on one hip and a revolver on the other, was part of the security detail for the meeting between the Minister of Indian Affairs and the Grand Council of Treaty #3 in March, 1996.

Tara was based at the Ontario Provincial Police detachment at Sioux Narrows and lived with her mother at Fred Kelly's home reserve of Sabaskong, about 150 kilometres southeast of Kenora.

A short time after Tara became a police officer, she came across a driver whose car had crashed into a moose on the main highway that connects Kenora to Fort Frances. It was one of her former teachers from the school at Sabaskong.

"I was in the cruiser alone and I pulled up and he turned around. 'It's me. Tara,' I said. I knew what he thought of me. He didn't see me as an officer. He saw me as Tara Kelly, the little girl in school. I asked him where the moose was and all that and he told me it was up the road. And then he said: 'Well, are you going to call a cop?' And I'm standing there, uniform, cruiser right behind me, lights flashing, and he just kind of laughed, like he just realized what he said. But he just saw me as Tara. That was it. He didn't see me as a cop.

"What he said, I just had to ignore, but it bothered me inside. Like you're trying to gain your confidence while you're out there doing this and I just dealt with it. I shot the moose. I had to. It had to be put away. It was just mangled, couldn't walk or anything. That was my first moose I ever shot. I like hunting, but I never went hunting that way."

Shortly after providing security at the meeting with the Minister of Indian Affairs and the Grand Council of Treaty #3, Tara was wearing a purple traditional Ojibway jingle dress [which features several rows of metal cones] at a pow wow at Sabaskong.

About 200 Ojibways were circling, shuffling, around the floor of the school gymnasium—they had moved inside because of the rain—keeping time to the beat of the drums and the singers. Dum dum, dum dum. Dum dum, dum dum. Round and round they went in traditional costumes with a multitude of colours and the jingles on the women's dresses going jing jing, jing jing. Jing jing, jing jing.

Tara's feet barely touched the floor. They just sort of kissed it as she circled the gym with an eagle feather fan clasped in her hand. One minute she's speeding down the highway in her police cruiser responding to an emergency call. The next moment she's on that gymnasium floor performing an Ojibway dance that goes back hundreds of years.

"It's a drum that you feel," she told me. "You're dancing to the drums, like you're feeling the dance. You know how people dance differently, the way they feel the drums. Yeah, it just makes you feel good especially when you hear the drums. There's differences in the drumming, like the old songs and the new songs. My brother's a drummer. It's just like you get power from it. Like when you're there it gives you a feeling of that's who you really are sort of thing, like this is where I belong. It's like a safe place."

Tara's mother took her to a lot of pow wows when she was growing up. "I grew up dancing in pow wows. My whole life is pow wows. I got family there. This is something that's normal, something you do all the time. I went to pow wows all the time, like every weekend if we could. You meet a lot of elders there, you get teachings from there and it's just meeting different people, like one whole big family getting together, like different families, but you're all one."

I was one of only a very few white people at the pow wow. At one point, early on in the afternoon, a muscular young Ojibway with tattoos on his forearms and both sides of his head shaved to make a Mohawk warrior haircut came up to me and, in a very threatening manner, asked me what I was doing there. When I told him I was just there as an observer, he asked who told me it was OK to do that. I told him that I had been invited to the pow wow.

"Oh, yeah, who invited you?" he demanded, rather belligerently. When I told him I'd been invited by Fred Kelly, a former chief of the Sabaskong band and Grand Chief of the Grand Council of Treaty #3, his whole attitude changed and he said of course I could stay. It turned out that Fred was his uncle.

"You know what," the young man said, "I spent my whole life in and out of institutions [training school and jail] and finally, when I was just a total mess, Fred took a hold of me, straightened my life out and to me there's only two people in this world that's worth anything and that's Fred and Peter [Fred's older brother]."

The mention of Fred's name had gained me safe passage to remain at the pow wow. I had been encircled by several hostile young Ojibway men and, since the atmosphere had changed for the better, I decided to tell them a story that had been told to me by Ojibway poet/writer Duke Redbird shortly after Prime Minister Pierre Elliott Trudeau brought the Canadian constitution home from England.

Here's some background. When the contiguous British colonies now known as the provinces of Ontario, Quebec, Nova Scotia and New Brunswick agreed to become one nation under British rule in 1867, the Canadian Constitution was kept in Britain. Any attempts to amend the constitution had to be approved by the British Parliament.

Prime Minister Trudeau succeeded in getting rid of that last piece of colonial baggage in 1982 when Queen Elizabeth II came over from England to sign the necessary papers so that, from that time forward, the British Parliament would have no say over Canada or its constitution.

Many native leaders were concerned about the impact patriating the constitution might have on their rights under the treaties and, during the time leading up to the actual patriation, they went to England to express their concerns to the Queen. Their concerns went unheeded and the constitution was patriated on schedule.

A year after the constitution was returned to Canada, some native leaders were in Ottawa where they were invited to meet the prime minister and some of his cabinet colleagues in preparation for a meeting that was going to be televised the following day. In telling this story, it is important to bear in mind that Prime Minister Trudeau did not believe in the concept of the inherent rights of the Aboriginal people or of their widely-expressed desire for self-government. In fact, he was adamantly opposed.

"We were all invited into the Cabinet room in Ottawa to discuss the agenda for the following day because we were going to be on television and it was going to be a public forum," Duke Redbird, a member of the Saugeen First Nation on the eastern shore of Lake Huron, told me. "So, the prime minister wanted to be briefed by the national leaders on what direction the discussion would take."

The Prime Minister asked them what was on their agenda, what they wanted to discuss with him at the meeting which was to be held on the following morning. Duke said the Native Council of Canada (an organization of Métis and non-status Indians formed after the National Indian Council dissolved) which he was representing at the meeting was interested in pursuing the question of self-determination.

"Trudeau went into a philosophical kind of discussion around the topic of self- determination and he said that self-determination was being fought for in places like Algeria and South Africa and Ireland, Libya and all kinds of places around the world. He went as far as to say that he supported the notion of self-determination," Duke told me.

"But then he said something to the effect that self-determination is broad and requires great sacrifice and he wanted to know how much blood was the native leadership prepared to shed for this idea because his government would not accept self-determination by native people.

"His final word on that was that the question of self-determination was a non-starter at that meeting. He said his government was not going to engage in discussions about self-determination and, if we were determined to pursue that, we'd better be, I'm paraphrasing now, we'd better be determined to fight for it because his government was not prepared to negotiate it.

"What that made me realize, and the other leadership there, was that we'd better be very responsible about what we tell our constituents because anybody's blood is going to be on our conscience and our hands if we are pushing the people to do something when we know very well that the final result can only be bloodshed and that it will be our people's blood that's going to be shed."

What the prime minister had said, in effect, was that, if Duke Redbird and his colleagues believed that the white man stole their lands at the end of a gun, that was the only way they were going to get it back. And, as was the case when Lieutenant-Governor Alexander Morris was travelling across western Canada in the 1870s making treaties with Queen Victoria's "red children", the whites had multiple times more guns and ammunition.

The young Ojibways at the pow wow listened intently as I told them about Duke Redbird and the prime minister. And then, the young man who first accosted me said: "You know, Trudeau was right. The time for talking is over. We've got a lot of angry young native people across this country. Let's bring it on."

His muscular young colleagues nodded their heads in agreement. They wanted to fight. They wanted to go to war to get back what their forefathers had lost. They were prepared to put their lives on the line for it.

When the Copenace family won the election and took control of the Band Council at Sabaskong in December, 1990, they fired all the Kellys who had been working for the band. Tara's sister and two cousins were among those who lost their jobs. "You can go and talk to people today [1997] and they'll say they had no right to fire these people," Tara told me. "They fired them just because they're Kellys."

This is not an uncommon problem on the reserves. Most of the Ojibway communities covered by Treaty #3, for example, are usually composed of no more than three or four different families. Control of the community's affairs passes back and forth between the different families.

Tara said her sister was on the band council at the time but the

Copenaces wouldn't tell her when the council was going to meet because they didn't want her to know what was going on. "We all went to the band officers, trying to settle this fight, this Copenace/Kelly thing. That's what they called it. The kids were fighting at school because they'd hear their parents talking about it so they don't like this kid because of this kid's parents. That's the reason why we pulled our kids out of the school, because of the fighting."

At one point, Tara's young niece was in the local grocery store and an adult Copenace started pushing her around because of the dispute. "Adults were picking on the kids. That's why we built a small school in my uncle's house. But then he was told he had to leave his house because he had 'all these people staying in there.' But they weren't staying there. They just had a school there.

"Anyway, he had to leave the house. The band, the chief and council, can kick out anybody they want. They're writing up all kinds of BCRs [band council resolutions], telling this person you're not allowed on this reserve any more. How would you react if you're put in a situation where your niece is pushed by an older lady and kids are fighting in school and nobody wants to talk about the problems? How the heck are you supposed to deal with it? And then they tell your uncle to move out of his house because he's putting a school in his basement for his kids to keep their education going and he's told to leave. I mean, they just have this authority where they [band council] can do anything and get rid of anyone."

Things degenerated to the stage where several of the families decided they had no option but to move back to the old reserve, off the road about eight kilometres north of Sabaskong, where they lived until Highway 71 was opened in 1936. The government moved the Ojibways to a new reserve at Sabaskong so they would have better access to hospitals and other amenities of modern life. It was to that old reserve in the bush that the families decided to return and start a new life together.

"They lived in tents all that summer, all winter," Tara recalled. "When they moved out there, there was nothing. There was just trees out there and there was just a clearing where the old reserve was. They built tents and they got lumber and all that to build a building.

It was a main building where everybody went to eat and they had a school there and what was taught there was a traditional way, the Ojibway language."

Tara said her mother, Mary, was really happy to be back at the old reserve where she grew up. "It was just like, this is her place. There's no electricity out there. They got a generator the following year I think."

They didn't have jobs because some of them had been fired when the Copenace family took over at Sabaskong. They had pulled their children from the school at Sabaskong but some teachers had moved with them back to the old reserve. They also had a former band manager and Tara's uncle who had been chief at one time. "They had everything out there. If you're talking about self-government, that was it. They started right from the bottom."

They wrote to the Department of Indian Affairs about their predicament but there was no response. When they tried to address the issue at a meeting of the Grand Council of Treaty #3 at the Best Western Lakeside Inn in Kenora, the Grand Chief—Fred Kelly's brother Peter—wouldn't let them speak. In fact, he told a Member of the Provincial Parliament who was attending the meeting that he didn't think he should recognize them or listen to what they had to say. They were on their own.

"They just put whatever food they had and put it together and tried to feed everybody," Tara said. "Everything was tough. I think they really survived because of the culture and there was a lot of healing. Like all the stuff that happened to them. Even I went through the healing."

Tara gives a lot of credit to Brian Tuesday, an Ojibway from the Big Grassy River reserve on the southeast side of the Lake of the Woods to whose memory this book is dedicated, for helping the families get through their first months back in the bush and rediscovering the traditional ways. "He's a very smart guy, he's very smart. Now there's one person that you can say really turned around because of the native culture and from moving out there."

Brian told me that he "crashed into reality when I came crashing down in '91" because, prior to that, he didn't give a damn about anything. "I didn't care what was happening down in the next house or the condition the kids were in. I just didn't give a damn because there was this notion that I was above all that. Even though I was abusing alcohol at the time, I still believed that I was above it all because I was educated in a white man's system [he had a Bachelor of Social Work degree from the University of Toronto with a major in English] and I was knowledgeable and doing a lot of things. That was the attitude. That was me and I was sober back in '91 when these people asked me to sit in on one of their meetings."

They told him that they were going to move away from the community because of the turmoil, the politics and the factionalism. He agreed to help them and, from that point on, he handled all of their correspondence and acted as their spokesperson. "At the time, I kind of doubted that they would leave their homes. I kind of doubted whether they'd go through with this. But, then, I got to know the people and I started to understand their determination and their commitment to create a better lifestyle, a better way of life and the primary reason for this was to avoid any further crises within the community because there was potential for violence, because there were already signs of where this thing was heading."

As Tara had mentioned earlier, there were long-standing feuds involving the different families, different factions, and that was what led to the Kellys being fired when the Copenace family took control of the Band Council. "That was all done without reason other than animosity, resentments," Brian Tuesday recalled. "Then from there it kind of boiled just underneath the surface. The potential for an eruption was always present and so, to avoid the type of violence that may occur, people moved into the bush and that was May 12, 1991."

Brian didn't think they were fully aware of what they were going to encounter out in the bush at the old reserve. Two weeks before the move, he was speaking to them and he went over what the move was going to entail and explained some of the things they were going to face.

"And I asked somebody, 'do you understand?' He said 'yeah'. 'Well are you going to go through with it?' He said 'yeah' so I said 'OK, I'll go with you.'

"I saw something in those people that I never saw anywhere before. First of all, they knew about my past drinking history. They knew my past because they saw me there, but they placed all their trust in me and they restored my self-dignity."

I asked Brian if he had a sense that they needed him. That they had a better chance of making a success of moving back into the bush if he was with them. "I don't know if it was a sense of needing me, but I think they understood that they needed somebody that could articulate their concerns, their aspirations and be able to express them on paper. But I don't think that was the primary reason why they asked me. I think in that span, from the middle of February or March to about the middle of April or the end of April, there was a bond that developed between us, a trust, a bond, even though I'm from a different clan."

What motivated him to go with them was, not so much that they needed him, but that he wanted to be part of this fresh new start. "Like I said, I'd been sober for two years prior to that, but I had the same attitudes and I had the same behaviour in the absence of alcohol. I was the same person, but I wasn't drunk and what essentially happened was they kept me sober and it just kept going and going up to today [1997], like I'm still sober. That's what happened to me personally. My dignity was restored. They placed all their trust in me so my self-esteem soared."

He quickly became the chief spokesperson for the small group and made presentations on their behalf at meetings of the regional chiefs, at workshops on domestic violence, and at a round table on aboriginal issues sponsored by the Royal Commission on Aboriginal Peoples — a $50 million consultation/research exercise the government had established in response to an armed standoff near Montreal, Quebec, between Mohawk warriors and the soldiers, tanks and helicopters, of Canada's Royal 22nd Regiment in 1990.

"What I was articulating or expressing at the time was the concerns of these people living in the bush back there in tents, what their aspirations were. But then we found out nobody even gave a damn. And here they're sitting in self-government workshops and attacking the people that actually did something about the social conditions and the political malfunction within that community. They were doing something about it. They went into the bush and they were expressing their independence and yet nobody came out to support us, nobody stood up in the self-government workshops and said 'well let's listen to these people, see what they have to offer.' Instead they were called malcontents, troublemakers, shit disturbers. The [Ojibway] leadership wouldn't listen."

Brian said native people have to find a way to take more control over their own lives. But, first, they have to get over the shame that too many feel about being native and develop a collective sense of self-esteem.

"Look at how we react to certain situations in life and that's that doubt or doubt of who we are and I find that very difficult to comprehend. Why can't we grasp this? We can see it in our kids every day and yet we deny what we see. We don't want to see that because then it focuses on us, what our attitudes are. When they talk about the past 30 years [since the 1965 march in Kenora], what has changed? Nothing, but we can't only look at the external, we have to look internally too. We can't continue to make these excuses. We can't do that, otherwise we'll never get out of this spinning in the sea, vicious circle, day in and day out and I myself have done that and I get tired of it. 'Can't get a job because I'm an Indian.' Those types of things.

"We have to get beyond that. We have to start focusing on what we have to offer instead of what does the government have to offer because they're not going to offer anything to begin with so why focus on it? Why say we want self-government? Why say that? Because the government is going to say no anyway. Why not just express it when they talk about it. The time for talk is over. I see that. It's over. All this collective rage must necessarily externalize, but how is it going to externalize? Is it going to be an externalizing violence or is it going to be externalizing in the ways that's going to produce beneficial results for the Anishinaabe? It doesn't necessarily have to have anything to do with guns and other types of weapons and that's where we're stuck.

"This term 'First Nation'. I don't know who came up with the term. But now there's all these different faces now. Like in the case in Treaty 3 here there'd be 25 different faces. So what the term, inadvertently I guess, has done was create this fragmentation. Each little community is a First Nation so now they can't get together to express this inherent right to self-government, the ability to determine our own future because each little community has their own ideas on how this is going to be implemented or what form it's going to take and they can't agree.

"It creates a perception that creates this confusion, this misunderstanding you're talking about and it's up to us to correct that misconception or this perception that we're projecting. We have to deal with the internal before we can deal with the external. We have to deal with that type of stuff and it's important that this is done as quickly as possible in the shortest time that it's possible and as soon as possible because the longer we wait and the longer we sit on the sidelines waiting for this self-government thing to all of a sudden materialize in front of us, the worse it's going to get.

"As far as this First Nation thing goes, to me, that means the Anishinaabe, the Cree, the Mohawks, Hurons, Algonquins. We're all separate nations, but the government wants do deal with us as a collective. At one point, not too long ago, contemporary society was very supportive of the Anishinaabe ritual of self-government. Now, today, they're becoming increasingly immune to the Anishinaabe aspiration.

They're becoming alienated by some of the things that have been happening in the last, in this past year, because I think we kind of missed an opportunity two or three years ago to really do something about what it is we want. What it is that we want to do. And I don't know when the opportunity will arise again, when society on a collective basis will support the Anishinaabe in their aspirations.

"Our biggest supporters when we moved back in the bush were from the white society. There was all this talk within the Indian community and yet nobody acts. White society became active because we were in tents and winter was coming."

Tara believed nothing could have been done to induce the families to return to their homes at Sabaskong instead of spending the winter in tents. "There was no going home. The idea for the move was permanent."

They asked around for some kind of shelter before the onset of winter, but they didn't get it. "We were still living in tents, crawling around on snow like crazy," Brian said.

What was the first winter like? "Fantastic. It was really good considering the shelter, considering the weather. Nobody ever got sick. There was no emergencies, no crises, no nothing. We didn't starve. We didn't freeze to death."

After a while, they put up little shacks and then they put up a main building to act as a meeting place and a place to eat. Some sympathetic white people provided them with a portable generator and all the wires and accessories that they would need to provide electricity for the tiny community.

"And so we survived there," Brian said. "By January, seven months, everybody was sober." Does that mean that some of the people who had moved back to the bush had drinking problems? "Yeah. There were abusers and drunks, alcoholics. But, by the seventh month, everybody was clean. We celebrated birthdays, we celebrated spring, we celebrated the fall, we celebrated the fallen snow. That's how we show our appreciation for what we discovered.

"Like I said earlier, they had no idea what they were going to encounter in the bush. What they encountered was the true self. They encountered their true self and that's how we achieved sobriety and that's how we achieved a new way of looking at life, a new way of living within family and to us that's self-determination.

"That's what self-determination is, trying to raise a healthy family and a healthy lifestyle. We're expressing it. That's self-government. We're a better family, another family, soon we have a community and then you have a nation and that to me is the only way that we're going to achieve this self-government. We can't be worried about what some politician is saying today, what they said in the past or what they are doing today. The hell with all that. You can't change our minds anyway. Let's change ourselves."

How did living in the bush affect the children? "I think they had the greatest time in their life. They had the best education that they ever received."

However, after the second year, a consensus developed that the children needed a "proper" education and, despite best efforts and good intentions, they weren't going to get it out there in the bush. But the parents were not going to put their children back into the school at Sabaskong either.

"We weren't wanted on the other reserve anymore," Tara said. "Nobody talked to you anymore. It's just, there was so much anger and so much, I don't know, everything. There was a lot of anger and there's still a lot of bitterness."

Most of them moved to the predominantly white community of Fort Frances, across the river from International Falls, Minnesota, got jobs and enrolled their children in local schools.

Brian said he would gladly move back to the bush and support himself by hunting and fishing all over again. "I'd do it any time. See, at one point, I said the kids were receiving the best possible education they could get in there and in the next breath I said, the pressure of schooling got too much. It's an apparent contradiction.

"And that's because we're conditioned to believe that white is better. That the white system is better. There are still influences, influences that affect us profoundly. Like, we're sitting by the campfire and all of a sudden I talk to them about education and I tell them that in the end it's not going to make a difference whether or not your kids are going to public school today or school at the reserve. It's not going to make any difference because what they're learning here is going to be their foundation for life and yet they took their kids back to the white school.

"And that's where the failure is. That's where we hit the wall and I think that's the greatest damage that the residential schools did. In spite of all the sexual abuse that was going on, I think it's that doubt that continues because we don't want to admit it. We'd rather talk about this is what this man did to me and this is what this priest did to me."

During the time that he was at St. Margaret's Indian Residential School in Fort Frances, Brian was frequently sexually abused by a priest and beaten regularly by a nun. The boys were separated from the girls in the yard by a wire fence and he was not allowed to approach that fence and talk to his sister. On more than one occasion, he stood helplessly on his side of the fence and watched as one of the nuns beat his little sister senseless.

Things were a bit better when they transferred him to St. Joseph's Indian Boarding School in Thunder Bay—about 350 kilometres farther east. No more sexual abuse. However, he did get beaten up pretty regularly by a big nun who used to whack him with a yardstick. She broke his right forearm once when he held it up to ward off the blows.

Brian never did recover from the horrible experiences he was subjected to in the Indian residential schools. His lack of self-esteem and profound sense of self-loathing was so strong that, when he was an adult, he used to smash mirrors in hotel washrooms with his fist because he didn't like the look of the tortured soul staring back at him.

"I know the effects of that, what it did to me when I was sexually abused. I know what it did to me. Now I can deal with it, but the doubts, the doubts are implanted in there. Even today they [native people] have to deal with their doubts. And, as I'm speaking to you today, I know what I'm talking about. It's there. It's present. The doubts are there. We can't deal with what might have been because it's non-existent.

"If we want to achieve something, then <u>we</u> have to do it. We can't depend on the external force to come in and help us do these things. We have to do it ourselves because I truly believe that all those resources to succeed are within us if we so choose to accept them and acknowledge them, but I don't feel that we're doing that and I think it has to do with this experience in the residential school system.

"For all the damage that's been done, for all the pain and hurt that it caused, we understand all that, we know that. We do experience it. But it did something else beyond that that we don't seem to be able to grasp and, to me, that's where the blockage is. I think it's the doubts.

"We have doubts now on our bounties. We have doubts now of our own institutions. We have doubts on our own expression. So, in other words, everything that we attempt to do I believe reflects the Western European ideology or philosophy.

"It took me a long time to understand, to know, what was driving me to deny my own identity, to create this illusion, this illusion of being who I am <u>not</u> and expending all that time and energy to maintain that illusion. If you put that on a collective basis, you can imagine the effect it has on our individuals, on our families, on our Indian communities and on our nations."

Brian, whose Ojibway spirit name was Tibishkopiness, was still sober back in 1994 when he picked up a pencil and wrote a poem in longhand while working as a guide at a fishing camp just north of Sabaskong. This is the poem he wrote.

THE BELL

In the child's mind he can hear it,
the sound of the bell.
Like embers of a dying fire rekindled, memories stir,
awakened, once again to revisit the madness of a time and
place almost beyond memory.
Fleeting images, glimpses of the unimaginable.
Like a shockwave, the child remembers.
Transfixed, he simply goes away to seek solitude in
 a world not of this place nor of this time.

Words echo.
"My child, my child, God has made a terrible mistake.
Come, I must recreate you into my own image."

The child sleeps, senses on full alert.
In the dorm, others of his kind, asleep on bunk beds, row on row,
pray that tonight madness will not visit.
A slight disturbance in the midnight air—movement!
Madness is on the prowl.
Who is the chosen?
A silent scream fractures the midnight calm.
The child freezes.
For tonight madness has chosen to visit upon him
the unimaginable.
Violated in mind, body and spirit, desecrated of the sanctity of his life,
the child simply ceases to be.

The years have passed.
On a hilltop a man sits, bottle in hand.
Hair once jet black betrays strands of white.
Lined with age, the face mirrors a life gone astray.
He waits and waits, not knowing what it is he waits for.
Darkness approaches.
Tortured by memories which haunt his mind, he tilts bottle to lips,
if only to seek solace in the stupor of cheap wine.

For the man there is nothing but the emptiness and the cheap,
meaningless, high of wine-induced euphoria.
Heaven!
He succumbs to the drunken sleep
to escape the hell of a tortured mind.

It is autumn.
The season of spectral colors, with brush in hand, paints
a beautiful portrait of scenic wonders across the landscape.
Myriads of different shades and hues clothe majestic trees
in their finest attire.

The wind plays upon a flute a beautiful and haunting melody.
Mesmerizing, the beautiful music entices the imagination
to alight on wings of melody.
To journey to distant lands and times
that never were.
The child cries.

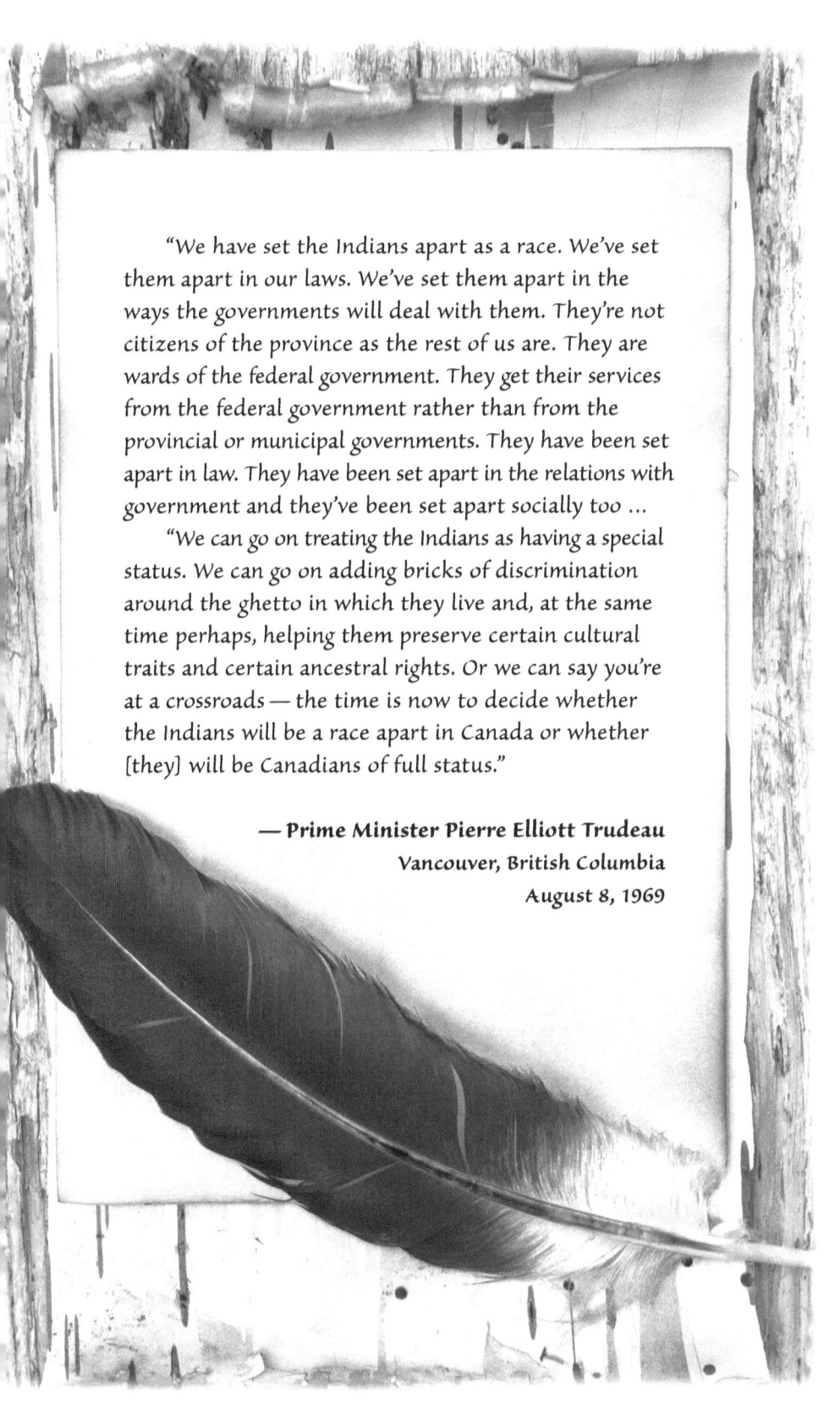

"We have set the Indians apart as a race. We've set them apart in our laws. We've set them apart in the ways the governments will deal with them. They're not citizens of the province as the rest of us are. They are wards of the federal government. They get their services from the federal government rather than from the provincial or municipal governments. They have been set apart in law. They have been set apart in the relations with government and they've been set apart socially too ...

"We can go on treating the Indians as having a special status. We can go on adding bricks of discrimination around the ghetto in which they live and, at the same time perhaps, helping them preserve certain cultural traits and certain ancestral rights. Or we can say you're at a crossroads — the time is now to decide whether the Indians will be a race apart in Canada or whether [they] will be Canadians of full status."

— Prime Minister Pierre Elliott Trudeau
Vancouver, British Columbia
August 8, 1969

Chapter 16

In June, 2007, I returned to the Kenora area to catch up with some of the Ojibway people I had interviewed for this book As the Air Canada jet flew northwest past Thunder Bay—travelling at about 700 kilometres per hour 38,000 feet up in the air—I could see the approximately 88,500 square kilometres of forest, lakes and rivers that are covered by Treaty #3 on the map on my TV screen. The green on the screen was pockmarked by thousands of little lakes and rivers. There was no open space anywhere. How on earth Lieutenant-Governor Alexander Morris got the idea that the Ojibway people could make a living farming among the bush, muskeg and rocks of this area is beyond me.

When the plane passed over Whiteshell Provincial Park, just west of the border between Ontario and Manitoba, the pockmarked picture on the TV screen changed abruptly. The myriad tiny lakes and rivers had been replaced by huge areas of fertile farmland with only two large lakes on the screen.

I could see the productive prairie farms spread out below me. Thousands of hectares of rich, fertile, land stretching for hundreds of kilometres as far as the eye could see. Roads laid out straight as arrows. Rivers winding through the wheat fields like big black snakes. An altogether different place in which to live and thrive.

It became readily apparent that the only real benefit to the Canadian government in negotiating Treaty #3 in 1873 was to provide a route from A to B—from Thunder Bay to Winnipeg.

I rented a car at the airport in Winnipeg and drove 200 kilometres east. As I drove down Main Street in Kenora, I thought about that snowy November day in 1965 when it was jam-packed with hundreds of Ojibways from the surrounding reserves protesting the conditions they were living under.

I passed the Kenricia Hotel where Andy White of Whitefish Bay was told there were no rooms available—three minutes before the white human rights officer he was with was told they did have rooms. And then I checked into Kenora's Best Western Lakeside Inn where Indian Affairs Minister Ron Irwin had met with the Grand Council of Treaty #3 in March, 1996.

After breakfast the next day, I drove north towards Whitedog. Rocks dynamited to bits to make way for the highway. Culverts crossing waterways and swamps. Hydro towers showing up on a regular basis taking electricity to the south.

As I approached the big dam and generating station about 20 kilometres south of Whitedog, I couldn't help but be impressed with the sheer size of it, and the electric power generated by the white waters rushing through its turbines.

A big black bear cast a suspicious eye on me as it crossed the road in front of my car to search for food at the dump on the outskirts of Whitedog. I learned later that the bears presented a major problem and many of the residents were quite fearful of them.

When I arrived at the school to catch up with Ron Roy McDonald, I was taken aback by the dilapidated shape it was in. The floor of the gym was buckled, partly because of flooding after the heating system failed one winter day and the pipes burst. Some parts of the furnace were so old that there were no replacements for them and the new parts would have to be machined.

The crumbling outer south wall had been braced by wooden trusses, which made the elementary classrooms look more like construction sites. Maintenance staff had reported that sparks were coming from the electric panel that was separating from the wall because of heaving caused by the foundation shifting and settling on its clay base. Staff were concerned about air quality and the school was subject to frequent closures.

About 20 students were using the front room of the teachers' residence as a classroom. The floor was unfinished and the students were using a makeshift table as a desk. The library and radio room had also been remodelled to serve as a classroom. Books that had been donated for the library were still sitting in the boxes they had arrived in because there wasn't enough room to put them on the shelves.

Overcrowding at the school had recently resulted in about 60 teenagers turning their backs on getting an education. As no one seemed to care whether or not they had an appropriate setting in which to learn, they had decided there was no real reason for them to care either.

Indian Affairs had been promising for years that funds would be provided to replace the decrepit old building which was plagued with mould and cracks. Treasury Board President Reg Alcock, a Liberal MP from Winnipeg, had promised that he, personally, would oversee construction of a new school. However, the Liberals lost power to the Conservatives in the election of January 23, 2006, and negotiations for the new school for Whitedog were sidelined.

When National Chief Phil Fontaine of the Assembly of First Nations visited the school in September, 2006, he was appalled at the conditions under which the students were attempting to learn.

Isaac Mandamin, who I told you about earlier in this book, was at that meeting in his capacity as chairman of Ojibway Child and Family Services. He told National Chief Fontaine that about 200 children had been removed from the community of approximately 900 residents by the Children's Aid Society and placed in foster care. If those children were allowed to return home to Whitedog, he said, that would put even more pressure on the school.

School staff told Fontaine that 70 per cent of their 300 students were under the age of 11 and that current conditions did not allow the school administration to pursue plans for providing adult education courses. Government representatives at the meeting promised that construction of an $18 million new school would be completed by the following year. It wasn't.

When I interviewed Ron McDonald again during that June, 2007, visit he was interim principal of the old school. "This is my main career," he told me. "By profession I'm a school teacher."

Ron attended teacher's college and got his licence to teach in 1979. From 1981 to 1995, he taught at the school in Whitedog, served as chief of the band council and then returned to teaching. He said running the school was like being the chief again. He was responsible for the operation of the place, had instituted a breakfast program, now had two school buses, and was in the process of starting a parent-teacher association.

He also wanted to provide instruction in Ojibway as most of the kids arrived at kindergarten unable to speak a word of their native language. "We're losing the language fast."

He was still very attached to his birthplace at One Man Lake, which remained under 50 feet of water, and had a cabin up there where he spent weekends with his wife and kids. He said the beach there was as good as anything in the Caribbean. "I've got a kayak now," he said rather excitedly. ""I really like it."

I noticed a framed copy of the Canadian Charter of Rights and Freedoms hanging on the office wall. "That sign was put there by a white principal," Ron said. "If I had my way, it wouldn't even have gone up because of the abuses and the historical genocides and all that. The gaps that are happening right now in terms of housing, jobs, stability, economic development, resource benefit sharing. I'm just leaving it up there because I'm only interim principal."

He spoke bitterly of the many times drunken Ojibways who had passed out on the town dock in Kenora were tossed into the lake. An Ojibway passed out in an alley would be severely beaten.

"Poverty is a big issue," he said. "Where are they when we need them? How does the Canadian Charter of Rights and Freedoms link to our present problem with treaties and all that? That's why I feel it doesn't apply to me because I'm not even being recognized. This Canadian Charter of Rights and Freedoms ignores a minority. It ignores certain minorities, for example, aboriginal people. In fact, this constitution or this Charter of Rights has an invisible Indian syndrome. They don't even acknowledge us.

"We already have a Charter of Rights. We already have sovereignty. Take One Man Lake, for example. We had a system of government where we were governed by a drum, by the staff of that drum, by the clan system of the day. Whether they were Sturgeon clan or whether you belonged with the Loon clan. That's how we governed ourselves. Our constitution, our government, was based on that. We don't have any ties with that Charter of Rights and Freedoms and that's why I say I don't recognize it."

During the time Ron McDonald was chief, he organized a 28-day walk from Whitedog to Ottawa in 2001 to draw attention to the problems that were plaguing his community.

"We walked all the way and Robert Nault [long-term Liberal Member of Parliament for Kenora-Rainy River] was the Minister of Indian Affairs at that time. We walked and walked for twenty-eight days. There were about 30 of us when we started out but it dwindled down to half by the time we reached Thunder Bay. The 15 stuck it through until the end."

What was the purpose of the walk? "We walked for housing. We walked for suicides. We walked for policing. We wanted a police station here," he told me during the 2007 interview. "We walked for an improvement plan for the community. We walked for a healing lodge for this community, and a teaching lodge as well. We walked for a treatment centre. We wanted an overall improvement of the school. We wanted a new school."

Ron said the Minister of Indian Affairs was impressed by the commitment they had shown by walking all the way from Whitedog to Ottawa and supported their demands. "He was behind us 100 per cent. He gave us a letter of approval at his level and the new school was supposed to have been built two years ago."

It didn't get built, he said, because he was replaced by another chief who did not see getting a new school as a high priority. "His priority was forestry and clear cutting so he put the new school aside until the last day in office. So now it's starting up again and I'm going to make sure as a [band] councillor that the new school gets to be a priority again."

Back in the early 1970s, Indian Affairs' officials would retire for a good steak dinner at the Minaki Lodge—a former world-class luxury resort frequented by millionaire Winnipeg grain merchants and other wealthy guests—after providing Ron McDonald's father with one more reason why his band couldn't raise mink to supply the fur factory that was being operated by the band at Whitefish Bay.

The lodge was built in 1914 by the Grand Trunk Pacific Railway near the railway bridge that crosses the Winnipeg River. The company went bankrupt and was nationalized as part of Canadian National Railways.

After the lodge burned down in 1925, it was rebuilt to an even more lavish scale by Scottish stone masons, Swedish log cutters and English gardeners. Thirty trainloads of soil were shipped from a farm in Manitoba to create a nine-hole golf course on the rocky terrain. The lodge had a 14-metre-high cathedral ceiling.

Minaki Lodge thrived as a luxury wilderness resort until after the Second World War. However, the CNR decided it could make more money moving freight across Canada than it could with passengers and sold the lodge in the early 1950s.

Ownership of the lodge passed through many hands. The government of Ontario owned it between 1974 and 1983 and spent an estimated $50 million on renovations and upgrading before selling it to a hotel chain for $4 million.

In 1994, the Ojibways of Whitedog paid $3.5 million out of the $8 million they received as compensation for the mercury poisoning of their lakes and rivers to purchase the lodge.

According to an article in the *Winnipeg Free Press*, the band lost $6 million operating the lodge before selling it to a Texas businessman for $1.5 million in 1998.

"Minaki Lodge, to us who opposed the purchase, was a white elephant," Ron McDonald told me during that interview in 2007. "No matter how much money was pumped in there, they weren't going to make a profit. Several groups had tried to make a go of it, including Canadian National Railways and then the government of Ontario.

"I was a member of council and I opposed the Minaki Lodge deal because, first of all, what were we getting ourselves into? I wanted to see a feasibility study first. I wanted to see a forecast of what's going to happen if we do take it over. What arrears and what liabilities are these people leaving us with at this Minaki Lodge?

"I said if we're going to purchase it let's have a referendum, let's have a community vote and see if we agree if we should buy it. Plus I need to see the feasibility study, forecast and all that before I agree with it. There was about three of us [on the band council] that didn't support it.

"This Minaki Lodge purchase was not done properly. The community was not consulted. There was no referendum on this decision to use our monies, our compensation monies, to purchase Minaki Lodge. It wasn't authorized and, in fact, today it's still being discussed by band members. And that's where our money went. Our settlement monies, all our revenues, assets from the [mercury poisoning] compensation all went to Minaki Lodge."

I remembered being at the lodge in 1997 and seeing local Ojibways criss-crossing the golf course with their clubs and carts. I asked Ron what it felt like to play on that golf course where all the rich people used to congregate?

"I felt really proud one day, sad the next day because there was no stability. But it felt good to be able to go in there and say 'hey I'm an owner here. I can go in any time I want to play golf' and I did a couple of times. I took advantage of it and I was really thrilled and I was thinking boy, you know, when I finished golfing that day and I said, holy cow just imagine there was aristocrats here, there were ambassadors here. There was royalty here and people from Winnipeg even, rich people from Winnipeg, used to golf here and here I am. It felt one day like I was on top of the world and the next day I was sad too because the community was not included in this whole process."

Josephine Mandamin, who I told you about earlier, died as a result of complications associated with diabetes in 2003. She had left Isaac and was living with her sister in Kenora. She'd been with Isaac for 39 years and they'd raised three sons and five daughters.

When I first met Josephine in 1996, diabetes had caused her to go almost blind in one eye. At the time of her death, she was pretty well blind in both eyes.

Ron McDonald was her nephew but they'd had a very strained relationship over the years mainly because of differences of opinion between Ron and Isaac on what was best for the Whitedog community. Isaac was all for buying Minaki Lodge, for example, and Ron was strongly opposed.

One day in 2003, when Ron was at the shopping mall in Kenora, Josephine's sister said: "Someone wants to see you and you'll be surprised to know who it is."

He found Josephine sitting on a bench.

"Is that you, Ronnie?" she asked looking up through eyes that could no longer see.

When he said that it was, she reached up and gave him a big hug.

"You are family," she whispered as she held him close to her.

She died a short time later.

Ron was quite emotional as he described those last moments with Josephine.

Like she said, they were family.

When I caught up with Isaac Mandamin during that brief visit in June, 2007, he was living in a small cabin down the road from the big log house he had shared with Josephine and their three sons and five daughters.

"I don't stay around the community," he told me with a mischievous grin. "I just come and change my socks and I'm off on the road again. I'm never home. A lot of people ask me when they finally get hold of me on the phone where are you? Where are you? I'm on the road."

As a very spiritual Ojibway elder, he was in demand at traditional funerals and other rituals. Much of his time was spent at Ojibway reservations in Minnesota — six hours south by car. "One of the things I tell people is that life goes on after death. When your time comes that's when you move to another world."

When I asked about Josephine, he said: "We worked together for 39 years, but one day it just blew up I guess and, after that, she lasted about two years." He described her as being in very bad shape at the time of her death. "She wasn't taking the medication she was supposed to be taking. That's what the doctor told me after. She wasn't taking what she was supposed to be taking and all of a sudden everything just came together."

There was a sense of loss on Isaac's face as he spoke about Josephine. A lot had changed since their early days together in the bush trapping beavers, picking blueberries and harvesting wild rice. Living the "nomads' life" as Josephine called it. The good life.

But that was before. Before the three communities were forced to live together at Whitedog after Ontario Hydro flooded their homes. Before their lakes and rivers were poisoned with methylmercury from the big pulp and paper mill at Dryden. Before the suicide epidemic of 1995.

When I suggested to Isaac that Whitedog looked more rundown in 2007 than it had when I first interviewed him in 1996, he used the analogy of a bird with only one wing. "If he's got two wings, well he's going to go straight. He's going to go ahead. But the way we are is just like a bird with one wing. Keeps going around in circles. Nothing ever gets done. That's the way I see it.

"Of course, some of the young people they don't notice it. They don't notice that. But me, as an old person, an old goat, I see these things happening. How come? It's very, very sad to see these things happening."

He said it made no sense at all to him that most of the people in Whitedog were relying on welfare despite the abundance of natural resources in their traditional territory. "We can't eat the fish according to Health Canada but the tourist operators are still selling the fish. They're still making money with sports fishing. But we can't make no money on it. So that's why I say we have to have a share in the resources. We have a lot of tourist businesses in the surrounding area. We could be sharing the profits of fishing licences and all that, stumpage [from logging], everything, mining. But we can't do it.

"If they gave us the right to manage our resources, cost sharing, everything, then we would go free. We don't have to bother the government any more. Don't have to bother towns or anything like that or charities. We don't have to bother those because we will be self-sufficient if we have all that. That's what is needed.

"But we're never going to change the way the system is right now. We get so much money from the feds with social services and the province and so much money for housing and welfare. I'll bet you if we had the full term of sharing resources, cost sharing, we wouldn't even have go to the welfare system for the community's social services. We wouldn't even look at them. That's the way I perceive what is needed."

Were there not discussions with the government about entering into resource sharing agreements and other means of self-support? "Just discussions and that's it. You might as well go and talk to a tree. You get the same answers because the government is controlled by civil servants and they don't want to let go what they have in their hand and, if they let go, somebody's going to be out of a job.

"Let's use the example of Kenora. If the native people of the surrounding area quit drinking overnight you'll see a hell of a lot of people in Kenora looking for jobs. That's what really keeps the economy going." Including funds to operate the school for 300 students, the Whitedog band was receiving approximately $13 million a year from the Canadian government in 2007.

Isaac expressed concern about the large number of children who had been removed from the community by the Children's Aid Society. "I don't know how many kids we have in care right across Canada. They're taken away when some of them were just born. They're going to lose everything. They're going to be worse off than we are.

"All these young fellows are now older guys. They all came from the [Ojibway] communities. They don't know who they are. They were taken away when they were small by CAS [Children's Aid Society]. They were put in homes. After 18 they were let go. 'Go home'. But they couldn't go home. They didn't know who they are so they started on drugs, alcohol, stealing, killing and that's why they went bad."

To address some of those concerns, several bands in the Treaty #3 area established Ojibway Child and Family Services—one of the key players in dealing with the suicide crisis of 1995. "We have our own aboriginal child and family services," Isaac said. "We just got a new mandate last July that we were recognized as an aboriginal child agency. So we didn't have to deal with the CAS. We have 14 bands in that association. In fact, I was the chairman of the board until last fall."

It also concerned him that so few people in Whitedog were able to speak Ojibway. "Take the school-age children. I'd say that 90 per cent of them don't understand their own language. When that's gone, then you better be ready to take the hard times. This is what we have right now and I could see what was happening. In 20 years time there won't be no such thing as treaty rights. That's the way I foresee. It's really something to think about. I know a lot of people don't think that way, but I think about it. What's going to happen?

"If the parents show respect for their language, then we wouldn't have this high percentage of young people not speaking their own language. The young kids today are always speaking English because of their parents. Everything will be English in this community. That's a fact we're facing right now."

On May 31, 1997, a large contingent of police arrived at Whitedog to deal with an intoxicated youth armed with a rifle. He was suicidal and threatened to kill himself. When the police arrived, the boy was sitting on the road with a rifle held under his chin. He got up several times and wandered around a bit and approached the officers, who had their guns drawn.

Isaac knew the boy and volunteered to speak to him and try to talk him down. "He had the gun in his mouth when I first approached him," he told me during that 2007 interview. "He was going to commit suicide. When you get to that stage, when you're being cornered, you got nothing else to do and that's when you think I might as well kill myself and get it over with."

Isaac realized he was putting his life at risk by approaching the boy. "All the guys around me had bullet vests and all I had was a T-shirt."

Some of his friends told him he was crazy for taking a chance like that. However, he knew the boy and was convinced he could talk him out of shooting himself or anyone else.

He sat down on the road, lit up a cigarette and gave one to the boy. "I knew the boy. I told him, you're not going to be hurt as much as you think. I know you think everybody hates you but they don't. Everybody loves you. You do this and your friends will be grieving for a long time. Talk, talk and talk about this, this and that, how it affects the community. Talking about his famly."

Three hours and many cigarettes later, the boy handed his gun to Isaac and surrendered to the police. For his act of bravery, Isaac was awarded a framed citation signed by the Commissioner of the Ontario Provincial Police.

When I asked Isaac about discrimination against Ojibway people in Kenora, he said: "I think it's been the same thing from way back. Never changed. Never changed. There's a lot of discrimination against people. But everybody knows my family in Kenora. They don't do anything with them. They talk nice to them because of who Isaac is."

You might recall me saying earlier in this book that Isaac had built up a very successful transportation business and was a well-respected individual who former Ontario Premier David Peterson had asked for advice when he was Opposition Leader.

Because of that, he was approached by key people in the Ontario Liberal Party in 2006 and asked to run against New Democratic Party Leader Howard Hampton who was the MPP for Kenora-Rainy River.

"They asked me could you be interested in throwing your hat in as a candidate? We need somebody that is well known in the whole riding and you've been there for a long time. You know everybody. Why don't you consider it? I told them I'd like to, but I'd have to ask my family first. So I asked my girls. I got five girls, and I asked them to see what they think and they said no. We need you here."

At one point in his younger years, Isaac had an opportunity to work for the Department of Indian Affairs as district manager for the Kenora area. "I spent about a year and a half on civil servant courses on my department so I had a chance to be the district manager in Kenora before they moved the office to Thunder Bay. I was approached and I asked my dad. My dad was alive at the time and I asked him, could I take that job, there's good money in it. Yeah he said there's good money in it, but what are you going to do about the chiefs? You go to the community and ask them what they want and you tell them I'll do it for you and when you get back at the office somebody's going to tell you 'no, no you can't do that' so you'd be lying to your own people."

Ron McDonald agreed with Isaac that, despite strenuous efforts and support within the community of a little more than 1,000, things didn't appear to have improved all that much since I interviewed him when he was chief in 1996. What went wrong?

"I look at the community in four parts," he told me in 2007. "Technology and resources on one side. Communication and relationship on the other. I look at things in four parts. The medicine wheel concept. Today we have good technology, we have good resources, we have fairly good communication now. Now that we have high-speed internet, we have web sites. We have telephone, faxes and all that. Video conferencing and all that. Today, however, we have a problem with relationships. That's the part this community needs to build, needs to create more stability.

"Right now as we speak there is no stability in this community because traffickers are controlling this community. The people that bootleg are controlling this community and it's being allowed to happen. I hate to say it, but our leadership has to step up to the plate and say 'hey we're going to stop this trafficking and bootlegging'.

"The relationship part has deteriorated again but, in terms of technology, the community has leaped forward. I was the one that got the water treatment plant going here and the sewage plant as well. The resources are still there, are still rich and waiting to be used for economic development.

"But then there's the politics. You have to realize that this community is made up of three parts, Whitedog, One Man Lake and Swan Lake, and, because of that, it seems like the relationships part of it is always a struggle. There's no stability."

He recounted the time in 1958 when the three communities were forced to live together in Whitedog because of the homes that were flooded by Ontario Hydro. "Ever since they've been forced to live together, there's always been this political rivalry, social unrest, instability, rampant drug abuse, substance abuse, alcohol abuse, suicides ever since."

And all of that was compounded by the fact that their lakes and rivers were poisoned by mercury from the big pulp and paper mill at Dryden. "The reason why they call it a mediation agreement is not only because it's an out-of- court settlement," Ron said. "It was the government's way of hiding the real issue. They didn't want to admit that they were at fault. They didn't want to admit they made a crime against humanity, particularly against Ojibwa people in this area.

"Not only was it corruption, hiding all this and not admitting that they made a mistake. They resorted to this mediation agreement by settling it out of court. People like me who were impacted by it should be able to go back to court and fight it."

You'll remember young Police Constable Tara Kelly who was part of the security detail when Indian Affairs Minister Ron Irwin met with the Grand Council of Treaty #3 at the Lakeside Inn in March, 1996.

When I got back to Kenora after interviewing Ron McDonald and Isaac Mandamin, Tara joined me for a catch up over coffee. She was now a community service officer with Treaty Three Police Service which was responsible for policing 28 Ojibway communities.

"We develop programs like delivering presentations to the communities," Tara told me. "We start building a relationship between the police and the communities. Show them that we're human. I'm trying to get all the little kids to realize that we're friends and a lot of them do. I remember when you would have kids run from the cruiser or try and hide. But, now, you've got them running up to the cruiser, waving, and smiling. I'm working on those types of relationships with the community and any concerns they have. Trying, hopefully, to develop something where we can attack the problems or work with them on a problem."

As part of her outreach activities, Tara often made presentations at the Ne Chee (Ojibway name for close friend or brother) Friendship Centre in Kenora. "They're having a role model day and I've been asked to represent the community service office of Treaty Three Police. Other presentations I've been doing are anti-bullying, strangers presenting danger to the little kids, marine safety and stuff like that."

It was clear that Tara really loved the career she had chosen and that the Kenora area was where she preferred to be. She'd served for two and a half years with a police force on Vancouver Island and had considered applying for a job with the police in Calgary. However, she was really proud to be part of the first native-administered police force in Treaty #3.

"I want to be part of first nations policing and now we have it here in Treaty Three. I remember years ago that's something they always talked about, that we should have our own police service and it's happened."

The Treaty Three Police Service certainly had its work cut out for it. Tara informed me in that 2007 interview that incidents involving suicide had increased considerably. "I find the suicide rate in our first nation youth higher. I deal with it more. We probably have more attempted suicide or uttering threats to commit suicide than we had before. I haven't gone a month without having a suicide or somebody threatening to commit suicide. Just had one yesterday."

Most of those attempting suicide were teenagers and the others were in their twenties and thirties. "There's a lot of repeats. You're bringing the same person in maybe two or three times in a year. A guy who's been drinking stabs himself in the chest and he's flown to the hospital in Winnipeg and then he's released. We got a girl that hanged herself with a T-shirt trying to kill herself. I went to see her at the hospital but she didn't want any help.

"We're always bringing people into the hospital. The doctors are always trying their best to give them the best treatment but they don't want them to go near them. Most of the time it's when they're drinking."

When I mentioned billboards I had seen along the highway saying it was wrong to hit a woman, Tara said they were getting more cases involving violence against Ojibway women because more and more women had acquired the courage to report the abuse. "Domestic violence has changed a lot. Our procedures and our policies have also changed. Women nowadays do report the violence more than they did in the past. It was always hush hush."

One problem with Tara's intense involvement with police work was that she was no longer connecting with her spiritual self by participating in pow wows or sweat lodges. "I never get to the pow wows, sweat lodges or ceremonies."

And, even if she could find the time, being a police officer meant that some people would rather that she didn't participate in the sweat. "What's said there stays there. But having a police officer present makes people uncomfortable to share. I respect that fact and, also, I don't feel comfortable going into a circle or a sweat when I have something to talk about in my personal life because later, when you go and deal with somebody [as a police officer], they're going to use that against you. I don't want to put myself in that position."

We talked briefly about the time back in 1991 when several families from Sabaskong moved back to the old reserve in the bush with Brian Tuesday because of the turmoil and potential for violence after the Copenace family took over the band council. "I miss that little community we had there," Tara said, "because everyone respected everyone. You know what I mean? It was so different and you felt comfortable there and you knew it was a safe place to go. You're always welcome and smiled at. It wasn't phoniness to your face."

Chapter 17

As I drove past the Kenora jail on my way to Whitefish Bay the next morning, I thought back to the time in 1997 when I interviewed former Manitou Rapids band councillor Calvin Bombay who had spent seven years counselling the Aboriginal inmates at the jail.

Calvin told me he learned a lot from the inmates and very quickly started to see things from their point of view. "They made me see things that I didn't see or, if I did see them, I had a different interpretation. It didn't take too long for me to start seeing the different things that were wrong with the system."

When he first started counselling the inmates in 1990, for example, he was given a program manual called Native Inmate Liquor Offender Program (NILOP). "Put yourself in the inmates' shoes," he asked me when I interviewed him in 1997. "The title is very judgmental. How can anybody feel good about this program? I wouldn't want to take it."

He asked the inmates to trust him and ignore the name of the program because he wasn't going to approach the job in that fashion. It took him five years to have the name changed to a very simple DEAL (Drugs, Education, Alcohol, Living) instead of NILOP (Native Inmate Liquor Offender Program).

"It's drugs, education, alcohol, living," he told me. "If you've got a problem in any of those four areas, there's only one way to resolve it and you've got to deal with it. Simple as that."

In counselling inmates with serious drinking problems, Calvin drew on a lifetime of experience with alcoholism. He recalled his dad telling him he was heading in the wrong direction when he started drinking in his teens.

"He said it's like heading into that brush there [I was interviewing him at a picnic table in a park outside of Kenora], all that thick bush, something like a jungle. He says that's the direction you're heading. And shortly after I sobered up in '84 it came to mind and I understood what my dad was talking about. For 30 years, it was like being lost in a jungle. It took that long for me to understand and it took that long to make sense.

"I'm lucky to be here. I guess you could say I almost paid with my life. In that 30 years, I did a lot of damage. Nothing that I'm proud of. I became a liar. I became a thief. I became a cheat. I got to a point where I had the nerve once to call myself a social drinker and, when I think about it, I laugh. I don't know the meaning of the word choice. Anytime Calvin took a drink, Calvin had to get drunk. It got to a point where it used to be one night and it became two nights and it just progressed to where you forget to go to work on Monday. It progressed to where I'd drink all week. Progressed to where I was actually drinking for months.

"If I'm drunk and I'm sick and I'm in jail, well, 'so and so made me do this'. I drank for 30 years and my wife and nobody else ever poured anything down my throat. But I blamed a lot of people. It's one of the easiest things that anybody can do. 'As long as I got somebody to blame, it's not my fault.'"

Calvin, who sobered up in 1984, told the inmates one of the first things they had to do was stop the blame game. "You've got to let go of the pointing of fingers. Let go this blaming of others. Are we just going to go through life pointing fingers and blaming? If we are, it's going to be a miserable life."

He described the way alcoholics often shut themselves off from reality because of their insecurities and lack of self-confidence. "We always build a wall around ourselves. We don't let anybody in and we don't allow ourselves to go out. That's our comfort zone and, every once in a while, it gets pretty damn lonely in there. If drinking is going to leave us insecure like that, then it's going to be a miserable life."

Inmates were serving up to four months for drinking offences when he first started at the jail on the outskirts of Kenora. The average age was 24. Three prisoners would be in each cell block and they were provided with individual beds and mattresses.

"I feel they're treated well," Calvin said, "even though I certainly wouldn't want to spend time in there. It's nice in there. It's clean and they're fed well. As far as the facilities go, sometimes I wish I was eating there, too."

All too often, Calvin told me, the alcoholic inmates "are victims of lack of parenting." More often than not, their parents had gone to the Indian residential schools and became alcoholics. "They're nice people. They're very nice people. It's just that they've got a drinking problem."

During the 10 years he'd been in Kenora, he had heard about the prejudice toward native people but had never experienced it himself. "Even though I've been here in Kenora for 10 years now, I have heard that over and over again from many, many people, the criticism, the prejudice here in Kenora. I guess in small ways I have seen it, but I certainly have never felt it."

Much of the prejudice and discrimination is related to a very small number of natives wandering the streets of Kenora. "One person can do a hell of a lot of damage. Take, for example, the street people. I would say probably about two dozen people create that image here in Kenora. Just the fact that they're Indian has a spin-off effect and personally myself I have never really actually encountered it. I have never encountered anything. When I first came to Kenora, I didn't like Kenora either."

He urged the inmates not to let deep-seated resentment dominate their lives. "There's too many people that live with resentments. You go out there and you blacken somebody's eye and you knock his teeth out. What did you gain? Is there any satisfaction? You sent this guy to the hospital and now you're in jail.

"That's what you call a lose-lose situation. And I say, let your resentment go. Just let it be. Sometimes it may be hard to swallow for a period of time, but it eventually comes to pass. Somebody may call you a wimp. So what?"

Andy White, the former chief of the Whitefish Bay band I told you about earlier in this book, had serious problems with alcohol. "My dad was an alcoholic so we were always hungry," he once told me. "When I was about 15, I became an instant alcoholic. You take your first drink and you never stop. That's the way I was. It gives you a lot of courage. It gives you this superman kind of thing. But it doesn't last long. You start drinking more and then, when you start sobering up, you go back."

Rediscovering his spiritual roots as an Ojibway played a key role in Andy's fight for sobriety. He was living in Kenora and participating in a pilot project run by the Addiction Research Foundation of Ontario. "We used a drum in the [Addiction Research Foundation] office. The elders would come to the sing-song. I was a greenhorn. I didn't even know how to sing [the traditional Ojibway songs] but my old uncle on my mother's side sat down with us. We started singing together and started getting people to get together. All of us came from different reserves. Every now and then somebody would get up and start talking about how alcohol is destroying our people. People enjoyed that and I think that's how the [traditional] drum came back into the circle."

Andy told me he remembered people doing the drum when he was a child but then there was a big gap where no one was doing the drum. "When alcohol hit most of the native communities, the native people themselves just left everything [like the drumming]."

When the addiction research centre in Kenora was scheduled to be shut down, the director suggested to Andy that he should move back to Whitefish Bay and work with alcoholics there. "I started approaching elders. I wanted to start the drum going again in all communities. When my uncle passed away, my older son who lives in Kenora and my great grandfather and grandfather used to sing around the drum and they used to tell us about the old history about the drum, about how the drum came to be.

"After a while, we started getting involved with old uncles. They started teaching us, telling us the history, the song. There was all these stories and traditional ways. My grandfather told me that I should have a traditional drum so they said this is how it's going to look and that's the way you're going to make the drum.

"I asked a lot of questions. How did the drum come to be? Who had the first drum? These old people they even gave us a song. They said that's the song that the Creator gave to the native people around this area. There was a real close connection between the spiritual ways and also the traditional ways of native people still living on earth.

"Our grandfathers told us about an old lady who had a dream of what was happening with the people, how they were destroying each other with wars. She had a dream of a drum that would be a peacemaker and, through her vision, she instructed the men how they would make the drum so that's what they did."

What was the first drum made of? "They used to tell us it was a hollow tree, because a long time ago they didn't have no tools. So they had a big tree that was rotten inside and they took out everything in the middle of the tree. They used moose skin. They had to take out the air and some of the meat. They'd scrape the hair off with a big bone.

"And then they would make something square, big enough for the hide to fit. They kind of tied up the hide on that square so it dries up. It would take them about two or three days to do that. Then they got a stick to pound the drum as the old lady had instructed them. They started hitting the drum and the next dream she had was people dancing around it. She saw men singing where the drum is sitting and then she gave them a special song. We sing it every now and then. The old lady got together the men and she had another dream telling them this is the way you're going to be doing it and this is the way that the people will be coming together and they will not destroy each other anymore.

"The dream she had was that, when they knew that another tribe was coming to have a war with them, they'd start doing this pow wow and singing and there would be dancing and, as these people coming to make a war start crawling towards the camp, they'd see that they were having a good time and they'd lay down their weapons and they'd start creeping towards the camp where they're having the pow wow and start to join in.

"Different tribes started joining that other tribe and having a dance and the elders think that probably took four days. They kind of pow wowed for four days with the different tribe without any problems, no fighting. I think they used to refer most to the Sioux people that came to this area. And, after four days, they went back. They had made peace and that's how the drum came about as a peacemaker."

One of the first things Andy did when he returned to Whitefish Bay was organize a pow wow. "People responded. Even people from Minnesota in the States came around to have a little pow wow with contests. I think the prize was 50 bucks or something like that and it just grew from there. Every reserve had their own little celebrations because people enjoyed watching what we were doing."

After passing the jail at the west end of Laurenson Lake, I continued down the highway along the north shore of Longbow Lake and headed south on Highway 71. The scenery was breathtakingly beautiful. Basically untouched, uninhabited, wilderness. God's country.

As I drove through Sioux Narrows, I looked at the Red Indian Lodge sign on the right side of the road with the huge face of the Indian chief in full headdress. Herb Hoffman (Eagle That Walks) had died at the age of 69 on February 6, 2004.

I continued down Highway 71 and turned left at Gaudry's Road to get to the Whitefish Bay community. After crossing the bridge at the narrows between Regina Bay and Dogpaw Lake and heading toward the band administration office on that sunny day in June, 2007, I saw the big log roundhouse Allan White had built down by the shore as part of the community's return to the traditional ways.

"It's a sacred building," Allan told me when I caught up with him that day. "it's a sacred site. We had to ask permission from the spirits. They provided the structural design, what we were supposed to do. So we did it exactly the way they wanted it done. That's where we hold our spiritual gatherings

"It's a meeting place for the people where they talk about the future, see where we're going. It's near the sacred islands and the spirits are there listening. That's the purpose of it. The elders speak to the spirits."

Allan is a very spiritual man and feels a special connection with the spirit world. He told me how, in spirit form, he once entered a beaver lodge and spoke to the beaver. "It's like in a dream. There's a layer, a second layer and a third layer. It's like a three-storey house. You don't see it when you look at it but there's a hole. You can see snow coming in. Not too many see that, but I've seen it."

Allan talked about how things had changed since he was a youngster. "It's so different from my time as a kid. When I talk to my kids, I say I was never spoon fed. Never had anything on a silver platter. I had to work hard as a six-year-old until today. I started making my own money when I was about eight years old when I used to go to my uncle's for harvest. He paid us and we'd buy shoes, we'd buy pants. If you didn't work, you go under. Today it's different, completely different. Today that's not the case. It's so different today and this is why I tell my kids it's important, very important, for you to take control of your life. It's no good to have welfare, can't depend on it because welfare will make you in disarray in life. You get to depend on something that's so easy. I had to work hard in order to feed my kids back in 1970. I had to work real hard. If you didn't work, you went hungry.

"But then welfare came in. That really buggered us up because it started to change. Today it's really hard because people depend so much on government housing. You can't feed your family with trapping. You can't feed your family with fishing. You can't even make it in lumber. Technology has taken over bush work. That's why the generation of today has to focus on their future."

Allan was very concerned about the recurring problem the community was having with suicides. "We were hit very hard since about 1996, '97. It took us quite a long time to come to grips with it. What causes the failures? The suicides. It took us years to really see our problem and it's the pain, it's a growing pain in the community. We had horrible, horrible, mishaps that happened for about 10 to 12 years.

"We're losing youth left and right committing suicide. That went on for about several years. I'm not saying that we have defeated it. It can erupt at any time."

After talking to Allan, I had a brief chat with Andy White at his office in the modern, well-equipped, health centre. He had no idea how much it had cost to build it.

Andy told me that Whitefish Bay had once been the central gathering point for all the Ojibways in the area. "Whitefish was a stopover for many communities. What they did was they made a big circle towards the Winnipeg River. Whitefish Bay people would take off from the community to collect food they could store for the winter. They'd also collect medicine, traditional medicine. They went around and they came around English River towards Dryden and they used to go from Dryden down this way. They came back up this way and Whitefish was the central focus and also the main source of food like whitefish, that's why it's called Whitefish Bay. Some of the elders were telling us that they'd stop here for a week or two. They did that every spring."

Andy's grandparents were originally from the Dryden area. His dad used to walk a trap line around Lobstick Bay. Andy left school after grade two and was working in the bush when he was 12. He was chief of the Whitefish Bay band for 14 years.

I drove back out to Highway 71 and headed south to Nestor Falls where I picked Brian Tuesday up at the supermarket across the road from his apartment. We drove to the lookout place on Highway 71 where Tara Kelly used to smudge her face with sage smoke on her way to the OPP detachment at Sioux Narrows.

We sat at a picnic table from where I looked down on Kagaki Lake and pictured Brian's ancestors paddling their canoes across it hundreds of years ago. He was very proud of the fact that, despite the demons he was always dealing with because of the horrible abuse he suffered in the Indian residential school system, he had, not including a couple of brief lapses, stayed sober for 18 years.

"I was a drunk but I've been sober for about 20 years," he told me.

"I kind of hit the ditch there for a while but I'm back on track again. We know we're going to trip somewhere along the line. We can't condemn each other for things we've done in the past."

In addition to his experience in the Indian residential schools, his previous drinking was very much a result of what he referred to as being a "colonized" Ojibway. "Drinking is one of the characteristics of a colonized person. That's just the way it is and we have to get over that. First, we have to understand that we're colonized. The way we think has been induced by the colonization process and now we have to get back to our own way of life.

"For a long time, in high school and all that, I denied my own people. And then, when I first went to a sweat lodge, there was a change in my head in the way I used to think, the way I conducted myself. That all changed. And I've been trying to stay on course over the last 20 years because I still see myself doing that stuff, still see myself drinking, and sometimes it's a depressing thought.

"That's what I had been dealing with for the last 20 years and, if you're going to deal with that history, it's going to consume you. You have to come to a point where you have to get rid of the shame and the embarrassment and all these other negative thoughts that go through your head if you want to move forward. You can't change what you did, but you can make amends for it."

Brian described something of what it was like to be enslaved by the bottle. "You don't care about anything. You have a bottle and the next drink is all that matters. I've been through all that but I've also learned a lot from my past. Destroying your body is not the answer to a good life. Destroying your mind, your spirit. That's essentially what addiction's doing."

When we spoke at the lookout place on Highway 71, it was only a couple of weeks before a national day of protest the Assembly of First Nations had called for June 29, 2007. Brian was aware that some natives were calling for violence and said that he could understand their motivation.

"We have to take a stand somewhere and, if it means violence, then so be it," he said as he dragged on a cigarette and looked out over Kagaki Lake. "They've been trying to kill us off for centuries and here's the opportunity for them to try it again.

"I don't know how long it's going to take before this social unrest becomes of a violent nature, whether within the communities or explode outwards into society in general. It's gonna happen. There's no doubt about that. It's going to happen. I thought it might've happened early in 2000. It really hasn't yet. It's still bubbling. I can see signs of it every once in a while.

"If things continue the way they're going right now, they're gonna have the same struggles I have, perhaps multiplied. And, for them to survive, we have to take extreme measures. Basically, that's what I see for the future.

"There's too many people starting to awaken to the idea that it doesn't have to be this way and, if it can't be changed from negotiation and peaceful measures, then what choice do they have? To me, whether I live or die is of no consequence to ensure that change is now or in the near future. I'm getting to that point in my life where everything is coming back to me. Every incident, every event in my life like a recall. Why did these things happen? Why didn't anybody do something about it, do anything about it at the time? So now I find myself thinking well what can I do now? And if it comes to a point where I have to be an active participant in measures that's going to come to violence I'll do it without hesitation.

"I will participate in whatever comes to be. I think the hopelessness that grips a lot of people is starting to just loosen up a bit as people start to awaken to the idea that life doesn't have to be this way. If there's something they can do about it, they would.

"We can't be kissing ass all our lives. I do not believe in negotiation and all that. We can't kiss ass to get a tiny slice of the pie. I'm getting old myself and I ain't going to be around much longer and I'd like to see my sons getting an education, I'd like to see them get some health care for my grandkids whenever they arrive.

"I know my rights as an Anishinaabe [Ojibway] person, as a human being, I know what my rights are. But who told me I had to live on a reservation? Is that a right? I'm Anishinaabe. We're the original people of this land. Why do we have to settle for second, third or fourth best? Negotiating to get a piece of the pie. As an Anishinaabe person, I've always had these rights."

As he looked back over time, Brian said he saw very little, if any, improvement in the lives of the Ojibway people. "I don't see any difference from 50 years ago to now. As a matter of fact, we might have had it better 50 years ago. The reserves are shrinking as the populations expand. You got three, four families per home. What's being done there? I don't see anything being done. They like to argue about treaty rights. What does that mean? I mean I don't know what it means either. We need the land. That's the basis of our life. We need land and, as our populations continue to expand, we'll be so crowded on these small reservations that something's gotta give.

"They signed an education agreement a few years back. It's limited the people. It's limited the amount of students we can send to university. The reservations, the members of these communities, are fighting over who's going to be sent where and who's going to go where. It's one of the stupidest things they ever did when they signed that agreement.

"I'm not talking in terms of myself and any personal gain. I'm talking about the communities in general and the membership, how they can improve community life, improve the social conditions, improve education. I didn't know they were negotiating for an education agreement. I didn't know what the contents of that agreement were, like the 'alternative funding' arrangement. What the hell is that?"

Brian said part of the problem was that there were too many voices at the table. Despite the fact that there was an Assembly of First Nations, there did not appear to be one clear voice speaking on behalf of all Aboriginals. "We can't be part-time Indians. We're either Anishinaabe or we're not in how we conduct ourselves. We can't be changing hats every five minutes. And it seems to me that the government preys on this mindset. We're fighting ourselves. We're not fighting for the oppressed. We're fighting ourselves. In the meantime, the oppressor sits back enjoying whatever is going on in our communities.

"Each little community negotiates their own self-government, their ideas of self-government. We can't seem to get together as a united voice that stands together to bring this point across to the governments that we will no longer stand by and see our people suffer, see our people robbed of their dignity, their livelihoods. And the way they [Children's Aid Societies] come after kids."

Like Annie Wilson at Manitou Rapids, Brian believed that learning to speak Ojibway was a necessary component in rediscovering their roots and traditional ways. "Language is the backbone of our nation. In speaking English instead of Ojibwa, you lose a lot of the meaning. It's not always the same as when you speak it in your own language. You need your culture, your language, customs, your traditions. If you don't have that, you've got nothing."

He recalled that, when former Prime Minister Pierre Elliott Trudeau was travelling out west at one time, he asked a chief how his people could be considered a nation when their own chief couldn't speak their native language.

"That's true. It had to make people think. We have to revive our languages in the way that our kids today can speak our language, understand our language. They have to know the customs and the traditions. These are what make us the Anishinaabe people."

He expressed regret about not being able to speak Ojibway and how that prevented him from understanding the ceremonies and the songs. "That's why I don't wear ribbon threads [at the pow wows]. I just can't quite get the deeper meaning of all the ribbon dress, the significance of each and all that. I've never been taught those things. When I go to ceremonies, I try to listen intently, but the deeper meanings always escape me. And that's a huge loss for me personally and for us as a nation. Because all these things dictate how we live, dictate how we conduct ourselves with people, with the land, with the animals. There's a huge part missing. When they say we're the keepers of the land, look at all the plastic bags littering the ground. Once a year they have a clean-up. So what does that say about our respect for ourselves and our respect for creation? Has that been lost? Essentially it has been lost. I mean, the idea is still there, but the action is missing.

"It's going to take a lot of work. I don't know if that's possible. We communicate in English in our communities. We do our ceremonies in English the majority of the time and the basic way of doing ceremonies has changed. So, in a sense, we have to re-learn as Anishinaabe people what, not individually, but collectively, we have to do. We have to relearn all our customs, all our traditions, our culture, our languages and then go from there."

Brian shared Bill Wuttunee's view that there was altogether too much focus on dressing up in the old costumes. "I don't need the ribbon shirts and parading around with a feather. I don't have to do that. Being Ojibway is more about the way we think, the way we live and follow our traditions. That's what makes us Anishinaabe. Not what we've got on. I could parade around in ribbon shirts and moccasins but that doesn't make me any more of an Anishinaabe person."

Chapter 18

After dropping Brian off at his apartment in Nestor Falls, I continued on down Highway 71 to spend some time with Chief Jim Leonard of the Rainy River First Nations at Manitou Rapids.

Jim told me he had been profoundly influenced by the armed standoff involving Mohawk Warriors and the Canadian army at Oka, just outside of Montreal, in August, 1990. "We were getting it live. Nobody was working. Everybody was glued to that television, waiting for the first shot to go off."

A company of the Royal 22nd Regiment had surrounded the Warriors and the women and children at the treatment centre on the Kanesatake reserve with razor wire and refused to let anyone in or out of the area. Additional troops and tanks and other military equipment were on standby in staging areas around Montreal. Military planes and helicopters flew overhead.

If the soldiers had moved in and started firing, Jim said, "all hell would've broken loose", and he would have been part of it. "Oh yeah, I was ready to die. I remember driving home [from Fort Frances] and thinking to myself if that's what happens, that's what happens. It was very, very, stressful, but I had made up my mind that's what I would do and I think a lot of people felt that same way.

"If the army would've moved in, there would've been civil war here. I've never told anyone this with the exception of my wife, but I was ready to die. I was ready to get up and join the revolution and I think people across the country, Indian people, all felt that same way, like it was something in your heart that was being taken away and it's our identity.

"I think you would have seen outbreaks all across the country. We probably would've lost, but I was ready to die and that's how strong I felt, even though I was brought up not to condone that type of activity.

"Of course, you have your radicals going around stirring the pot so to speak, but I think the everyday citizen felt the same way as I did. I talked to people about that since and they've indicated that they had those feelings, too. I think that's what would have happened."

Jim's words, tone and demeanor surprised me. During the 10 years I had known him, he had always been very laidback, very congenial. Kind of a gentle giant. I'd never have thought he was capable of violence. But it was clear that, for him, the Oka incident was a breaking point.

"If they would have taken that golf course [the town of Oka wanted to create a 9-hole golf course on disputed territory], then they would have taken something from each and every Indian person in Canada," he said, "and that's why, if the army would have moved in, then you would have seen a rebellion. The people in the office that I worked with all felt the same way."

"It's very, very, hard to explain if you're not an Indian person. We've been accustomed to giving and giving and giving and giving. All through this time, our rights are being eroded. Things we had in the past are being eroded. It's been slowly taken away from us and being replaced by the government's policy of assimilation. It's being replaced by other things. The more you take away, the less of an Indian person you become and there's got to be a point where you say 'no, no more'. When Oka happened, in my mind, the point had been reached where they weren't going to get any more from me. It was either let's stop it now or let's die because in a few years there'll be nothing left.

"We will never give up. It's hard to explain. It's part of something inside. We're Indian people. We're proud to be Indian people. No matter what is done to us, we're still Indian people. We'll always be that. It's unthinkable to give up.

"My mother talked to me one day and she said, in 100 years there'll be no Indians left. Every time you turn around, something's been taken from you. That's why the elders are saying now we've got to stop that. We've got to start to do it ourselves. We've got to start bringing our traditions back. We've got to start teaching our kids. I think that's some of the problem that our kids are having today. They've lost that identity. So we've got to try to bring them back, bring their identities back. Bring that equilibrium back."

Despite the fact he was ready to put his life on the line at the time of the Oka crisis, Jim said he had mixed feelings about the national day of protest the Assembly of First Nations had called for June, 29, 2007. "I'm not really sold on it. I've been throughout the country. I do travel a lot and I see money going into first nations [bands], a lot of money going into first nations. First nations are always saying it's never enough but, on the other hand, you see so much waste and poor spending practices, poor management.

"In fact, it happened here a couple of years ago. It's one of the reasons I came back. There was poor management going on and a lot of waste. I feel that the money we get from the government is sufficient. You just have to find ways to spend that money more efficiently and you have to take economic development opportunities as they come. Hopefully, in a couple of generations, you won't need Indian Affairs any more. The sooner we get away from Indian Affairs and the Canadian government the better."

Jim Leonard's mixed feelings about the 2007 National Day of Protest can be explained in part by his sense of pride and self-confidence and his understanding of how the world works. "Sure, I see the government cutting back on programs and every year the envelope gets smaller and smaller but I think that's the state of the world nowadays. You just have to make do with less because there's more people and we have to provide more services to the seniors and health care costs and so on. So it's a drain on the general economy and I don't know if Canada is conspiring against the first nations but my feeling is we just have to do the best with what we got. I agree with the protest, but in a sense you have to sit back and look in your own back yard. How can we spend what we have more efficiently, get a better bang for the buck?

"What we have to do as Aboriginal people is look at our existing structures and become more efficient and that's basically what we've attempted to do here. We've been told that, in order to do anything, we have to do it ourselves and if there's an opportunity there and we have the resources to look at that opportunity, we'll do it. We have to build an economic base here and our community knows we have to build that economic base to survive. Because the days of the government grants and hand-outs are over and we realize that. We have to build that economic base."

In building a stronger economic base, they would invest money from the $70 million they received in May, 2005, in compensation for the lands that were taken away from the seven Rainy River bands in the early 1900s.

"We had seven communities that lived along the Rainy River and that was the days of the farmers coming in," Jim said. "They wanted our land and so they just basically put us onto Manitou here and took our land away. That was the reason for the claim. We lost everything. We were told back then if you don't sign this piece of paper and move up, we're going to move you up anyway with a gun and burn your house down. What were these old guys supposed to do? 'Sign, sign the paper.' And so they moved here and I guess that's why the government agreed to settle the claim.

"We also received some land back. I think it was about two or three thousand acres. Part of the settlement was that we will be able to buy more land and return it to reserve status. Since then, we've been looking at economic development, trying to get more economic development.

"I'll give you one example. The cost of energy, hydro, gas, utility bills, today is skyrocketing. A lot of our community members were coming in within the last couple of years and asking if we could help them with their hydro bill. It's more than double or triple what it used to be. And they were saying since we have $70 million why don't we just subsidize the hydro bills?

"Council and myself don't feel that's right because you're throwing money away and it's never going to come back. So what we're looking at right now is putting up a couple of big wind turbines and paying for those out of the settlement and then using those profits or those revenues that that wind turbine generates and subsidize the home owner.

"You're always replenishing that supply because you have revenues coming in and you take a portion of those revenues and send out rebate cheques or something every few months to help the people. Those are the kinds of things we're looking at doing. The energy costs for natural gas for our small sawmill have increased to $14,000 a month. So we're looking at ways of converting a waste product into pellets to burn for the boilers. We talked to a guy some place in the state of Washington. They took steam turbines out of a ship for making power. We're looking at those possibilities. We're looking at ways to reduce energy costs."

You might recall earlier in this book where one of the elders thought former Chief Willie Wilson wanted to "turn us into Chinamen" when he suggested they should create wild rice paddies to compete with the farmers in Manitoba and Minnesota.

"Willie's become more and more traditional in the last few years," Jim told me during the interview in 2007. "He assists us in the traditional aspects of our everyday life. If some of the things we're doing are wrong, he'll point that out to us. It's a continuing relationship."

Calvin Bombay, the counsellor at the Kenora jail and former band councillor at Manitou Rapids, spoke highly of Willie. "I have a hell of a lot of respect for Willie," he told me when I interviewed him in 1997. "As a matter of fact, Willie was the one that really rebuilt our community. If it wasn't for him, we'd probably still be living along the highway without the conveniences of life. Willie made life more comfortable for people and he took a lot of flack going through that process, not so much by the people, but from his own family. He's got a nephew who works for Treaty Three who ran against him for several elections.

"I give credit to Willie for a lot of my abilities, if you want to call them that. I give credit to a lot of people that I refer to as my teachers and Willie was one of them. I spent 10 years on council with Willie and I learnt a lot of things from Willie."

You might also recall how Annie Wilson held on to the Ojibway language despite the efforts of the white nuns at St. Margaret's Indian Residential School in Fort Frances to erase it from her memory.

"The nun would make me stand up and say 'I'll not speak my language again' if I got caught speaking my language. That's what she would make me do. 'I'll not speak my language', from nine o'clock till midnight at night I had to repeat that. From nine in the evening till midnight, I had to repeat that for a whole month. That was my punishment for speaking my language. And, at the back of my mind, I said 'No. It's going to stay there.'"

The last time I saw Annie she was proudly dancing in traditional Ojibway dress to the sound of the drums and the singers at a pow wow at Manitou Rapids in June, 2007,—five months before she turned 82. "Yeah, I always had the language," she told me on the day before the pow wow. "They tried to make me lose it in the boarding school, but I didn't listen to that because I knew it was going to help me later. I could learn English any time but, to lose my language, that's something else. I wanted to keep it. I didn't want to lose it. I didn't want to lose the way I spoke to the Creator. I knew both ways so that's why I kept it because I knew I had to use it someday. That's what I'm teaching young people now with prayer and all that kind of stuff."

When I interviewed Jim Leonard before the pow wow got under way, he talked about how Annie and some of the other elders had been helping the community restore some of the Ojibway culture and traditions. "The elders want some of that back. We want it back and we're going to get it back."

I asked what motivated elders like Annie Wilson to want to get back to the traditional Ojibway ceremonies and traditions. "I think it was movements like Oka and those types of things," Jim said. "The elders saw that we were losing and losing. The fish stocks were being depleted, hunting charges were being laid, governments were becoming oppressive. We lost everything. Everything that we were was being destroyed.

"You start hearing about the abuses in the residential schools and things like that. Native issues became more important to the Canadian public because of a lot of these things that were happening and consequently the elders saw that as the opportunity to start to demand from the chief and councils in the communities to look at our history and that's what we did.

"We've been here for thousands of years and we'll still be here tomorrow. We've survived this long. We've become somewhat independent. We have our existing businesses, our employment and we're not dependent on increases in government funding. We'll survive."

Chapter 19

On Wednesday, October 12, 2011, Ron McDonald led a large group of dignitaries, community residents and students from the dilapidated old school at Whitedog to the new $25 million Mizhakiiwetung Memorial School—named after Ron's father Roy.

"It's a monumental moment in the history of Wabaseemoong," Ron, who was now the school's principal, said at the grand opening ceremony. "Education is now a priority in our community. Students will not turn their backs on school. I can't really even put into words how emotionally charged and ecstatic the kids are."

The new school had 16 fully-equipped classrooms and could accommodate 460 students from kindergarten to Grade 12. There was an outdoor hockey rink, baseball diamond, multi-purpose track and a gymnasium.

When I caught up with Ron on my last visit to Whitedog in June, 2013, he was proudly overseeing the graduation ceremonies. The gymnasium was packed with well-dressed parents and their children. Almost everyone seemed to have a cell phone they were taking pictures with. You could feel the excitement in the air. The sense of pride and accomplishment.

Banners on the wall proclaimed championships young people

from Whitedog had won. Anishinaabe Winter Games. Snow shoeing championship. Broomball champions.

An elder was on stage blessing the ceremonies with a prayer in Ojibway but hardly anyone was paying attention to him. Traditional drummers led the procession of officials, dignitaries and students into the gym which was bedecked with balloons and colored stars.

And then the different classes were called up to receive their certificates. Youngsters wearing gowns and academic caps with tassels had big beams on their faces. There was hardly a blond hair in the bunch. They all looked 100% Ojibway.

When Ron McDonald took his turn at the podium, he emphasized the importance of the Ojibway language and declared: "No one will ever again ban us from speaking our language." Right after that, they handed out the native language proficiency awards

As I drove south toward Kenora, I thought back to my last visit with Isaac Mandamin in 2010. I'd been told that he had been admitted to Lake of the Woods District Hospital because of "complications" but I wasn't told what those complications were.

When I got to the hospital on that trip, there was a man sitting in a wheelchair at the front entrance. Both legs had been amputated above the knee. Inside, I saw several people with parts of their legs missing. Diabetes.

When I got to Isaac's room, he was curled up on the bed like a baby. Like a small bear with its leg caught in a steel trap. His right leg had been amputated just below the knee.

He was on the phone talking to his sister in Ojibway and didn't notice me when I first entered the room. He yawned as he looked toward me and scratched his tummy. His bare left foot looked quite discolored and the nails were yellow.

He told me he'd had diabetes for about 30 years and things had deteriorated over the last couple of years. Doctors had removed a blister on his toe a couple of months earlier. When he got another blister, they told him they would have to cut his leg off at the knee. However, he said he was quite optimistic about travelling around in his van again because they were going to provide him with a prosthesis.

Isaac, a very proud man, was obviously deeply embarrassed at me seeing him in the sorry state that he was in. It looked like the life had pretty well gone out of him. I couldn't imagine what an immense psychological and emotional trauma he must have been going through.

When I was at Manitou Rapids a couple of days later, Chief Jim Leonard told me there was an epidemic of Ojibway people having parts of their limbs amputated because of complications caused by diabetes. One of his councillors was scheduled to have his left leg amputated at the hospital in Thunder Bay. Isaac Mandamin was not the exception that proved the rule.

And now, almost three years later, I was about to pay Isaac another visit. The nurse at Birchwood Terrace Nursing Home told me he was in the very last room on the right at the end of the corridor on the first floor.

He was sitting in his wheelchair with his back to the door looking out the window at the cars and trucks passing by on Lakeview Drive.

"Hi, Isaac," I said. "It's Robert MacBain."

As he turned slowly towards me, I saw that his right leg had now been cut off almost to the groin. It was highly unlikely that Isaac would ever walk again.

Driving past Brian Tuesday's apartment in Nestor Falls on that June, 2010, trip on my way to spend some time with Chief Jim Leonard at Manitou Rapids, I thought back to my visit with Brian in June, 2007. He was in pretty good shape when we talked at the lookout place on Highway 71. Still living on the edge. But sober.

But then, a year later, someone suggested he should file a claim with the Truth and Reconciliation Commission as a survivor of the Indian residential school system.

In preparing his submission with his lawyer, all of the horrible childhood memories of sexual and physical abuse that had remained buried deep in his consciousness bubbled up to the surface. He started drinking again. Heavily.

While he was awarded $179,000 in compensation for the abuse that was inflicted upon him, he didn't derive a nickel's worth of benefit out of it. He was still drinking when he got the settlement cheque and handed the money over to his ex-wife who lived just up the road at the Sabaskong reserve. She promptly bought herself a $52,000 Buick SUV, got a new boat and built a porch around her house.

When I last saw Brian in September, 2010, he was in pretty bad shape. He was flat broke and survived on fish he got from a commercial fisherman he helped out every morning. He looked quite gaunt. A lot like the tortured old man in the poem he wrote when he was sober back in 1994.

I gave him a ride to Fort Frances to visit one of his sons who had been in and out of hospital for several years. Brian's hair flew in the wind as he took his son out for a spin on his wheelchair. His wife's luxury SUV was parked outside the hospital.

When we had coffee in Nestor Falls on the last morning, Brian gave me a photocopy of the poem he wrote about being sexually abused when he was still sober back in 1994. He also loaned me his copy of *When Rabbit Howls,* a book about a two-year-old child who created an inner world to escape the horror of violent abuse and shield her from the pain. As an adult, she had 92 split personalities. The book clearly meant a lot to Brian.

I gave him some money and a windbreaker I had bought for him and said I'd see him again in the spring. Brian died alone in his small apartment at Nestor Falls less than four months later. His son told me he'd suffered a massive brain aneurism. He was 66.

When I spoke to Chief Jim Leonard during our last visit in June, 2013, he had put aside the wind turbine idea in favour of solar panels. He said further investigation had shown that the profit from the wind turbine project would have been marginal. They were in negotiations with a big German firm to partner on a $130 million project that would have 200,000 panels producing 25 megawatts of electricity.

They were also exploring ways of supplying Ojibways in Minnesota with cheaper drugs from Canada. Jim said the Jay Treaty of 1796 gave Ojibways the right to trade goods across the border without paying duty.

Article III of the Jay Treaty says natives on both sides of the border have the right "freely to pass and repass, by land or inland navigation into the respective territories and countries of the two parties on the continent of America ... and freely carry on trade and commerce with each other."

"They're paying $150 a month for blood pressure pills," Jim said. "We can get them for $30." He said they were working with a couple of doctors in Toronto and a pharmacy in Thunder Bay.

The 15,000 to 18,000 employees working at the 13 casinos the Ojibways operated in Minnesota presented a ready-made market for blood pressure pills and medication for diabetes and other chronic diseases. If the drug deal went ahead, it would be another example of the trading relationship Jim's band had developed with Ojibways in Minnesota and Wisconsin. They'd been selling sturgeon to the White Earth band in Minnesota since the late 1990s.

"We've become friends," Jim told me in 2007. "A couple of weeks ago they brought a bus load of their elders and kids up here. So we're going to go down tomorrow and talk to the tribal council, the tribal chairman, and see if we can form a more formal relationship, a friendship and maybe share resources somehow. We're trying to open up the doors."

Judging by the ambitious deals Jim was working on in 2013, he had succeeded in opening quite a few doors.

Like Josephine and Isaac Mandamin, Andy White and Bill Wuttunee, Jim Leonard believed the bureaucrats at Indians Affairs exercised far too much control over the lives of the native people.

"I often say that guys like [former Indian Affairs minister] Ron

Irwin wanted to do something back in those days, but the bureaucracy just swallowed up the whole initiative," he said. "We often say we'd like to get it back to where it was when Irwin was here, but it's just so bureaucratic right now.

"I have a lot of respect for Ron Irwin and then when Jane Stewart [minister during 1997–99] came in she was following the same program that Irwin had and I met her a couple of times. I had a lot of respect for her. She did provide us with some assistance in our developments here.

"After that, when [Bob] Nault came in, we thought hey, we got it made, we got somebody from the local area that's our minister. Unfortunately Nault had a lot of plans, a lot of big ideas and dreams, but he never did follow through with them. The bureaucracy swallowed them and consequently nothing happened with Nault.

"So everything just went downhill from Irwin's time and Jane Stewart tried to carry on what Irwin was trying then Nault came in with big plans and the bureaucracy just swallowed them alive."

I asked Jim if he thought Bob Nault had the right approach when he was Minister of Indian Affairs. "I think he had it right and he had it in his heart that he wanted to do well. But he just didn't. For whatever reason, the bureaucracy turned against him and anything that he would commit to was overturned by the bureaucracy. There was either no money or whatever. Nothing seemed to click for him."

When I got back to Kenora's Best Western Lakeside Inn on the last night of that trip in June, 2013, I went to the restaurant at the top of the hotel, got a table by the window, and looked out over the Lake of the Woods as the sun set in the west.

Boats were criss-crossing Rat Portage Bay. Houseboats were moored at the end of the town dock. A freight train with hundreds of double-decked containers and tank cars headed west over Hospital Bridge. A single-engine Cessna roared over the hotel roof and landed on the water below.

As I looked south across the Lake of the Woods, I had visions of Ojibways canoeing up from Rainy River to negotiate Treaty #3 with

Lieutenant-Governor Alexander Morris in September, 1873. It took three days for a 16-man freighter canoe to get from Manitou Rapids to the Northwest Angle.

I thought about Isaac Mandamin alone in his room at the long-term care facility across the bay mourning the loss of his right leg. I wondered how many times he'd paddled his canoe from Whitedog to Kenora and back.

I thought about the future of the bright young kids showing off their certificates at the graduation ceremony at the Mizhakiiwetung Memorial School earlier that week. There's nothing in the way of employment opportunities for them at Whitedog.

Like Bill Wuttunee said, it would probably be in their best interest to move to where the jobs are and make the transition to an urban lifestyle.

I remembered the many times I had stayed at that hotel when I was providing public relations counsel and service to the Department of Indian Affairs in the early 1970s.

At one point, I turned to one of the department's senior economic development officers in Toronto and said: "We're spending $400 million a year on the Indians but nothing seems to change. Nothing's getting better for the Indian people." He smiled and said: "It isn't supposed to." That took me by surprise.

Why would he say something like that? "It's conscience money," he replied. "People feel bad about what's happened to the Indians and they want to feel something's being done about it. When the minister stands in his place in the House and says we're spending $400 million a year [as compared to the estimated $7.9 billion spent in 2013–2014], they say that's good. Then they go back to their TV and watch Archie Bunker in *All in the Family*."

That reminded me of blunt-spoken Arthur Laing from Vancouver who became Minister of Indian Affairs in 1966. In his maiden address to Parliament, Laing said seven ministers had held the portfolio before him and they were all abject failures.

Then he smiled and said: "I don't intend to be the exception that proves the rule."

He wasn't.

Bibliography

Beyond the Indian Act — Tom Flanagan, Christopher Alcantara and Andre Le Dressay, McGill-Queen's University Press, 2011

Canada and its Future — The United Church House, 1967

First Peoples in Canada — Alan D. McMillan and Eldon Yellowhorn, Douglas & McIntyre, 2004

History of the Ojibway People — William W. Warren, Minnesota Historical Society Press, 1885

Our Home OR Native Land — Melvin H. Smith, Q.C., Stoddart, 1996

Red Man's America — Ruth M. Underhill, The University of Chicago Press, 1971

Royal Commission on Aboriginal Peoples, 1996 report

Ruffled Feathers — William I. C. Wuttunee, Bell Books, Ltd., 1971

The Ojibwa of Southern Ontario — Peter S. Schmalz, University of Toronto Press, 1991

The Treaties of Canada with the Indians of Manitoba and the North-West Territories — Alexander Morris, Belford, Clarke & Co., 1880

Acknowledgements

I am deeply indebted to the Ojibways of Whitedog, Whitefish Bay, Sabaskong and Manitou Rapids in northwestern Ontario who generously took time away from their busy lives to share their knowledge and experience with me. I am also indebted to former chiefs Andrew Delisle and Gene Lahache from the Mohawk community of Kahnawake across the river from Montreal. Cree lawyer Bill Wuttunee, Winnipeg entrepreneur Marion Ironquill Meadmore and long-time civil servant Jean Cuthand were most generous with their time.

Ojibway poet Duke Redbird and Sol Sanderson, former president of the Federation of Saskatchewan Indians, also increased my understanding of the issues I wrote about in this book.

Herb Hoffman of the Red Indian Lodge on the Lake of the Woods and former Trudeau cabinet minister Martin O'Connell were also kind enough to share their opinions and perspective.

Considerable benefit was derived from reading *The Ojibwa of Southern Ontario* by Peter S. Schmalz, *History of the Ojibway People* by William Whipple Warren, *First Peoples in Canada* by Alan D. McMillan and Eldon Yellowhorn and, most important of all, *The Treaties of Canada with the Indians of Manitoba and the North-West Territories* by former Lieutenant-Governor Alexander Morris.

A paper published by the Manitoba Historical Society in the fall of 1989 written by Sarah Carter of St. John's College, University of Manitoba, put the spotlight on the dislocation Aboriginals in Manitoba suffered at the hands of land speculators and corrupt government officials.

The paper Cree lawyer Delia Opekokew prepared for the Federation of Saskatchewan Indians in 1980 provided further evidence of the failure on the part of the Canadian government to meet some of its responsibilities under the terms of the treaties.

Further insight into the making of Treaty #3 was derived from reading a well-documented paper lawyer Sara J. Mainville prepared for the Grand Council of Treaty #3 in September, 2012.

Above all, I am grateful for the love and support of my wife of 34 years — former International Cooperation Minister Maria Minna. As always, Maria's constructive comments and suggestions were helpful in keeping me on track.

I also appreciate enjoying the good health and sharpness of mind in my 80th year which enabled me to rework and republish the 2015 edition of *Their Home and Native Land* and get started on my next two books.

—Robert MacBain

About the Author

Scottish-born Toronto author Robert Macbain spent more than fifty years in journalism, politics and public relations. During that time, he built up a vast deposit of knowledge, experience and perspective.

His first novel, *Two Lives Crossing*, was published in 2013. He is currently at work on a non-fiction book about the Indian residential schools and one about the 2006 Mohawk protests/blockades at Caledonia, Ontario.

Robert MacBain lives in the Upper Beach area of Toronto with his wife of 34 years—former International Cooperation Minister Maria Minna.

His eldest son Cameron lives in Brentwood Bay, British Columbia. Youngest son Andrew lives in Surrey, BC, with his wife Veronica and MacBain's six grandchildren.

www.ingramcontent.com/pod-product-compliance
Lightning Source LLC
Chambersburg PA
CBHW020606300426
44113CB00007B/529